AF478218

BEYOND CRAFT

DECORATIVE ARTS FROM THE LEATRICE S. AND MELVIN B. EAGLE COLLECTION

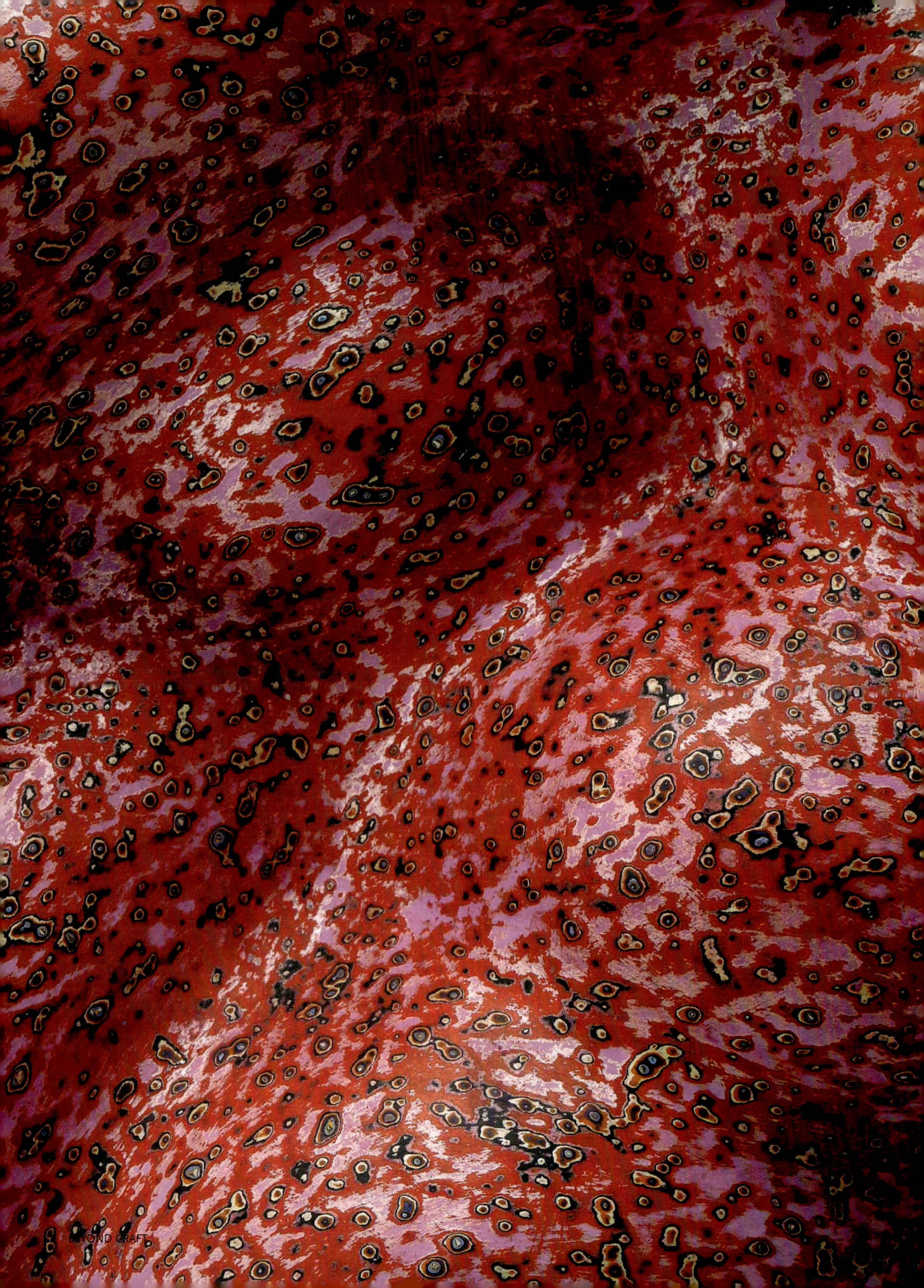
BEYOND CRAFT

BEYOND CRAFT

DECORATIVE ARTS FROM THE LEATRICE S. AND MELVIN B. EAGLE COLLECTION

Cindi Strauss

with contributions
by Janet Koplos
and Susie J. Silbert

THE MUSEUM OF FINE ARTS, HOUSTON

DISTRIBUTED BY YALE UNIVERSITY PRESS,
NEW HAVEN AND LONDON

This catalogue was published to coincide with the exhibition *Beyond Craft: Decorative Arts from the Leatrice S. and Melvin B. Eagle Collection*, organized by the Museum of Fine Arts, Houston, from February 23 to May 26, 2014. Other exhibition venues include the Mint Museum of Craft + Design from September 6, 2014, to February 22, 2015, and the Canton Museum of Art from August 27 to October 25, 2015.

This exhibition is organized by the Museum of Fine Arts, Houston.

Generous funding is provided by:
The Margaret Cooke Skidmore Exhibition Endowment
Friends of Leatrice S. and Melvin B. Eagle

Publications Director: Diane Lovejoy
Editor: Heather Brand
Indexer: Kay Banning
Book designer: Phenon Finley-Smiley
Printer: Masterpiece Litho, Inc., Houston, TX

Distributed by
Yale University Press, New Haven and London
yalebooks.com/art

Library of Congress Cataloging-in-Publication Data

Museum of Fine Arts, Houston.
Beyond craft : decorative arts from the Leatrice S. and Melvin B. Eagle collection / Cindi Strauss ; with contributions by Janet Koplos and Susie J. Silbert.

pages cm

Summary: "This beautifully illustrated catalogue showcases for the first time the work of about forty leading American decorative artists of the mid- to late twentieth century represented in the Eagle collection."—Provided by publisher.

"This catalogue was published to coincide with the exhibition Beyond Craft: Decorative Arts from the Leatrice S. and Melvin B. Eagle Collection, organized by the Museum of Fine Arts, Houston, from February 23 to May 26, 2014."

Includes bibliographical references and index.
ISBN 978-0-300-20410-0 (pbk.)

1. Decorative arts—United States—History—20th century—Exhibitions.
2. Eagle, Melvin B.—Art collections—Exhibitions. 3. Eagle, Leatrice S.—Art collections—Exhibitions. 4. Decorative arts—Private collections—Texas—Houston—Exhibitions. 5. Museum of Fine Arts, Houston—Exhibitions.

I. Strauss, Cindi. II. Koplos, Janet. III. Silbert, Susie J. IV. Title.

NK808.M87 2014
745.0973'0747641411—dc23
2013041697

Cover: Robert Arneson, *Golden Triangle / Us Guys*, 1991, earthenware, The Leatrice S. and Melvin B. Eagle Collection, gift of Leatrice and Melvin Eagle, 2011.970. Cover art © Estate of Robert Arneson / Licensed by VAGA, New York, NY

Page 2: Ken Price, *Sag* (detail), 2007, painted clay, The Leatrice S. and Melvin B. Eagle Collection, museum purchase funded by the Caroline Wiess Law Accessions Endowment Fund, 2010.2110.

Page 6: Ralph Bacerra, *Teapot* (detail), 2000, whiteware, The Leatrice S. and Melvin B. Eagle Collection, museum purchase funded by the Caroline Wiess Law Accessions Endowment Fund, 2010.2031.A–.C.

Page 18: Earl Pardon, *Pin* (detail), 1960, sterling silver, 14k gold, shell, colored stones, and enamel, The Leatrice S. and Melvin B. Eagle Collection, museum purchase funded by the Caroline Wiess Law Accessions Endowment Fund, 2010.2104.

Page 34: Cynthia Schira, *Borderland* (detail), 1986, cotton, linen, rayon, and mixed fibers, The Leatrice S. and Melvin B. Eagle Collection, museum purchase funded by the Caroline Wiess Law Accessions Endowment Fund, 2010.2130.

Page 140: Tom Patti, *Spectral Panel* (detail), 1997, glass, The Leatrice S. and Melvin B. Eagle Collection, museum purchase funded by the Caroline Wiess Law Accessions Endowment Fund, 2010.2109.

CONTENTS

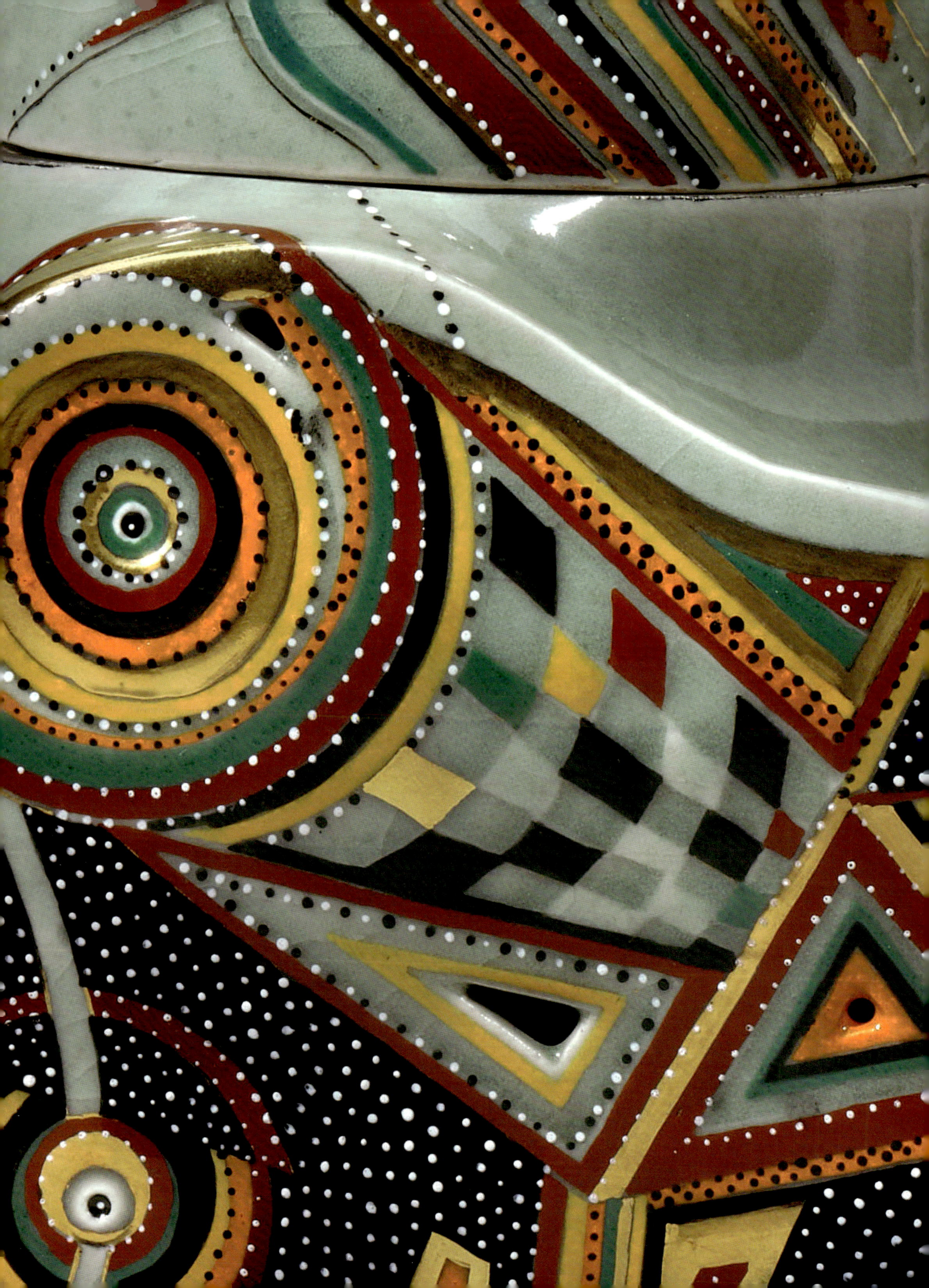

Gary Tinterow,
Director, The Museum of Fine Arts, Houston

Over the past decade, the Museum of Fine Arts, Houston, has actively acquired and exhibited modern and contemporary decorative arts, particularly singular works made by studio artists since World War II. Through our programs and publications, we celebrate the creativity and innovation of makers and their work as we explore their contributions within and beyond the craft movement.

One of our most significant acquisitions in this field is the Leatrice S. and Melvin B. Eagle collection of ceramics, fiber art, furniture, glass, jewelry, and works on paper. Assembled by Lee and Mel Eagle from the 1960s to today, this collection highlights seminal artists such as Robert Arneson, Olga de Amaral, Wendell Castle, Ron Nagle, Albert Paley, Ken Price, Adrian Saxe, and Peter Voulkos as well as less-familiar figures such as Jack Earl, Frank Fleming, and Takeshi Yasuda. The Eagles were adventurous collectors at a time when the boundaries between high art and studio craft were challenged by cognoscenti and prescient dealers; the result is a distinctive collection that reflects the technical innovations and shifting tastes of the last half century.

Thanks to the support of the Board of Trustees and director Peter C. Marzio, the Museum acquired 170 works from the Eagles in 2010, through purchase and partial gift. Cindi Strauss, curator, modern and contemporary decorative arts and design, undertook the ensuing exhibition and produced this exemplary catalogue.

We are delighted that a selection of works from the Eagle collection will travel to the Mint Museum of Craft + Design in Charlotte, North Carolina, and the Canton Museum of Art in Canton, Ohio, since Lee and Mel Eagle have long-standing ties with both museums. We thank Dr. Kathleen V. Jameson, president, and Annie Carlano, director, Craft + Design, at the Mint Museum of Art, M. J. Albacete, director of the Canton Museum of Art, and the staff members of both institutions for their collaboration in this endeavor.

Parting with a collection built over a lifetime is a difficult and delicate task. We are grateful that Lee and Mel Eagle entrusted the Museum with the care of these fascinating objects, and we look forward to sharing them with the widest possible public.

ACKNOWLEDGMENTS

Cindi Strauss,
*Curator of Modern and Contemporary Decorative Arts
and Design, The Museum of Fine Arts, Houston*

In 2004, over tea in New York, Sara Morgan, an MFAH trustee, great friend, and fellow collector, introduced me to Lee and Mel Eagle. For a few hours, we spoke about the current issues facing the field of contemporary craft and our hopes for the future. We formed a connection that developed into a wonderful friendship. A few years later, in 2010, the Eagles made final what we had been discussing for some time: their extraordinary collection would find a permanent home at the MFAH. I am grateful to them for entrusting their works to the museum and for welcoming me into their lives these past nine years.

Members of the Board of Trustees of the Museum of Fine Arts, Houston, supported the acquisition of this extraordinary collection and its subsequent exhibition and catalogue from the beginning. I am also indebted to the members of the museum's decorative arts subcommittee whose participation in the acquisition process made this project possible. Jane Gillies and Ingrid Seyb, object conservators; Julie Bakke, chief registrar; David Aylsworth, former collection registrar; Geoffrey Dare, associate registrar; and the museum's preparators have shepherded the collection from its inception. Gary Tinterow inherited this project when he became the director of the museum in 2012 and has been steadfast in his support. Gwendolyn H. Goffe, former associate director, finance; Amy Purvis, chief development officer; Deborah Roldán, assistant director, exhibitions; Jon Evans, chief librarian; Lynn Wexler, associate librarian; Marty Stein, Donna Kleist, and Flora Brooks in the image library; Margaret Mims, associate director, Jay Heuman, and Sara Wheeler in the education department; and Mary Haus and Amy Lowman in the marketing and public relations department also deserve thanks.

The exhibition was magnificently designed by Bill Cochrane in the exhibition design department. Frances Trahan deserves special recognition for her superb mounts, and Brooke Barclay in the matting and framing department handled all the needs for the works on paper. Diane Lovejoy, publications director, and Heather Brand, editor, were fantastic colleagues, as always, and shaped the text brilliantly. Thomas R. DuBrock and Will Michels provided new photography to illustrate this catalogue handsomely. Phenon Finley-Smiley, head of graphics at the museum, created the beautiful design for the catalogue.

I am particularly grateful to Janet Koplos for her thought-provoking essay, which seriously analyzes the period during which most of the objects in the Eagles' collection were made. Janet was given a tall order and rose to the occasion; her essay is a major contribution to the field. Susie J. Silbert researched and condensed incredible amounts of information for her entries on selected artists. Her writings reflect the clarity of her thoughts and her ability to home in on salient details. Anna Walker, Windgate Foundation Curatorial Fellow in Contemporary Craft, put in many hours assisting with the organization of and research for the exhibition. She also cheerfully helped with a myriad of other tasks

and is an indispendible colleague. Christine
Gervais, associate curator for decorative
arts, was, as ever, a phenomenal sounding
board in regard to this project. I thank
her for all her support. I must also thank
Rebecca Dunham, former curatorial assistant,
prints and drawings, for her help with the
works on paper in the collection. Former
decorative arts curatorial assistant Rebecca
Elliot and research volunteer Gehane
Huckaby were also instrumental in gathering
important contextual sources for the pieces
in the collection.

The museum is pleased to be partnering
with the Mint Museum of Craft + Design
and the Canton Museum of Art on this
exhibition. Kathleen Jameson, director, and
Annie Carlano, senior curator, of the Mint
Museum, and M. J. Albacete, director, and
Lynnda Arrasmith, curator, of the Canton
Museum of Art, and their staff members
have been great colleagues.

The museum's relationship with the Eagles
began and took shape under the directorship
of the late Peter C. Marzio. His belief in the
importance of this material was inspirational,
and I will be forever grateful for his support.
Finally, I would like to thank my husband,
Chris, and my son, Dashiell, for their love
and patience during my absences from home
while working on this project. I could not
have accomplished it without them.

Lee and Mel Eagle

This catalogue illustrates and expounds on a group of objects that represents the fruits of a forty-year journey of learning, acquisition, and enjoyment. As we reflect on this period, we realize that what is now a collection was assembled based on instinct and a bit of bravado, and without a master plan. The ceramic objects that we began acquiring in the 1960s were entirely functional; we preferred them to the factory-made dishes and containers that we had used early in our marriage. Later, in the mid-1970s, while Lee was becoming a functional potter and then the owner of a ceramic supply company, she attended lectures, workshops, and conferences where she became familiar with a number of the prominent ceramists, including Don Reitz, Robert Turner, and Michael Cardew, whose works are illustrated in this catalogue.

Many other connections, such as with Ralph Bacerra, Rick Dillingham, and Adrian Saxe, resulted from our close working relationship with the American Hand Gallery in Washington, D.C. We began buying these artists' works, most of which were not intended for functional use, and our enjoyment of these objects in our home led us to expand our horizons in the direction of even more sculptural works in the 1980s. At the same time, we began a long affiliation with the James Renwick Alliance, the support group for the Renwick Gallery of the Smithsonian American Art Museum. Through the Renwick, we began an education process that extended our range of

interests to objects in all studio-art media: furniture, jewelry, fiber, and glass. In the 1990s, we worked closely with the Mint Museum in Charlotte, North Carolina, during the launch of its Museum of Craft + Design, to help establish the Founders' Circle support group. Through this initiative, we interacted with a broad range of artists, their work, and many American studio-art collectors. In addition, Lee's involvement with the American Craft Council, where she served as chairperson, gave us exposure to the full spectrum of the studio arts. Since the 1990s, we have been even more focused on works that have made a strong artistic statement, including those by such artists as Olga de Amaral, Robert Arneson, Stephen De Staebler, Ken Price, Frank Stella, and Peter Voulkos.

The works in the collection are clearly focused on the period of the 1970s and 1980s. During this time, a subset of makers who previously had been comfortable working within the restrictions implicit in the field of "crafts" began working in ways that would set them apart. Ceramicists such as Peter Voulkos and others from the West Coast; adventurous jewelers from Philadelphia and elsewhere; glass workers creating a new language of expression just ten years after Harvey Littleton and Dominic Labino had ignited an American studio-glass movement; and others in the movement freed themselves from the externally imposed restraints of "crafts" to forge a new path that ultimately has merged with the broader regime of the arts.

Examples from just the last few years of the level of recognition that these trailblazing artists have succeeded in realizing abound. Their work has become accepted in most of the major museums of America and is shown in one-person shows, major comprehensive exhibitions, and galleries featuring twentieth-century art. The makers whose works we acquired in the most casual settings thirty-five years ago are now getting recognition that we could never have imagined then. We are truly excited for these artists, who, because we acquired their work years ago, are now joining the exceptional permanent collection of the Museum of Fine Arts, Houston.

Over the past four decades, we did not acquire art with the intention of building a focused collection. Instead, our decisions centered for the most part on enhancing our home, creating a beautiful and stimulating environment that would be a source of daily pleasure. Visitors to our home, including museum directors, curators, and gallery owners, were ultimately the ones to open our eyes to the fact that we had succeeded in assembling a group of art objects that could stand on its own as a collection in a museum. This assessment proved true when the Museum of Fine Arts, Houston, accessioned about 170 works from our collection in 2010, and we are still taken aback that our personal penchant for acquiring art has resulted in a coherent group of works that may now be enjoyed by a larger public. It can certainly be said that ours was an accidental collection.

We are amazed and pleased that our works have found a home at the Museum of Fine Arts, Houston, and that this catalogue has become a reality. We hope that the exposure benefits the artists, all of whom are deserving of recognition. We also thank the museum, its late director, Peter Marzio, its current director, Gary Tinterow, and Cindi Strauss, assistant director, programming, and curator, modern and contemporary decorative arts and design, for their efforts and for the resources that have been and will be dedicated to the process of educating and enlightening the museum's audiences in what we feel strongly is an important movement in American art.

After the works featured in this catalogue left our home in late 2010, we had assumed that we would not continue to acquire. However, that has turned out to not be the case. For us, the search for objects that enhance the enjoyment of life is an ongoing process. It is part of what keeps us excited about being alive.

INTRODUCTION

Cindi Strauss,
*Curator of Modern and Contemporary Decorative Arts
and Design, The Museum of Fine Arts, Houston*

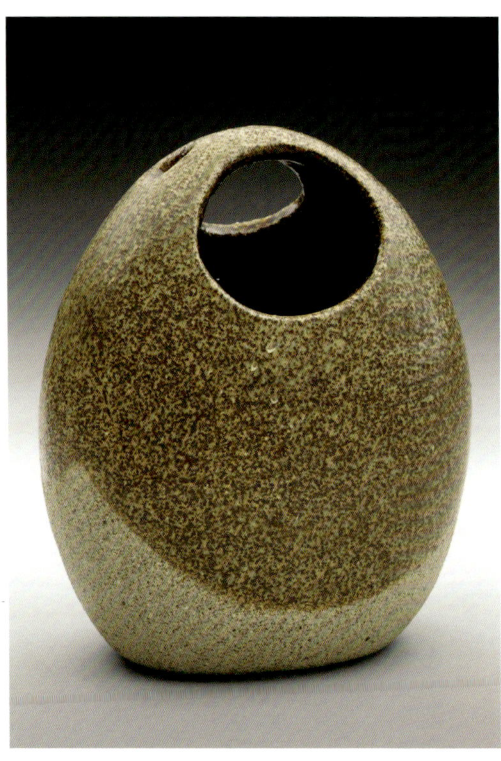

FIGURE 1
JANE PARSHALL
Untitled, 1960
Stoneware
7 1/4 x 6 1/4 x 4 1/8 inches
(18.4 x 15.9 x 10.5 cm)
The Leatrice S. and Melvin B.
Eagle Collection, museum
purchase funded by the
Caroline Wiess Law
Accessions Endowment Fund
2010.2108

If you ask most collectors about the piece that launched their lifelong commitment to collecting art, you likely will receive the details not only of the acquisition but also of the role that the acquisition played in the future development of their collection. Some collectors consciously and systematically build collections, whereas others organically grow theirs without a particular strategy and are often surprised to find themselves labeled as collectors. For Lee and Mel Eagle, both of these pathways are central to their story. As they remarked in their statement for this catalogue, the Eagles consider themselves accidental collectors. Certainly this was true for the first decades of their collecting, but as they became sophisticated

observers of the field over time, their preferences took shape and opportunities for acquisitions increased, resulting in a museum-quality collection of ceramics, fiber works, furniture, jewelry, and prints, paintings, and drawings.

It all began with clay, a medium that remains at the heart of the Eagles' collection. Lee's early training as a ceramist led to a lifetime devotion to clay, a passion that Mel has shared with her over the years. This passion resulted in their first purchase as a young married couple, a Jane Parshall stoneware vase acquired in Lee's hometown of Cleveland at the Cleveland Museum of Art's 1960 *May Show* (fig. 1). They did not know then that this simple purchase would ignite a larger passion, one that would grow beyond living with objects to encompass a deep respect for art and artists as well as a lifelong commitment to promoting and supporting their work through institutional and personal involvement.

One of the most significant manifestations of the Eagles' interest in clay was the 1973 establishment of Eagle Ceramics, a business that made available the materials, tools, equipment, and educational resources for the making and teaching of ceramics. Over the next eleven years, their company became the second-largest supplier in the United States, conducting business with individual artists, universities, educational programs, and others. In addition to its success as a business, Eagle Ceramics became a vehicle through which the Eagles came in contact with many important artists of the period. For example, the firm sold Paul Soldner's pottery wheels, leading them to meet him and collect his work. It also supplied Montgomery College, in their home state of Maryland, with materials for its ceramic program, which provided entrée to the college's workshops and lectures. Artists such as Michael Cardew, Toshiko Takaezu, Robert Turner, and Stephen De Staebler, among others, had presented their work at Montgomery, and Lee, in particular, had begun to develop her keen eye for form, technique, and aesthetics from watching them. Acquisitions of pieces soon followed. For example, Turner became a favorite of the Eagles' daughter, Alissa, after she had watched one such demonstration, ultimately leading to the acquisition of two vessels for the collection.[1]

Montgomery College, under the direction of Richard Mower, continued to play a central role in the Eagles' development as collectors through its participation with Eagle Ceramics and the American Hand Gallery in Washington, D.C., in a series of workshops, lectures, and exhibitions called "Making It in Clay," held from 1979 to 1983. The Eagles and the American Hand Gallery owner, Ken Deavers, and its manager, Ed Nash, drew up a list of artists to invite to give a lecture and workshop at Montgomery College (and later at the Corcoran School of Art), to be followed by a selling exhibition at the American Hand Gallery. For Lee, these events enabled her to meet artists who were on her wish list.[2] Indeed, the twenty-nine artists who participated in these exhibitions included many whose works the Eagles began to collect in-depth, beginning with their first purchases through the "Making It in Clay" shows. Ralph Bacerra, Don Reitz, Adrian Saxe, and Michael Cardew have remained touchstones for the Eagles both because of the immediate connection they

felt to their work upon first seeing it as well as because of the friendships, many lifelong, that resulted from their initial meetings. Other participating artists, such as Val Murat Cushing, Rick Dillingham, David Leach, and Mineo Mizuno, also found their ceramics acquired by the Eagles.

For many of these artists, the "Making It in Clay" exhibitions were a watershed event. Bacerra credited the American Hand Gallery and its shows as providing a strong collector base for his work (fig. 2).[3] Cushing recalled the line of people waiting for his exhibition opening, which extended around the block from the gallery and resulted in many sales.[4] Saxe's 1980 exhibition sold out, as did four of the six "Making It in Clay" shows from that year.[5] The Washington, D.C., area was quickly becoming a hotbed of ceramic collectors, the Eagles included.

At the time of these exhibitions, the Eagles were also deeply involved with the Renwick Gallery of the Smithsonian American Art Museum in Washington, D.C., and its support group, the James Renwick Alliance. Mel was president of the alliance from 1991 to 1993. Michael Monroe, former curator-in-charge of the Renwick Gallery, first met the Eagles in 1974 when he joined the staff of the institution and became close friends with them, a friendship that continues to this day. The Renwick Gallery, established in 1972, was one of the few museums

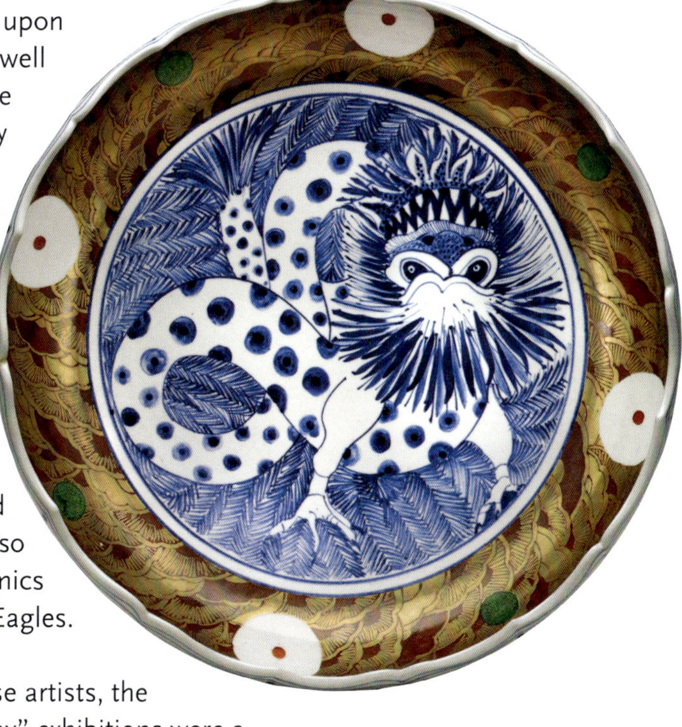

in America that seriously examined contemporary craft at the time. According to Monroe, it "became a focal point and magnet for audiences locally, nationally and internationally who were hungry for examples of and information on craft and design at a level not previously experienced. Although the Eagles' first love for collecting ceramics was already established, their appreciation of the Gallery's mission of rotating exhibitions and educational programming exposed them to works in other craft media such as wood, fiber, metal, and glass, all of which inspired and influenced them to expand their collection to its present form."[6]

Monroe watched the Eagles' collection evolve over the next few decades and worked closely with them as members of the James Renwick Alliance and as individual patrons of the gallery. The Eagles were especially dedicated to helping Monroe build the Renwick Gallery's collection of ceramics. "They were diligent in their efforts to keep me informed of the whereabouts of important pieces that would make excellent candidates for inclusion. When I sought approval from the [James Renwick] Alliance for funding, Mel and Lee were exceptionally knowledgeable and provided encouragement," said Monroe. "The Eagles' advocacy was invaluable to me as curator, not only for

their knowledge and connoisseurship, but as highly respected collectors within the local, regional and national community of craft collectors."[7]

The Eagles' involvement with the Renwick Gallery, like their later establishment of the Founders' Circle for the Mint Museum of Craft + Design's collection in Charlotte, North Carolina, also provided them with a sense of community as they encountered like-minded collectors from across the United States who also belonged to the group. Travel with the Renwick Alliance in the United States afforded additional opportunities to meet artists and visit their studios. In most cases, these visits enhanced the Eagles' existing knowledge of an artist, such as Stephen De Staebler, but in other cases the trips offered an introduction or access to an artist for the first time and often resulted in acquisitions, as with Sam Maloof.[8] Lee's many years of board service to the National Council on Education in the Ceramic Arts (NCECA), the American Craft Council, and Anderson Ranch Arts Center in Snowmass, Colorado, also provided exposure to and a vehicle for friendships with artists working in a variety of media.

In addition, other travels significantly influenced the Eagles' collection. For example, a business trip to Los Angeles serendipitously occurred at the same time as an auction of the collection of the Craft and Folk Art Museum, providing an opportunity to acquire two fiber works by Olga de Amaral and glass by Richard Marquis and Therman Statom. On a trip to Japan, they visited the Kyoto home and studio of Kawai Kanjirō and, according to Mel, were "taken by the beauty and the depth of his creativity, not only in ceramics but in other media as well."[9] They also visited the town of Mashiko, where they met Shimaoka Tatsuzō and other artists of the region (fig. 3).

FIGURE 3
SHIMAOKA TATSUZŌ
Plate with Rope Design, 1980
Stoneware
1 3/4 x 10 1/2 inches diameter
(4.4 x 26.7 cm)
The Leatrice S. and Melvin B. Eagle Collection, museum purchase funded by the Caroline Wiess Law Accessions Endowment Fund
2010.2135

This trip, combined with Lee's interest in the message of the book *The Unknown Craftsman: A Japanese Insight into Beauty* (1989) by Yanagi Sōetsu, one of Kawai's partners in establishing the *mingei* (folk art) movement in Japan, formed the basis of their Japanese ceramic collection. In addition to finding the objects "to be aesthetically pleasing, beautifully crafted and decorated objects that we wanted to live with," Mel stated that they were also interested in "the connections of these particular artists' work to [American and British ceramic] history."[10] Their interest in tying American ceramic history to that of Japan and England resulted in acquisitions of works by Edmund de Waal and Takeshi Yasuda that complemented the Eagles' earlier acquisitions of pieces by Michael Cardew, David Leach, and Hamada Shōji.

As the Eagles' collection grew in the 1990s and early 2000s, a directed acquisition program began to take hold, formed by years of study, exposure to artists, galleries, museums, and other collections. Discernible patterns emerged: a preference for color; content and message; outstanding technique in individual works; and a focus on artists who occupied a time-tested leadership role in their field.[11] The Eagles' significant holdings in West Coast ceramics, particularly those made in the 1960s and 1970s during the heyday of the Funk movement, coalesced clearly, as did strong collection subsets in jewelry, fiber, and furniture that provided comparative contexts for the ceramics holdings (fig. 4).

As they honed their collection, the Eagles also began to turn their advocacy and energy toward the more philosophical issues that challenged the field. As a member and then chair of the board of trustees of the American Craft Council from 1999 to 2006, Lee spearheaded a campaign to broaden the scope of the council's activities, encouraging the organization to once again become a leader in the field by highlighting new ways of making, encouraging critical discourse, and breaking down the ideological barriers that had ossified craft's history and its role in the larger art world. The culmination of this work was the 2006 "Shaping the Future of Craft" National Leadership Conference, which took place in Houston and was attended by more than six hundred artists and practitioners, educators, museum and arts professionals, gallerists and business owners, and writers and critics. This conference provoked some of the most spirited, engaging, and refreshing dialogues about craft in years.

Peter C. Marzio, the late former director of the Museum of Fine Arts, Houston, referred to contemporary craft as "objects of cultural significance," acknowledging the way that these pieces have been perceived historically and contemporaneously in many cultures.

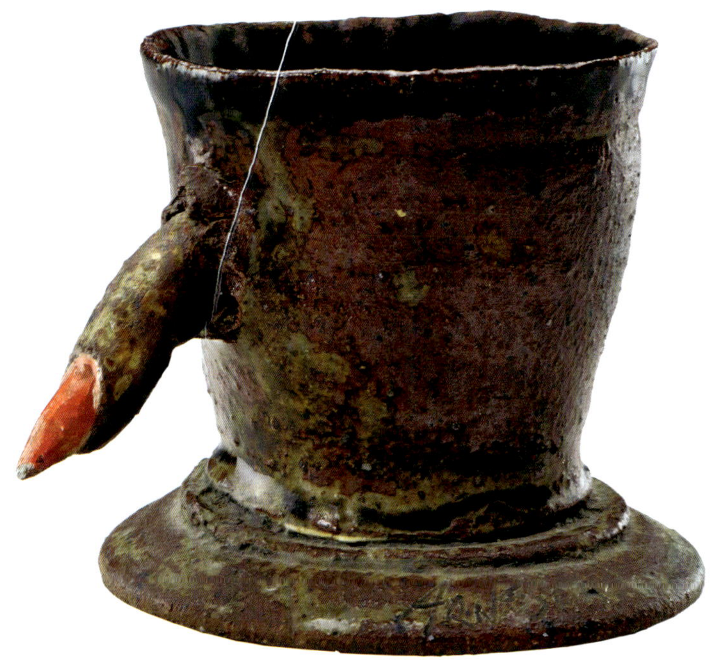

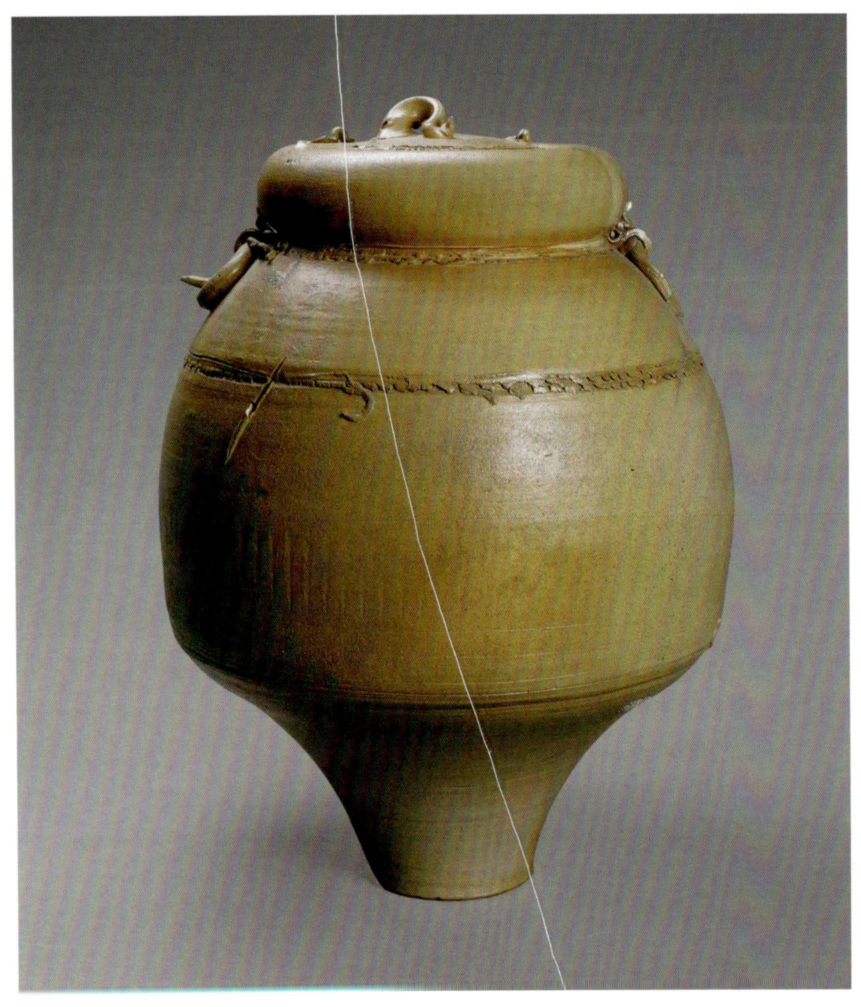

His public exasperation with the hierarchical divisions in the art world and its institutions at the "Shaping the Future of Craft" conference was a call to arms for many, including the Eagles, who responded to Marzio's words with a gift of an untitled vessel by Don Reitz to the museum that same year (fig. 5).[12] Ultimately, the museum's embrace of craft as an equal art form, its welcoming of a diversity of mediums in its gallery presentations, and its focus on artistic excellence, not labels or categories, are what led to the Eagles' choice of the museum as the new home for their collection in 2010.[13]

Since that time, the Eagle collection has fit seamlessly into the Museum of Fine Arts, Houston, enhancing its strengths in ceramics, glass, and jewelry, and filling major gaps in fiber and furniture. These works have been featured in numerous presentations of the permanent collection, providing glimpses into its riches. Now, for the first time, the public will see the collection as a whole, experience the power of these individual objects, and appreciate the Eagles' vision as collectors.

NOTES

1 Lee and Mel Eagle, interview by the author, July 26, 2010.

2 Ibid.

3 Ralph Bacerra, "Oral History Interview with Frank Lloyd, April 12 and 19, 2004," Nanette L. Laitman Documentation Project for Craft and Decorative Arts in America, Archives of American Art, Smithsonian Institution, Washington, D.C. Available online at http://www.aaa.si.edu/collections/interviews/oral-history-interview-ralph-bacerra-12942.

4 Val Cushing, "Oral History Interview with Margaret Carney, April 16, 2001," Nanette L. Laitman Documentation Project for Craft and Decorative Arts in America, Archives of American Art, Smithsonian Institution, Washington, D.C. Available online at http://www.aaa.si.edu/collections/interviews/oral-history-interview-val-cushing-12255.

5 Florence Rubenfeld, "American Hand," *American Craft* 41, no. 1 (February/March 1981): 40–41.

6 Michael Monroe, in an e-mail to the author, July 8, 2013.

7 Ibid.

8 Lee and Mel Eagle, interview by the author, July 26, 2010.

9 Mel Eagle, in an e-mail to the author, August 11, 2010.

10 Ibid.

11 Mel Eagle, in an e-mail to the author, July 9, 2013.

12 For a complete transcription of Peter Marzio's talk, see Monica Hampton and Lily Kane, eds., *Shaping the Future of Craft: 2006 National Leadership Conference* (New York: American Craft Council, 2007), 43–47.

13 Lee Eagle, in an e-mail to the author, July 20, 2012.

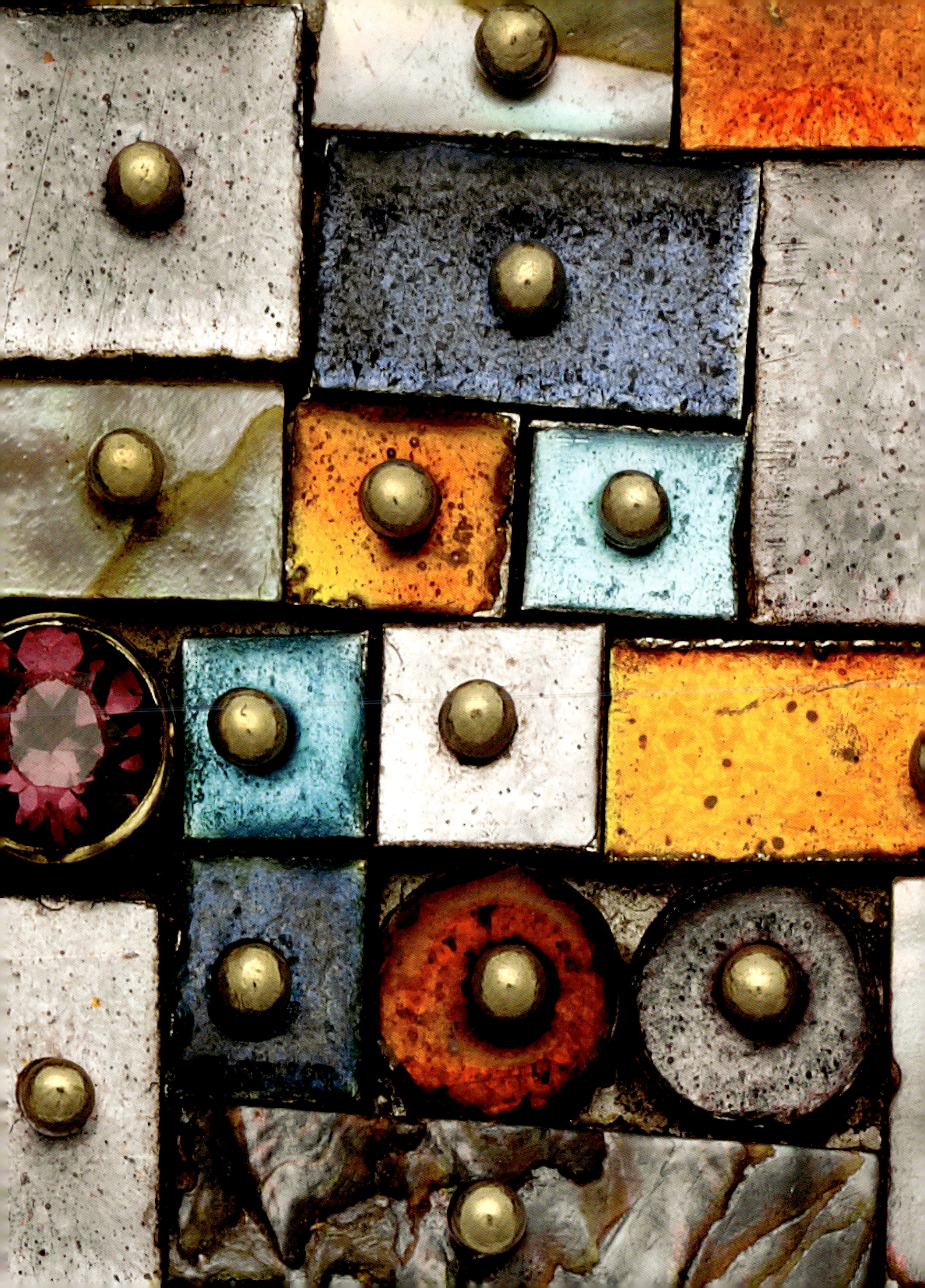

TOWARD AN IDEOLOGY OF CRAFT

Janet Koplos

VOCABULARY LESSONS

In the decades following World War II, as crafts burgeoned in America, vocabulary became a concern. It was to some degree a matter of identity: what exactly did "crafts" mean in the middle of the twentieth century? What were the motivations of people working under that label, and how did crafts (ceramics, textiles, jewelry, metalwork, wood, and glass) differ from any other sort of visual art? If invention rather than tradition was crafts' primary allegiance, did the work need a new name?

In the 1960s, another question was raised. By then crafts were thoroughly embedded in academia, no longer learned by apprenticeship. Standing shoulder to shoulder with painters and sculptors, craftspeople not surprisingly adopted some of the same goals, from social commentary to shock. They longed for critical discourse, beyond mere reportorial or human-interest writing.[1] The subsequent discussion, however, consisted more often of lamenting the lack of a critical language than proposing a vocabulary or applying art terms to see what fit, what did not, and what might be learned from the contrast.

The question of critical language endures, although there has been some clarification over the years. Utilitarian work and production work sold in quantities and at modest prices at fairs or shows have mostly disappeared from the critical sphere. Craft galleries went through decades of ascendancy and advocacy but are now fading as crafts move increasingly into art galleries. In this context, crafts can be seen to offer physical directness, to communicate evidence of process, and to employ an inward focus in which one work inspires the next, rather than outside events or issues being the motivation. It seems that intuition and implicitness are the gifts of crafts in a world where other forms of expression are deliberate and explicit and where the art establishment favors "content" that can be verbalized rather than the visual aspects that more universally define art.[2] Sociologists and philosophers have offered new perspectives, including the ideas that making is a form of thinking and that the labor involved is part of the meaning of the work.[3] New attention has come from young scholars exploring the ideology of crafts and examining history through various lenses, such as feminism.[4] The ongoing confusion and debate, it could be argued, are signs of the vitality of the field.

The art world is not a great deal clearer about such issues. In the twentieth century, it debated the artistic validity of photography, computer-based art, and new media; whether video was collectible; the role of text; the inclusion of performance; the relevance of painting; and more, arguing about everything as a matter of course. Also, in recent decades, the art world has lacked a dominant style. Though this stylistic void was of some concern in the 1970s, now one can, in retrospect, recognize the emergence of pluralism, which rules to this day. The historian Jonathan Fineberg has noted, "Broadly speaking, the pluralism of the seventies grew out of a widespread late-sixties assault on hierarchies of authority, political as well as cultural, in favor of the uniqueness of each individual's experience as an equal (and mobile) component of the cultural whole."[5] So the absence of a preeminent movement in fact defined the time, as the doors of the art world were opening to women and non-Western artists, among others. The crafts have likewise been pluralistic, if less articulate about politics or theory, and have long been receptive to the aesthetics of other cultures and to the expertise of immigrants. English metalsmiths were dominant in America in the early twentieth century, and a few decades later, American ceramic development was led by Austrian, German, and Finnish immigrants, whereas the postwar period was swept by a wave of Japanese influence.

LOOKING FOR THEMES AND STYLES

One way to uncover the main issues of late-twentieth-century crafts is to look at the primary evidence: preserved works. Private collections like that of Mel and Lee Eagle, which naturally reflect individual preferences and are not comprehensive, may be supplemented by examination of exhibition catalogues and books of the time. These sources reveal stylistic shifts, new techniques, status concerns, and arguments about the role of tradition, for example.

Craft exhibition catalogues were rudimentary until the 1970s and often consisted of a few black-and-white photos accompanied by a short text, or no text at all. The curatorial focus of these exhibitions could be perceived only in the choice of featured works, which almost always celebrated variety. New York's Museum of Contemporary Crafts (MCC) opened in 1956 with the general exhibition *Craftsmanship in a Changing World*, followed by survey exhibitions, such as *Furniture by Craftsmen* (1957). Presenting handmade

and mostly functional objects neither as historical artifacts nor as anthropological specimens, MCC modeled itself after art museums. As modest as the title *Furniture by Craftsmen* sounds, the word "craftsmen" actually marked a change, replacing the term "designer-craftsmen," which implied an association with industry.[6]

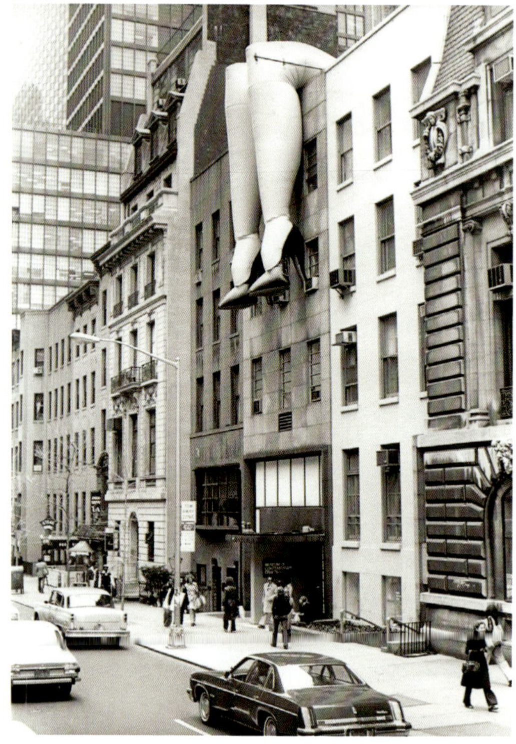

Crowd-pleasing shows were an early staple, the height (or nadir) being *Cookies and Breads: The Baker's Art* (1965), which ventured the claim that a creative process and decorative aesthetic could be discovered anywhere. Even later shows that focused on inedible objects, such as *Homage to the Bag* (1975) and *The Great American Foot* (1978), did not explore the implications of form or the nature of utility but offered assortments easy for the public to digest (fig. 1). This strategy was practical for promoting a new institution and for bringing attention to a little-examined field, and was not unusual. Even the Museum of Modern Art allowed painters freedom from thematic strictures by organizing nonspecific shows such as *16 Americans* (1959), and museums still curate "soft" subjects to reach a population larger than the art cognoscenti. (Consider the Guggenheim Museum's 1998 exhibition *The Art of the Motorcycle* and the Museum of Arts and Design's 2012 presentation *The Art of Scent, 1889–2012*.) The MCC also presented small individual-artist shows, a few retrospective exhibitions, and the award-centered *Young Americans* shows—a type absent from the national playing field today. The museum occasionally came close to defining a category, perhaps with *Fantasy Furniture* (1966) and almost certainly with curator (later director) Paul J. Smith's *Woven Forms* (1963). That show introduced large-scale fiber sculptures and identified a new emphasis on dimensional shaping (fig. 2).

Smith also had a hand in the most important traveling show of the 1960s and 1970s, *Objects: USA*, aiding curator Lee Nordness. Opening in Washington, D.C., the exhibition traveled to twenty-two American museums and then abroad. Nordness and Smith did not choose any particular style or subject but concentrated on works by the younger generation. The show has been described as the first to focus on nonproduction crafts (that is, one-of-a-kind and often nonfunctional objects). Nordness did not want to call participants craftsmen, so he dubbed them "object makers."[7] The term was not widely adopted.

Most museum shows that responded to the vastly increasing numbers of makers and consumers of crafts likewise surveyed the field or addressed the breadth of one medium in the sort of exhibition I call "see what (clay) can do" and another writer calls a "show-everyone extravaganza."[8]

Newness was the emphasis. The Smithsonian's Renwick Gallery began its

craft and decorative arts program in 1972 with a show called *Woodenworks* that distinguished itself by focusing on the work of just five preeminent furniture makers, rather than multitudes.[9] In general, museum exhibitions did not name movements because the field did not develop in that way,[10] nor did they focus on formal analysis of works. They surveyed the entire crafts field, or a single medium, or a single technique.

Two important shows of the 1960s, however, were thematic. *Abstract Expressionist Ceramics* (1966) and *Funk* (1967), both organized in California, addressed current work. The title

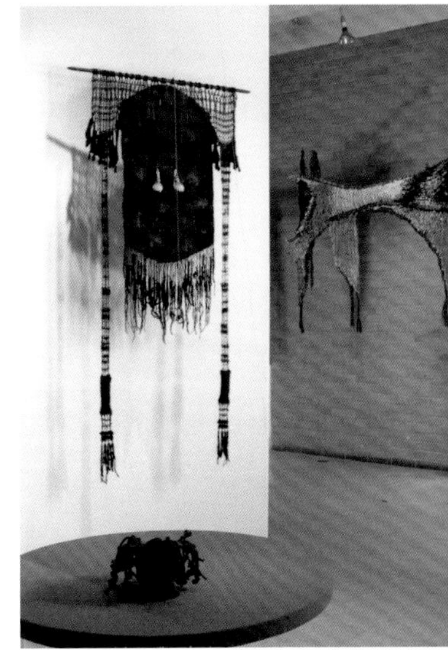

of the former was a convenience used by critic John Coplans, an early champion of the California "clay revolution." Regrettably, the terminology "Abstract Expressionist"— besides being inappropriate for such included artists as Ron Nagle—became a problem because it categorized new ceramics in terms of a near-passé painting style rather than in the context of its own history. Ceramics were an integral part of the all-medium art exhibition curated by Peter Selz (fig. 3). "Funk art is hot rather than cool; it is committed rather than disengaged; it is bizarre rather than formal; it is sensuous; and frequently it is quite ugly and ungainly. Although usually three-dimensional, it is

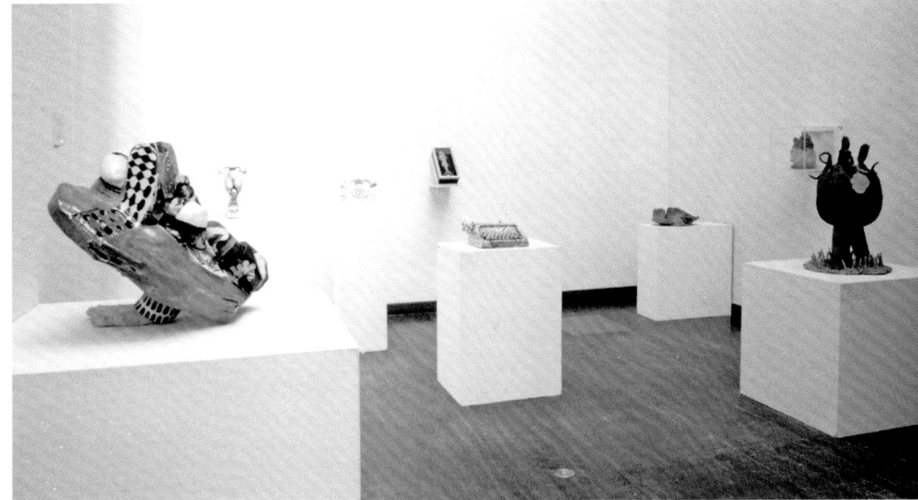

FIGURE 2
Installation view of the exhibition *Woven Forms*, Museum of Contemporary Crafts, New York City, 1963.

FIGURE 3
Installation view of the exhibition *Funk*, Berkeley Art Museum, California, 1967.

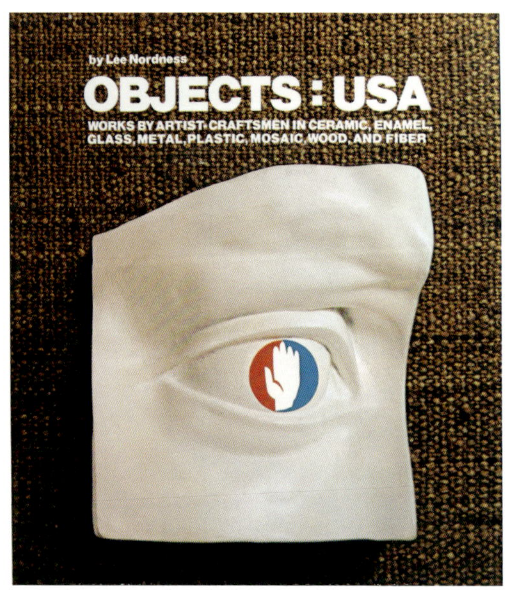

non-sculptural in any traditional way, and irreverent in attitude. It is symbolic in content and evocative in feeling," he wrote.[11] He added that Funk artists "enjoy and often exploit the vulgarity of the contemporary man-made environment and speak in a visual vernacular."[12] Both "Abstract Expressionist" and "Funk" are terms that remain in use in crafts, and Funk is sometimes expanded to include any vulgar and amusing work. It is noteworthy that these instances of curatorial clarity developed outside the crafts field.

Individuals also named themes or styles. The collector and gallerist Garth Clark came up with the descriptor "Super-Object" for highly refined ceramic work, but it did not stick.[13] The artist Sheila Hicks proposed the term Substantialism to reflect crafts-people's devotion to their medium.[14] For whatever reason—maybe just because the field did not aspire to categories or really want to develop a language—this term, too, faded away.

Another way to get a handle on late-twentieth-century crafts is to enumerate changes that generated excitement. Among the innovations were sculptural furniture, sculptural fiber, free-form glass, body jewelry, large-scale ceramics, and wood turning in the 1960s; alternative-material and aggressive jewelry plus basketry and blacksmithing in the 1970s; and virtuoso ceramics and glass in the 1980s. However, most of these examples are not specific or distinctive enough to define a style, body jewelry being the closest.[15]

Style, an identifiable appearance not limited by function, is closely associated with the fashion industry but has been part of art's pursuit of the new as well. The familiar chronology in the art world is that Abstract Expressionism emerged in the 1940s and 1950s, followed by Pop, Minimalism, and Post-Minimalism. However, in the years since then the picture is less clear. The 1970s, as they were lived, seemed amorphous, styleless. Pattern and Decoration (P&D) in the mid-1970s was probably the last defined stylistic movement, after which were only occasional flashes of group identity, such as the "Pictures Generation" in the 1980s. P&D adopted some craft materials and a decorative, color-and-pattern-obsessed aesthetic, but the other movements have only a weak connection to crafts. Although some describe individual bodies of work, these approaches have not carried over into identifiable groups of craft practitioners. The "dematerialization of the art object" around 1970 is the exact opposite of craft values, and Minimalism's industrial approach is the reverse of crafts' concurrent move toward virtuosity.[16]

This poor correspondence between art movements and craft works suggests that the craft field does not simply follow art's lead. Postmodernism may be the most transferrable term, but it originates in architecture and design, with less application in painting and sculpture and less in crafts. Although Peter Shire's ceramics

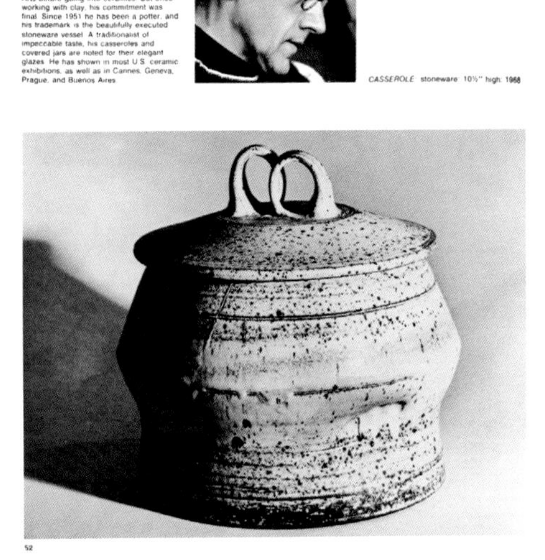

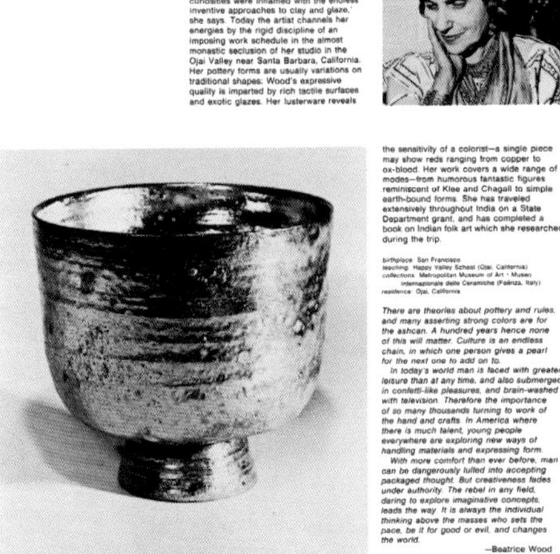

FIGURE 5
Interior spread from *Objects: USA*, by Lee Nordness (New York: Viking Press, 1970).

in association with the Memphis group unquestionably qualified as Postmodern, and some studio furniture shares such characteristic features as aggregation, high color, and geometric contrasts, the best-known book applying the term to ceramics was too broad to be illuminating.[17] However, even if art movements do not apply to crafts, cultural phenomena of a given time may appear equally in both art and craft, from the antiwar sentiments of the 1960s to ecology in the 1990s. Money affected both art and crafts in the 1980s in conjunction with a Wall Street boom by increasing the number of collectors and raising the prices that they were willing to pay. Art critics then feared "that art no longer opposed consumer culture."[18] Nevertheless, crafts came closer to being happily integrated into mainstream consumer culture (the buying culture) at that time than during its various periods as an alternative practice.[19]

Craft books and catalogues dating from the postwar decades reveal the styles of the times, visually if not verbally. Among the most useful overviews are the 1970 *Objects: USA* catalogue, Julie Hall's 1977 book *Tradition and Change: The New American Craftsman*, and the 1986 catalogue *American Craft Today: Poetry of the Physical*. All three are extensively illustrated and give a curated view of their decade. But they make no more than a cursory attempt to name the styles or state artists' ideas. How should this absence of characterizing and the already noted lack of categorizing be explained? Were the forms too new to be conceptually grouped? Were there no associations of like minds back then? Did the field not welcome such consideration, either in general or in details? Had it not yet attracted the critics or scholars who would do that work? Or perhaps were the authors ahead of their time in accepting diversity and in believing that stylistic boundaries need not be drawn? All three publications offer great numbers of works, throngs rather than select choices, and the writers seem disinclined to name masterpieces or develop a canon.

The three hundred artists represented in *Objects: USA* were chosen to emphasize diversity of method, style, and generation—chosen, in other words, for their differentness from each other (fig. 4). The catalogue grouped them by medium (fig. 5). Mosaic

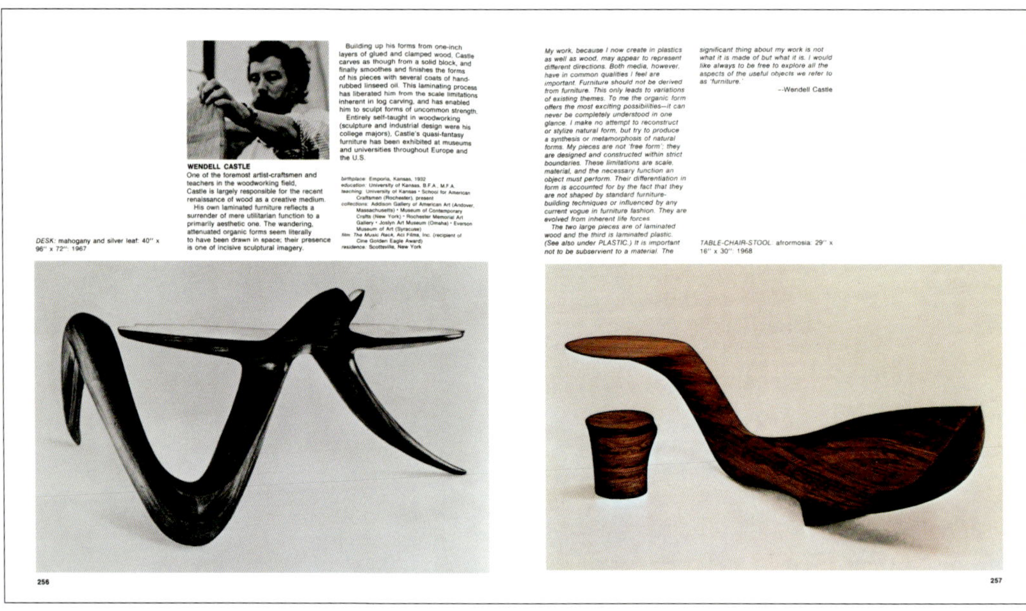

WENDELL CASTLE
One of the foremost artist-craftsmen and teachers in the woodworking field, Castle is largely responsible for the recent renaissance of wood as a creative medium.

His own laminated furniture reflects a surrender of mere utilitarian function to a primarily aesthetic one. The wandering, attenuated organic forms seem literally to have been drawn in space; their presence is one of incisive sculptural imagery.

Building up his forms from one-inch layers of glued and clamped wood, Castle carves as though from a solid block, and finally smoothes and finishes the forms of his pieces with several coats of hand-rubbed linseed oil. This laminating process has liberated him from the scale limitations inherent in log carving, and has enabled him to sculpt forms of uncommon strength.

Entirely self-taught in woodworking (sculpture and industrial design were his college majors), Castle's quasi-fantasy furniture has been exhibited at museums and universities throughout Europe and the U.S.

birthplace: Emporia, Kansas, 1932
education: University of Kansas, B.F.A., M.F.A.
teaching: University of Kansas · School for American Craftsmen (Rochester), present
collections: Addison Gallery of American Art (Andover, Massachusetts) · Museum of Contemporary Crafts (New York) · Rochester Memorial Art Gallery · Joslyn Art Museum (Omaha) · Everson Museum of Art (Syracuse)
film: The Music Rack, Aci Films, Inc. (recipient of Cine Golden Eagle Award)
residence: Scottsville, New York

My work, because I now create in plastics as well as wood, may appear to represent different directions. Both media, however, have in common qualities I feel are important. Furniture should not be derived from furniture. This only leads to variations of existing themes. To me the organic form offers the most exciting possibilities—it can never be completely understood in one glance. I make no attempt to reconstruct or stylize natural form, but try to produce a synthesis or metamorphosis of natural forms. My pieces are not 'free form'; they are designed and constructed within strict boundaries. These limitations are scale, material, and the necessary function an object must perform. Their differentiation in form is accounted for by the fact that they are not shaped by standard furniture-building techniques or influenced by any current vogue in furniture fashion. They are evolved from inherent life forces.

The two large pieces are of laminated wood and the third is laminated plastic. (See also under PLASTIC.) It is important not to be subservient to a material. The significant thing about my work is not what it is made of but what it is. I would like always to be free to explore all the aspects of the useful objects we refer to as 'furniture.'

—Wendell Castle

DESK: mahogany and silver leaf: 40" x 96" x 72": 1967

TABLE-CHAIR-STOOL: afrormosia: 29" x 16" x 30": 1968

256   257

---

and plastic are nonexistent categories today, and enamel, a promising medium then, is now minor.

Across all mediums, only the most basic language is consistently applied: the phrase "excellence of execution" (craftsmanship) was often used, and so was the word "exploring" (an art intention). Those were the polarities of the 1960s: sticking to traditional measures of quality or searching for the new. At that time, sturdy pottery was common, and throwing lines were prominent. Teapots were accompanied by low, wide teacups with saucers. Figurative work was practically nonexistent, though it would become dominant by the end of the century—a clear demonstration of how preferences change. Conceptual work was rare. A few artists addressed personal or political subject matter. Some sculpture, particularly Funk, riffed on contemporary culture. Peter Voulkos and Toshiko Takaezu were leaders in making sculptures for which "vessel" is too modest a description.

For glass, *Objects: USA* presented both engineered works (before the 1962 Toledo workshops that reintroduced the medium) and emergent spontaneous and experi-mental efforts.[20] Metalwork at the time was conventional, with a few organic shapes in silver conveying modernity. Jewelry presented a far greater range, emphasizing strikingly sculptural forms. Other works of the 1960s incorporated found materials and plastics, used industrial techniques to create innovative surfaces, or worked at a new scale in old techniques. Leading-edge crafts emphasized structure and repetition, dynamic movement, or "magical" energies.

Objects: USA did not include much wood, featuring only two turners and eleven furniture or object makers, though most of them are still regarded as major figures. The most common aesthetic was organic, but some makers juxtaposed functional and almost Pop elements, combined fantasy and whimsy, or deviated from the planed edge and found attractive visual effects in decay (fig. 6). The fiber selection in *Objects: USA* included a great range of formats and surfaces, many by makers who are forgotten today. Experimental works often retained the visible structure of weaving but violated expectations of material or scale. Dense and colorful patterning that might be described as psychedelic came from dye, stitchery, and collaging or piecing. Some works responded to historical and ethnic textiles. Color effects were systematic or painterly. A few makers pursued personal expression in spiritual directions. The 1960s marked an adventurous and intensely inventive period in textiles that has not been repeated (although the 1970s came close in its sheer volume of innovation including basketry, felting, hand-papermaking, and "wearables," and the new emphasis on surface design included Asian dyeing techniques and industrial photo-transfer methods). Attention to extremes of scale was heightened by the large dimensions required by the prestigious Lausanne Biennial in Switzerland, and by a series of British shows that recognized and encouraged miniatures.[21]

Objects: USA was immediately regarded as a landmark exhibition, and it retains that status today. The number of works and the exposure allowed by its extensive tour made the show important. Nordness and Smith had the advantage of working in simpler times, when there was less institutional bureaucracy, so they could respond quickly to what was happening. The show also gained its outsize importance because Nordness persuaded its sponsor, the Johnson's Wax Company, to buy the entire contents of the show and donate works to the museums that hosted the exhibition; these works thus stayed in the public realm, and many became popular and critical icons (for example, Arline M. Fisch's outsize *Body Ornament* in the collection of the Museum of Arts and Design). Nordness and Smith's decision not to honor the senior figures in the field but to emphasize the young probably arose from Smith's youth and Nordness's closeness to the art world as a New York dealer.[22] It paid off. *Objects: USA* put an imprimatur on the careers of its featured artists for any collector who needed such reassurance (although in the crafts, most collectors are moved by

impulse rather than status). As these artists matured, they continued to cite the show in their curriculum vitae, endorsing it in return. Although an exhibition this large would inevitably have some duds and some hits, the curators must be given credit for having a good eye.

For all mediums, the 1970s was a period of stretching in new directions. Rose Slivka, editor of *Craft Horizons* magazine, in writing an article called "Affirmation: The American Craftsman," made the case with poetic romanticism: "The cry is for a new humanism and resistance to increasing mechanization of thought, of feeling, of work. The presence of the craftsman in this emerging new humanism is crucial."[23] At the same time, commercial, whimsical, and avant-garde forms were challenging the utilitarian and traditional.

The first field-surveying books were published in the 1970s, notably *Tradition and Change*. Hall divided her book into nine chapters. The headings, while better than nothing, are not mutually exclusive, so placement of an artist seems nearly arbitrary. The first chapter, "For Use and Beauty," could have included three-quarters of the makers in the book. "A Decade of Funk" is valid and clear; other chapters address abstraction, fantasy, icons, and identity. All of these broad themes have played out over the years. However, only one of the five artists included in the small "Identity and Issue" chapter represents what is now called ethnic identity.[24]

Surprisingly, Hall recognized neither feminism nor gender identity in the crafts in 1977 (she placed Patti Warashina in the "Fantasy" chapter and omitted Howard Kottler), although crafts and art were both affected by these social issues, which have remained major themes in crafts. Some artists in other chapters make

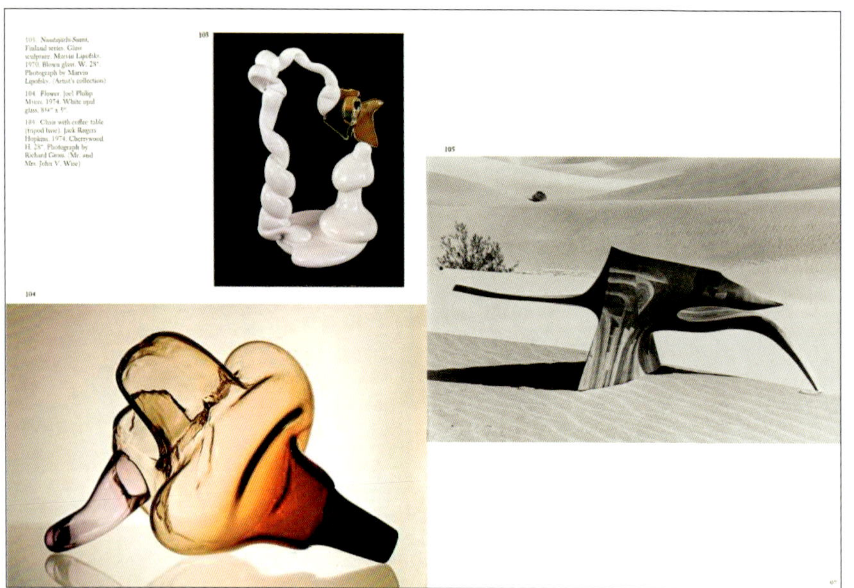

FIGURE 7
Interior spread from *Tradition and Change: The New American Craftsman*, by Julie Hall (New York: Dutton, 1977).

and was to become a major theme in other materials as well. Another missing category is illusion, especially 3-D illusion and especially in ceramics.

This book bore the burden of being the first of its type. Hall had no basis for comparison and few resources for the text, which is vastly longer than Nordness's introductory essay. Her hundred-plus artists are very well chosen; in retrospect only two or three do not qualify as major figures in their medium. The failures of the book are in the admirable risks it took, rare instances of categorization that now seem inadequate, yet can evoke useful distinctions.

sociopolitical commentary, an increasingly common approach. In the "Public Spaces" chapter, the textile works—then popular in corporate lobbies and hotel atriums—put color and repetitive structure to work, rather than imagery. Those qualities are abstract, and maybe that neutrality suited America's pluralistic society. "Icons for Our Time," implying yet avoiding the term spiritual, includes most mediums, with some perceptive and some surprising choices.[25]

Organic form was widespread in the 1970s. In furniture and wooden vessels, "organic" meant rounded edges, curved legs, and minimized geometry; in ceramics, it meant bulbous forms, tactile surfaces, and layered effects that suggested nature; in glass, it came from blowing and from still-limited skills; and in jewelry, it manifested in thin edges, ripples or twists, and actual feathers in addition to forms evoking creatures of the sea and air (fig. 7). Nonprecious materials and industrial techniques were used in most mediums. Another look of the period was baroque entanglements and complexity in textiles, ceramics, and blacksmithing. Hall made no reference to the body, which was already a subject in jewelry

Poetry of the Physical, capturing the 1980s, included 286 artists and cited their "plurality of purpose" (fig. 8).[26] Paul Smith noted in his essay that beauty continued to be honored in the crafts. That observation can lead today's readers to the thought that the art world, suddenly discussing beauty in the 1990s at the instigation of Dave Hickey,[27] was late to the issue. Smith cited interest in modern design and historical styles and ended by saying that the object is the message and that the viewer must puzzle out the poetry of the physical (a conclusion that could be read as either an open door or a cop-out). Edward Lucie-Smith's essay placed craft historically and ideologically. *Poetry of the Physical* made less effort to categorize than *Tradition and Change* did. It used two groupings by purpose ("Statement" and "Use") and two by form ("Vessel" and "Adornment"—the latter meaning jewelry and clothing). Yet in retrospect, the 1980s work shows striking differences from that of the 1960s and 1970s: namely, a drastic expansion of "content" and a new orientation toward photographic documentation.[28]

The catalogue immediately introduces the idea of virtuosity, which is particularly associated with Adrian Saxe's ceramics. Such works elicit a "wow" from the viewer and show the vast improvement in skills in the crafts over the postwar period. Although Lucie-Smith said little about the exhibited work, he used the word "narrative" in a reference to Wendell Castle—and this term would be employed increasingly broadly in the coming years. In *Poetry of the Physical*, works that made a statement or implied a story are numerous. Commentary comes in a range of exactness from explicit to subtly suggested; in ceramics these extremes might be represented by Michael Lucero's historical or environmental references and Jack Earl's shaggy-dog stories, which in his early work were laboriously lettered onto the work or a label (fig. 9).

Animal metaphors multiplied in the 1980s, with animals as expressions of human emotion, mostly disturbing. Also flourishing was the depiction of vulnerable bodies, usually stylized rather than precisely representational. Organic abstraction continued to be important. Geometric abstraction was a minority interest in basketry and in other materials, though it appeared regularly in John Mason's ceramic oeuvre. Two other notable interests of the decade were the ritual or spiritual and the evocation of place, either a landscape or a looser spatial configuration.

Poetry of the Physical selections reflected the energy in studio furniture in the 1980s. Though artists still showed a preference for softened, rounded forms, they also created some forms that were crisper and some that shaped architectural space, and they produced disparate assemblies that fit one definition of Postmodernism, although that term is not applied in this catalogue. The latter works ranged from mildly disjunctive

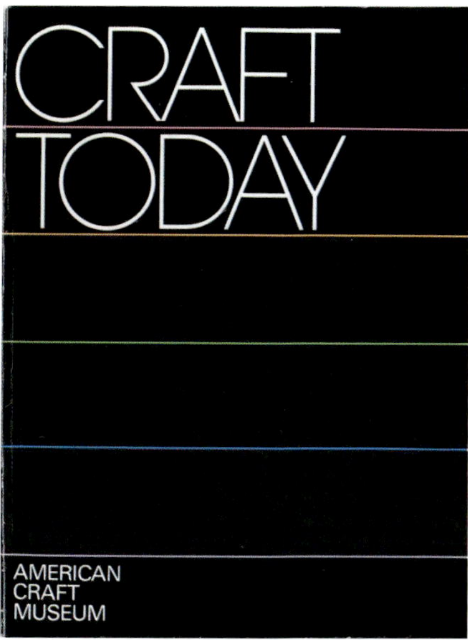

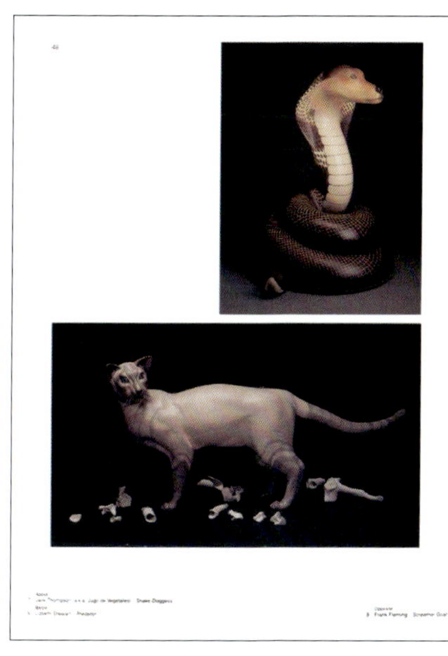

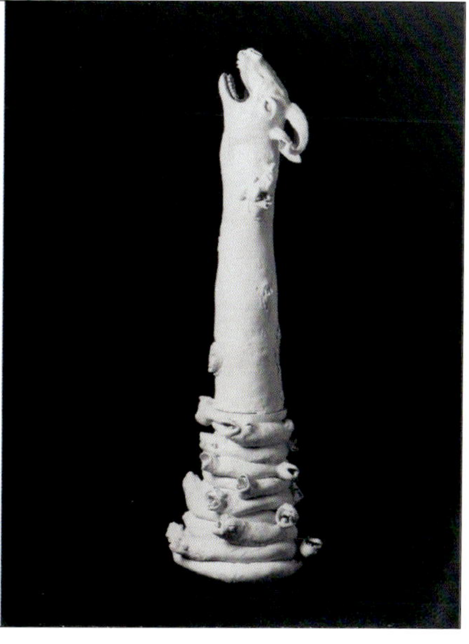

to jokey. Figurative furniture, adopting human or animal shape, was another feature of the decade, along with large-scale ironwork in which Albert Paley was and continues to be a leading practitioner.

The catalogue's "Vessel" category, which was dominated by ceramics but included glass, textiles, and wood, showed nearly every 1980s stylistic approach cited so far. Saxe's continuing masterful ceramic works were high points. Here, Postmodernism might be recognized in exaggerated vertical

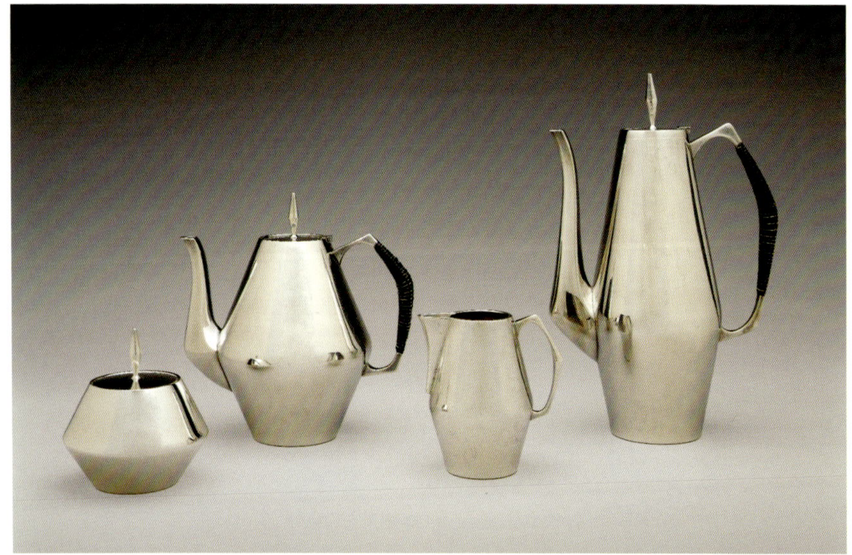

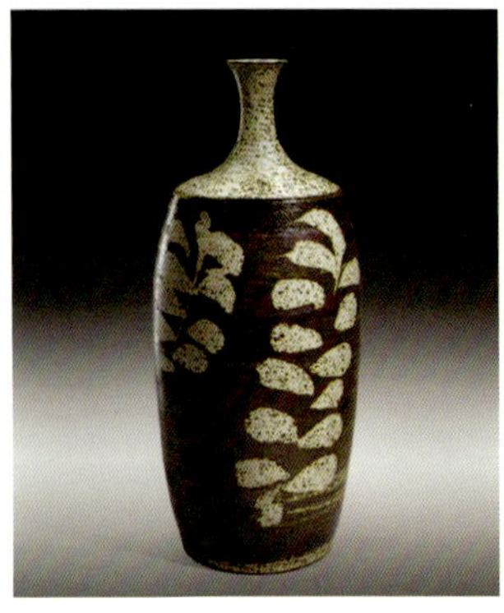

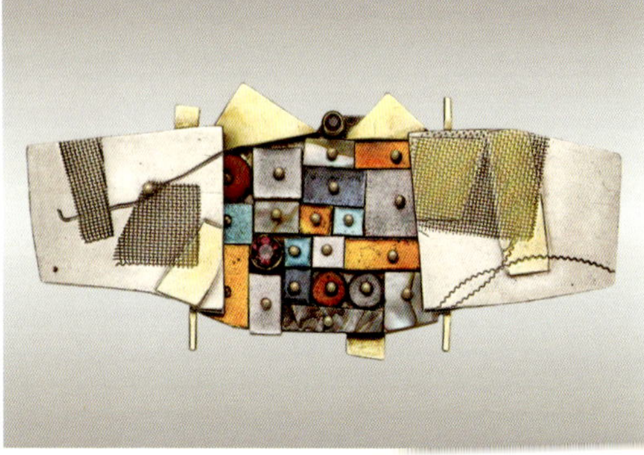

CLOCKWISE FROM TOP:
FIGURE 10
JOHN AXEL PRIP
Manufactured by Reed & Barton,
*"The Diamond" Tea and
Coffee Service*, 1960
Sterling silver and plastic
2010.2263.1–.4
(Checklist no. 108)

FIGURE 11
EARL PARDON
Pin, 1960
Sterling silver, 14k gold,
colored stones, and enamel
2010.2104
(Checklist no. 99)

FIGURE 12
PETER VOULKOS
Vase, 1952–53
Stoneware
2010.2156
(Checklist no. 162)

intensely patterned surfaces was also frequent in the 1980s. The Eagles' 1979 and 1980 works by Ralph Bacerra are fine examples, highly and precisely decorated (see checklist nos. 20–23). Sometimes pattern acknowledged crafts' constant exchange across cultures or alluded to the passage of time. It also offered the sheer physical pleasure of repetition.

Like *Objects: USA, Poetry of the Physical* was an enormous show. It did not travel so extensively, nor was it purchased in its entirety, but again the works were well chosen. Most likely the credit for that should go to Smith, since Lucie-Smith is an art historian, not a curator or critic. His notable contribution was the twenty-five-page historical essay that gave the catalogue some scholarly weight, whereas Smith's introductory essay was brief. In addition to biographies of the artists, the back matter included a chronology of American crafts from 1851 to 1986, which, along with Lucie-Smith's essay, marked the craft world's increasing sense of its own history. This catalogue has become a classic likely because its production quality magnified the solid selections. The book is slightly oversize, and many of the images occupy a full page. The images are spectacularly sharp and the color precise, making study of the catalogue a sensual and therefore memorable experience.

forms that look assembled rather than unified, presumably commenting on our precarious cultural integrity in a polyglot, multicultural, high-speed culture. They drew from history, but then, crafts have always done so; the exaggeration of elements was common in ceramics and may relate not to Postmodernism but to challenging conventions: pots about pots.

Many works in all mediums displayed their own process of making so that the viewer could share it kinesthetically. This formal expressiveness demonstrated what is now recognized as the concept of "making is thinking." Likewise, the celebration of the material itself as a sensuous, beautiful, engrossing collaboration with nature, rather than an imposition upon it, remained a strong philosophical motivation in craft works. On the other hand, the artifice of

THE EAGLE COLLECTION

No personal collection ever presents a perfect historical chronology, and the choices of private collectors are likely to be swayed by different factors than the choices of curators or writers. Nevertheless, the Eagles collected major types of work and pieces by major artists that illustrate important points in the decades addressed by *Objects: USA, Tradition and Change*, and *Poetry of the Physical*. An impressive conservative example in the Eagle collection is John Prip's 1960 design for a four-piece silver tea service manufactured by Reed & Barton (fig. 10). Prip's European education and apprenticeship experience prepared him to conceive such elegant objects, which were already becoming outdated when this set was given to the Eagles as a wedding present. The lifestyles that accommodated silver steadily diminished in the twentieth century, and no other object in their collection has this formality.

Prip was included in *Objects: USA*, as was Earl Pardon. The collection includes several pieces of jewelry by Pardon (fig. 11), whose mastery of color, primarily through enamel, might be equated with the contemporaneous Color Field painters or the eccentric colorist Friedensreich Hundertwasser. In ceramics, the Eagles' favored medium, the collection represents many phases of Voulkos's work, from a refined vase of 1952–53 with wax-resist decoration (fig. 12) to a signature 1973 platter with "pass-throughs" to a massive 1999 stack form that is playfully titled *The Eagle Has Landed* (see checklist nos. 159 and 166). They acquired fewer Takaezu pieces, but excellent ones: the exquisitely gentle and pale, small *Bottle* (1980), the deeply colored spherical *Purple Moon* (1999), and the later five-and-a-half-foot-tall *Zeus* from her Saratoga firings (see checklist nos. 152–154).

The Eagles' collection includes early work by two of the furniture masters included in *Objects: USA*. Sam Maloof is the maker of a 1968 walnut-and-leather rocking chair, attenuated yet sturdy, elegant yet comfortable, a signature work yet an epitome of "serving" form (see checklist no. 78). His chair shows sensitivity to the warmth and character of wood, a common attitude in studio furniture then. Wendell Castle created both of-the-moment, lighthearted forms in fiberglass, such as his tooth-shaped *Molar Chair* (the Eagles' version is a 1965 love seat titled *Molar Couch,* fig. 13), and

dazzling sculptural work made by carving laminated layers of wood to avoid rectilinear structure. His 1975 *Lectern* is all curves and balanced weight, animated yet serene (see checklist no. 31).

Maloof's and Castle's works also appear in *Tradition and Change*. In addition, the book includes Michael Frimkess, whose *Neck and Neck* (1977) in the Eagle collection shows the Greek form and provocative subject matter in its decoration that Hall cites (see checklist no. 60). Adrian Saxe is among the artists whom the Eagles collected in depth. His *Antelope Jars* of 1979 and 1980 demonstrate his fine skills, tight control, the illusion of incongruous materials or unexpected scale and suggestion of symbolism or subject matter (fig. 14). Another artist whom Hall selected, and who is also extensively represented in the Eagle

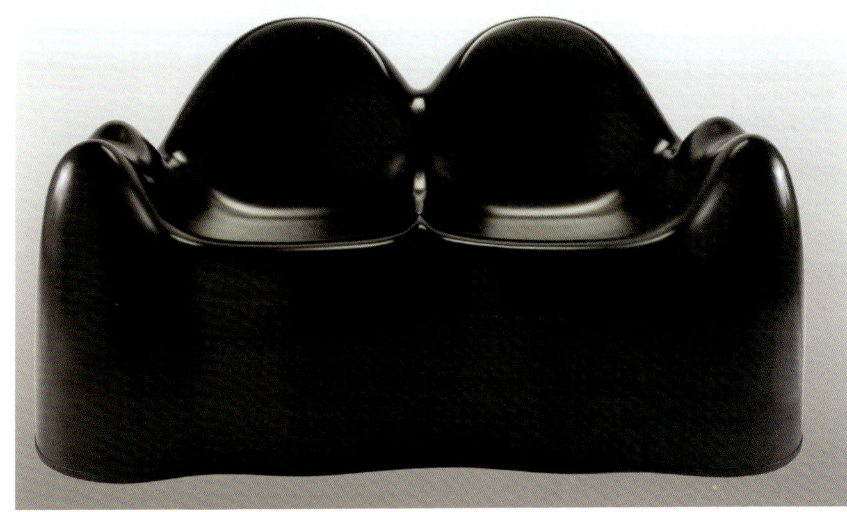

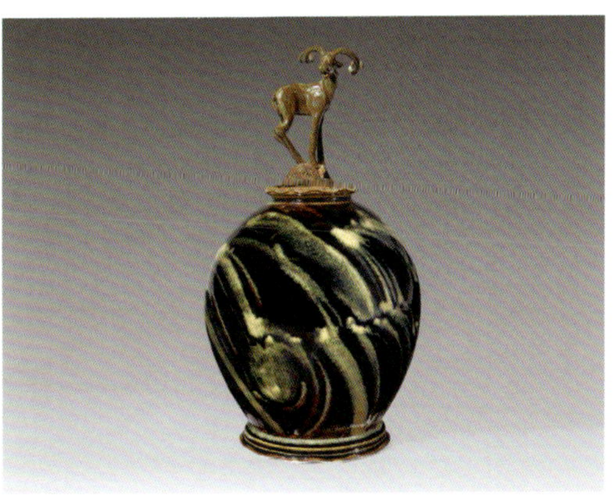

FIGURE 13
WENDELL CASTLE
Molar Couch, 1965
Fiberglass
2010.2042
(Checklist no. 32)

FIGURE 14
ADRIAN SAXE
Antelope Jar, 1979
Porcelain and stoneware
2010.2121.A,.B
(Checklist no. 119)

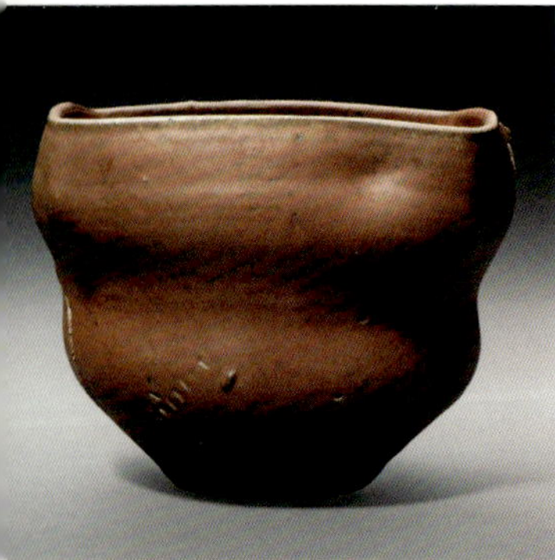

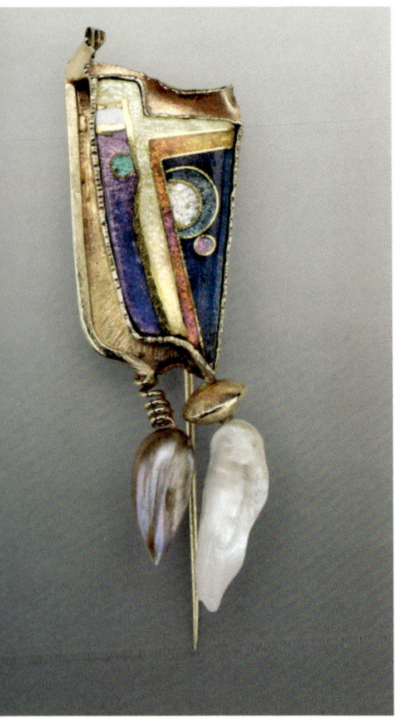

collection, is Paul Soldner. A 1979 vase typifies his raku technique and the stenciled imagery extracted from American popular culture for which he is known (see checklist no. 138). Robert Turner, whose ceramics Hall discusses in "Icons for Our Time," is represented in the collection by *Bowl Squared* (1978), which exemplifies his universalizing soft geometry in a modest scale that implies the monumental (fig. 15). Marilyn Levine's trompe l'oeil satchel of clay that appears to be leather also dates from this decade (see checklist no. 74). Of the artists included in *Poetry of the Physical*, the Eagle collection includes Stephen De Staebler's attenuated *Standing Figure with Segmented Knee* (1982), a columnar fragment that communicates stoic endurance and the passage of time (see checklist no. 36). Ruth Duckworth is represented by several works, including two bifurcated spherical sculptures from 1980 and 1981 that are evocative of landscape or female genitalia (see checklist nos. 47 and 48). In William Harper's jewelry, such as *September Sketch #5* (1985), exotic materials or natural objects such as shells and coral combine with colorful enamel patterns to suggest tribal inspiration (fig. 16). In the several Rick Dillingham works from the 1970s and 1980s in the collection, emphasis on piecing and strong, simple markings evoke Native American shards and refer to damage over time and the optimism of repair (see checklist nos. 39–44).

Although these correspondences reinforce the validity of both the publications and the collection, the divergences are also interesting and important. The Eagles also collected earlier or later works by the artists included in these decade-emphasizing publications, and they also collected artists not included in the books, which suggests the fecundity of the field. No one show or book can encompass all the good work—work that repays the attention a viewer gives to it.

IDEOLOGIES

The academic examination of modern and contemporary crafts is on the upswing now, with scholarly journals, history books, and collections of writings, although the number of critical reviews giving close readings of particular works has declined. The field continues to puzzle over its identity. In 1977 Hall cited characteristics of the field: a thread of tradition, connections across media boundaries, how training defines identity, and a professional community interacting through workshops and periodicals, among others.[29] She wrote that one of the primary frictions in art versus craft was the issue of function, and that makers either gave up function or, contrarily, asserted that art "does not require an erasure of the services [the work] can perform on another level."[30] (With the art world producing functional works today, one would hope that this never-logical objection to function would vanish at last.) Regarding the question of quantities versus uniqueness, she observed, "Serially produced objects do not necessarily lack resourcefulness, impact, or beauty."[31] (This issue, too, seems rendered moot ever since John Coplans examined repetitive painting in the exhibition and catalogue *Serial Imagery* in 1968.)

Hall also quoted ceramist Paul Soldner, who told her, "When we get a pot in the Whitney, then we will really be somewhere."[32] Soon thereafter, in 1979, the Whitney Biennial featured a unit of Ken Price's *Happy's Curios*, an evocation of Mexican folk pottery, and two years later, his work was presented in *Ceramic Sculpture: Six Artists* at the Whitney along with works by five other artists, all represented in the Eagle collection.[33] Soldner's remark reflects the same unfortunate attitude seen in painters and sculptors throughout the United States who think that New York is the only measure of success. The New York art world was the greatest center of activity during the late twentieth century, but it was slow to accept feminist art, slow to take up non-Western artists, and was conservative and provincial in its own complex way. Crafts, especially ceramics, were already widely accepted almost everywhere except in New York museums. However, craft practitioners are inclined to magnify every personal slight and not to recognize that those slights typically come from second-tier figures uncertain of their own standing (with the exception of an occasional incorrigibly neo-conservative critic such as Hilton Kramer).

This mild paranoia continues today, but perhaps to a lesser degree. With the small steps of these exhibitions and books, the craft world has gradually recognized the strengths of its own history and identity, and in the last decade the larger art world has increasingly reflected that realization. Lucie-Smith wrote that "craft provides the individual with the satisfaction of imposing himself on the material world, a feeling that has deep roots in the American pioneer spirit" and "the practice of craft is an effective means of self-realization."[34] All the writers cited in this essay were working toward an ideology of craft. Another major contribution, associated with yet another big survey show, came from Tulsa's Philbrook Museum: *The Eloquent Object* in 1988. Most important was the accompanying thick catalogue with essays by its curator, Marcia Manhart, museum curators Jonathan Fairbanks and Mary Jane Jacob, critics John Perreault and Lucy Lippard, and others. The contributing authors made an exceptional effort to pinpoint issues and provide a short history of postwar crafts. The catalogue handles social and political statements gingerly, and it fails to stylistically categorize, but the essays admirably deal with invention, dismiss distinctions between fine and minor arts as fictions in the cold light of history,[35] and look at painters and sculptors working in craft mediums. Perhaps the most significant essays are the last two, by Ronda Kasl on the creation of fictional worlds, and by Edwin L. Wade on recognizing the spiritual. Both are narrowly focused and deeply analytical, models for future scholarship in their consideration of a theme and examination of the works of a small number of artists. Neither was a common practice in crafts catalogues before that time.

The 1980s were a turning point in both curating and critical writing through addressing innovation, formal characteristics, meanings, and relationship to contemporary culture. Yet while the writing became more analytical, the work itself continued to resist stylistic categorization. Nowadays, the choice to work with the hands, rather than virtually, stems from a philosophical and physical motivation, from curiosity about how things work, and pleasure in acquiring skills. How that approach plays out in a "look" is not the issue. The freedom of crafts and the sensuous response of a material are what allow makers to be as individualistic as they wish. Beginning with the bedrock principle of direct making, craftspeople can produce objects to use, to wear, or to view, in whatever manner is gratifying and meaningful to them and to those who collect the works. Although the issue of forging a cohesive critical vocabulary for crafts remains unresolved, perhaps this lack of vocabulary could be viewed as an asset rather than a hindrance—providing an undefined, unbounded arena in which crafts' themes, styles, and ideologies may continue to advance within the larger realm of art.

1   Some claim that crafts are "never covered," but that is not true. Art magazines in the first half of the twentieth century reported on all mediums, the midcentury California "clay revolution" was extensively analyzed in *Artforum* magazine, Peter Voulkos and John Mason both had feature articles in *Art in America* in 1979, and Ken Price was on the cover in 1980, to cite just a few examples.

2   See Jacques Maquet, *Introduction to Aesthetic Anthropology* (Reading, MA: Addison-Wesley Publishing, 1971), in which he makes the case that "contemplation rather than cognition, form rather than content" are the universals of aesthetic expression, even if some cultures at some times privilege other aspects (p. 36).

3   See, for example, Richard Sennett, *The Craftsman* (New Haven, CT: Yale University Press, 2008), and Matthew B. Crawford, *Shop Class as Soulcraft: An Inquiry into the Value of Work* (New York: Penguin Press, 2009).

4   Elissa Auther and Maria Elena Buszek are prime examples. Glenn Adamson, Jenni Sorkin, and Dennis Stevens are other young scholars giving in-depth attention to the history and current issues of crafts.

5   Jonathan Fineberg, *Art Since 1940: Strategies of Being*, 3rd ed. (Saddle River, NJ: Prentice Hall, 2011), 360.

6   For example, in 1953, the American Craftsmen's Educational Council sponsored *Designer Craftsmen U.S.A.* in conjunction with the Brooklyn Museum.

7   Julie Hall, *Tradition and Change: The New American Craftsman* (New York: E. P. Dutton, 1977), 18.

8   Sandy Ballatore, "The Art Fabric: Mainstream," *American Craft* 41, no. 4 (August/September 1981): 39.

9   In reviewing the 1970s, I found a title that seemed to suggest a conceptually thematic show in that contentious time: the Brooklyn Museum mounted an exhibition called *Attitudes*. But no, the museum went on to describe it as just a "lively grouping." *Craft Horizons* 30, no. 6 (December 1970): 64.

10 An exception is the wood-fire movement, which is a community and an aesthetic. In fact, ceramics change in appearance with each change in firing; the growth of low-fire clays and glazes and electric firing gave new options for color, for example, although they did not generate a community.

11 Peter Selz, *Funk* (Berkeley, CA: University Art Museum, 1967), 3.

12 Ibid., 5.

13 The Super-Object was characterized by unbounded preciousness, carefully considered execution, and meticulous craftsmanship that denies any expressionist use of the materials. See Garth Clark and Margie Hughto, *A Century of Ceramics in the United States, 1878–1978* (New York: E. P. Dutton, 1979), 201.

14 "Sheila Hicks: Holey Socks, Darned Sheets and Phase IV," in *Fiberworks Symposium on Contemporary Textile Art* (Berkeley, CA: Fiberworks, 1978), 6–9.

15 See Donald J. Willcox, *Body Jewelry: International Perspectives* (Chicago: H. Regnery, 1973). The term is associated with piercing today.

16 The term comes from Lucy Lippard in *Six Years: The Dematerialization of the Art Object, 1966–1972* (Berkeley: University of California Press, 1973) and other writings.

17 See Mark Del Vecchio, *Postmodern Ceramics*, with an introduction by Garth Clark (New York: Thames & Hudson, 2007).

18 Alison Pearlman, *Unpackaging Art of the 1980s* (Chicago: University of Chicago Press, 2003), 9.

19 The major alternative periods to everyday commerce might include subsistence work during the Great Depression, the post–World War II influx of veterans into the crafts for its more self-determined lifestyle, and 1960s counterculture crafts. We should also recall the original anti-industry motivation of the Arts and Crafts movement when it began in England.

20 The ceramist Harvey Littleton, with the cooperation of the Toledo Museum of Art, organized two workshops in 1962 to demonstrate that glass could be employed expressively by an individual working alone. The expressive part has held over time, but as individuals developed their skills, the tendency has been to revert to cooperative teams that share the burden of the expensive process.

21 The British Craft Center held a series of shows featuring small-scale works beginning in 1974.

22 Emphasizing the vitality of young makers is still a curatorial strategy. See the Renwick Gallery's 2012 show *Forty Under Forty*, for example.

23 Rose Slivka, "Affirmation: The American Craftsman," *Craft Horizons* 30, no. 6 (December 1970): 11.

24 The artist cited is Native American jeweler Charles Loloma. The others in the chapter are Larry Foster for stained glass on an ecological theme, Mary Ann Scherr's health-monitoring jewelry, Gary Griffin's jewelry and metalwork using machinery, and Michael Frimkess's political-commentary ceramics.

25 Dominic Di Mare, Walter Nottingham, Lenore Tawney, and perhaps William Harper are predictable inclusions, Richard DeVore, Robert Turner, Ferne Jacobs, and James Carpenter less so.

26 Paul J. Smith and Edward Lucie-Smith, *American Craft Today: Poetry of the Physical* (New York: American Craft Museum and Weidenfeld & Nicolson, 1986), 13.

27 See Dave Hickey, *The Invisible Dragon: Four Essays On Beauty* (Los Angeles: Art Issues Press, 1993).

28 I lived abroad in the late 1980s, and on a trip home, looking at a ceramics show at the American Craft Museum, I was struck by the fact that, although the objects were three-dimensional and shown on pedestals, they had a frontal orientation, a best view, just right for a photograph.

29 Hall, *Tradition and Change*, 9.

30 Ibid., 10.

31 Ibid.

32 Ibid., 11.

33 They were: Peter Voulkos, John Mason, Robert Arneson, David Gilhooly, and Richard Shaw.

34 Lucie-Smith, *American Craft Today*, 36.

35 Penelope Hunter-Stiebel, "The Craft Object in Western Culture," in Marcia Manhart and Tom Manhart, eds., *The Eloquent Object: The Evolution of American Art in Craft Media Since 1945* (Tulsa: The Philbrook Museum of Art, 1987), 139.

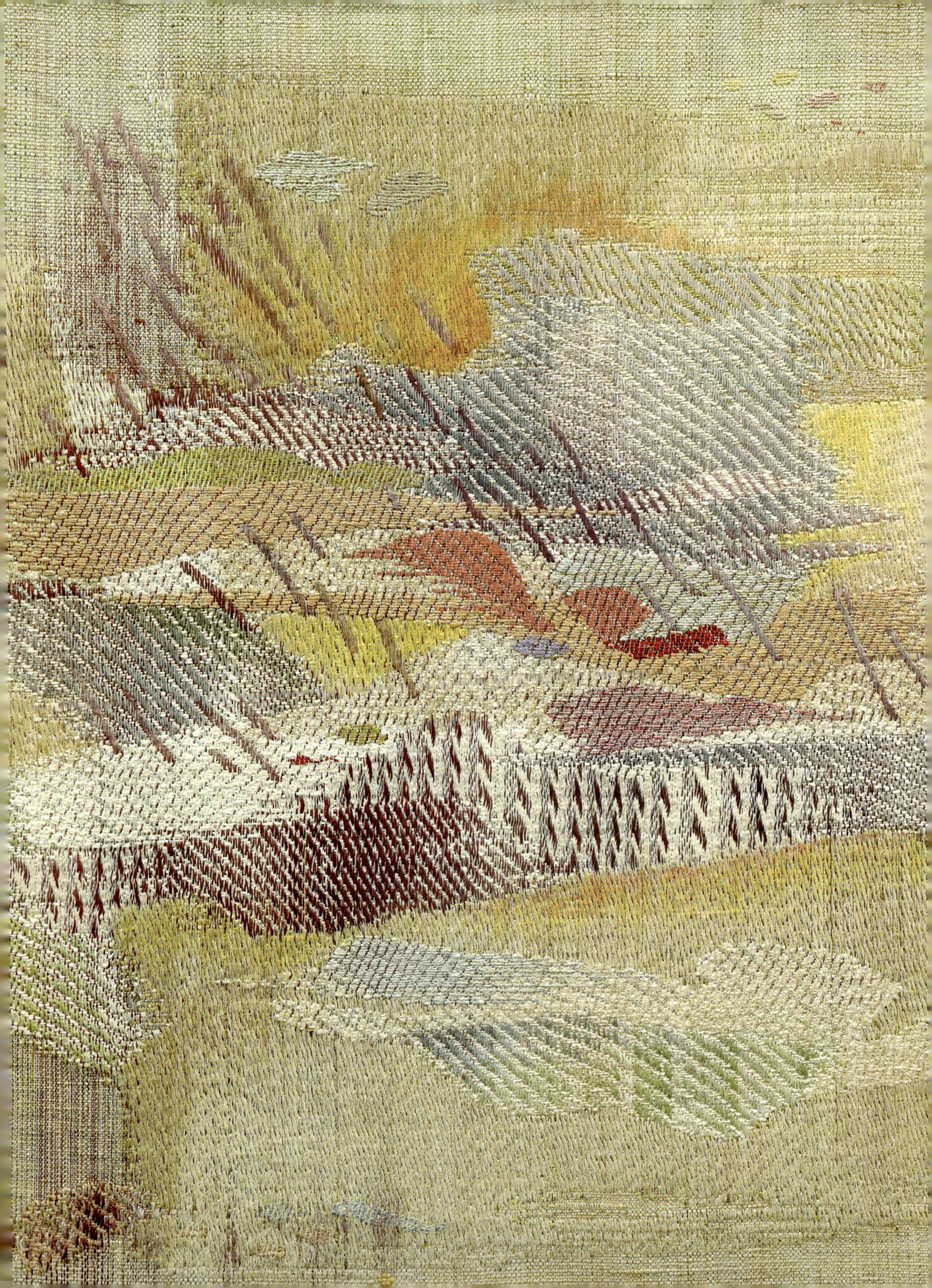

FEATURED WORKS

OLGA DE AMARAL
Colombian, born 1932

Olga de Amaral studied architectural design in her native Colombia before matriculating at the Cranbrook Academy of Art in Bloomfield Hills, Michigan, in the early 1950s to study textiles with Marianne Strengell. These dual pursuits have greatly informed the nature of her works. More than just a collection of carefully composed threads, Amaral's tapestries are opulent meditations on the transformative possibilities of space. Like the most successful edifices, her weavings use structure and ornament to create an encompassing sense of shelter, warmth, and contemplation.

In part, the affective power of Amaral's architectural interventions derives from her sensuous use of color, scale, and tactility to evoke elements of the natural environment. With their often monumental size and impressive repetition, seemingly beyond the bounds of human manipulation, her pieces impact the eye with the same visual and emotional force as their namesakes, cliffs, clouds, stele, and shadows, converting the viewer to Amaral's abstract vision of the Colombian landscape. No less persuasive are the gradations of grays, reds, and blues or the glimmering silver and gold that she has employed increasingly since 1970. Her culturally resonant use of color references the scarred surfaces of cliffs, the differing shadows of clouds before the sun, and the hallowed spaces of Pre-Columbian altars, cathedrals, and religious icons. In more recent works, Amaral has brought the union of nature and culture even closer together, impregnating her textiles with clay before gilding.

Amaral has mined the traditional history and landscape of Colombia for both aesthetic and technical inspiration since the outset of her career. However, rather than operate in a revivalist aesthetic, her objects utilize native history to create a modern sentiment, locating her production within the history of both Latin American modernism and the fiber art movement. SJS

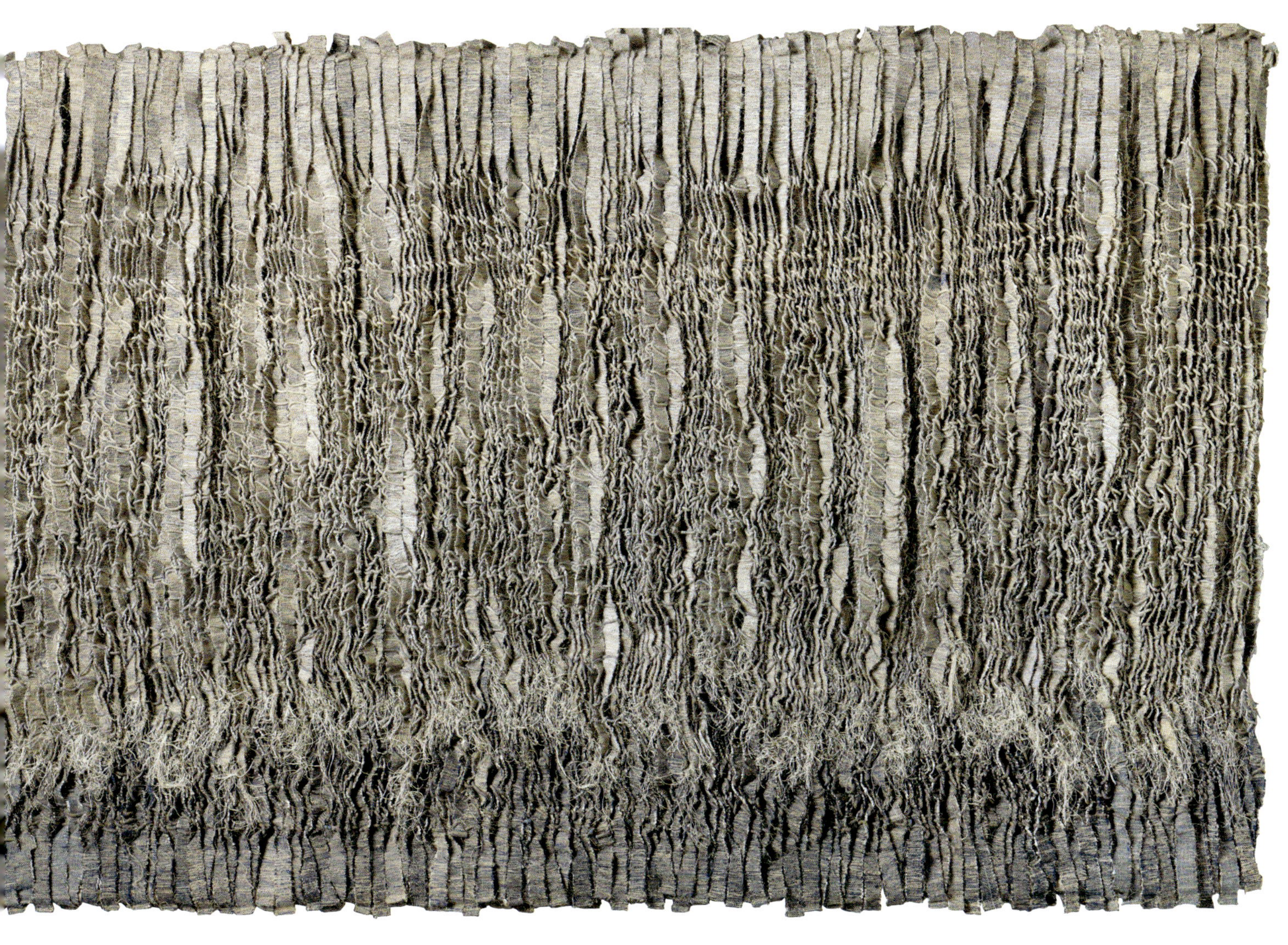

PLATE 1

RISCOS Y TIEMPO
1985
Fiber
47 x 75 inches (119.4 x 190.5 cm)
The Leatrice S. and Melvin B.
Eagle Collection, gift of
Leatrice and Melvin Eagle
2010.2262

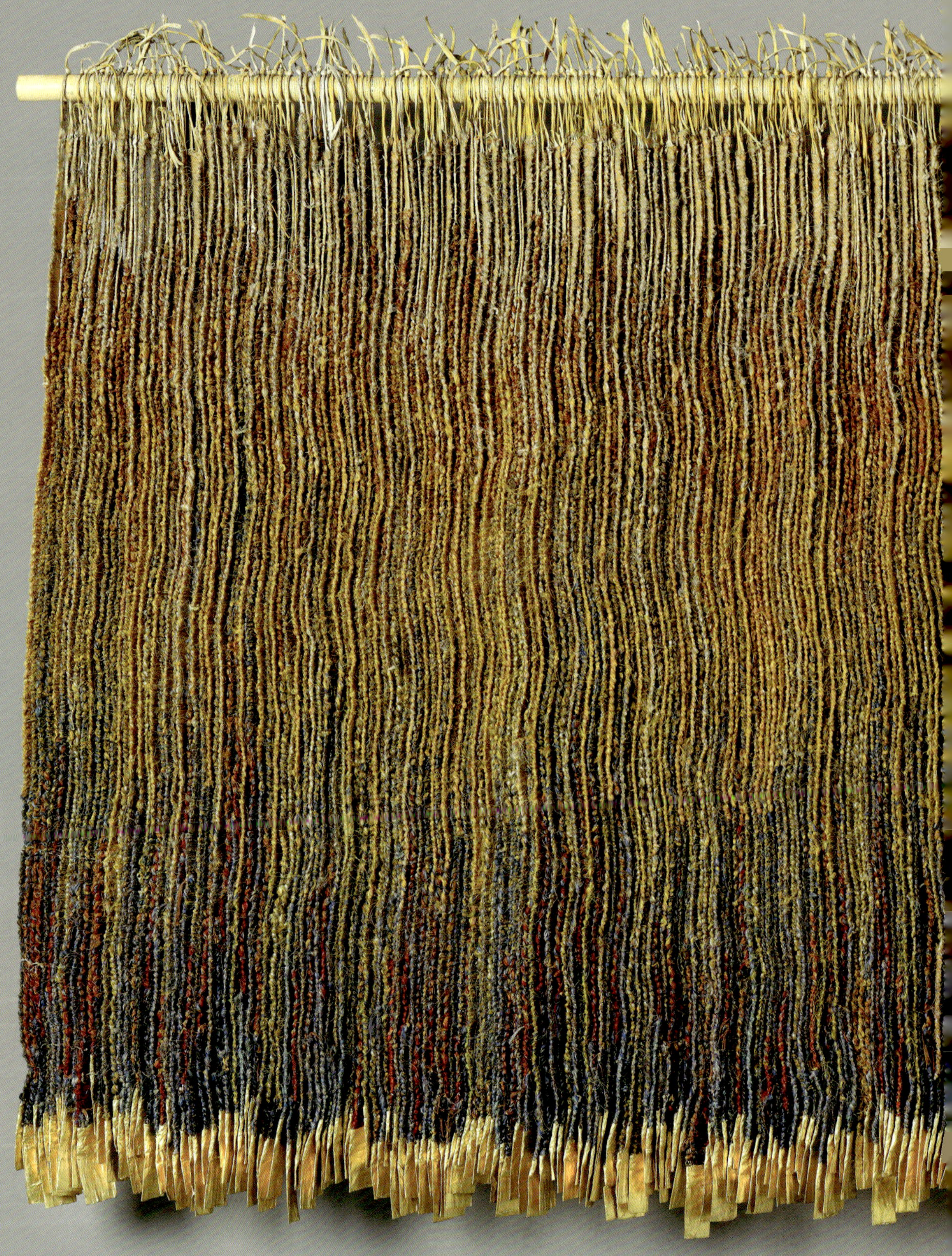

OLGA DE AMARAL

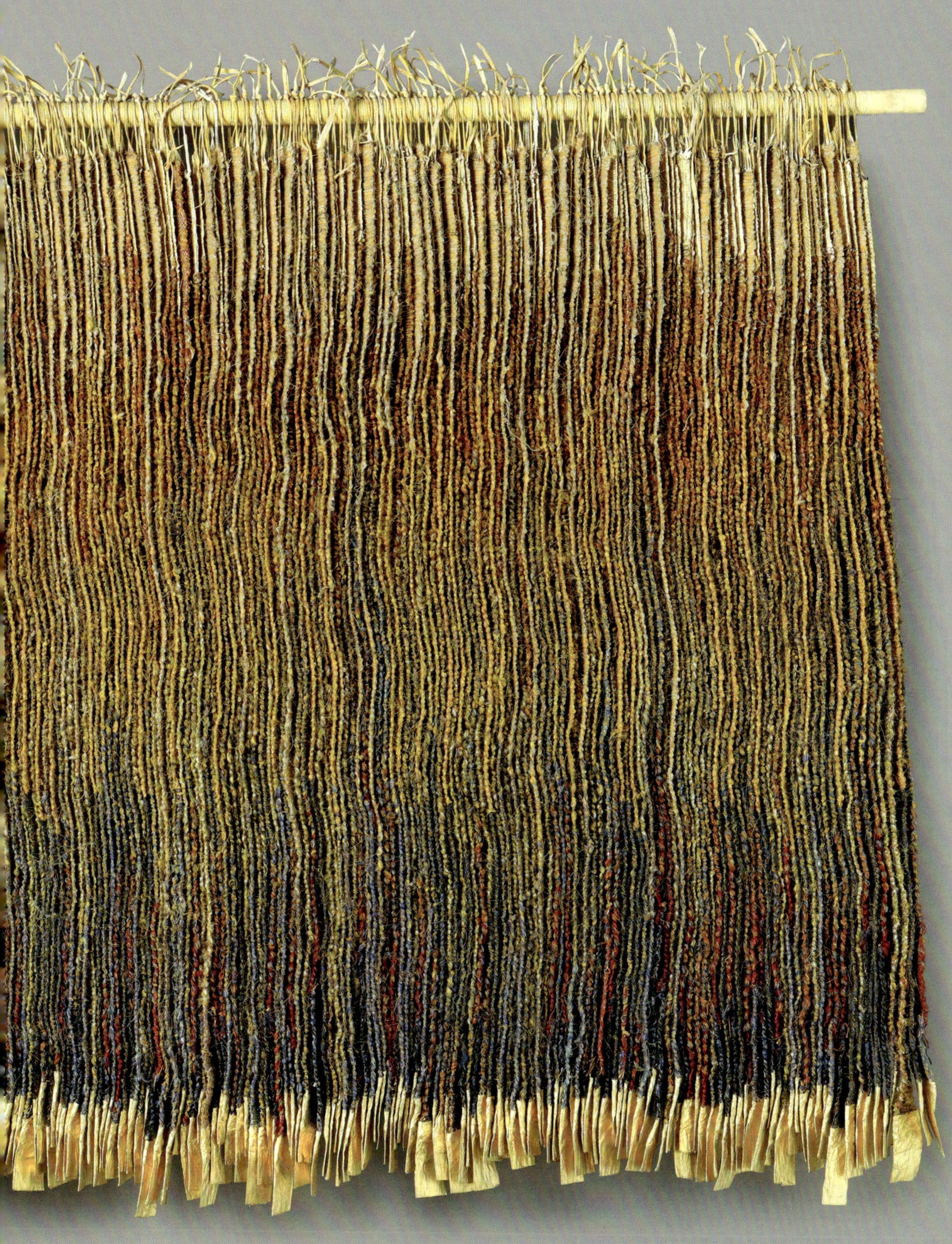

ROBERT ARNESON
American, 1930–1992

PLATE 3

CHINA TROPHY
1964
Ceramic
18 5/8 x 11 1/4 x 7 3/4 inches
(47.3 x 28.6 x 19.7 cm)
The Leatrice S. and
Melvin B. Eagle Collection,
museum purchase funded
by the Caroline Wiess Law
Accessions Endowment Fund
2010.2021

Northern California native Robert Arneson was one of the most influential artists in postwar American ceramics and a leader in the development of the San Francisco Bay Area artistic culture of the late twentieth century. Known as the progenitor of California Funk ceramics due to his scatological, political, and darkly humorous social sculptures that he began making in the early 1960s, Arneson influenced generations of ceramicists from his post at the University of California, Davis, where he taught from 1962 to 1991.

Between 1956 and 1958, Arneson studied with the technically rigorous utilitarian potters Edith Heath, Anthony Prieto, and Herbert Sanders, building his reputation on thrown stoneware vessels. Yet he was increasingly drawn to the expressionist sculpture of Peter Voulkos and its promise of autonomy from the strictures of functional craft. After a brief period working in an Abstract Expressionist style in the late 1950s, Arneson uncovered the Pop-infused Funk aesthetic that would mark his contribution to ceramic sculpture while giving a demonstration at the California State Fair in 1961. There, he threw a small ceramic bottle, which he capped with a clay bottle cap and labeled "No Deposit, No Return." This repositioning of a ceramic object to make satirical a statement would become his dominant mode of expression.

Throughout the 1960s and early 1970s, Arneson utilized everyday objects, such as toilets, bricks, and trophies (as in *China Trophy* of 1964), in pieces that were vulgar, transgressive, humorous, and poignant. Gloppy and bright, these asymmetrical sculptures crossed the boundaries of the designer-craftsman ceramic tradition and critiqued middle-class values of propriety and good taste. In the 1970s, Arneson turned to self-portraiture both in his drawings and three-dimensional works to comment on art, art making, politics, and social issues. He utilized his own image to represent an everyman experiencing the issues he critiqued, presenting these works on ceramic columns, in diptychs and triptychs, as seen in *Golden Triangle / Us Guys* (1991), and as large heads. Arneson has explained his choice of himself as a model, stating, "I'm the easiest person to abuse without offending. . . . It's really dealing with the plastic nature of the expression and not the inherent sense of character."[1] SJS

NOTE

1   Robert Arneson, interview by the San Francisco Museum of Modern Art, December 1994, available online at www.sfmoma.org/explore/multimedia/videos/330.

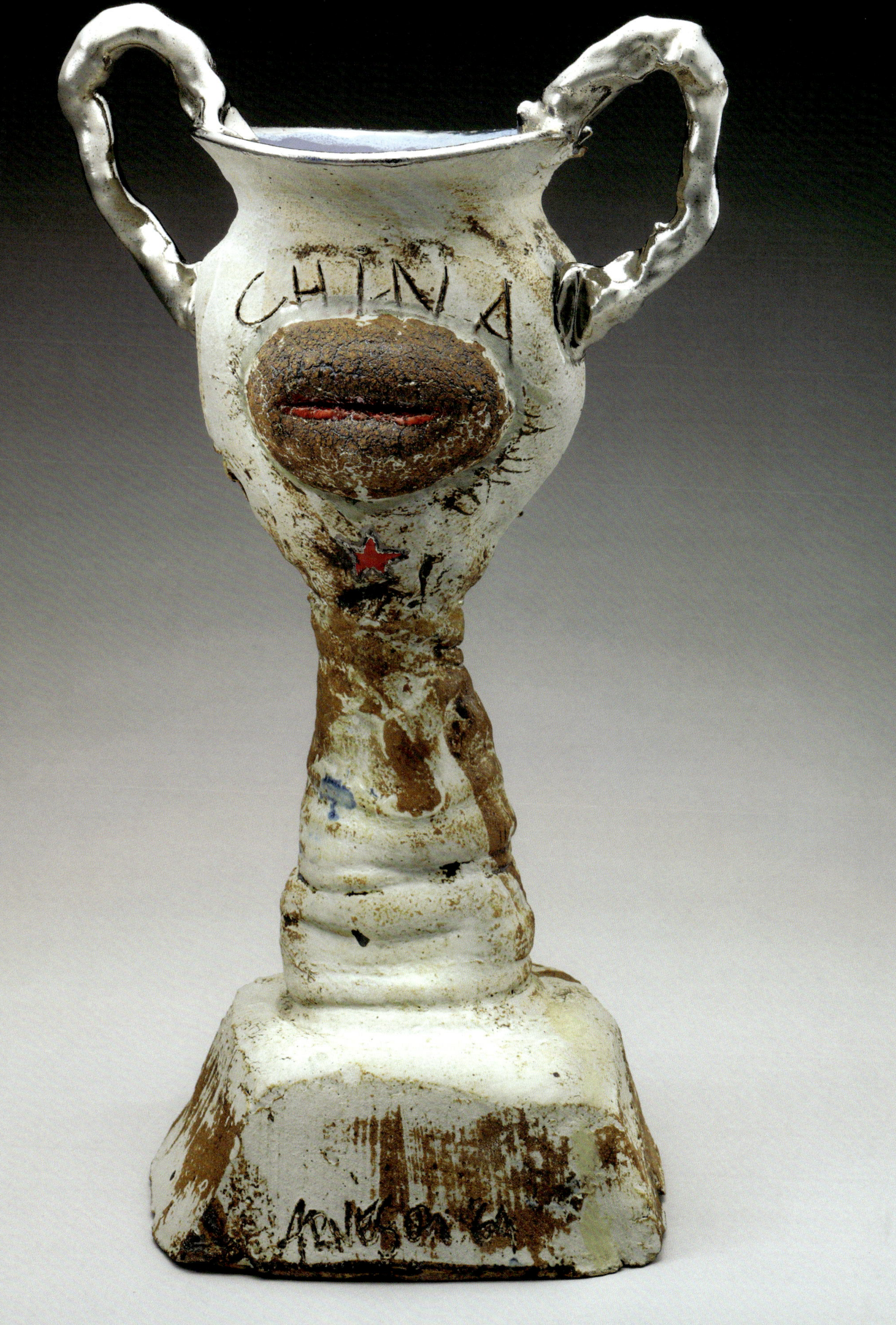

CHINA

ROBERT ARNESON

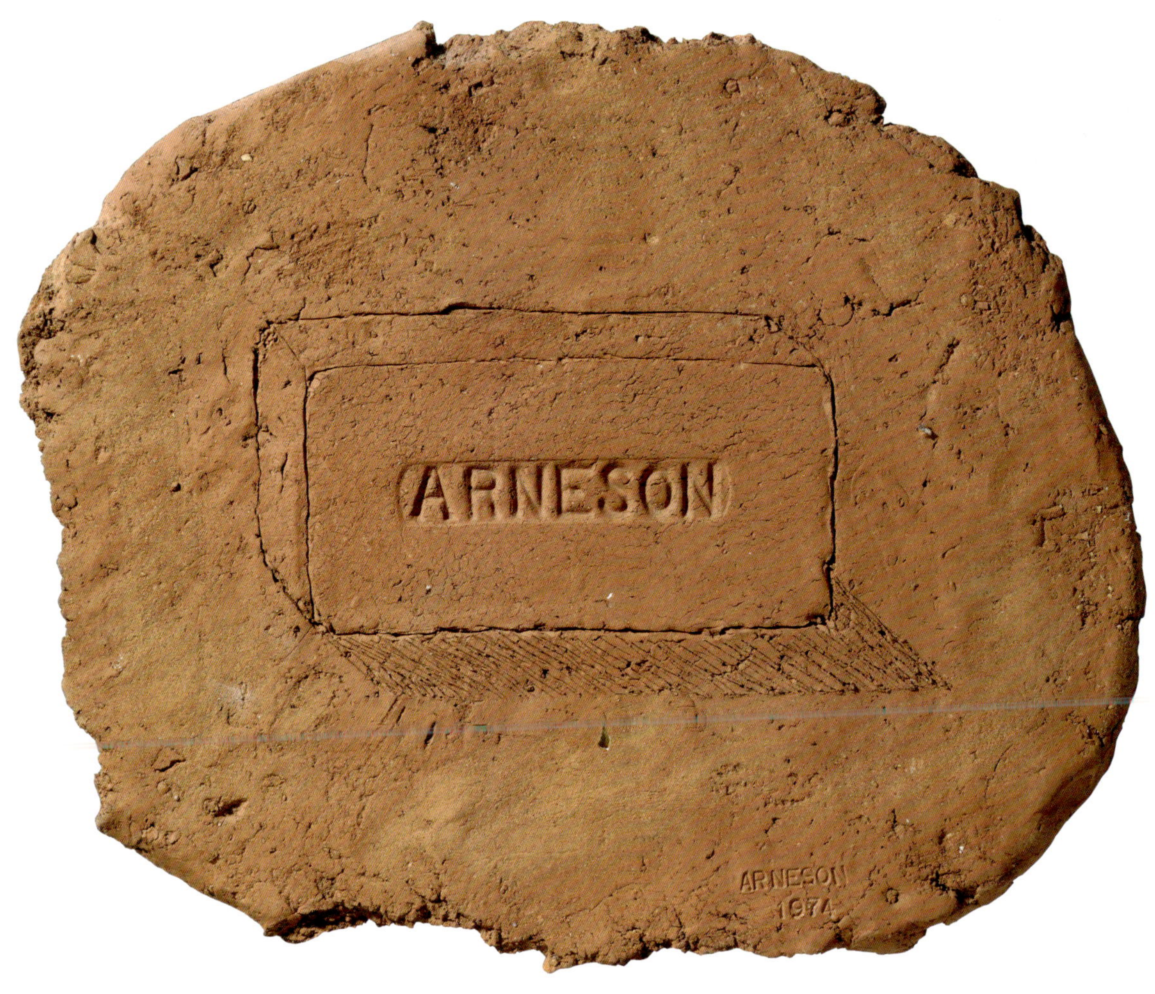

PLATE **4**

BRICK

1974
Ceramic
15 x 17 7/8 x 1 5/8 inches
(38.1 x 45.4 x 4.1 cm)
The Leatrice S. and
Melvin B. Eagle Collection,
museum purchase funded
by the Caroline Wiess Law
Accessions Endowment Fund
2010.2023

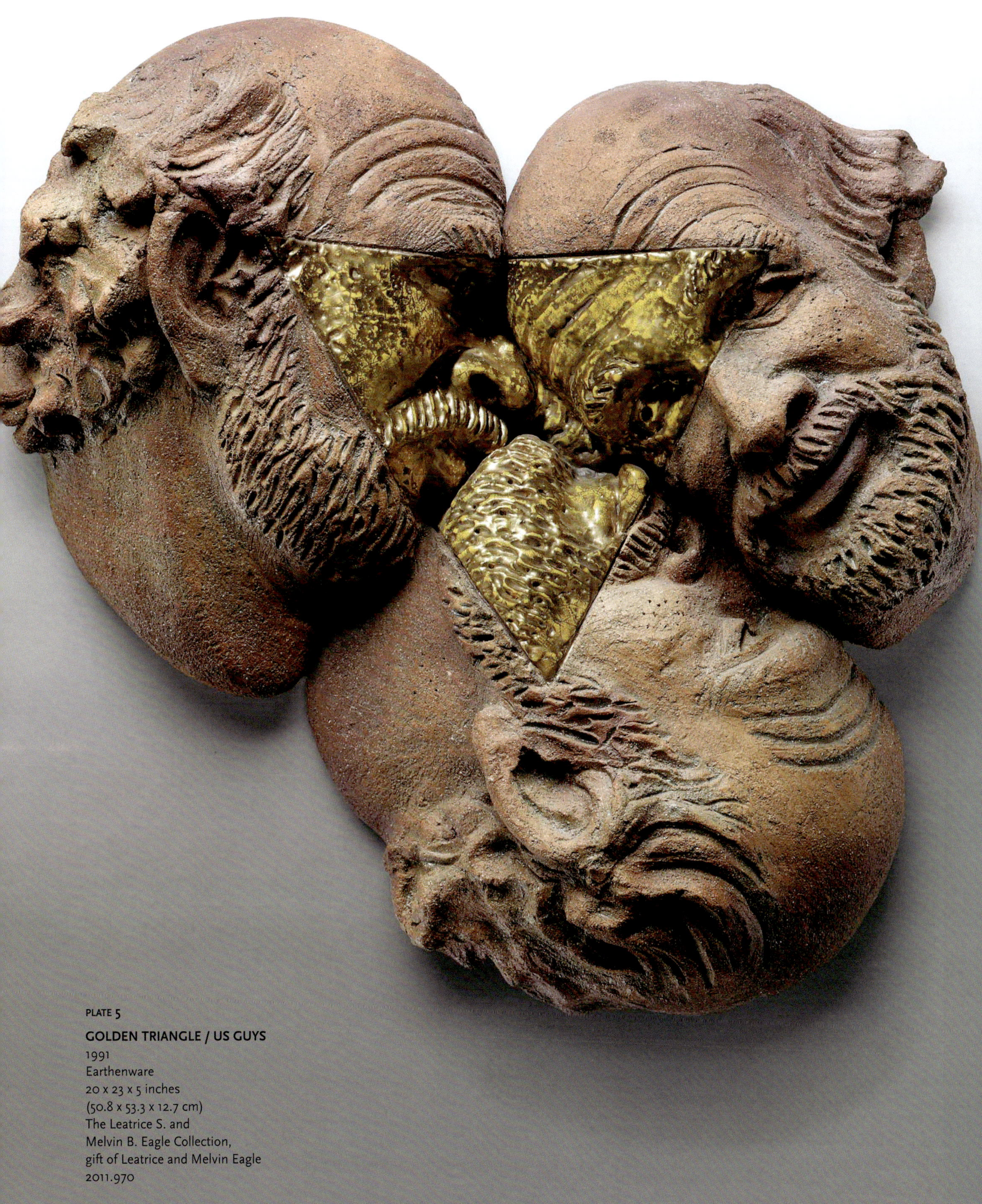

PLATE 5

GOLDEN TRIANGLE / US GUYS
1991
Earthenware
20 x 23 x 5 inches
(50.8 x 53.3 x 12.7 cm)
The Leatrice S. and
Melvin B. Eagle Collection,
gift of Leatrice and Melvin Eagle
2011.970

RUDY AUTIO
American, 1926–2007

While a founding resident at the Archie Bray Foundation for Ceramic Art in Helena, Montana, in the early 1950s, Rudy Autio constructed large, narrative relief murals whose monumental size mirrored the ambitions of the nascent medium. Autio invested his stridently figured reliefs with confident lines and conventionalized forms that owed a debt to the public works of artists such as Diego Rivera and Viktor Schreckengost.[1] Like the works of these social realists, Autio's bold, large-scale ceramic objects were designed to carry a message through their very presence.

Before long, Autio abandoned the murals in favor of large, hand-built vessels with sculptural appendages, which he incised with watery, dreamlike images of nudes and horses. Later, Autio explored this sensuous subject matter in vivid drawings that reflected the artist's affinity for the art of Henri Matisse. Though the form of his works had changed, the muscular handling and confident bearing of Autio's objects and drawings had not; through their quiet power, they convey messages of romance and the American West.

Throughout his career, Autio pursued two major passions: pride of place and the development of studio ceramics. The first can be seen in his commitment to subject matter that mythologizes and celebrates the open landscape of his native Montana and later in his numerous trips to work in the ceramic factories of his ancestral home of Finland. His dedication to the burgeoning field of ceramics is evident in his role in the founding of the Archie Bray Foundation for Ceramic Art with his friend Peter Voulkos as well as in his mentorship of the legions of students that passed through his program at the University of Montana during his twenty-seven years of teaching. SJS

NOTE

1   "Oral History Interview with Rudy Autio," October 10, 1983–January 28, 1984, Archives of American Art, Smithsonian Institution, available online at http://www.aaa.si.edu/ collections/ interviews/oral-history-interview-rudy-autio-11713.

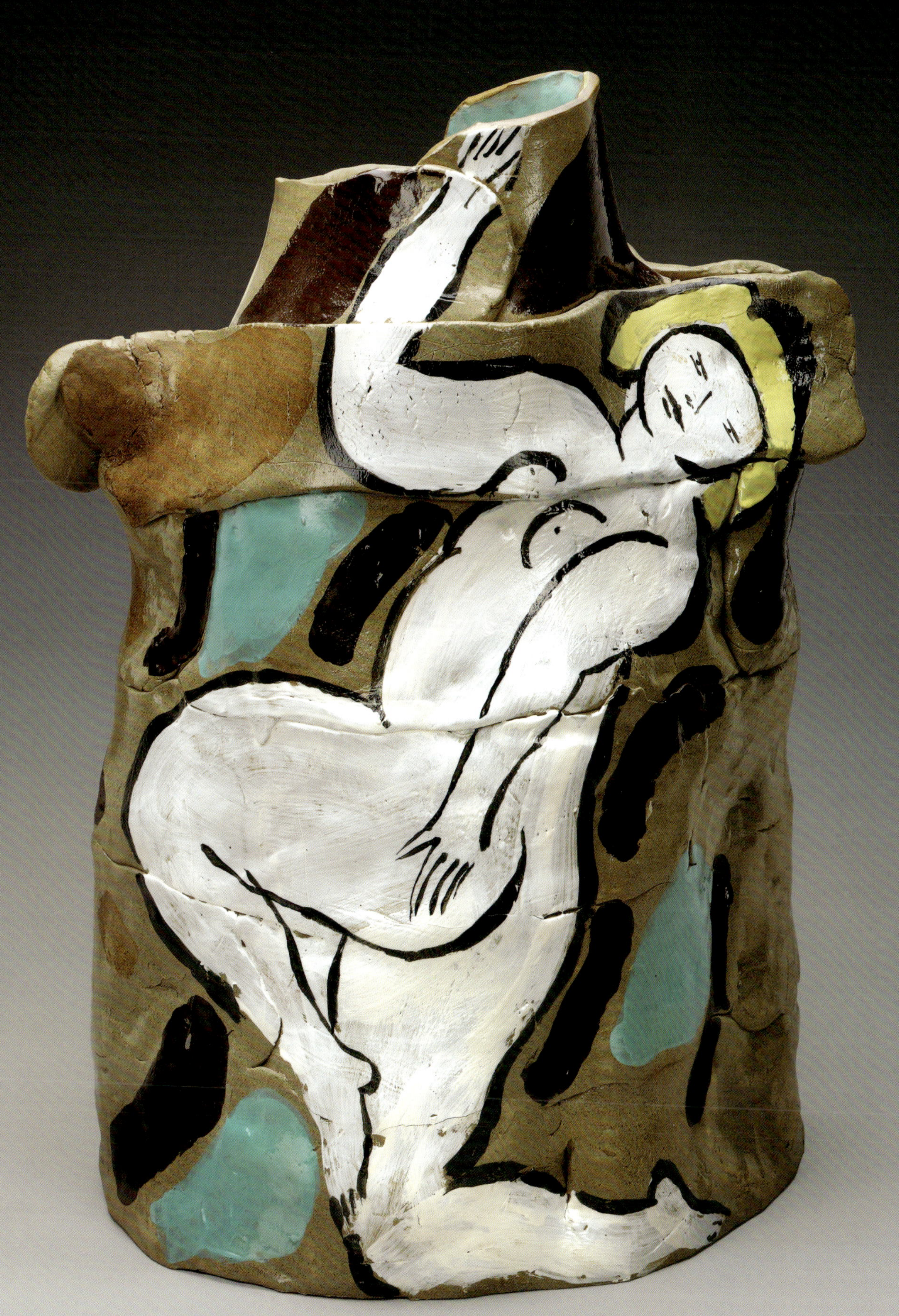

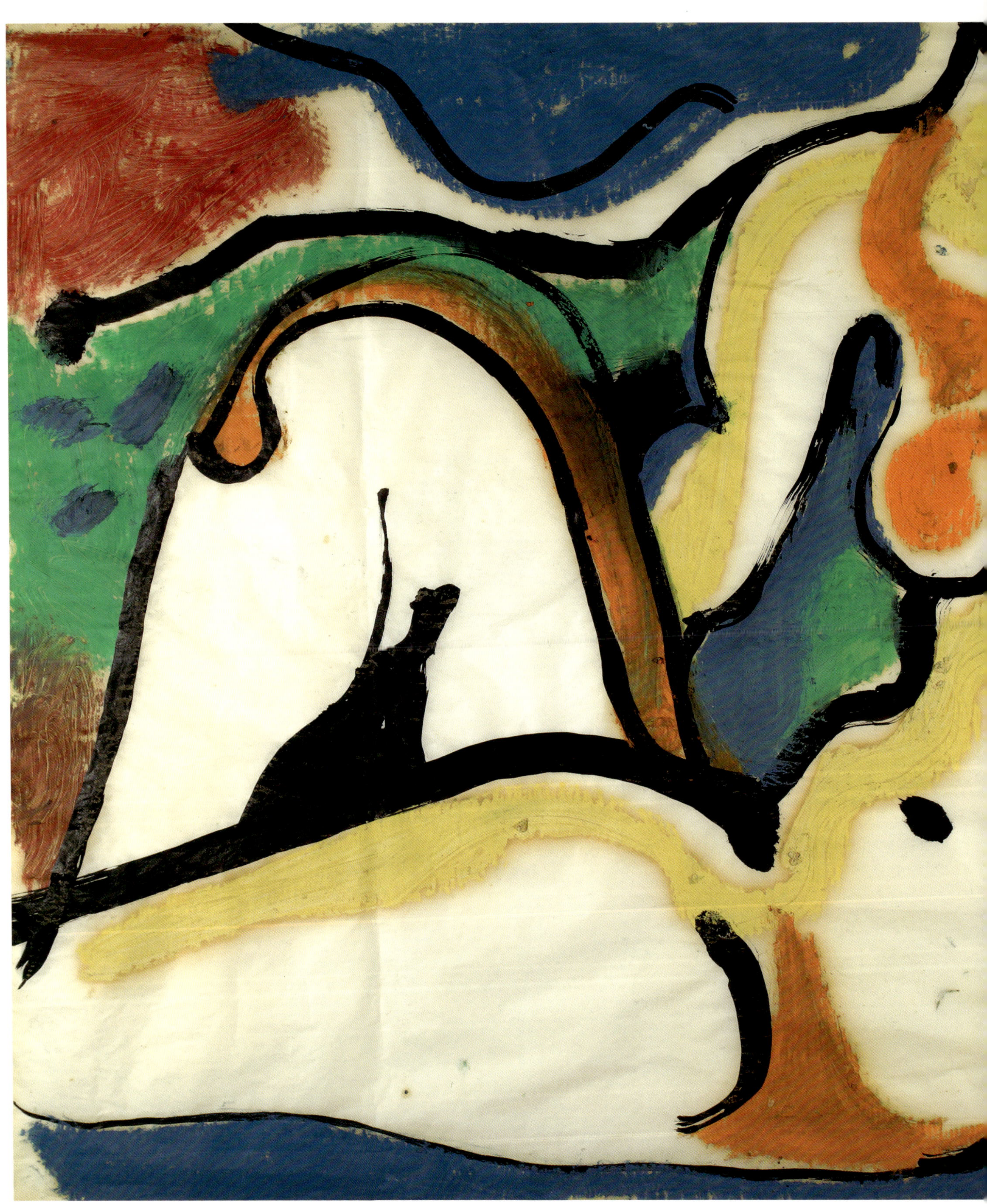

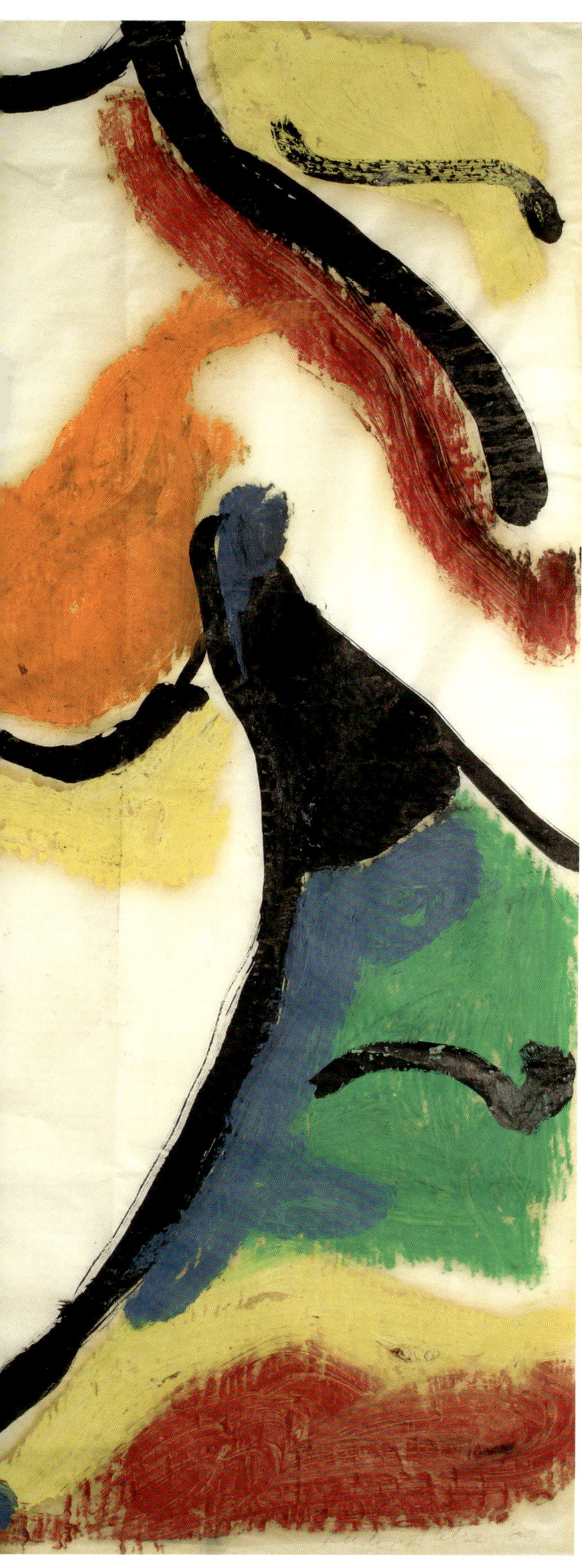

PLATE **7**

TORSO
1980
Oil crayon and tempera
on paper
25 x 32 inches (63.5 x 81.3 cm)
The Leatrice S. and
Melvin B. Eagle Collection,
museum purchase funded
by the Caroline Wiess Law
Accessions Endowment Fund
2010.2259

PLATE 8

IRIS PLATTER
1980
Stoneware
2 3/4 x 21 3/4 inches diameter
(7 x 55.2 cm)
The Leatrice S. and
Melvin B. Eagle Collection,
gift of Leatrice and Melvin Eagle
2010.2261

PLATE 9

TEAPOT
2000
Whiteware
18 1/4 x 11 1/2 x 5 1/2 inches
(46.4 x 29.2 x 14 cm)
The Leatrice S. and
Melvin B. Eagle Collection,
museum purchase funded by
the Caroline Wiess Law
Accessions Endowment Fund
2010.2031.A–.C

Few studio ceramicists were as concerned with the symphonic possibilities of surface as was Ralph Bacerra. Reveling in layered color and pattern, Bacerra composed exquisite polychrome geometries over a host of sculptural forms. When he first developed this ornamental approach in the early 1970s, it represented a break with the reductive formalism of an earlier era, exemplified in the pottery of Bacerra's teacher and friend Vivika Heino. But as novel as his objects appeared, both they and the processes Bacerra used to complete them were never very far removed from the history of his material.

Formally, Bacerra's works are rooted in and reference the breadth of ceramic's utilitarian tradition. Lidded vessels, platters, teapots, and occasionally even ancient ritual objects, such as funerary sculptures of camels from Tang-dynasty China, form the basis of his ornamental musings.[1] Bacerra's ceramic literacy is exemplified on the surfaces of his pieces. His masterful command of low-fire glazes, a proficiency developed through close study of the Japanese and Chinese precedents that inform his works, allowed Bacerra to create visual textures that both mask and enhance the forms they adorn.[2]

Bacerra was more than just an excellent ceramicist, however. By all accounts, he was also a gifted professor, teaching first at his alma mater Chouinard Art Institute (now California Institute of the Arts) and later at Otis College of Art and Design in the program initiated by Peter Voulkos. The legacy of his commitment to excellence and his deep technical knowledge can be seen in the accomplished works of his students such as Adrian Saxe, who is also included in this catalogue. SJS

NOTES
1 Elaine Levin, *West Coast Clay Spectrum Artists* (Los Angeles: Security Pacific Bank, 1979), 3.
2 Frank Lloyd, "Oral History Interview with Ralph Bacerra," April 7–19, 2004, Oral Histories, Archives of American Art, Smithsonian Institution, available online at http://www.aaa.si.edu/collections/interviews/oral-history-interview-ralph-bacerra-12942.

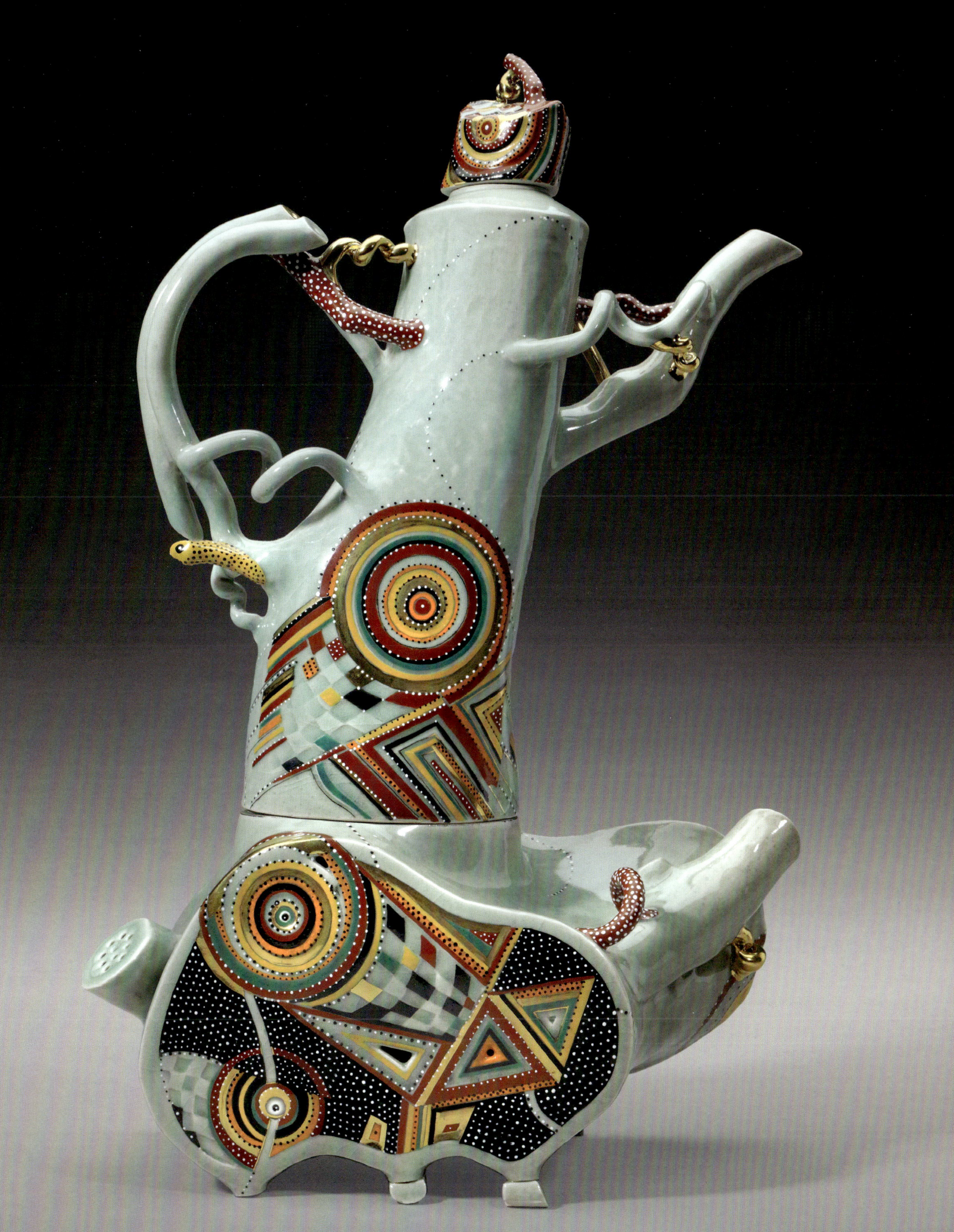

CLAYTON BAILEY
American, born 1939

For more than half a century, Clayton Bailey has been creating irreverent, humorous sculptures in clay and metal. After graduating from the University of Wisconsin–Madison, where he studied with Toshiko Takaezu, Bailey spent four years teaching at the University of Wisconsin–Whitewater. In 1968 he moved to California to serve as Robert Arneson's sabbatical replacement at the University of California, Davis. Bailey, who had already achieved renown for his joyfully transgressive sculptures, such the wormlike urinals with voluptuous lips and breasts that he called *Night Pots*, integrated well into the Funk-infused milieu of Bay Area ceramics, and he soon relocated to the area permanently.[1]

At the heart of Bailey's sculptures is an embrace of the absurd and an affinity with the roadside attraction. Together with his mad-scientist alter ego, Dr. Gladstone, Bailey has created a range of objects that are equal measures science, technology, and fun. *Burping Bowls*, which Bailey began producing in 1969, capture the essence of this spirit. These bowls use an aquarium pump embedded in water to compress air within a sculpted ceramic creature. The air causes the cartoonish creature to rise within its tank and generates a belching sound.[2]

These pieces' impudent embrace of bodily function mimics the scatological humor of Arneson, among other Funk ceramics practitioners. However, whereas Arneson positioned his work within the practices and history of the fine arts, Bailey aligns his output with that of outsider artists, carnival hucksters, and other folk champions. SJS

NOTES

1 G. Joan DePaoli and Clayton Bailey, *Clayton Bailey: Happenings in the Circus of Life* (Davis, CA: John Natsoulas Press, 2000), 29.

2 Ibid., 37.

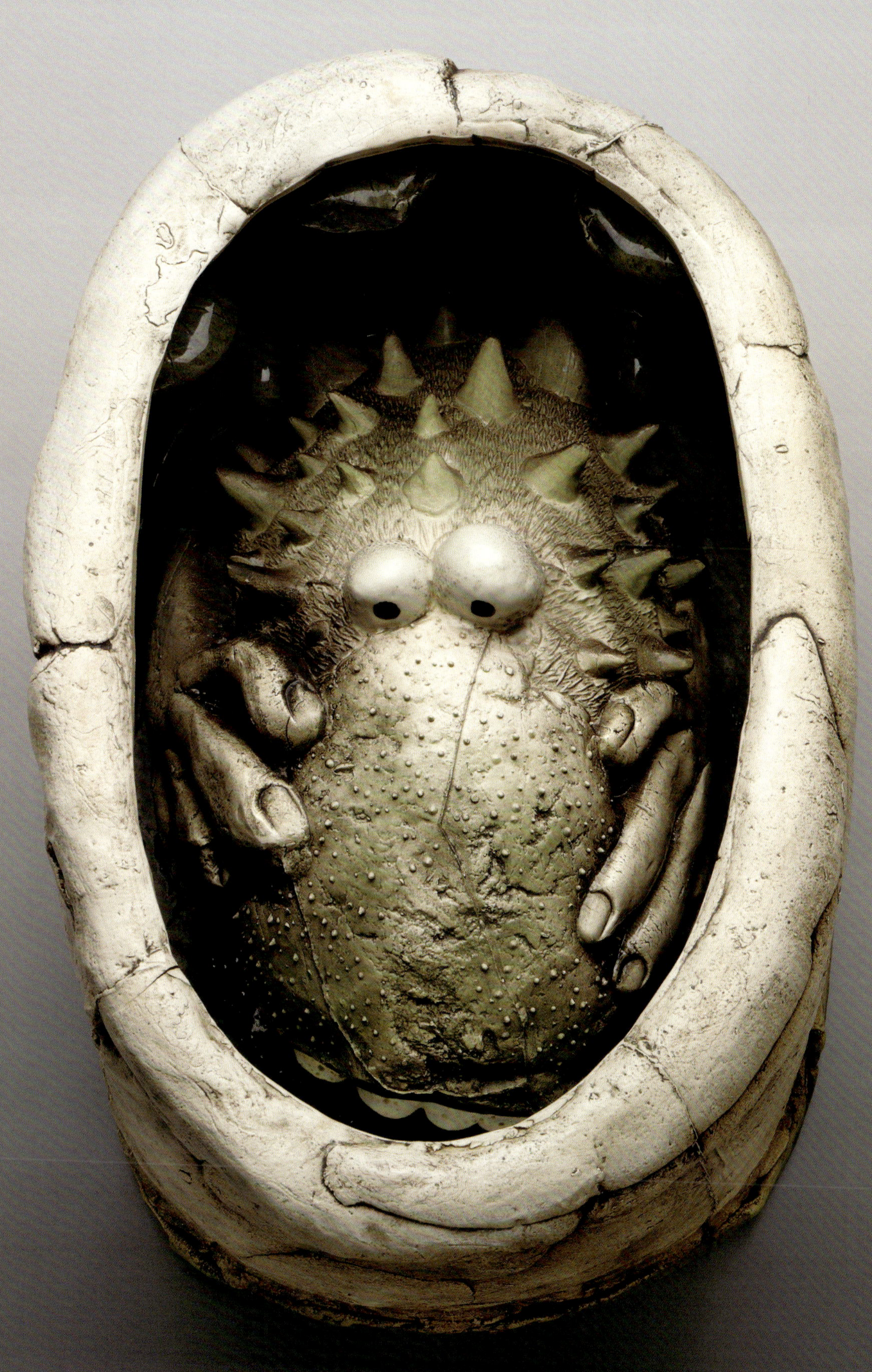

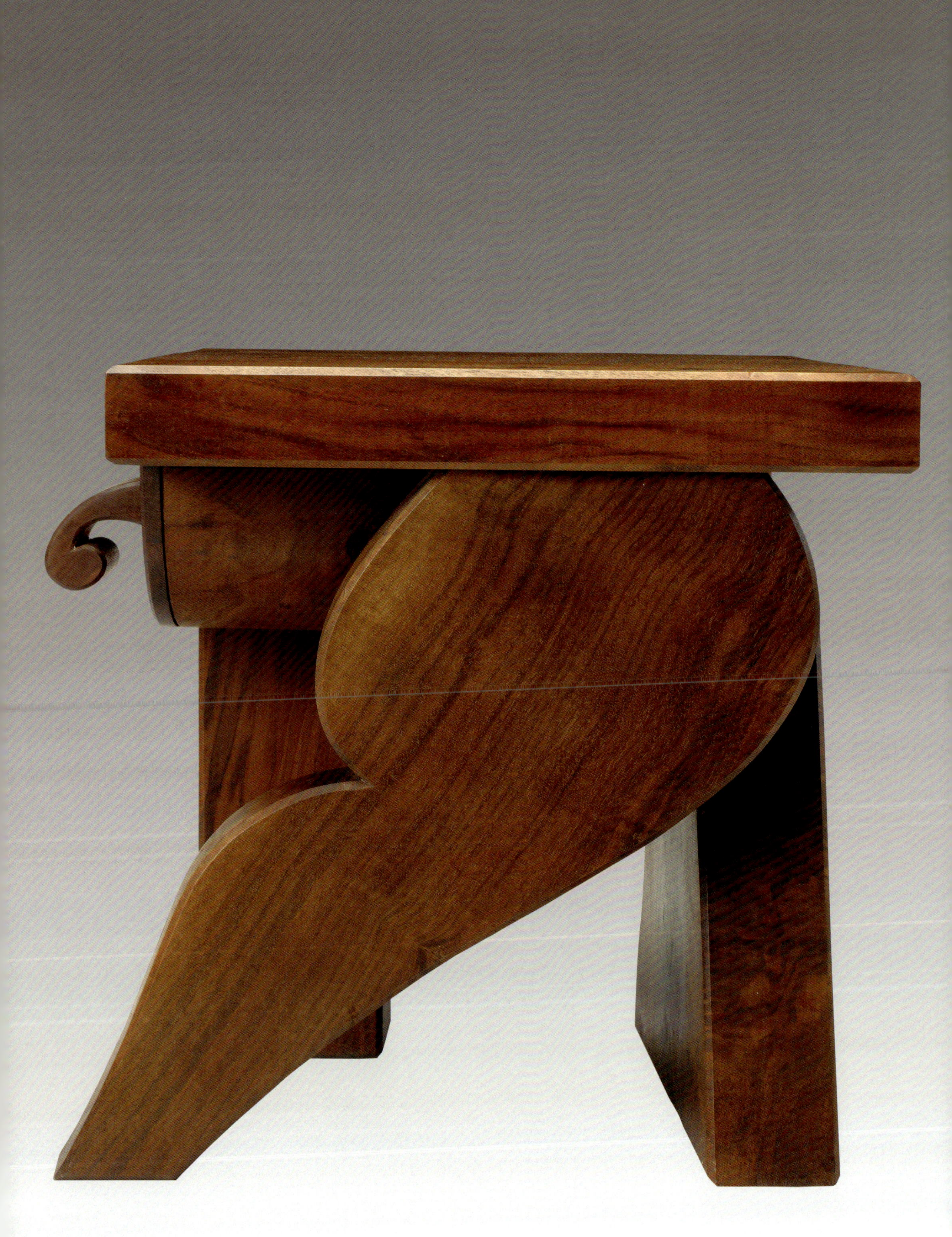

GARRY KNOX BENNETT
American, born 1934

Garry Knox Bennett ushered in a new era in furniture making with his unorthodox approach to materials and techniques, in particular his advocacy throughout the 1980s and 1990s for the incorporation of new materials such as Formica ColorCore, aluminum, and particleboard.[1] Bennett's interest is not only in expanding the pantheon of permissible materials but also in broadening the possible conceptions, meanings, and implications of studio furniture.

By incorporating historical investigation, pastiche, reinterpretation, and humor in his forms, Bennett has filtered nearly every category of furniture, from tables to lamps and most recently chairs, through a Postmodernist conceptual treatment whose recombinations upend traditional logic. For example, seizing the essential irony of the trestle table's visual weightiness with its intended portability, Bennett created a number of interpretations juxtaposing heavy mismatched legs with light, airy tops. This inquiry into the relationship of parts to the whole, and of component to overall function, remains central to his objects. In works such as *Side Table* (1997), three different types of table legs appear to jostle together in their support of the diminutive tabletop.

Along with furniture makers such as Alphonse Mattia and fellow Californians John Cederquist and Wendy Maruyama, Bennett has been at the forefront of a movement to incorporate more conceptual layers into the field of studio furniture. Reverberations from this push, which mirrors the advances in ceramics by his West Coast contemporaries Robert Arneson and Peter Voulkos, can be felt in educational furniture programs throughout the country. SJS

NOTE
1   Cheryl White, "Garry Knox Bennett," *American Craft* 61, no. 5 (November 2001): 60–64.

PLATE 11

SIDE TABLE
1997
Walnut
18 x 16 x 17 inches
(45.7 x 40.6 x 43.2 cm)
The Leatrice S. and
Melvin B. Eagle Collection,
museum purchase funded
by the Caroline Wiess Law
Accessions Endowment Fund
2010.2036.A, .B

ROBERT BRADY
American, born 1946

At first glance, the quiet sophistication of Robert Brady's wood and ceramic figures belies the artist's background as a potter of utilitarian forms. Their meditative stolidity, evocative of the centering process at the heart of wheel throwing, suggests a kind of inward-gazing self-containment, with each work conveying a spiritual quest for self-realization. Read this way, Brady's figures can be seen as embodiments of the psychological aspect of vessel making. They are explorations of interiority, even as the artist left the vessel form in favor of sculpture.

Brady was first introduced to clay as a teenager and instantly knew that he would have a lifelong engagement with the medium. He stumbled into woodwork later, when his desire to create long, attenuated forms led him to seek new materials. He was attracted to wood for its strength, warmth, and tone, as well as to wood-working techniques. The use of wood connects Brady's pieces with the indigenous antecedents that he finds so compelling and with the work of Elie Nadelman, a modernist sculptor of the early twentieth century known for his affinity for folk art.

Brady attended the California College of the Arts and the University of California, Davis, in the late 1960s and early 1970s, during the height of the Bay Area ceramic scene. Despite its occasional humorous references, Brady's output resonates more with the spiritual intensity seen in the work of Stephen De Staebler than that of his professor Robert Arneson. SJS

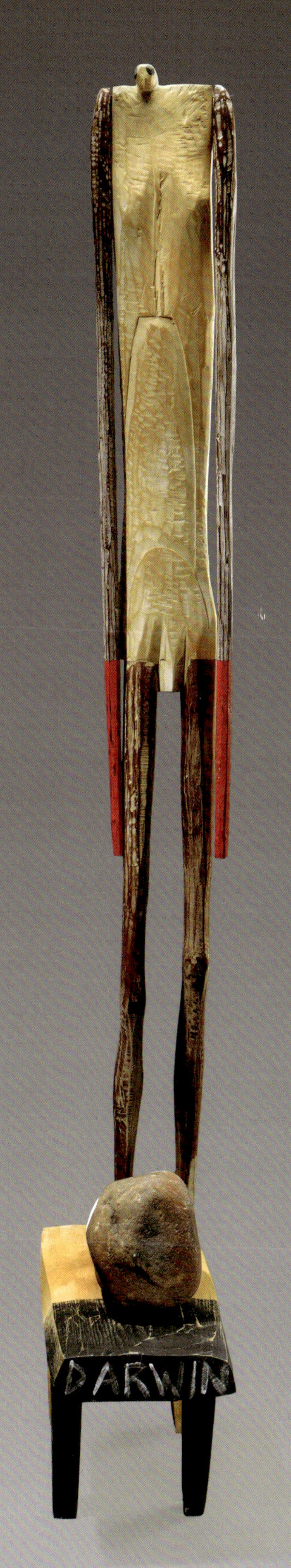
DARWIN

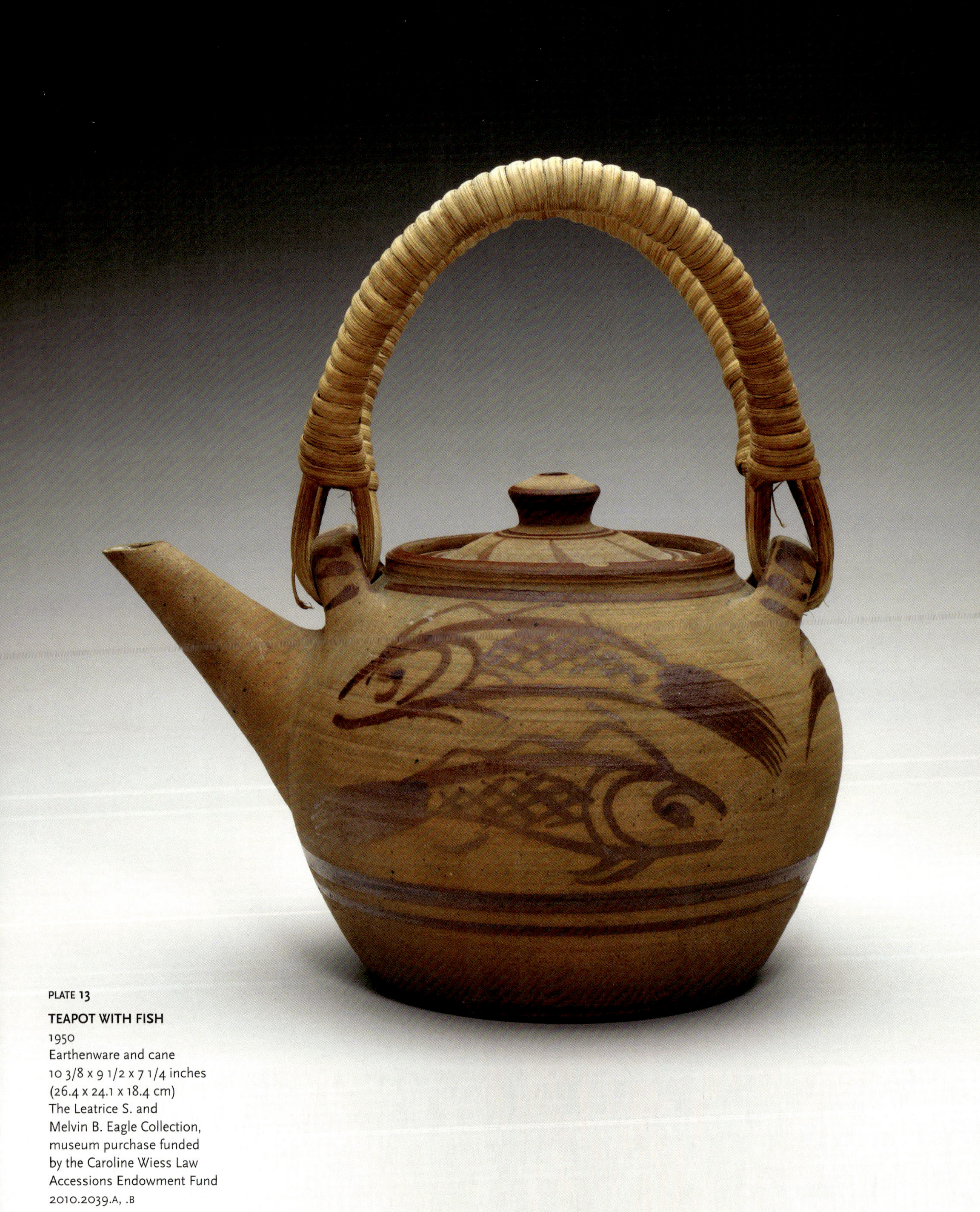

PLATE 13

TEAPOT WITH FISH
1950
Earthenware and cane
10 3/8 x 9 1/2 x 7 1/4 inches
(26.4 x 24.1 x 18.4 cm)
The Leatrice S. and
Melvin B. Eagle Collection,
museum purchase funded
by the Caroline Wiess Law
Accessions Endowment Fund
2010.2039.A, .B

MICHAEL CARDEW
British, 1901–1988

Michael Cardew was a first-generation British studio potter renowned for the directness of his utilitarian forms, his embodiment of the craftsman ideal, and his widespread advocacy for the medium. In the 1920s, he apprenticed with Bernard Leach, the highly influential "father" of studio pottery. Together with Leach and the Japanese master potter Hamada Shōji, Cardew helped revive British slipware traditions of the eighteenth century, eventually establishing two potteries, Winchcombe and Wenford Bridge, to carry out his designs.

Cardew spent more than twenty years working in potteries in the West African countries of Ghana and Nigeria. Initially, he traveled to Ghana as a civil servant tasked with heading a small factory in Alajo that produced tableware and other glazed items for the British Army and local industry.[1] Soon, however, he moved to a rural pottery-making village and, along with three of his best students from Alajo, began using local materials to make stoneware vessels that recalled indigenous ceramics in both form and bold decoration but retained an individualistic sensibility. This process mirrored his early days in Britain and foreshadowed his subsequent work at the Abuja pottery in Nigeria.

Cardew is notable for his commitment throughout his career to his distinctive formal language, even while adapting and borrowing those of other cultures. The roots of his broad interest can be seen in his earliest ceramic training with Leach and Hamada. His aim was not to create exact replicas of the older work but rather to draw inspiration from the process and methodology. With his interminable drive to recover older traditions as a basis for modern modes of working, Cardew has been an inspiration to generations of British, African, and American artists of the twentieth century and today. SJS

NOTE
1 Tanya Harrod, " 'The Breath of Reality': Michael Cardew and the Development of Studio Pottery in the 1930s and 1940s," *Journal of Design History* 2, no. 2/3 (January 1, 1989): 152.

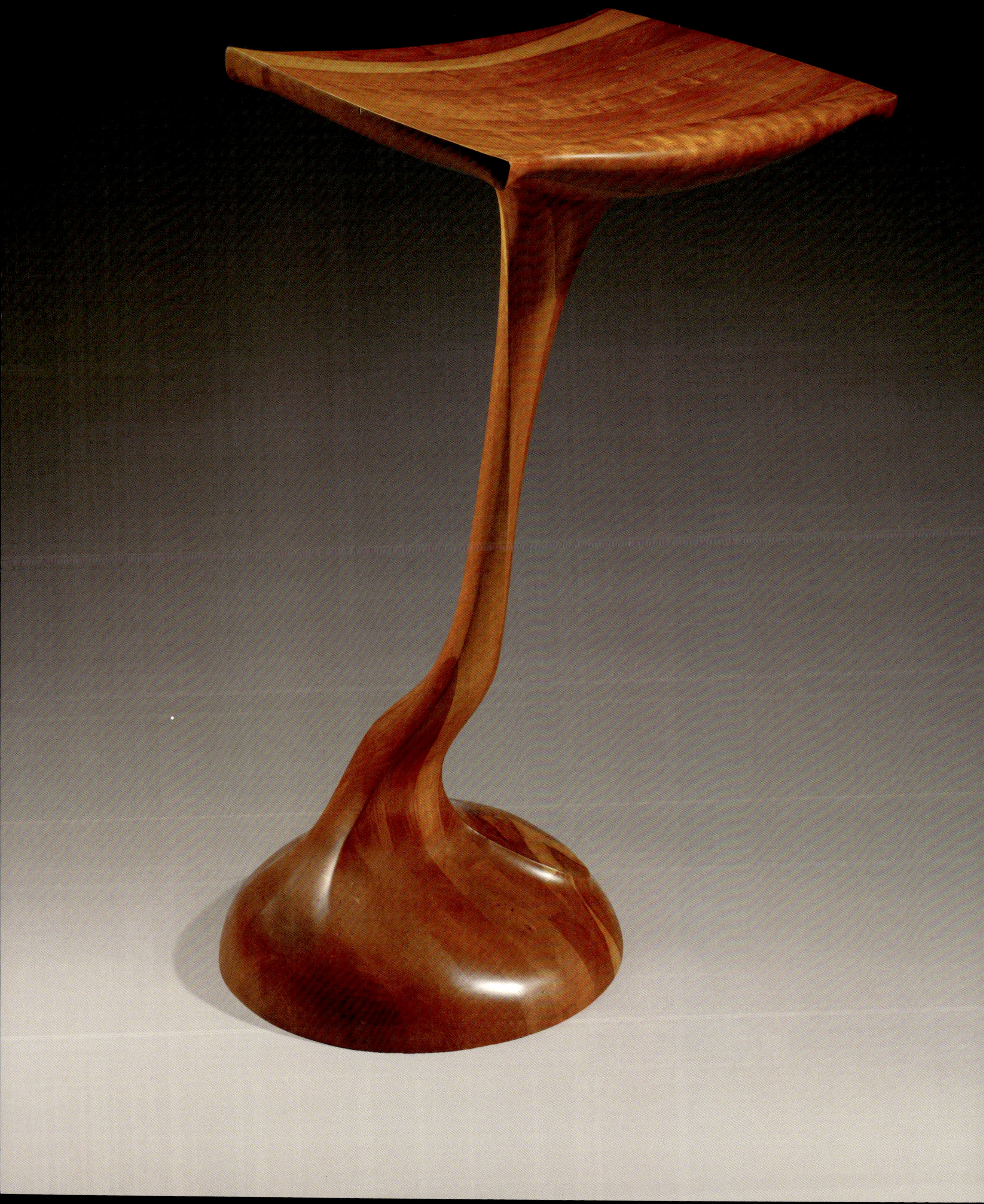

WENDELL CASTLE
American, born 1932

Wendell Castle has been a leader in contemporary furniture since the early 1960s, when, propelled by a desire to make expressive, biomorphic shapes, he began laminating blocks of cherry, walnut, and other hardwoods to create forms from which to carve. He was appropriating a technique that, although well known to wood sculptors for the strength it affords the material, was outside the realm of furniture making until Castle's experimentation. Castle embraced the potential of this process by using it to create bold sculptural works as large as his acclaimed 1965 *Library Sculpture*, which integrated two chairs and a desk into its twisting central column, as well as smaller works such as his series of lecterns and music and dictionary stands, in which he transformed wood to appear like a molten, free-flowing substance. Castle's innovation was quickly embraced by the growing cadre of academically trained furniture makers emerging from university programs such as that of the Rochester Institute of Technology in New York, whose staff Castle joined in 1962, looking to blur divisions between craft, art, and design.

Castle has been a pioneer in this regard, utilizing his training in sculpture and industrial design as a springboard to incorporate new ideas and materials into his practice. In addition to his appropriation of slab lamination, Castle is renowned for his innovative use of plastics and fiberglass beginning in the late 1960s.[1] The brilliant colors and seemingly endless formal possibilities of these materials allowed the artist to move beyond the limitations of wood, bringing his work as well as the field of studio furniture more fully into the realm of sculpture. SJS

NOTE

1 Edward S. Cooke, *The Maker's Hand: American Studio Furniture, 1940–1990* (Boston: MFA Publications, a division of the Museum of Fine Arts, 2003), 115.

STEPHEN DE STAEBLER
American, 1933–2011

PLATE **16**

**STANDING FIGURE WITH
SEGMENTED KNEE**
1983
Bronze
93 1/2 x 12 3/4 x 21 1/2 inches
(237.5 x 32.4 x 54.6 cm)
The Leatrice S. and
Melvin B. Eagle Collection,
museum purchase funded
by the Caroline Wiess Law
Accessions Endowment Fund
2010.2048

Craggy and marred, with subtly colored surfaces in pinks, creams, and grays suggestive of human flesh, rust, and fire, Stephen De Staebler's sculptures in ceramic and bronze record the artist's long preoccupation with the relationship between the human body and the earth. His figures appear timeworn, broken down, and partially reclaimed. These are contemplative objects; they beckon viewers to examine their mortality. Yet just as the relics of ancient cultures signal the transience of life even while attesting to its persistence, De Staebler's works are palliative and reassuring.

While an undergraduate in theology, De Staebler experimented with the visual expression of his interests, studying first with the painters Robert Motherwell and Ben Shahn at Black Mountain College in North Carolina and with the ceramicist Hui Ka-Kwong at the Brooklyn Museum School in New York.[1] However, not until he entered the dynamic environment of Peter Voulkos's studio at the University of California, Berkeley, in 1959 did he develop an approach that combined the abstract expressionism of Motherwell, the empathy of Shahn, and the materiality of Hui.[2]

De Staebler's early pieces incorporated the physicality of Voulkos's work and the ambitious scale of that of Harold Paris, a largely self-taught artist who joined the staff of the University of California, Berkeley, in 1960. Soon, however, the artist's abiding interest in the spiritual and religious moderated his impulse for grandeur. With their fragmented bodies partially embedded in their surrounding matrices, these mature pieces emphasize the mortality of flesh and the immortality of landscape. SJS

NOTES
1 Garth Clark, *American Ceramics, 1876 to the Present*, rev. ed. (New York: Abbeville Press, 1987), 260.
2 De Staebler came to University of California, Berkeley, in 1958, but Voulkos's arrival in 1959 is what sparked De Staebler's creative output. See Timothy Burgard, "Stephen De Staebler: Humanist in an Existential Age," in Stephen De Staebler et al., *Matter and Spirit: Stephen De Staebler* (San Francisco: Fine Arts Museums of San Francisco; Berkeley: University of California Press, 2012), 25.

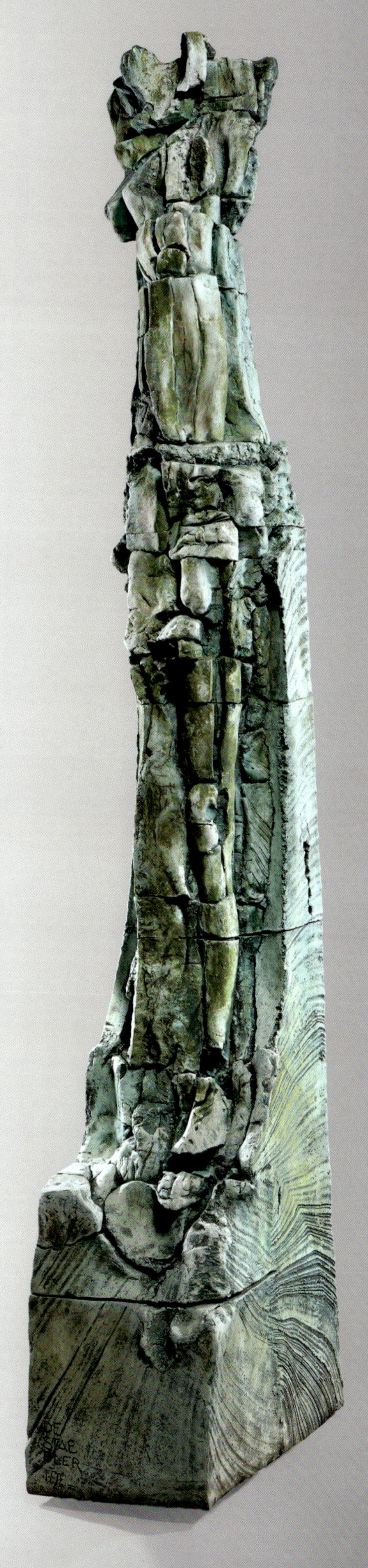

PLATE **17**

FIGURE COLUMN I
2001
Stoneware
75 x 11 1/2 x 12 1/4 inches
(190.5 x 29.2 x 31.1 cm)
The Leatrice S. and
Melvin B. Eagle Collection,
museum purchase funded
by the Caroline Wiess Law
Accessions Endowment Fund
2010.2047

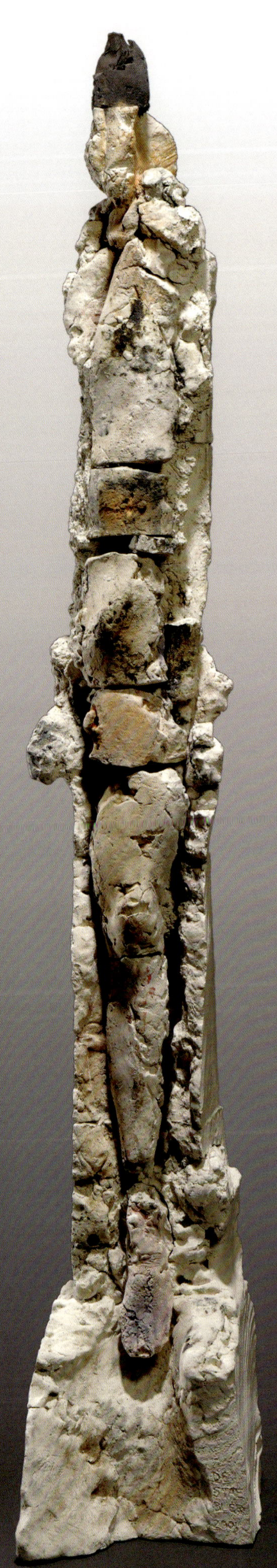

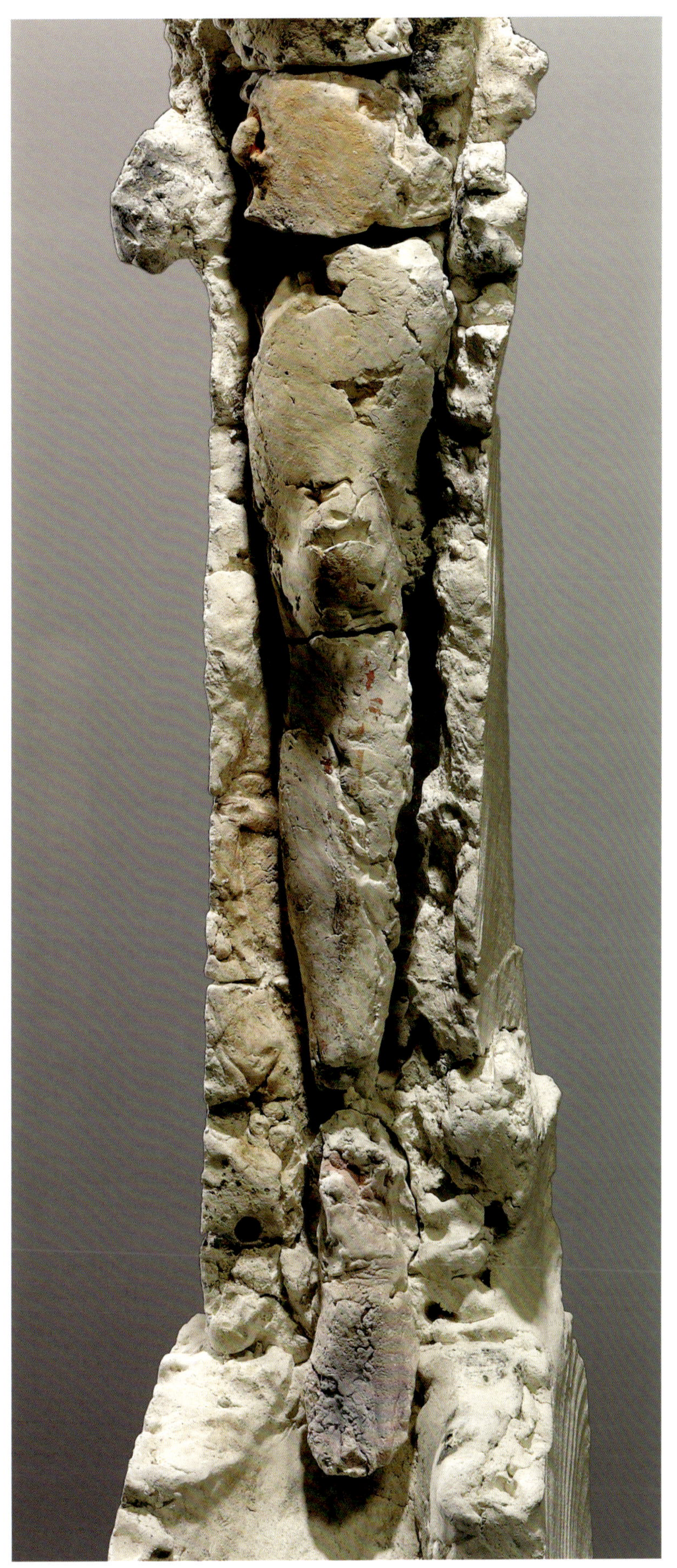

RICK DILLINGHAM
American, 1952–1994

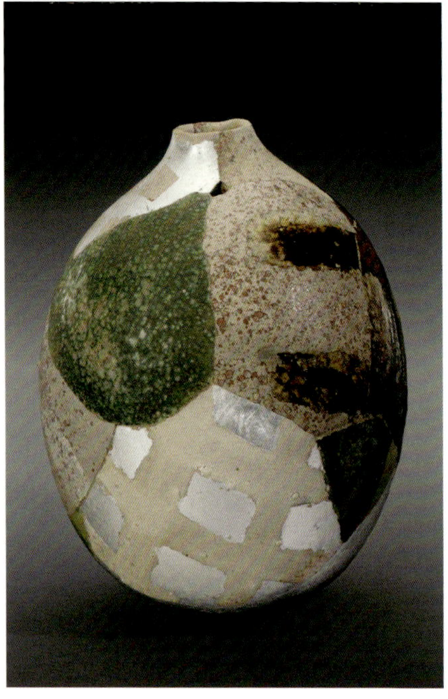

PLATE **18**

VESSEL
1985
Raku
6 1/4 x 5 1/8 inches diameter
(15.9 x 13 cm)
The Leatrice S. and
Melvin B. Eagle Collection,
museum purchase funded
by the Caroline Wiess Law
Accessions Endowment Fund
2010.2053

PLATE **19**

VESSEL
1985
Raku
23 x 13 1/2 x 13 1/4 inches
(58.4 x 34.3 x 33.7 cm)
The Leatrice S. and
Melvin B. Eagle Collection,
museum purchase funded
by the Caroline Wiess Law
Accessions Endowment Fund
2010.2051.A, .B

Rick Dillingham's short-lived career produced a body of work that was distinctive in its aesthetic and mature in its conception. While a student at the University of New Mexico, Dillingham worked as a ceramics restorer at the Maxwell Museum of Anthropology. His work there introduced him to Native American and ancient ceramics, and gave him valuable experience in repairing and reassembling the shards of broken ceramic forms.

Dillingham's work as a restorer and his recognition of the new patterns that could emerge from recombining broken pieces altered more than his viewpoint. When, out of frustration, Dillingham broke a pot of his own, he drew on his experience at the anthropology museum to repair it, thereby creating a new ceramic archetype that would sustain him for the rest of his career.

Dillingham's process remained the same once he determined his course for a slab- or coil-built vessel. He broke biscuit-fired forms into shards, decorated both sides of the shards with stripes, zigzags, spirals, or other motifs in bold colors and metallics, and refired and reassembled the individual pieces. The only deviation in his process was whether he fired the pots in an electric kiln or whether he raku- or dung-fired them to achieve varied surfaces. Dillingham's simple shapes were the perfect vehicle for these symbols and motifs; their soft contours balanced the calligraphic and loose nature of his decoration. Over the years, only their scale and presentation changed as he incorporated metal or decorated ceramic stands for the vessels. CS

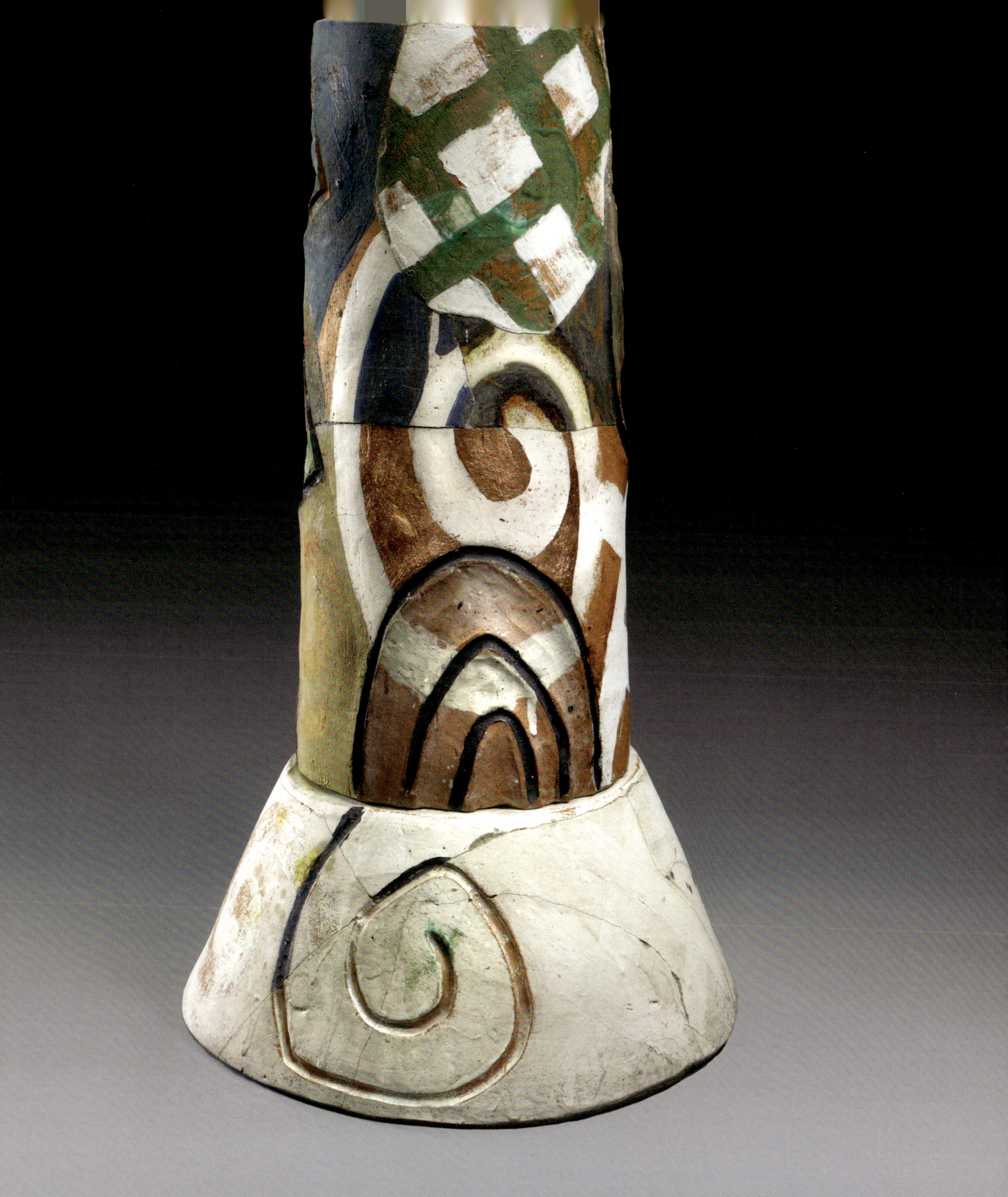

RUTH DUCKWORTH
American, born Germany, 1919–2009

PLATE **20**

VESSEL: SPLIT # R81-735801
c. 1981
Stoneware
18 1/2 x 19 1/2 x 21 inches
(47 x 49.5 x 53.3 cm)
The Leatrice S. and
Melvin B. Eagle Collection,
museum purchase funded
by the Caroline Wiess Law
Accessions Endowment Fund
2010.2057

Though Ruth Duckworth was born and reared in Germany, her life in England was what created opportunities for mentoring and friendship, each of which would affect her artistic development. Duckworth's association with the British ceramics artists Lucie Rie and Hans Coper and her admiration of the work of sculptors such as Constantin Brancusi, Henry Moore, Barbara Hepworth, Jean Arp, and others helped her to develop forms whose aesthetic ranged from abstract representation to the purely organic. In 1964 Duckworth relocated to Chicago from England to take a teaching position at the University of Chicago. The move to the United States coincided with a shift in her work's direction: large-scale, organic sculptures began to emerge from her studio, and a freer use of texture and symmetry pervaded her vessels and sculptures.

Duckworth began her renowned *Mama Pot* series in the late 1970s and continued working on the idea through the 1990s. The series name is derived from a reaction that a young boy had to one of her divided vessels, saying "nice mama, nice mama" to the pot.[1] The *Mama Pots* evolved from Duckworth's early experiments in slab-building large-scale vessels. Their apertures and rhythms are evocative of the female body, with shapes, curves, and folds that speak to the contours of femininity, and their bisected forms emphasize the tension between interior and exterior, and between solid and void. Like many of Duckworth's stoneware pieces, the *Mama Pots* have irregular surfaces and a palette varying from earth tones to darker colored glazes.

One of the most remarkable aspects of Duckworth's practice was her ability to renew forms over a long period of time. As Garth Clark wrote on the occasion of an exhibition celebrating her career at age eighty, "[Duckworth] has kept a constant balance, resisting novelty and eccentricity in her quest for innovation, yet working experimentally with a vocabulary that she knows well and which gives her voice its unique blend of authority and intuition."[2] CS

NOTES

1 Jo Lauria, "Modernist Impulses in the Work of Ruth Duckworth," in Jo Lauria and Tony Birks, *Ruth Duckworth: Modernist Sculptor* (Hampshire, England: Lund Humphries, 2005), 85.

2 Garth Clark, *Ruth Duckworth at 80* (New York: Garth Clark Gallery, 1999), 25.

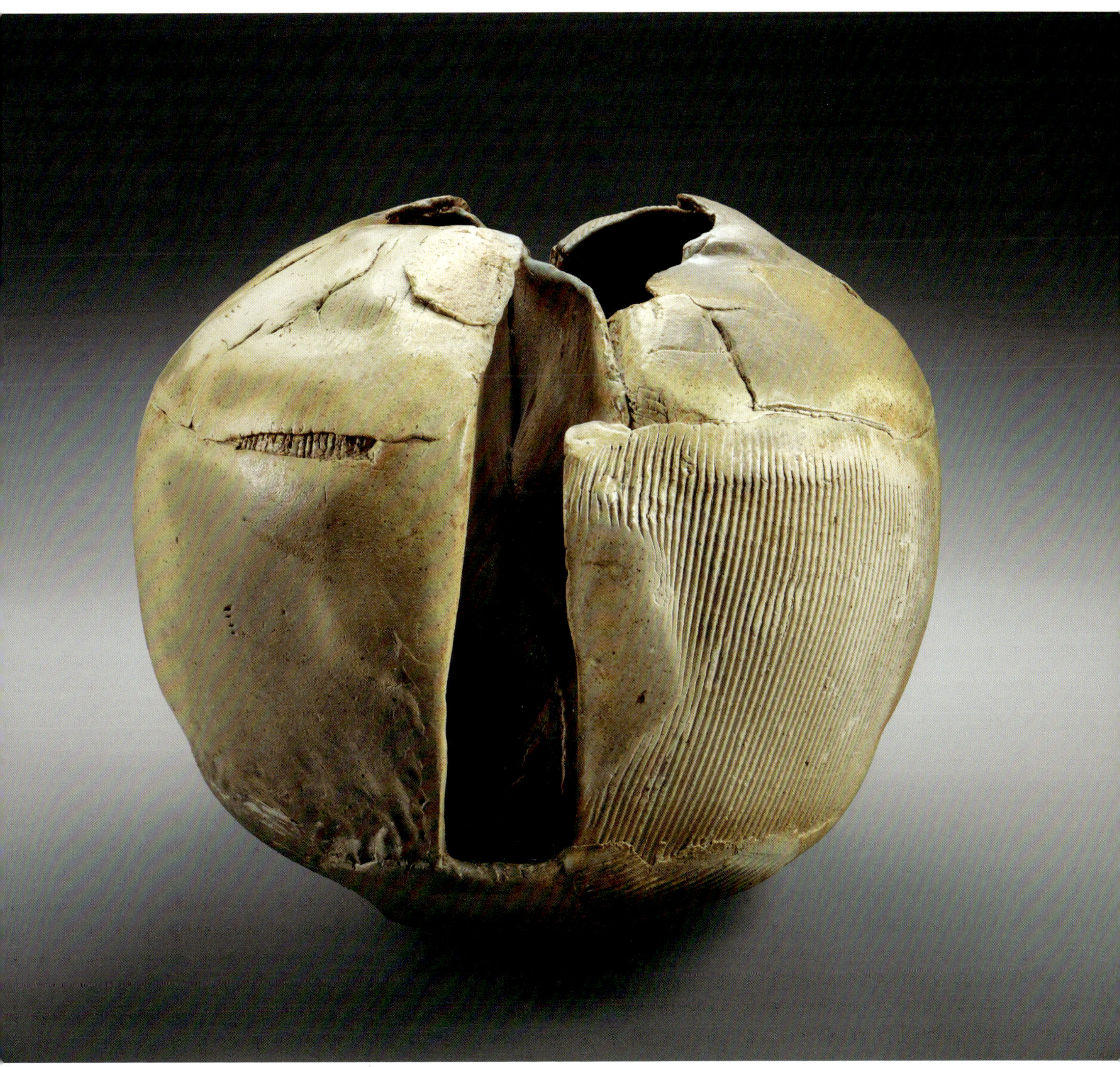

ROBERT EBENDORF
American, born 1938

Robert Ebendorf is renowned equally for his technical and aesthetic contributions to the field of jewelry, which have been marked by innovative thinking and a passion for materials. A highly respected professor of jewelry and metalwork, he has mentored legions of American jewelry artists during his long teaching career at the University of Georgia (1967–71), the State University of New York, New Paltz (1971–89), and East Carolina University in Greenville, North Carolina (1997 to the present). Even after an almost fifty-year career, he remains active and open to new inspiration.

Ebendorf works with precious metals, gemstones, alternative materials, found objects, and drawings. He favors strong visual patterns and juxtapositions of color and texture in his jewelry, and his wide-ranging aesthetic includes Scandinavian influences, pop culture, narrative imagery, and text elements, as well as themes ranging from religion to memory. Many of the objects that he creates have personal associations and meanings.

Some of Ebendorf's pieces are imbued with a wry sense of humor, but others are serious in their content and message. Another genre in his oeuvre consists of jewelry that explores shape, material, and color, whereas other works highlight imagery that simply appeals to the artist. Despite this diversity, Ebendorf's pieces are distinctive and identifiable in their tone and quality. This aesthetic essence pervades his jewelry, allowing it to transcend beyond ornament. CS

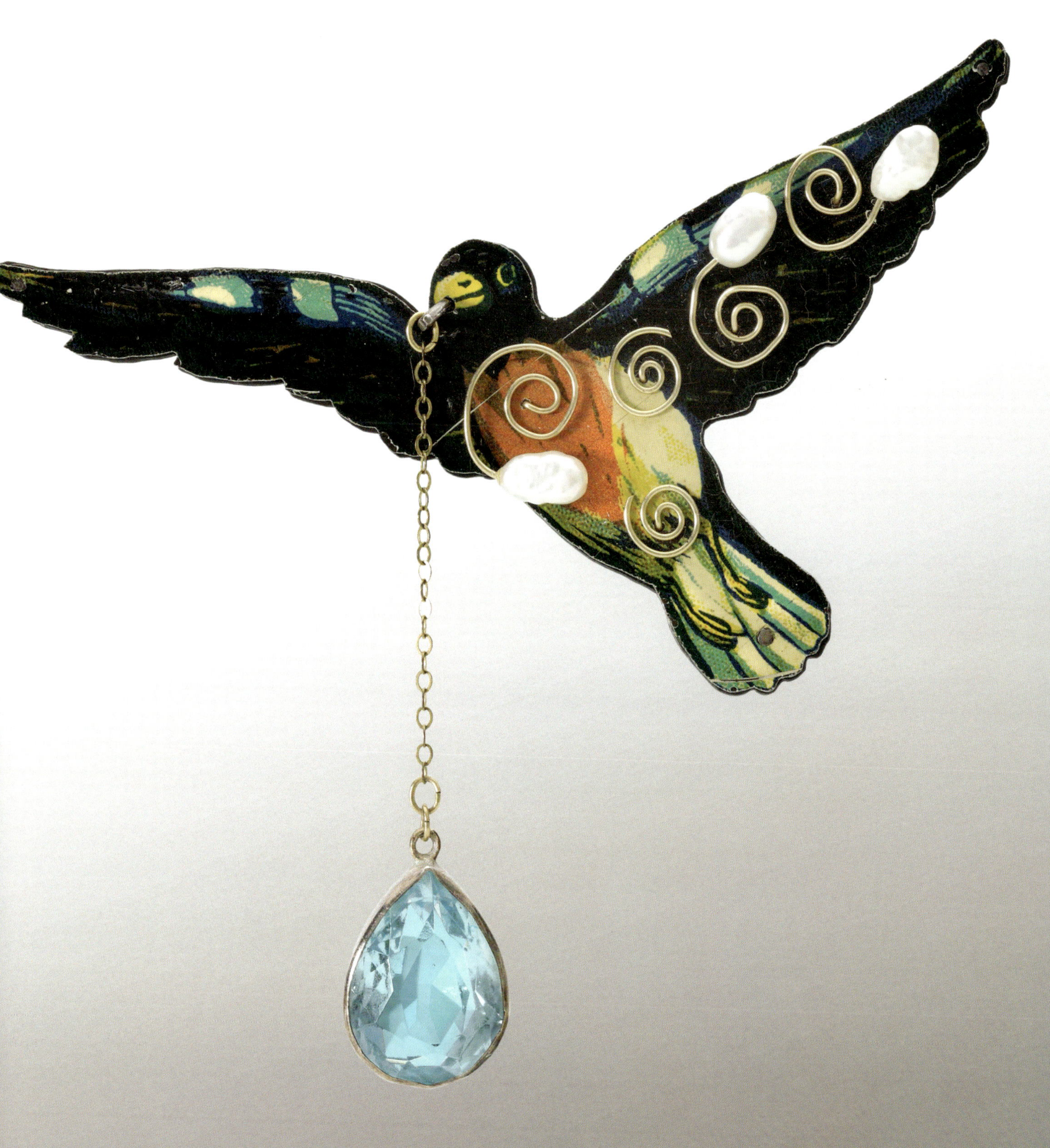

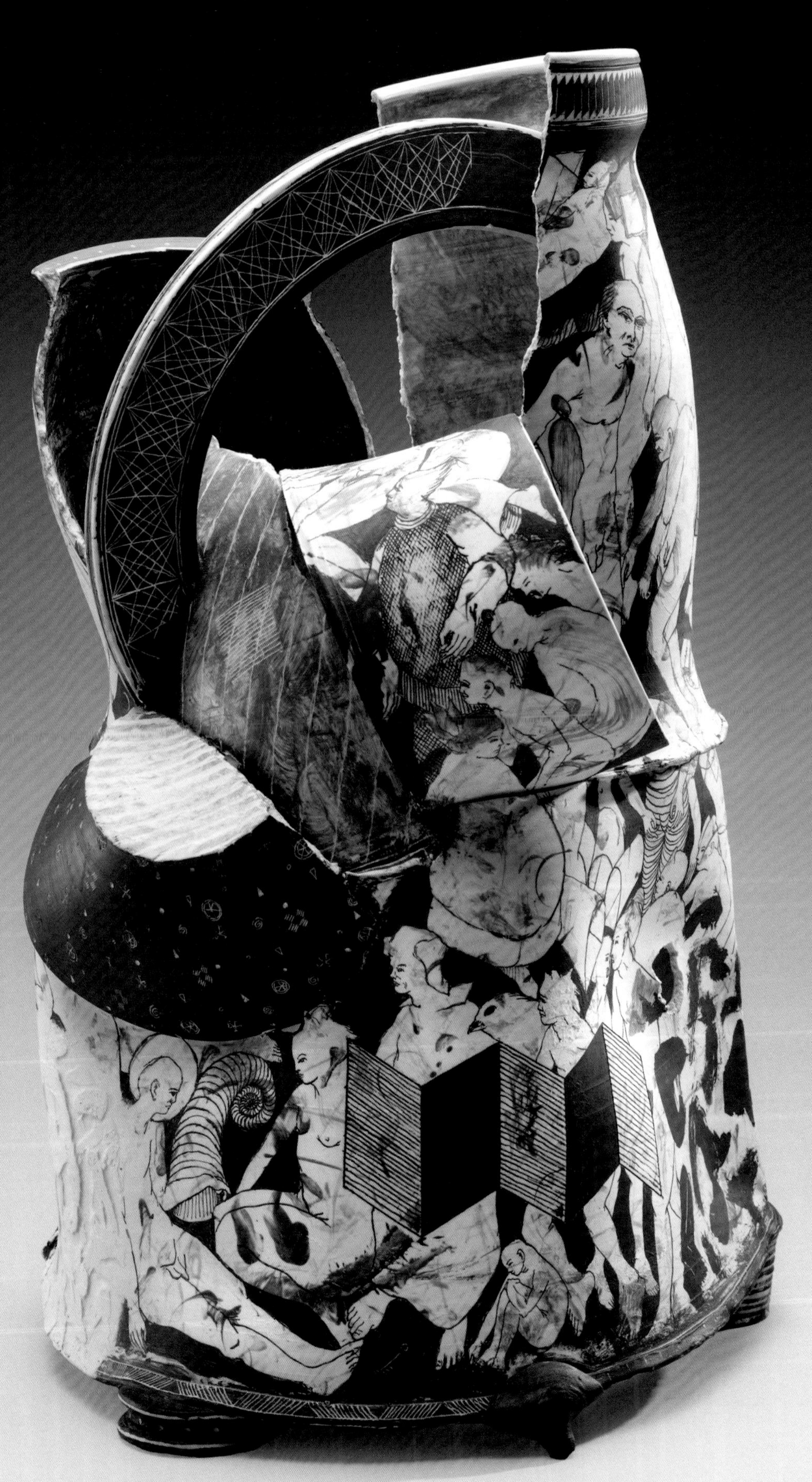

EDWARD S. EBERLE
American, born 1944

Edward S. Eberle uses black *terra sigillata*, a technique and material dating to ancient Rome and Greece, to draw on porcelain. A master potter, his wheel-thrown pieces vary from traditional containers to architectonic forms. Many incorporate deconstructed elements to become hybrids of both types. These pieces, such as *Fire Hat and Full Moon* (2002), emphasize movement and the layering of information and allow the artist to interrupt or punctuate the visual program in dynamic ways.

Eberle paints intuitively so that his process remains spontaneous and improvisational. His early pieces of the 1980s were small in scale, with singular images paired with geometric motifs. The placement of the illustrations was deliberate, leaving plenty of undecorated surface area on each work. By the 1990s and 2000s, Eberle's forms, such as the example in the Eagle collection, had become larger, more architectonic, and more complex in their decoration and narratives, ultimately resulting in ornamentation that entirely covered the vessel. Nude figures, animals, and symbols flow into one another with overlapping limbs and movements, generating distinctive spatial and perspective effects. Eberle often references elements of the human condition, mythology, and symbolism in his pieces, but can just as easily offer few clues to a work's meaning. CS

PLATE **22**

FIRE HAT AND FULL MOON
2002
Porcelain
22 3/8 x 15 x 13 1/2 inches
(56.8 x 38.1 x 34.3 cm)
The Leatrice S. and
Melvin B. Eagle Collection,
museum purchase funded
by the Caroline Wiess Law
Accessions Endowment Fund
2010.2063

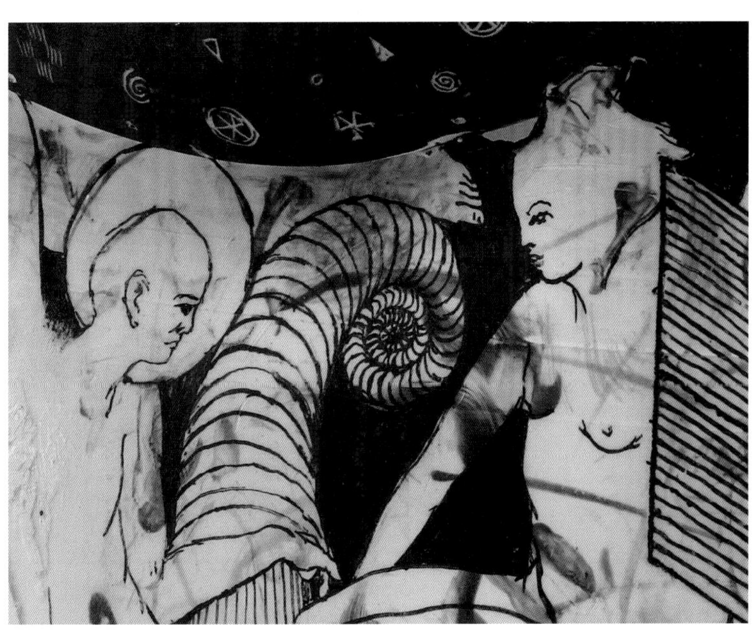

FRANK FLEMING
American, born 1940

Frank Fleming is a sculptor who works within a narrative tradition. A lifelong resident of Alabama, the artist is known for a signature style that reflects his southern heritage in its down-home folk sensibility and elegantly understated aesthetic. Fleming's sculptures act as a bridge between mythological fantasy and everyday life. In their cultivation of a private imaginative realm, Fleming's sculptures have a relationship to the alternate worlds of West Coast ceramicists such as Clayton Bailey and David Gilhooly. Indeed, a formative experience of Fleming's youth was a 1972 trip to the San Francisco Bay Area, which brought him in contact with Robert Arneson and his circle at the University of California, Davis.[1] For a brief period following this trip, Fleming made Funk sculptures of open-faced sandwiches in polychrome colors but ultimately settled on using stark white porcelain, colored only by its own shadows.

Fleming then began creating goat- and penguin-men, dressed in carefully wrought suits of clothing, who appeared as characters in a drama of the artist's own telling. Though emblems of the outside world, such as a staff, umbrella, or suitcases, often accompany Fleming's figures, his stories are ambiguous, allowing viewers to read into them what they will. On the motivation behind this ambiguity, the artist has commented, "It's most important for each of us to be able to turn inward—to listen, hear, and respond to the personal myths that might (but not necessarily do) dwell inside us."[2] SJS

NOTES
1 R. M. N. McAusland, "Frank Fleming's Fantasy in Porcelain," *American Artist* 43, no. 441 (April 1979): 60.
2 Frank Fleming, *Personal Mythologies, Frank Fleming: Birmingham Museum of Art, 3 October–14 November, 1982, Morgan Gallery, Kansas City, 3–28 December, 1982,* exhibition brochure (Birmingham: Birmingham Museum of Art, 1982), 1.

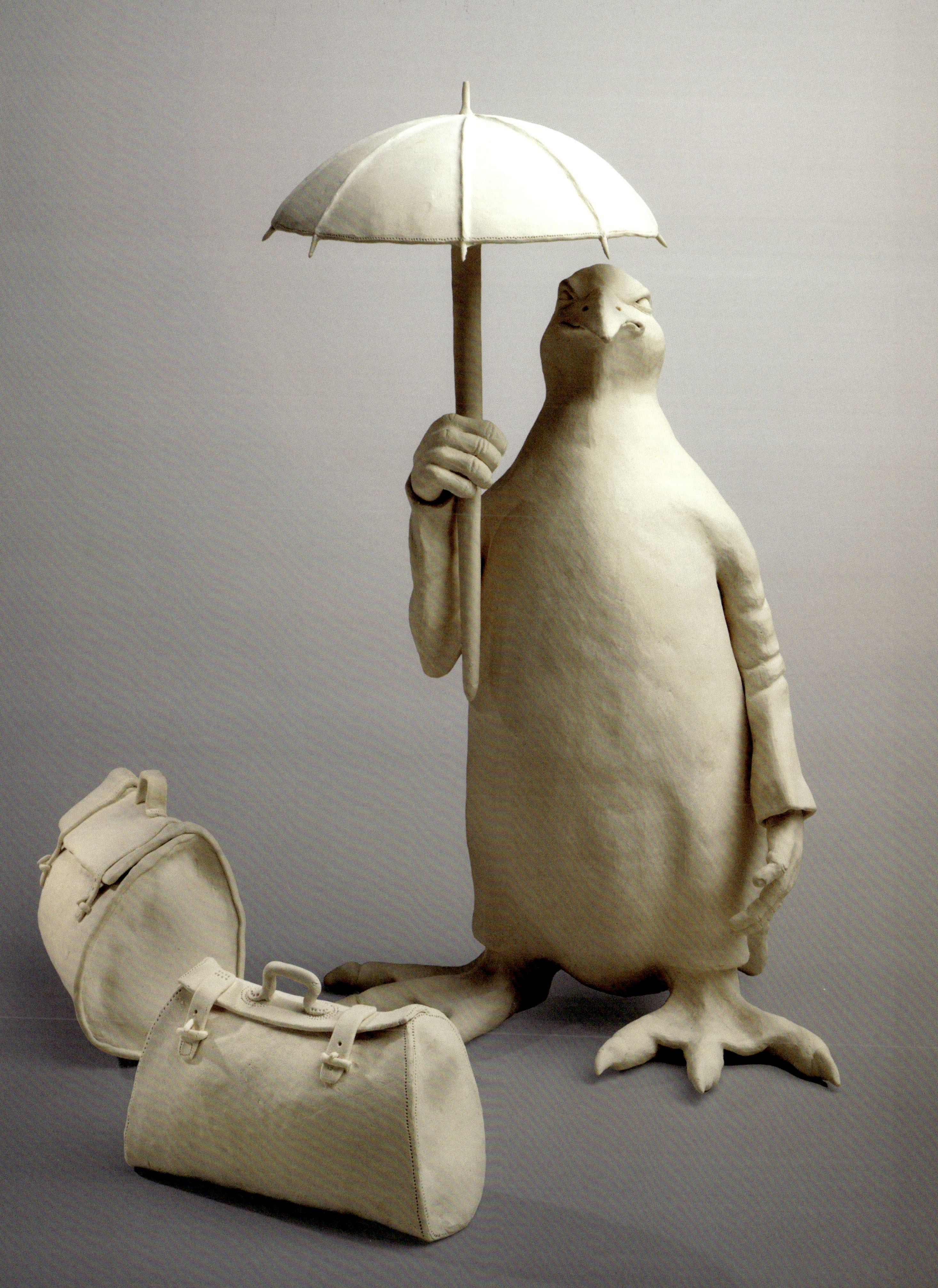

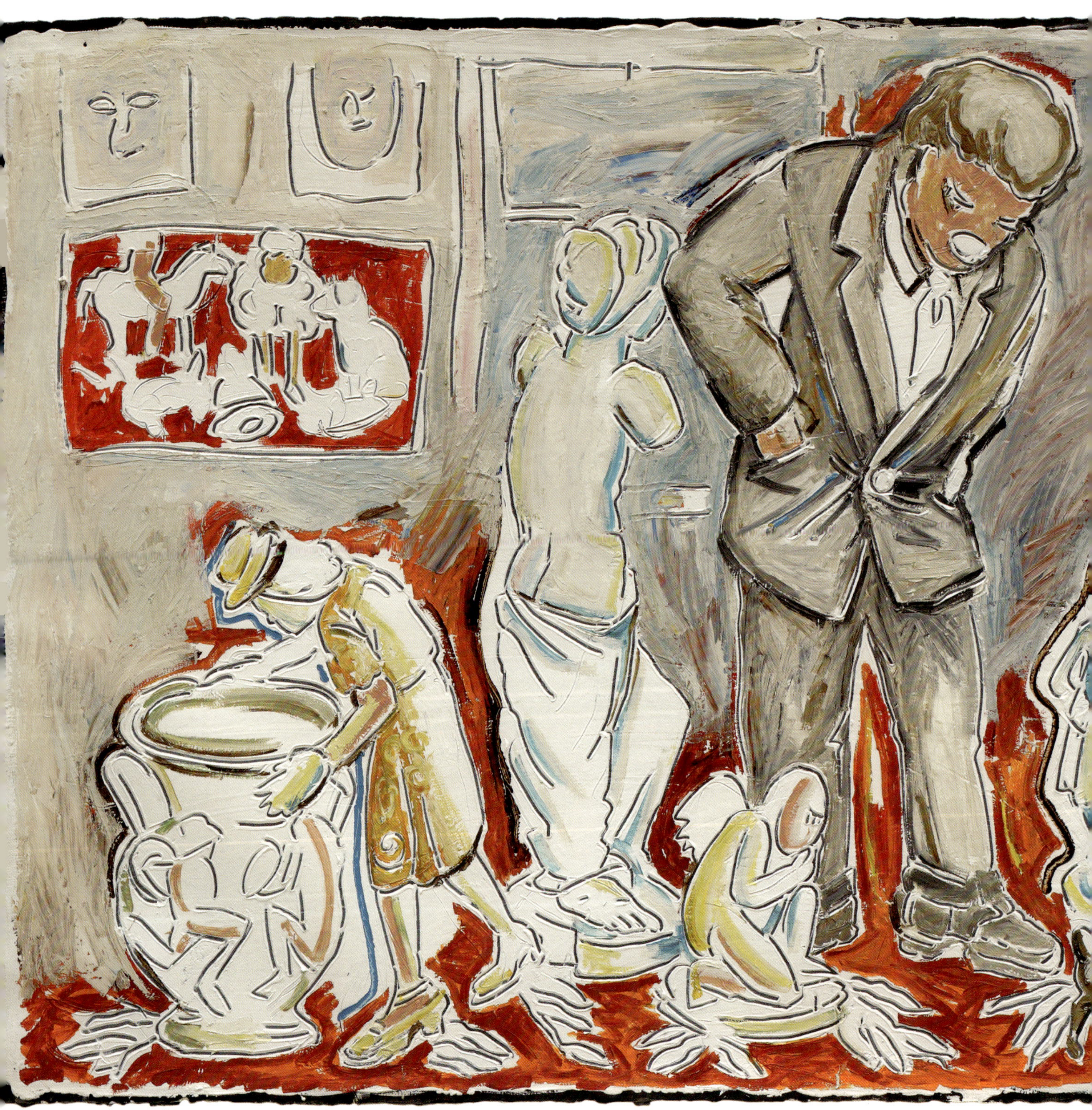

In her sculptures, assemblages, paintings, and photographs, Viola Frey combined observations on American culture and personal iconography to create a distinctive body of work. Although her formal and informal education as a painter and ceramicist took place in the 1950s, Frey truly came of age as an artist in the 1960s, when she moved to San Francisco from New York. This change brought her into contact with the leading figurative artists of the time as well as with the leading ceramicists, thereby fueling her artistic growth.

By the mid- to late 1970s, the flea-market and thrift-store bric-a-brac figurines and objects that Frey had been accumulating since childhood began to serve as powerful inspirations for her large-scale figural sculptures and smaller assemblages. These pieces are thought-provoking and often arresting in their forthrightness. In the assemblages, she juxtaposed men and women with objects, animals, and other shapes to create a dialogue about male–female relationships, religion, politics, and other social causes. One figure is never sacrificed for another; instead, they work together to create a harmonious composition. Frey's work most often features bold colors, ranging from electric hues to saturated tones, that are used to enhance and define form and space. Color makes Frey's work come alive. It brings a humanistic quality to the pieces as well as power and authenticity—qualities that, along with their realistic forms, transform the sculptures into riveting works of art. CS

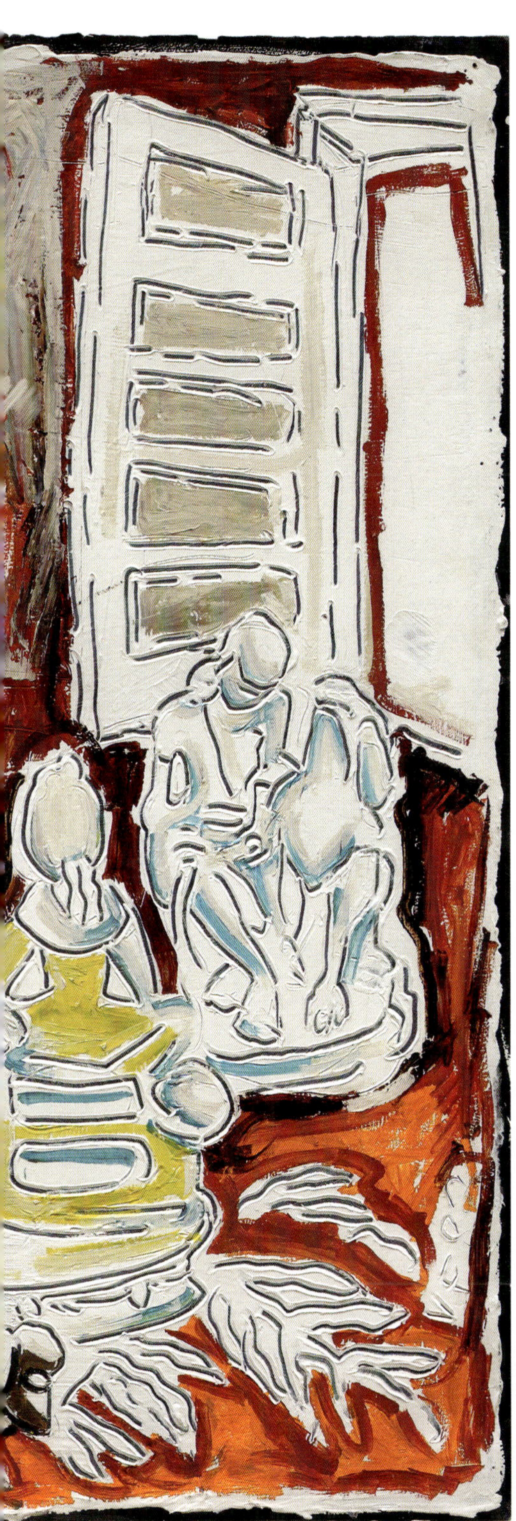

PLATE **24**

WOMEN UNDERNEATH STUDIO
1982
Oil on paper
40 x 60 inches (101.6 x 152.4 cm)
The Leatrice S. and
Melvin B. Eagle Collection,
museum purchase funded
by the Caroline Wiess Law
Accessions Endowment Fund
2010.2066

VIOLA FREY

PLATE 25

**SEATED MANIKIN MAN
AND VENUS**

1975
Ceramic
32 1/2 x 16 x 14 inches
(82.6 x 40.6 x 35.6 cm)
The Leatrice S. and
Melvin B. Eagle Collection,
museum purchase funded
by the Caroline Wiess Law
Accessions Endowment Fund
2010.2068

PLATE 26

**WESTERN CIVILIZATION
(CLOWN CARE)**

1997
Ceramic
31 1/4 x 24 x 14 1/2 inches
(79.4 x 61 x 36.8 cm)
The Leatrice S. and
Melvin B. Eagle Collection,
museum purchase funded
by the Caroline Wiess Law
Accessions Endowment Fund
2010.2067.A, .B

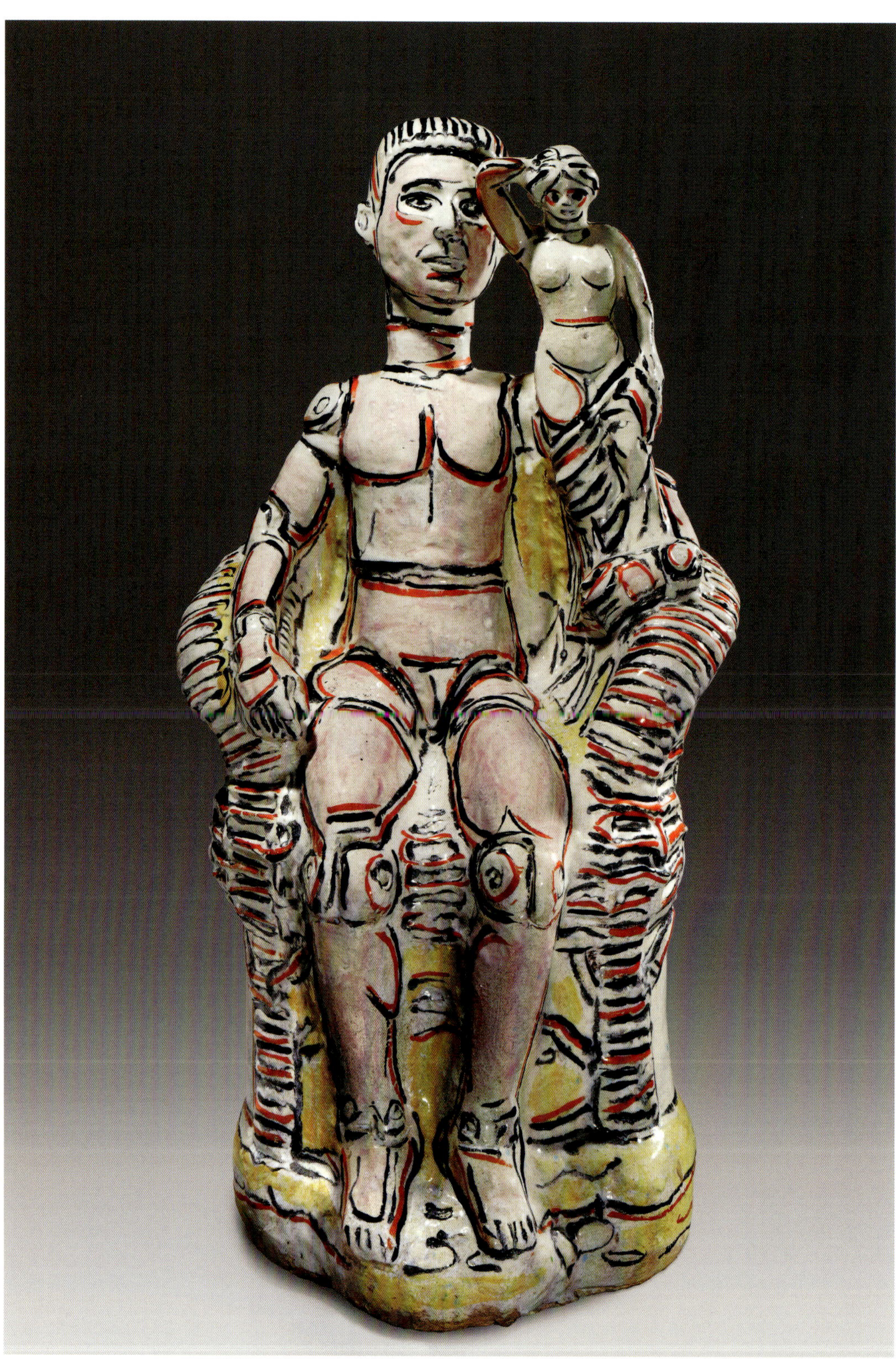

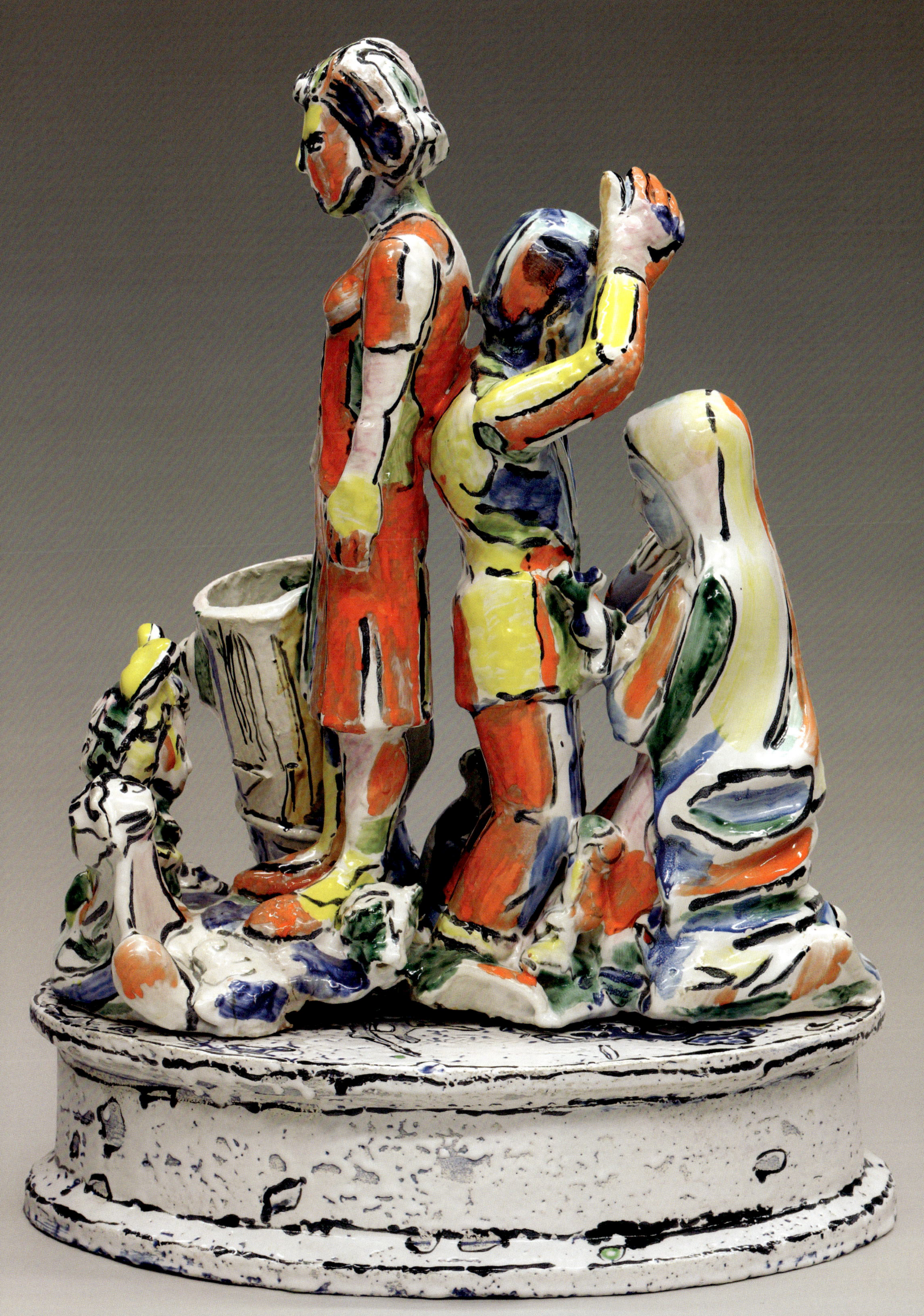

MICHAEL FRIMKESS
American, born 1937

MAGDALENA FRIMKESS
American, born Venezuela, 1929

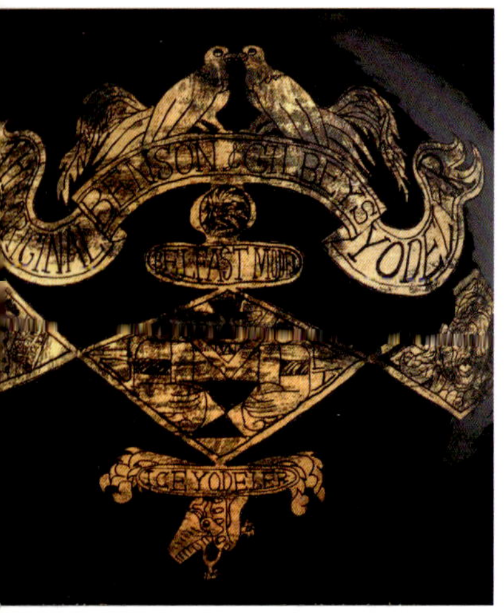

Along with Robert Arneson, Michael Frimkess is credited as being one of the first postwar ceramicists to introduce overtly political themes into his work.[1] The youngest of Peter Voulkos's students at the Los Angeles County Art Institute (now Otis College of Art and Design) in Los Angeles, California, where he studied from 1956 to 1957, Frimkess first dabbled in Abstract Expressionist sculpture before moving to the East Coast in 1963, where he worked in a commercial pottery in Pennsylvania. There, he was introduced to a dry-throwing technique, and he was also encouraged to study ancient vessels at the Metropolitan Museum of Art in New York City.[2]

Based on these studies, in the mid-1960s Frimkess initiated an ongoing series called *Melting Pots* that recontextualized ancient pottery forms, such as Chinese ginger jars, Greek amphorae, and Roman kraters, by melding traditional ceramic forms of the past with contemporary illustrations that provide commentary on the present. The somewhat cartoonish illustrations on Frimkess's vessels decry pollution, war, overpopulation, and racism. However, their didactic quality is relieved by a pervasive sense of humor, evident in inclusions such as the faux label on the reverse side of *Neck and Neck* (1977), advertising the "ice yodelers" of the fictional Benson & Gilbey's company.[3] The lighthearted amalgamation of Frimkess's imagery reflects the countercultural milieu of the mid-century Los Angeles art scene as well as the interests and aesthetic of his wife, Magdalena Frimkess, who has painted the majority of the vessels, including this one, since 1971. SJS

NOTES

1 Paul Mathieu, *Sex Pots: Eroticism in Ceramics* (New Brunswick, NJ: Rutgers University Press; London: A&C Black, 2003), 82.

2 "Oral History Interview with Michael and Magdalena Suarez Frimkess, 2001 March 8– April 17," Oral Histories, Archives of American Art, Smithsonian Institution, available online at http://www.aaa.si.edu/collections/.

3 Garth Clark, *A Century of Ceramics in the United States, 1878–1978: A Study of Its Development* (New York: E. P. Dutton, 1979), 267.

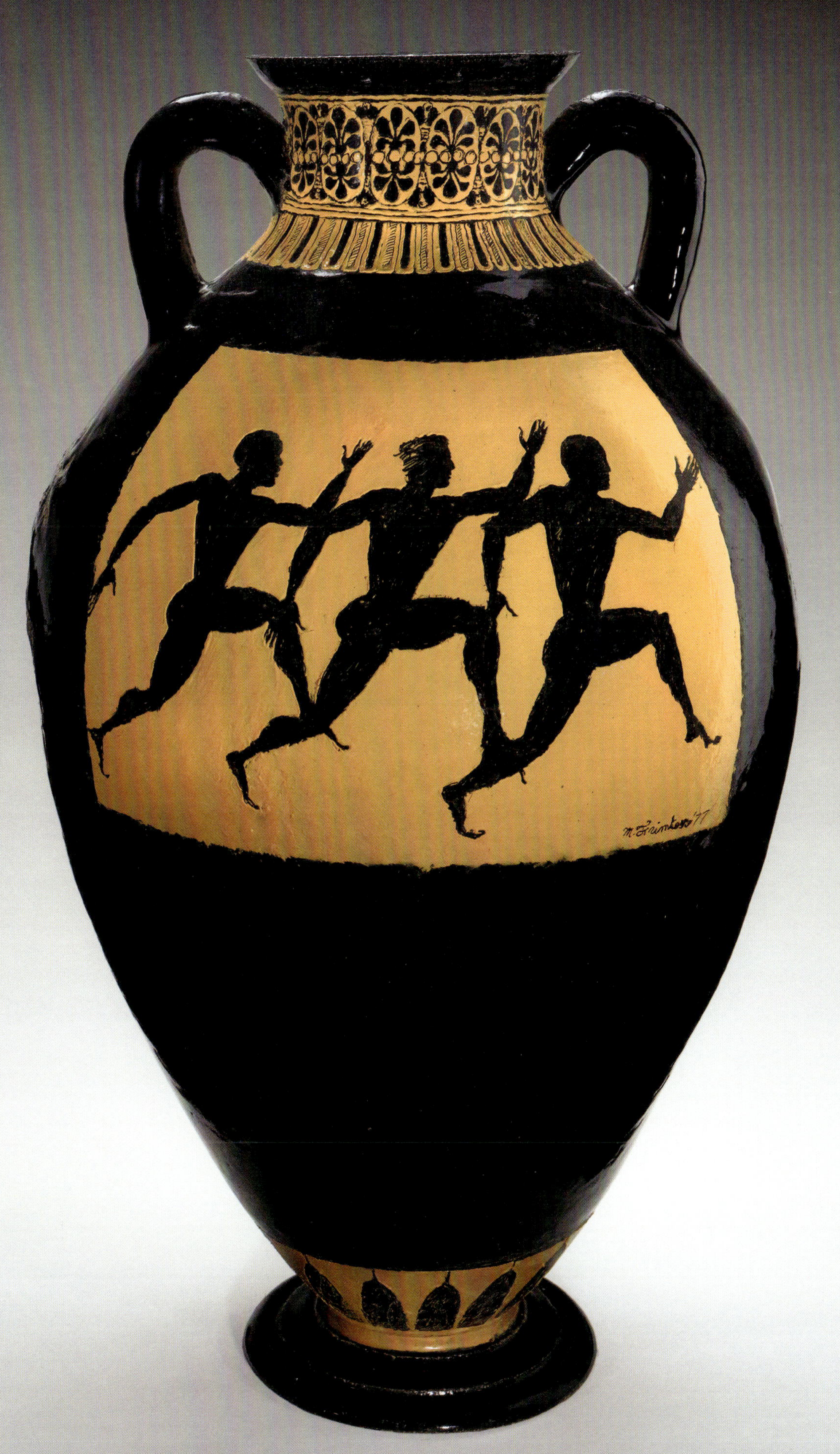

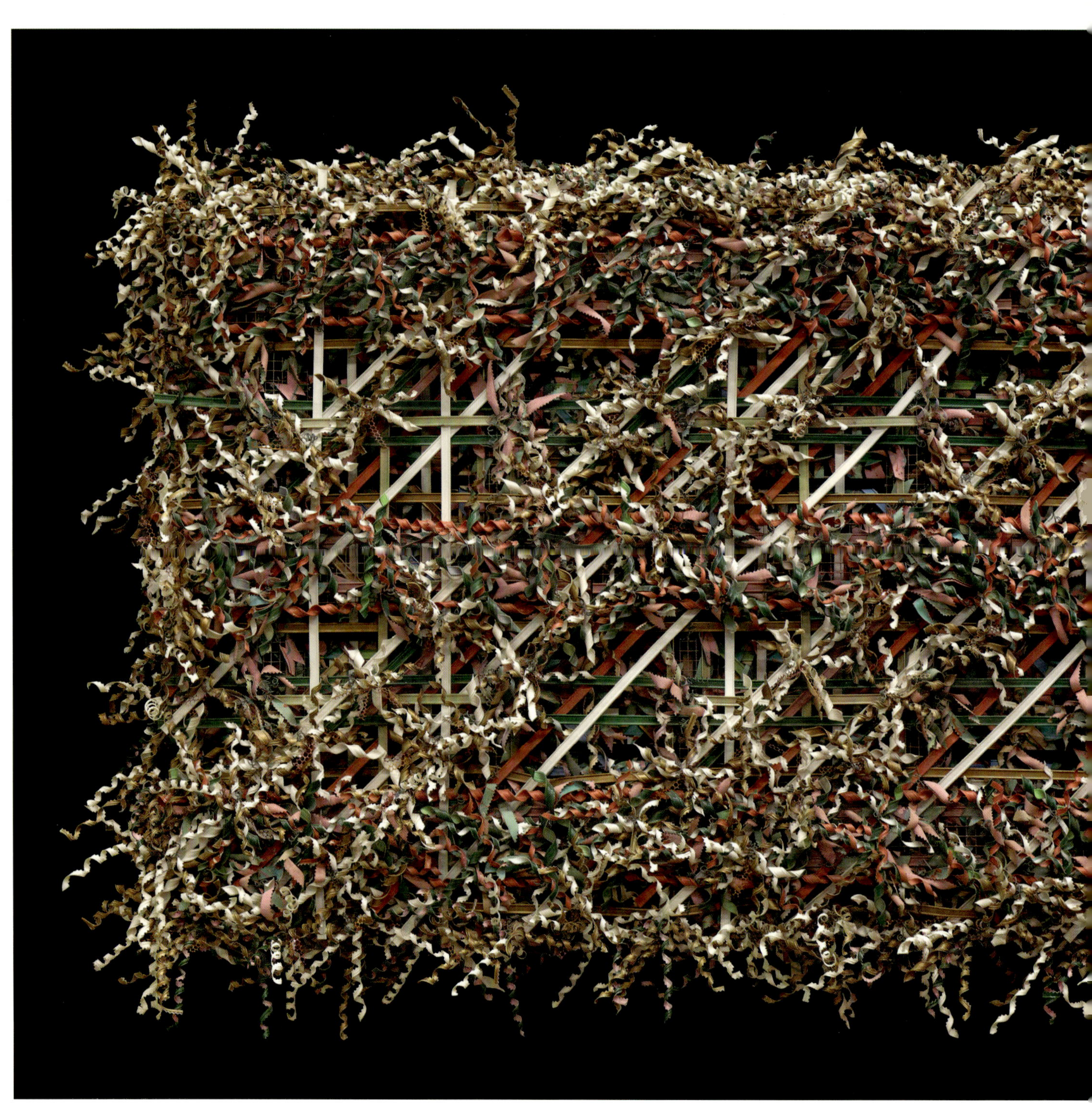

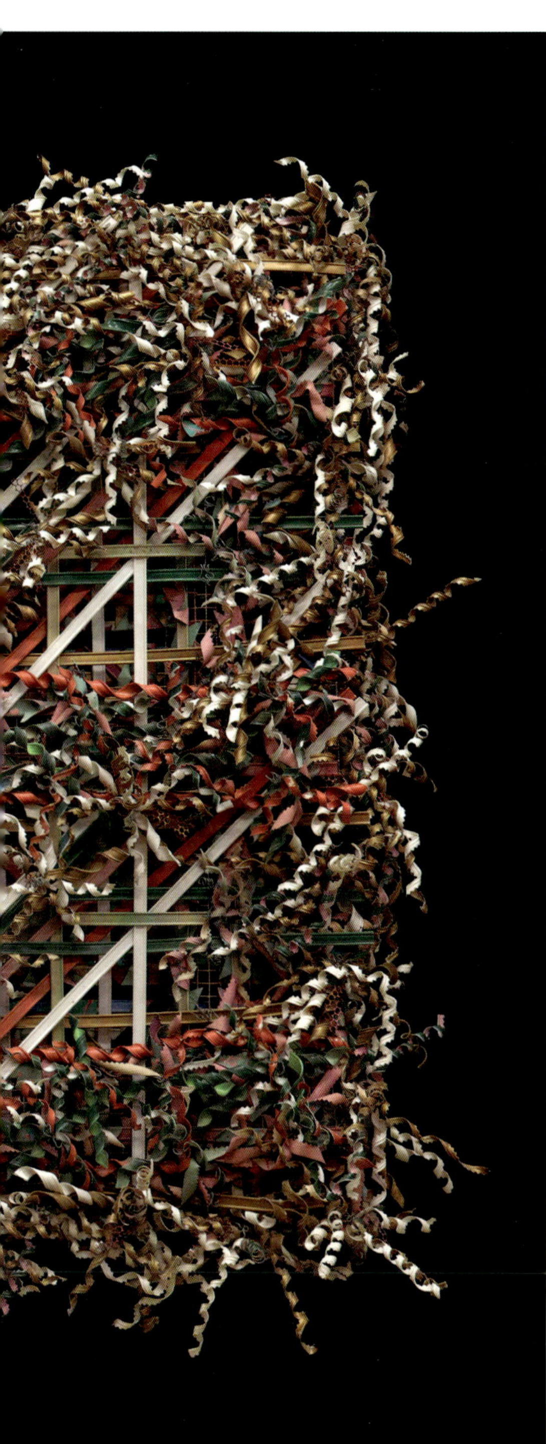

JOHN GARRETT
American, born 1950

A pioneer of the "new basketry," John Garrett has been creating innovative woven forms utilizing nontraditional materials for more than forty years. He constructs highly complex, visually rich baskets, wall hangings, and installations, employing a diverse palette that includes plastics, colored vinyl, copper flashing, hardware cloth (a type of welded wire mesh), and deconstructed tin cans, among others items. Despite the variety of his output, Garrett's process is remarkably similar for all categories of work. Nearly all of his forms begin as flat panels, some of which he later manipulates into sculptural formations.

In fact, Garrett's first introduction to baskets came through the field of weaving, which shares a similar methodology. While a student at Claremont Men's College (now Claremont McKenna College), Garrett took courses with Neda Al-Hilali at Scripps College. Inspired by Al-Hilali's use of unconventional materials, such as paper and metal, as well as by the groundbreaking fiber-art exhibition *Deliberate Entanglements* at the University of California, Los Angeles, in 1971–72, Garrett began experimenting with discarded and cast-off materials. Through much of the 1970s and 1980s, he used bright plastics and highly colored vinyl to create intricately layered patterns, such as those seen in *Desert Garden Gate* (1985). For Garrett, the use of these materials was rooted in landscape; the information overload created by their vibrant color and contrasting patterns reflected Los Angeles' "culture of excess" and carried a residue of use. In 1990, when Garrett moved back to his home state of New Mexico, his work became more muted, taking on the burnt metallic tones of the desert landscape. SJS

PLATE 28

DESERT GARDEN GATE
1985
Plastic and wire mesh
45 x 70 1/2 x 10 inches
(114.3 x 179.1 x 25.4 cm)
The Leatrice S. and
Melvin B. Eagle Collection,
museum purchase funded
by the Caroline Wiess Law
Accessions Endowment Fund
2010.2070

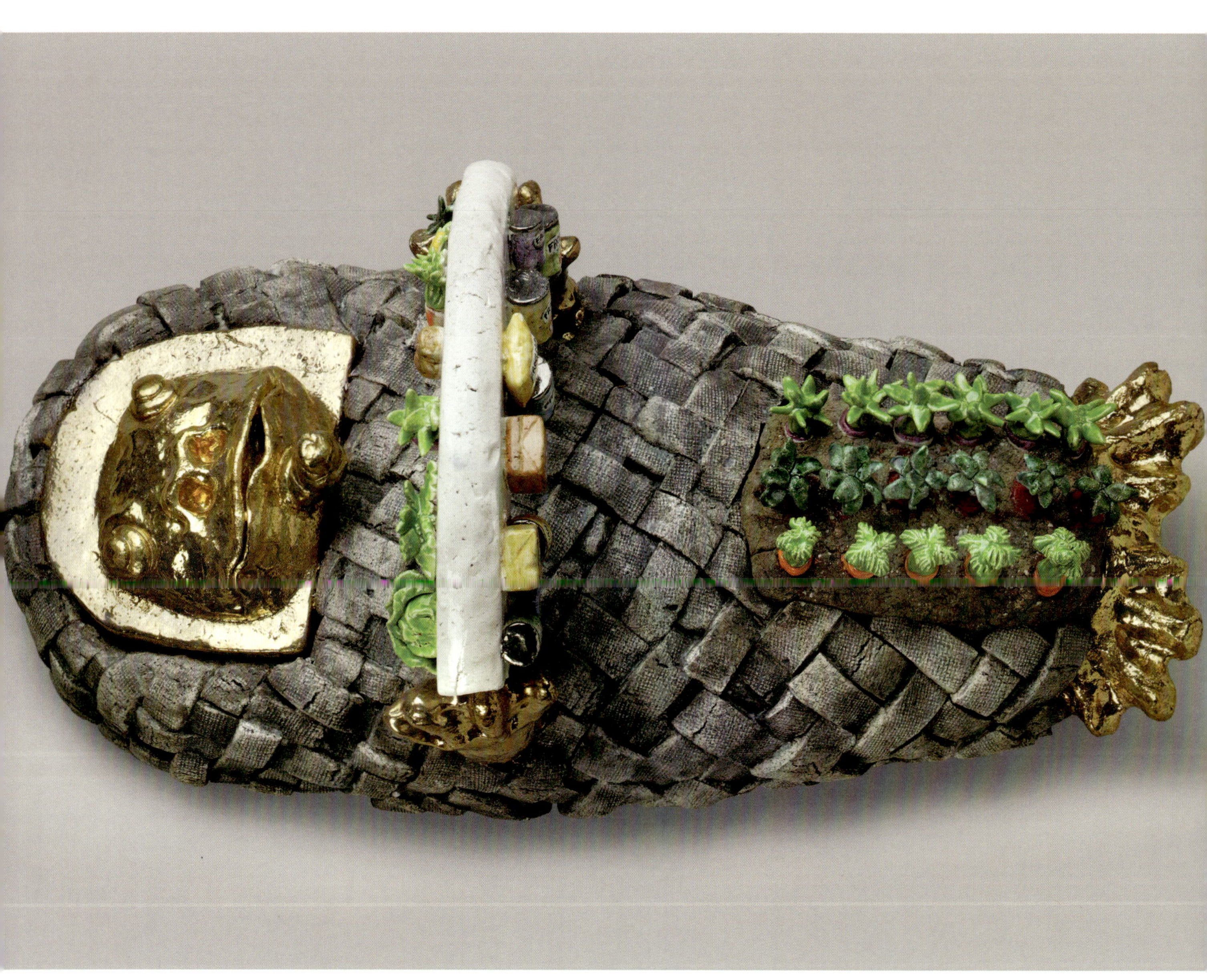

DAVID GILHOOLY
American, 1943–2013

From the late 1960s through the early 1970s, David Gilhooly created a parallel world, complete with its own cosmology, deities, political system, and culture. Populated primarily by frogs, Gilhooly's narrative sculptures document the daily rituals of this consumerist and fertility-obsessed culture. He used this "frog world" as a foil for the contemporary world and as a platform from which to comment on the excesses of American culture, with special reference to the art world and American consumption patterns.

With their absurdist subject matter and elaborately imagined cosmology, the objects from this series incorporate much of the approach at the center of Funk art. The artist's free handling of material and his choice of ostentatious, straight-out-of-the-bottle glazes connect this work to that of hobby-craft practitioners; his use of figuration references kitschy ceramic figurines; and his satirical commentary on the excesses of contemporary culture (represented in the frog world by an overabundance of food and sex) reflects the countercultural bent of the San Francisco Bay Area in the late 1960s. Indeed, Gilhooly's ironic humor owes much to his professor Robert Arneson at the University of California, Davis.

Despite the dystopian overtones of his particular vision, the strident colors and easily accessible imagery of his work found a wide audience throughout the 1970s.[1] Along with Arneson, Clayton Bailey, Paul Soldner, and others, Gilhooly was one of the foremost exponents of Funk ceramics. Although Gilhooly eventually stopped producing works on the theme of the frog world, the completeness of his endeavor remains a milestone in the development of a sculptural voice in American ceramics. SJS

NOTE

1   In fact, according to ceramic historian Garth Clark, Gilhooly was "without doubt the most exhibited ceramic artist in the United States" throughout the 1970s. Garth Clark, *American Ceramics, 1876 to the Present*, rev. ed. (New York: Abbeville Press, 1987), 278.

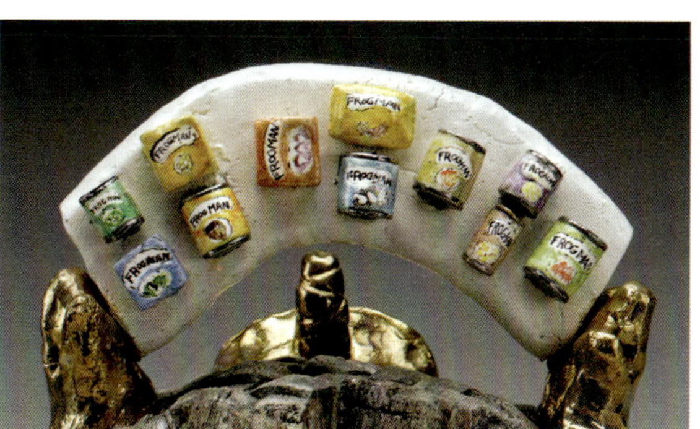

WILLIAM HARPER
American, born 1944

The exquisite detail, masterful technique, and commitment to content in William Harper's works over five decades have cemented his position at the forefront of American studio jewelry. An avid colorist, Harper first explored painting when he entered Case Western Reserve University in Ohio in the mid-1960s. Soon, however, he developed an interest in enameling, encouraged by his professors Kenneth Bateman, lauded as the "dean of enameling," and the jeweler John Paul Miller.

After experimenting with a wide range of techniques, Harper homed in on cloisonné in 1970. An ancient process, cloisonné employs thin strips of metal—in Harper's case primarily gold—to differentiate areas of colored vitreous enamel. Characteristic of Harper's works is a graphic application of the cloison wire, which he manipulates freehand in order to retain the power and immediacy of a hand-drawn line. He then layers lush combinations of opaque and transparent enamels into these frames to create brilliant, multicolored brooches, neck pieces, and earrings.

The metallurgic process of enameling, which marries copper, gold, and silver with the base material of glass, is a perfect corollary to Harper's attraction to alchemy, mysticism, and the tangible remnants of religious ritual. The breadth of his interest in these subjects, which spans West African tribal arts, European Catholic practices, and ancient divination rights, is evident in his titles such as *The Magician's Chain*, *Pagan Baby*, and *The Ecstasy of St. Theresa*, as well as in the forms of his objects. In addition to incorporating enameled elements, his pieces often drip with pearls, bones, semiprecious stones, and articulated gold charms, as if invested with apotropaic powers. SJS

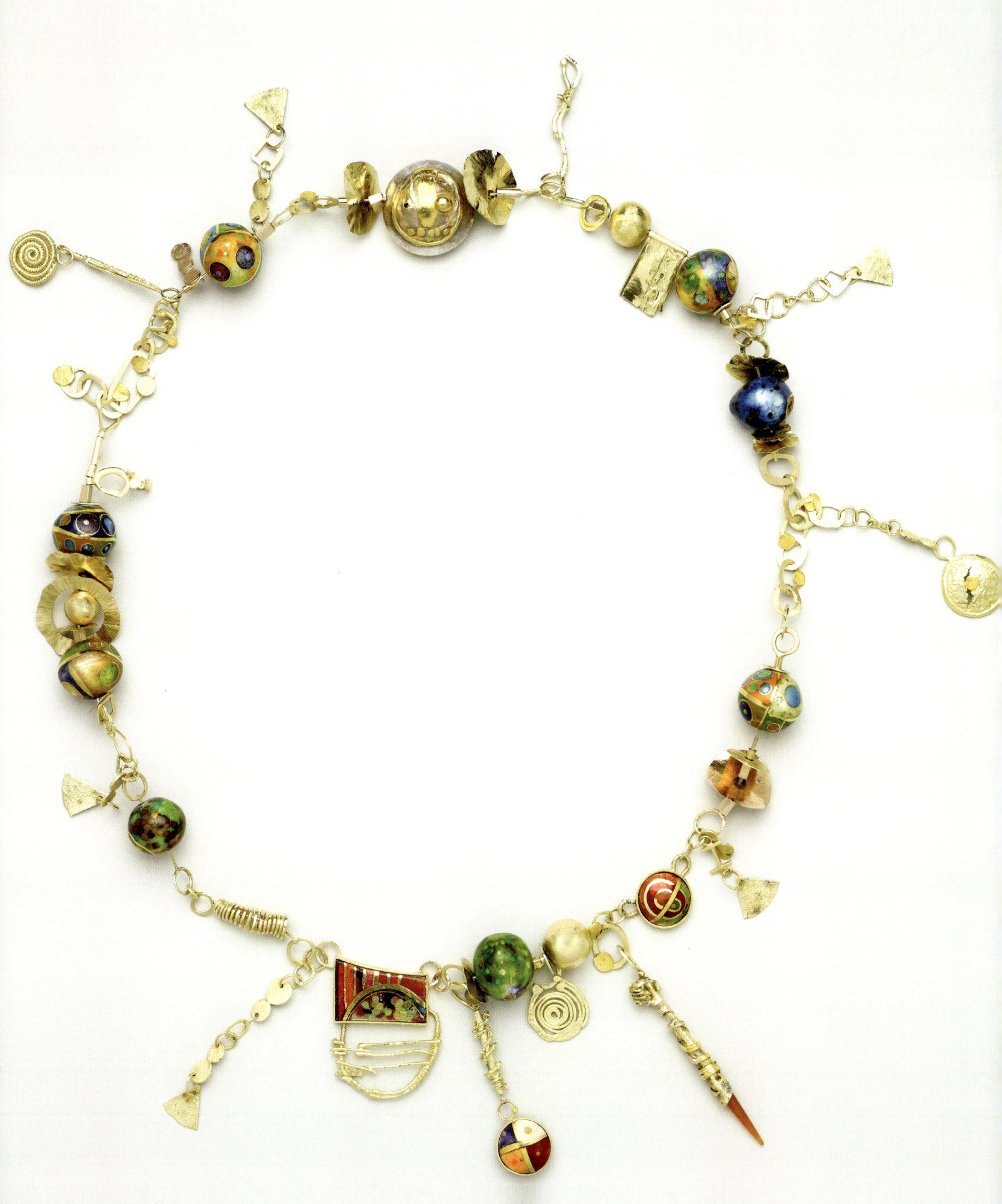

PLATE **31**

FLEA MARKET BAG
1971
Stoneware and string
12 3/4 x 17 1/4 x 9 inches
(32.4 x 43.8 x 22.9 cm)
The Leatrice S. and
Melvin B. Eagle Collection,
museum purchase funded
by the Caroline Wiess Law
Accessions Endowment Fund
2010.2083

For thirty-five years, Marilyn Anne Levine explored the mimetic possibilities of clay in masterful trompe l'oeil versions of old leather bags, belts, jackets, and shoes. What Levine sought in the ragged, torn up, decrepit, and cracked was not verisimilitude to individual objects per se, but rather a sense of universality achieved through specificity. With carefully scratched surfaces, artfully composed ripples and folds, and dutifully reproduced tears and broken straps, Levine's exacting representations of age are surrogates for the human presence and the accumulation of time.

Originally trained as a chemist in Canada, Levine moved to San Francisco in 1969 to pursue an MA and MFA in ceramics at the University of California, Berkeley, during the tenure of Peter Voulkos. Drawn less to Voulkos's abstract expressionism than to the Funk sensibilities of her thesis adviser, Jim Melchert, and of Robert Arneson, professor at the University of California, Davis, Levine initially constructed humorous sculptures of everyday objects. In 1970 a gift of a pair of scarred old boots, torn and burned through use in a foundry, redirected her interests. By her thesis exhibition in 1971, she had fully embarked on her signature investigation of wear and use.[1] Levine's work was unlike that of any other ceramicist of her generation. She continued exploring ceramics in this vein until her death in 2005. SJS

NOTE
1   Marilyn Levine, *Marilyn Levine: A Decade of Ceramic Sculpture, January 13 to March 8, 1981, Institute of Contemporary Art, Boston, Massachusetts* (Boston: Institute of Contemporary Art, 1981), 4.

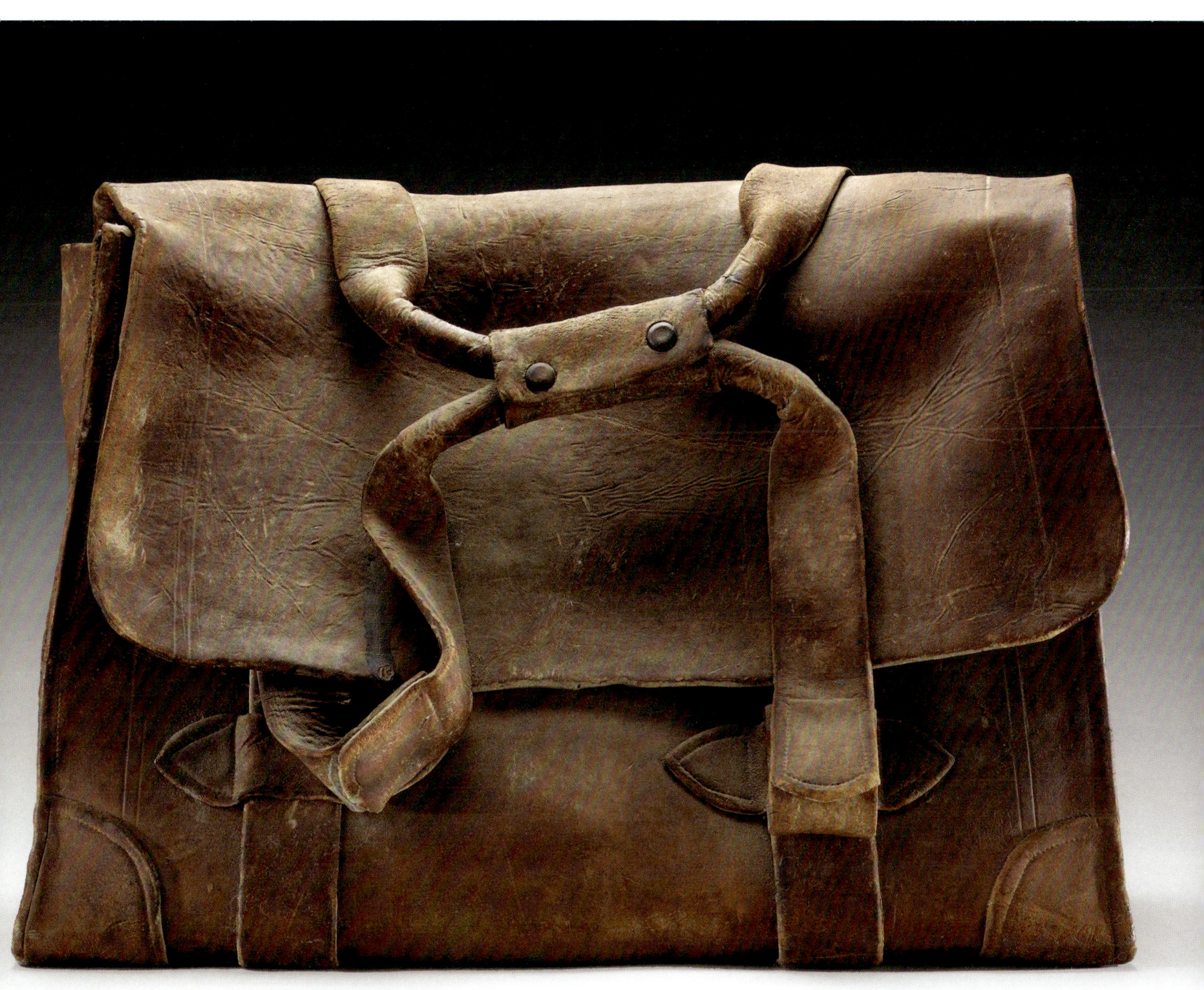

MICHAEL LUCERO
American, born 1953

Michael Lucero uses clay as a vehicle for complex painting, symbolic and metaphorical meaning, and cross-cultural commentary. His ceramics often take hybrid forms; part figure and part vessel, they reference a wide range of geographic cultures, art history, popular culture, and the artist's own personal thoughts on history. A keen sense of color, pattern, and whimsy is reflected in each of Lucero's pieces, as is his interest in challenging scale.

Lucero primarily works in series, with one series often leading him into another. He has said of these series, "They each speak to me. When the idea evolves to such a height, I know that it has to move on to something more complicated."[1] Lucero's early series *Shards* and *Totems* were of grand scale and featured ceramic heads and vessels in monumental configurations that either hung from the ceiling or were stacked on the floor. Reacting against those forms, he created the *Dreamers* series (1984–86), involving ceramic heads whose painted imagery references the unconscious and land iconography, and whose raised pedestals were drawn from pueblo architecture. In 1986 Lucero ceased working in clay for a brief time, instead creating bronze sculptures, such as the *Night Train—Dreamer*, for the next few years. By 1990 he had rediscovered ceramics and began working with a visual vocabulary that drew on Pre-Columbian sources. In 1997 he began the *Reclamation* series, from which *Lion* in the Eagle collection comes. This series, which he continues to expand upon to this day, combines found objects with clay to create new forms. Lucero has said that, for this body of work, he wants to "reclaim [the object's] status as a valuable, meaningful symbol but in a contemporary context."[2] This reframing of objects and images pervades all of his ceramics, resulting in dynamic forms that challenge preconceived ideas about ceramic art. CS

NOTES
1 Mark Richard Leach and Michael Lucero, "That Was the World and It Still Is!: A Conversation with Michael Lucero," in *Michael Lucero: Sculpture 1976–1995* (Charlotte, NC: Mint Museum of Craft and Design, 1996), 34.
2 Ibid.

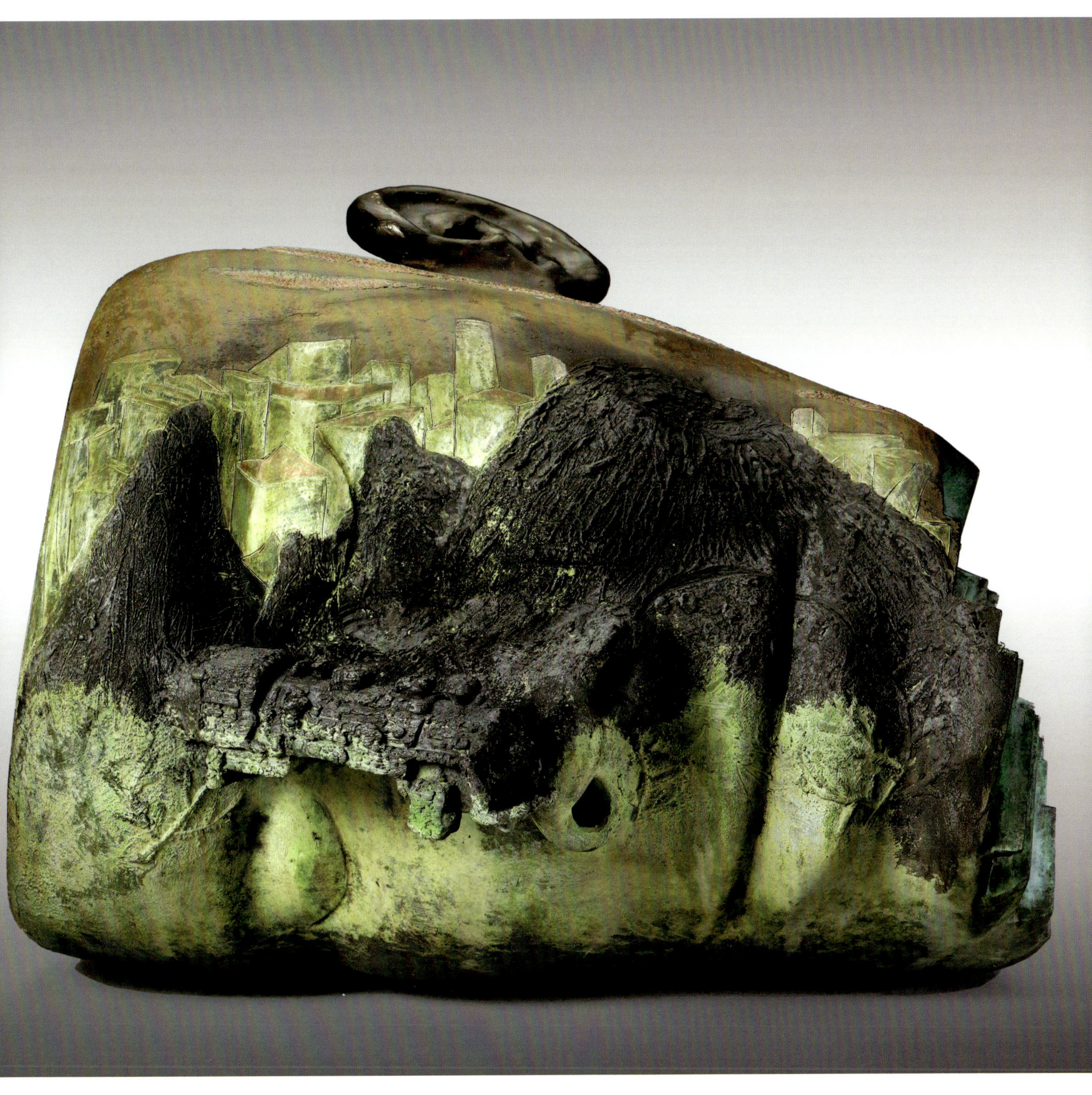

MICHAEL LUCERO

PLATE 33

LION, from the series
RECLAMATION
1997
White earthenware
and found object
29 x 23 x 13 inches
(73.7 x 58.4 x 33 cm)
The Leatrice S. and
Melvin B. Eagle Collection,
museum purchase funded
by the Caroline Wiess Law
Accessions Endowment Fund
2010.2084.A–.C

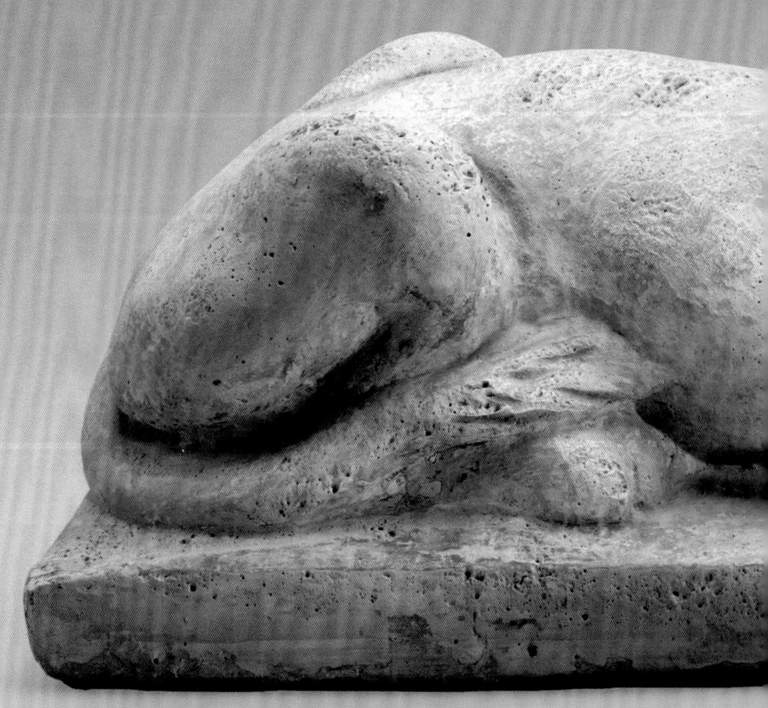

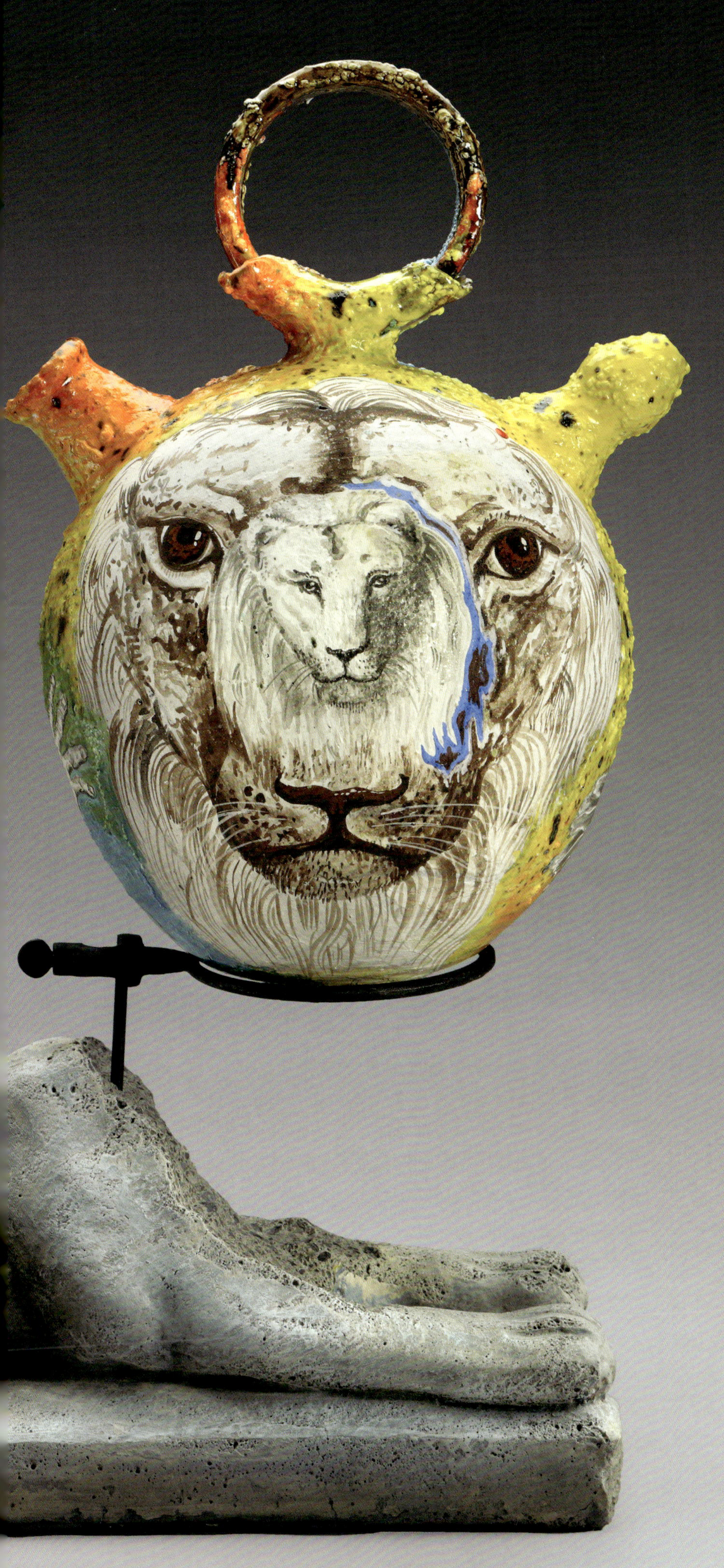

SAM MALOOF
American, 1916–2009

PLATE 34

ROCKING CHAIR
Upholstered by Ballard
Upholstering, American
1968
Walnut and leather
45 x 27 1/4 x 42 3/8 inches
(114.3 x 69.2 x 107.6 cm)
The Leatrice S. and
Melvin B. Eagle Collection,
gift of Leatrice and Melvin Eagle
2009.1704

From his rise to prominence in the 1950s and continuing beyond his death in 2009, Sam Maloof has been revered as an icon of studio furniture and the craftsman's way of life. A graphic designer whose first foray into woodworking came out of the necessity of furnishing an apartment for him and his young wife, Maloof went on to pioneer a style of construction that valued integrity of materials over mass-production and quality of life above all.

From his hand-built home in Alto Loma, California, Maloof and a small group of assistants laboriously produced his interpretations of classic forms of chairs, tables, case furniture, and the like. Maloof, who considered himself a woodworker rather than an artist, insisted on a very hands-on process, completing the bulk of the pieces himself before enlisting others in their finishing. This method was designed to ensure high quality but resulted in a relatively low output. Yet Maloof declined several offers to license his designs, stating, "For me, it is not enough to be a designer only. I want to be able to work a piece of wood into an object that contributes something beautiful and useful to our everyday living."[1]

Nevertheless, the world of industrial design had an outsize influence on his career. His work was often featured within the context of California design, and denizens from that world frequently became his clients. For instance, the designer and ergonomics authority Henry Dreyfuss was an early supporter, commissioning twenty-five pieces for his home.[2] Later, Dreyfuss would encourage Maloof to create rocking chairs, sparking a lifelong investigation into what would become his most iconic form. SJS

NOTES
1   Jeremy Elwell Adamson, *The Furniture of Sam Maloof* (Washington, D.C.: Smithsonian American Art Museum; New York: W. W. Norton, 2001), 92.

2   Ibid., 34.

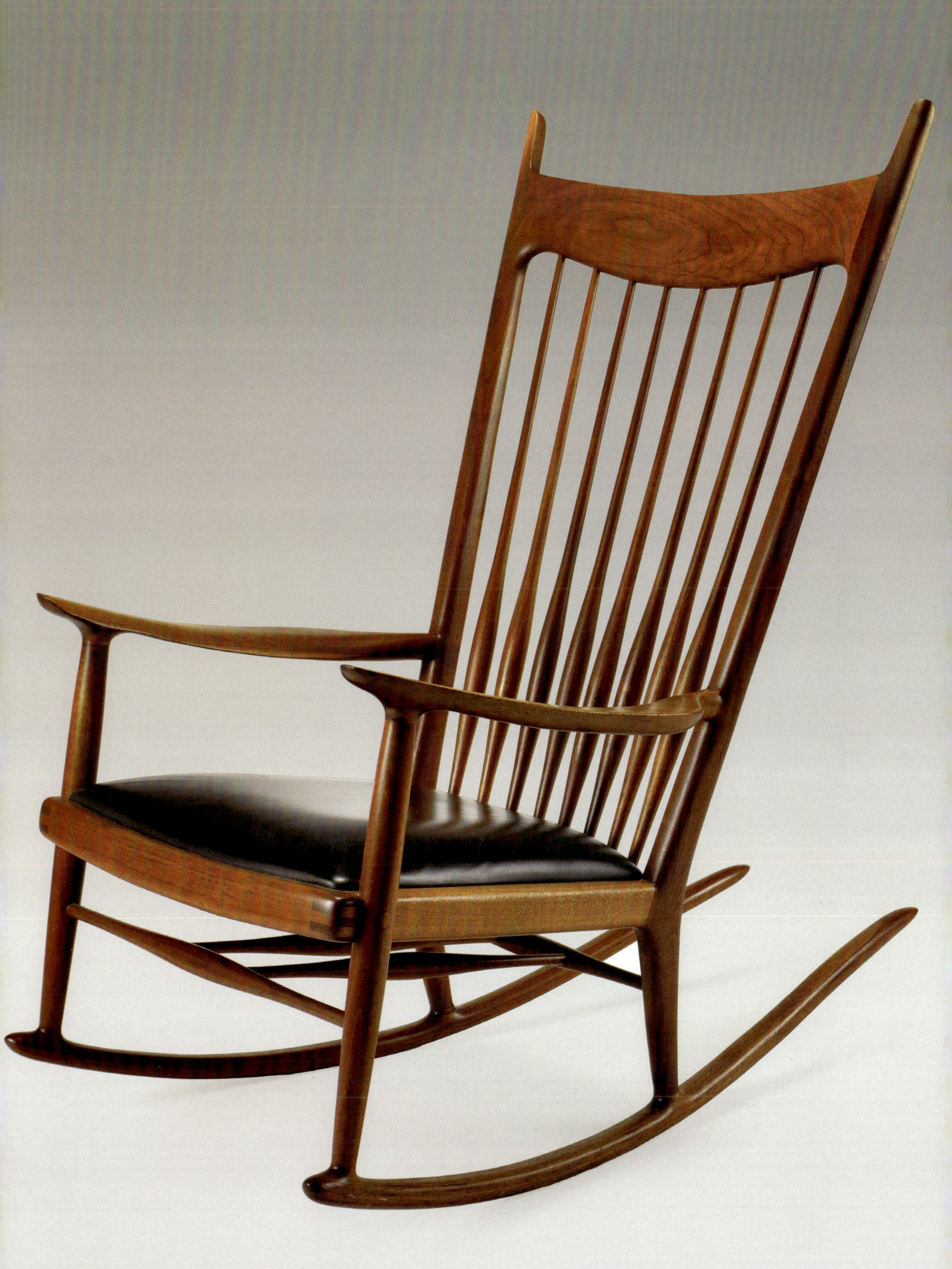

SAM MALOOF

PLATE 35

DESK
1975
Walnut
29 1/2 x 72 x 36 inches
(74.9 x 182.9 x 91.4 cm)
The Leatrice S. and
Melvin B. Eagle Collection,
museum purchase funded
by the Caroline Wiess Law
Accessions Endowment Fund
2010.2087.A–.K

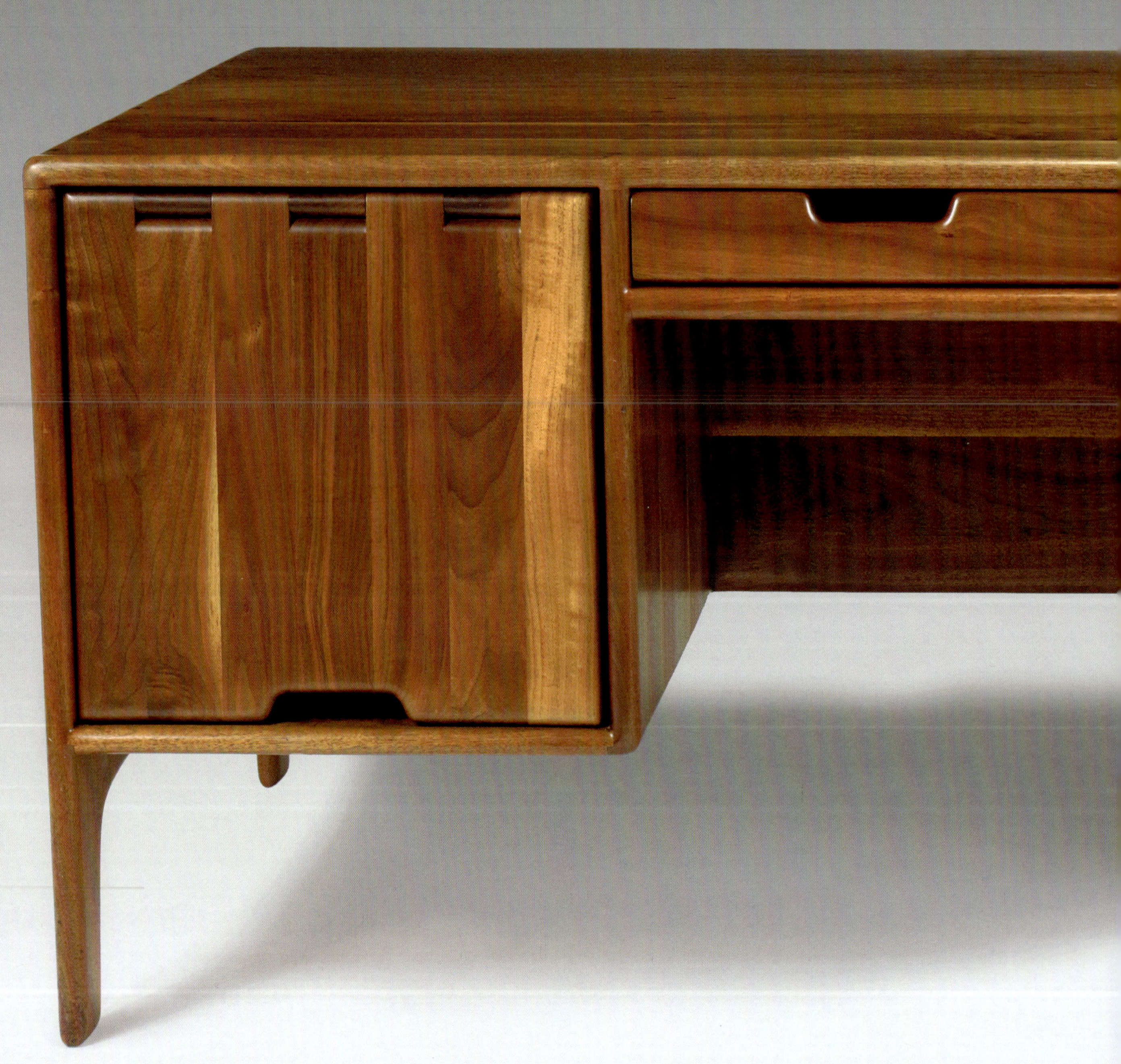

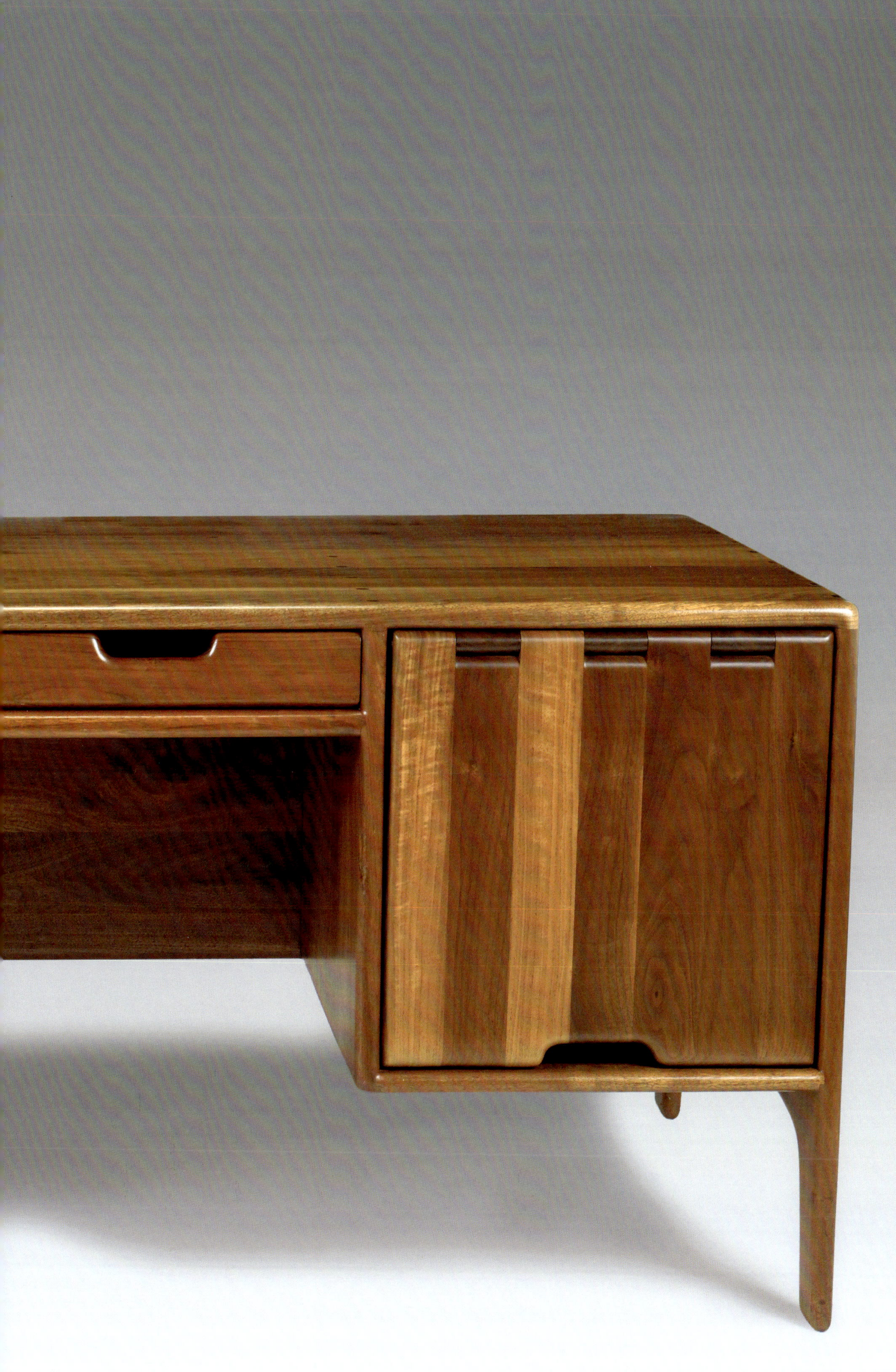

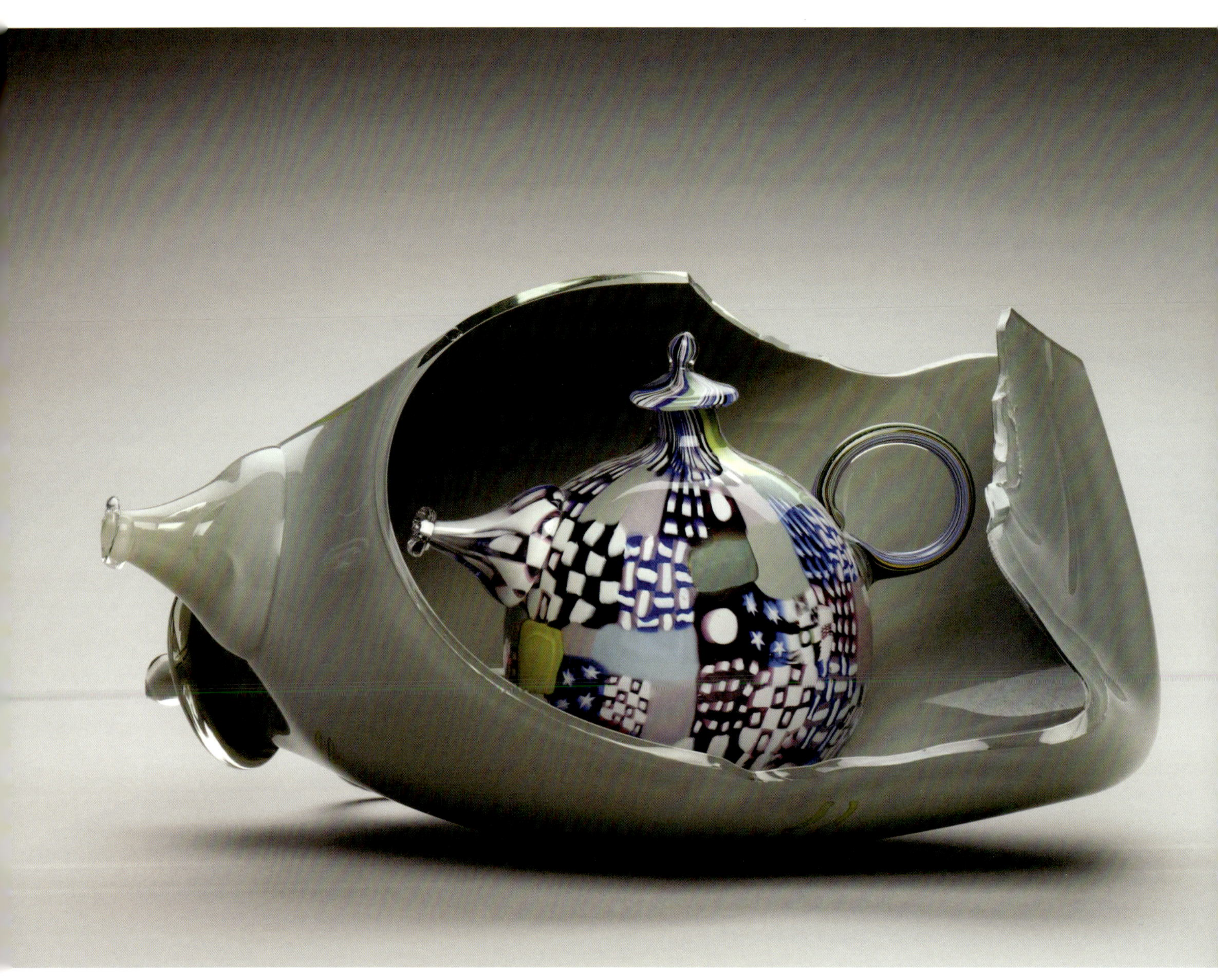

BROKEN GREY #1
1979
Glass
5 3/8 x 10 1/4 x 7 inches
(13.7 x 26 x 17.8 cm)
The Leatrice S. and
Melvin B. Eagle Collection,
gift of Leatrice and Melvin Eagle
2011.972

RICHARD MARQUIS
American, born 1945

Richard Marquis combines a historian's interest in technique, a collector's love of Americana, and a humorist's sense of form in the riotous glass sculptures that he has been making since the 1960s. Like many in the first generation of studio glass artists, Marquis came to glass circuitously, studying architecture and then ceramics at the University of California, Berkeley, before being introduced to glass there as an assistant to Marvin Lipofsky in 1964.

Though glasswork eventually became his primary means of expression, Marquis's conceptual training in ceramics was central to his development as an artist. At Berkeley, he studied with Peter Voulkos, whose dynamism infuses Marquis's work, and with Ron Nagle, whose involvement in the Finish Fetish school of ceramics is reflected in the slick coloration and diminutive size of Marquis's pieces. The creative milieu of the Bay Area also introduced him to the Funk aesthetic of Robert Arneson and David Gilhooly, whose irreverent sense of humor can be seen in Marquis's juxtaposition of disparate components and in the implied looseness in his handling of materials.[1]

When Marquis became Marvin Lipofsky's assistant in setting up Berkeley's first glassblowing program in 1964, the medium was in its infancy within the fine-arts realm. With little information about the material available in the United States, Marquis applied for and received a Fulbright-Hayes grant to study at the legendary Venini glass factory in Murano, Italy, in 1969. While there, he investigated the ancient process of murrine, a technique for reproducing complex patterns in rods of colored glass that can be cut, assembled, and blown to create objects with great visual complexity. Marquis's rediscovery and subsequent introduction of this technique into American studio glass is certainly one of his most enduring achievements, but even more impressive is his ability to adapt this process to his own lively aesthetic vision. SJS

NOTE
1   Cindi Strauss, *Pioneers of Contemporary Glass: Highlights from the Barbara and Dennis DuBois Collection* (Houston: The Museum of Fine Arts, Houston, 2009), 43.

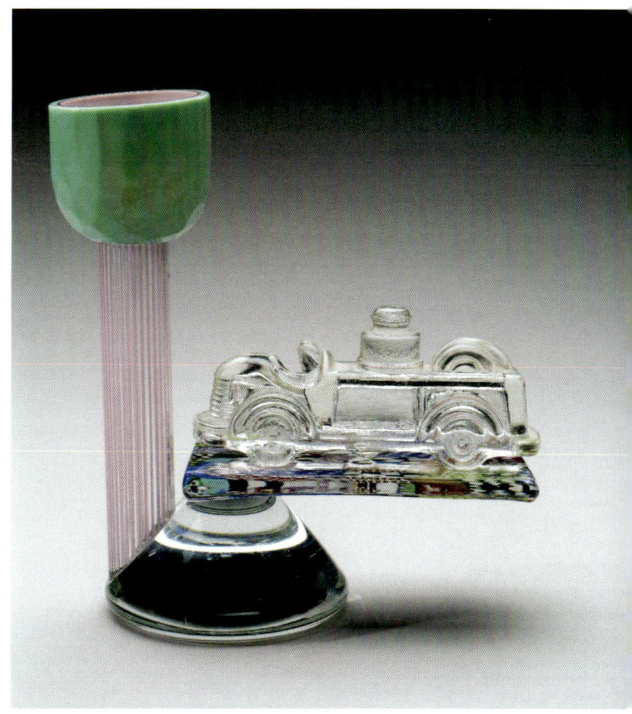

FIRE ENGINE CUP
1980
Glass
7 x 6 3/4 x 3 3/8 inches
(17.8 x 17 x 8.6 cm)
The Leatrice S. and
Melvin B. Eagle Collection,
museum purchase funded
by the Caroline Wiess Law
Accessions Endowment Fund
2010.2090.A, .B

JOHN MASON
American, born 1927

PLATE **38**

TORQUE VESSEL
1986
Stoneware
44 x 21 x 22 inches
(111.8 x 53.3 x 55.9 cm)
The Leatrice S. and Melvin
B. Eagle Collection, gift of
Leatrice and Melvin Eagle
2007.1785

A pioneer of contemporary ceramics, John Mason has been a leading force in ceramic sculpture for more than six decades. As a student of Peter Voulkos's at the Los Angeles County Art Institute (now Otis College of Art and Design) in the mid-1950s, Mason initially adopted that artist's affinity for Abstract Expressionism, gaining significant attention for his muscular sculptures and expansive ceramic walls, whose massive scale was unprecedented in clay.

In the 1960s, perhaps inspired by the conceptual art milieu at the Ferus Gallery, where he had shown since it opened in 1957, Mason began to move away from the emotional chaos of Abstract Expressionism.[1] Utilizing a restrained minimalism that would become his signature, Mason embarked on a series based on the cross or "X" form. These pieces, which were increasingly devoid of surface manipulation, culminated in 1966 in *Red X* and *Yellow Cross*, large, pristine works glazed in brilliant, flat glazes.

The strict geometry and unmodulated coloration of *Red X* and *Yellow Cross* prefigure Mason's mathematically based, site-specific installations of the 1970s, whose size and precision took him away from the ceramic medium, as well as the *Torque Vessels* that signaled his return to ceramics in the 1980s. These meticulously constructed, architectonic vessels manipulate the viewer's sense of space with twisting prismatic forms and subtle linear glaze patterns, uniting the artist's interest in perception and surface in a format that he continues to explore to this day. SJS

NOTE
1 Ben Marks, "John Mason's Conceptual Journey," *American Craft* 50, no. 6 (December 1990): 37.

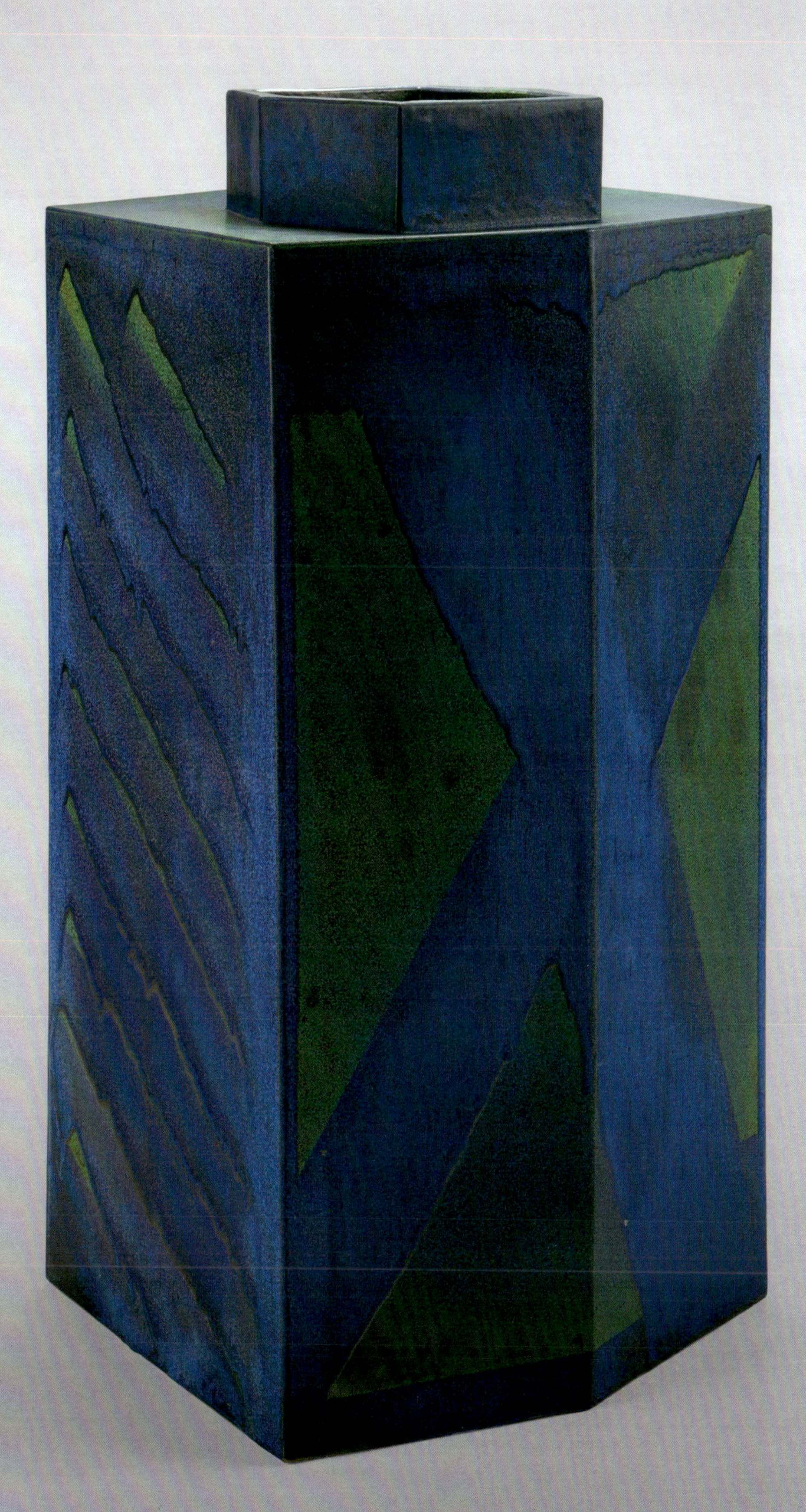

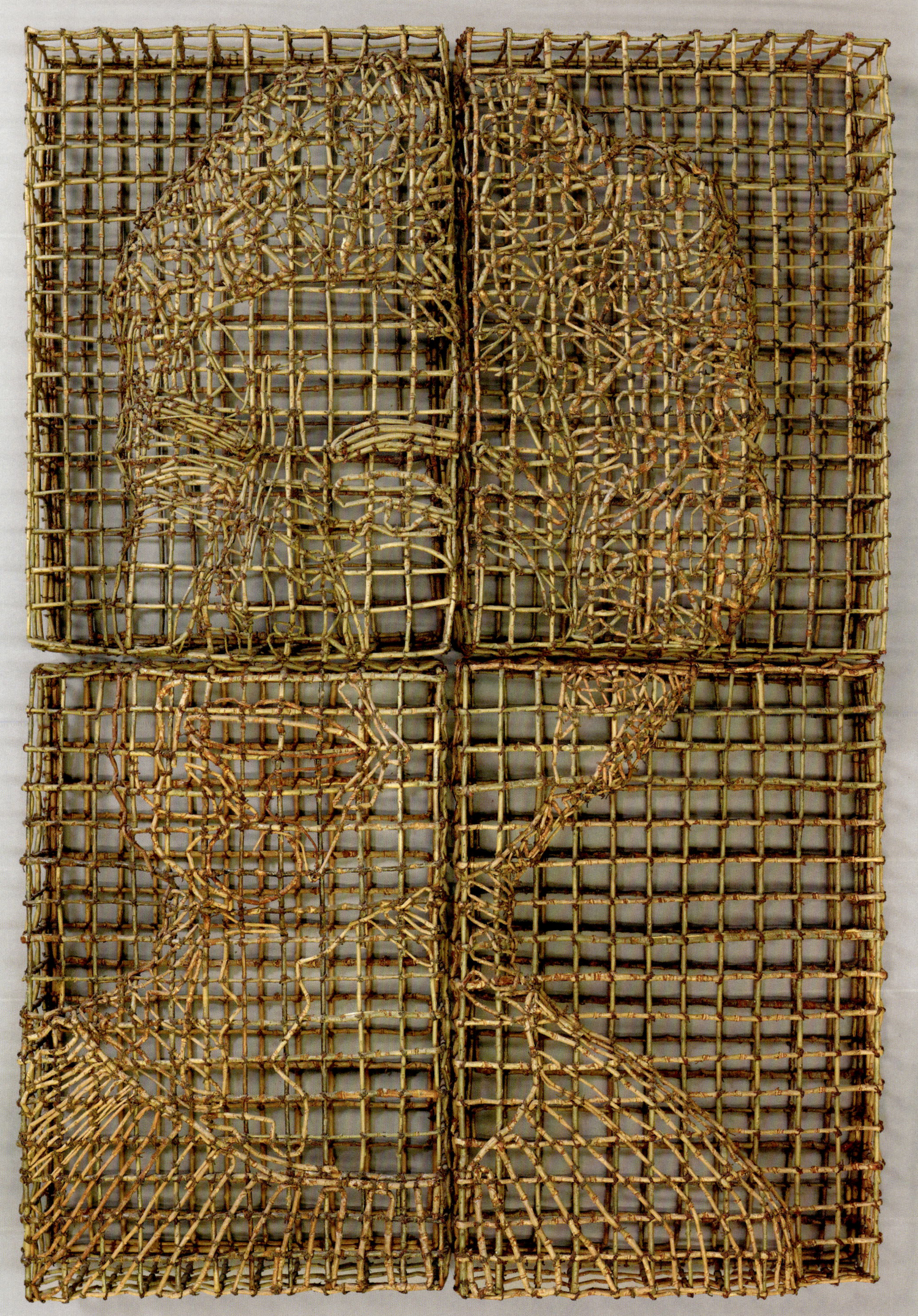

JOHN MCQUEEN
American, born 1943

Since the early 1970s, when a Native American basket of architectural proportions first caught his eye at the New Mexico State Fair, John McQueen has explored the physical and conceptual possibilities of basketry. At first, McQueen was drawn to the natural materials traditionally associated with the process; the willow, pine, and reeds allied strongly with his sculptural interest in sod and adobe. Soon, however, his focus shifted to both the symbolic function of baskets as containers and the conceptual possibilities suggested by basketry's integral structure.

McQueen has said that his early output centered on his notion that, in basket making, "the subject is the object," due to the inherent marriage of process and form.[1] With this premise, McQueen embarked on a thorough exploration of the structural possibilities of basketry. By complicating the rigid structure of over-under weaving, he completed chaotically woven objects in basswood, yucca, and ash, explored the often awkward forms of trees in a series plaited directly over logs salvaged from his firewood pile, and utilized materials as diverse as burdock burrs and sewn spruce bark in his compositions.

In time, McQueen's focus broadened to incorporate the functional aspect of baskets as containers. He approached this concept with signature ambition, expanding his interpretation of containment to include words, sentences, and figures alongside more conventional vessel forms. With a boldly gridded background offset by the curving organic lines of a face, *Self-Portrait* represents an intermediate phase in the development of this body of work. Still tethered by the structural regularity of a basket-woven structure, this piece's two-dimensional format and figuration signal the artist's new direction. Later, McQueen would utilize this hybrid technique to create life-size figurative sculptures and room-size installations that amplify the concerns of the vessel with their presence and scale. SJS

NOTE
1   John McQueen, as quoted in *Baskets Now: USA* (Little Rock: Arkansas Arts Center, 2002), 68.

PLATE 39

SELF-PORTRAIT
1998
Willow and waxed string
41 1/2 x 29 1/4 x 7 1/2 inches
(105.4 x 74.3 x 19.1 cm)
The Leatrice S. and
Melvin B. Eagle Collection,
museum purchase funded
by the Caroline Wiess Law
Accessions Endowment Fund
2010.2091.A–.D

RON NAGLE
American, born 1939

PLATE 40

KNUCKLEHEAD JR.

2000
Earthenware with overglaze
3 1/2 x 5 1/8 x 3 3/4 inches
(8.9 x 13 x 9.7 cm)
The Leatrice S. and
Melvin B. Eagle Collection,
museum purchase funded
by the Caroline Wiess Law
Accessions Endowment Fund
2010.2094.A, .B

The intimate scale of Ron Nagle's ceramics stems from his early work as a jeweler. First introduced to the contemporary art and ceramics scenes of California in San Francisco and Los Angeles, Nagle is known for his devotion to the cup form, which he has consistently explored since the 1970s. Initially influenced by the work of Ken Price that he had viewed at Los Angeles' Ferus Gallery, Nagle also began creating cuplike sculptures that contained few vestiges of function and became more abstracted over the years.

Nagle's cups appear in a diverse variety of colors and textures and often have humorous underpinnings that draw from his observations on life. His work shows the constant influence of the coloration of California architecture and landscape, brightly saturated Mexican hues of the 1950s, the primary colors of craft-shop china paints, and the lacquer paints used on automobiles. Nagle applies numerous layers of overglaze enamels on his cups, which gives greater depth to his colors. Planes of color are also delineated through drawn borders. These planes contrast with the overall palette and bring a pop of color to the foreground of the composition. Nagle often enhances the surface of his cups with texture, which derives from his interest in the stucco architecture of his native California and the glaze drips and blobs commonly seen on Japanese ceramics.

Nagle intends for his cups to be viewed from a single perspective so that the viewer engages with them as graphic forms rather than solely as three-dimensional objects. This forced perspective allows for broader conclusions to be drawn about the nature of the work, and reveals Nagle's artistry and his ability to renew a form over time. CS

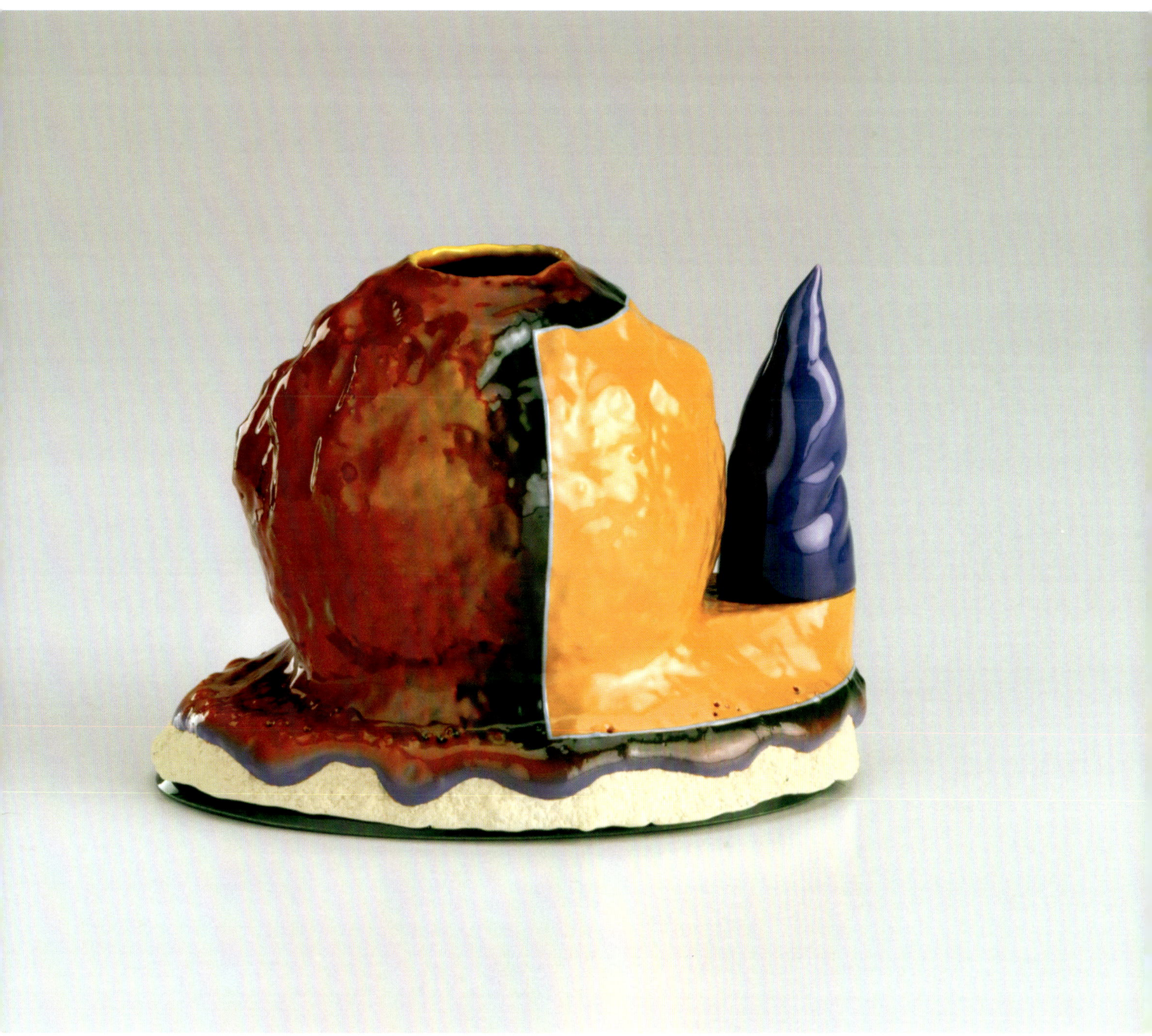

ALBERT PALEY
American, born 1944

More than anyone else working in the United States today, Albert Paley can be credited with giving the art of blacksmithing a contemporary voice. For more than forty years, he has pursued a sensuously ornamental body of work that includes architectural commissions, freestanding sculptures, and domestic objects such as tables, desks, and lamps. The sweeping forms and fluidity of his designs, which perfectly express the molten character of the material, represent a progression from the rectilinear symmetry and emphasis on joinery of historical precedents.

In part, this break with tradition can be attributed to the artist's own nonlinear path. Paley began his career in jewelry by studying with Stanley Lechtzin in the highly innovative climate of the Tyler School of Art at Temple University in Philadelphia. He achieved breakout success for his evocative, ornate pieces that sought to delineate the body rather than simply augment it.

In the early 1970s, concurrent with his jewelry production, Paley and his former professor began experimenting with blacksmithing.[1] By 1978, despite critical acclaim, Paley stopped producing jewelry entirely, invigorated by the challenge of blacksmithing and the possibilities for large-scale production that it afforded. An important commission of gates for the Renwick Gallery of the Smithsonian American Art Museum in 1973 accelerated this change in direction and elevated him to national prominence.

Constant throughout Paley's oeuvre is his highly developed visual language, which incorporates lyrical lines, a range of textures, colors, and materials, and adventurous forms in jewelry; the swags, twists, and tapers of traditional blacksmithing; and ribbons and festoons that emphasize the fluidity of hot iron. This lively vocabulary invests his objects with a palpable energy, as if, as the historian and critic Edward Lucie-Smith has suggested, they are like a "living organic thing."[2] SJS

NOTES

1   In a quest for information, Paley and Lechtzin went to the local library to check out books on blacksmithing, only to find that the books had last been checked out in the early 1900s. Edward Lucie-Smith, *The Art of Albert Paley: Iron, Bronze, Steel* (New York: Abrams, 1996), 26.

2   Ibid., 43.

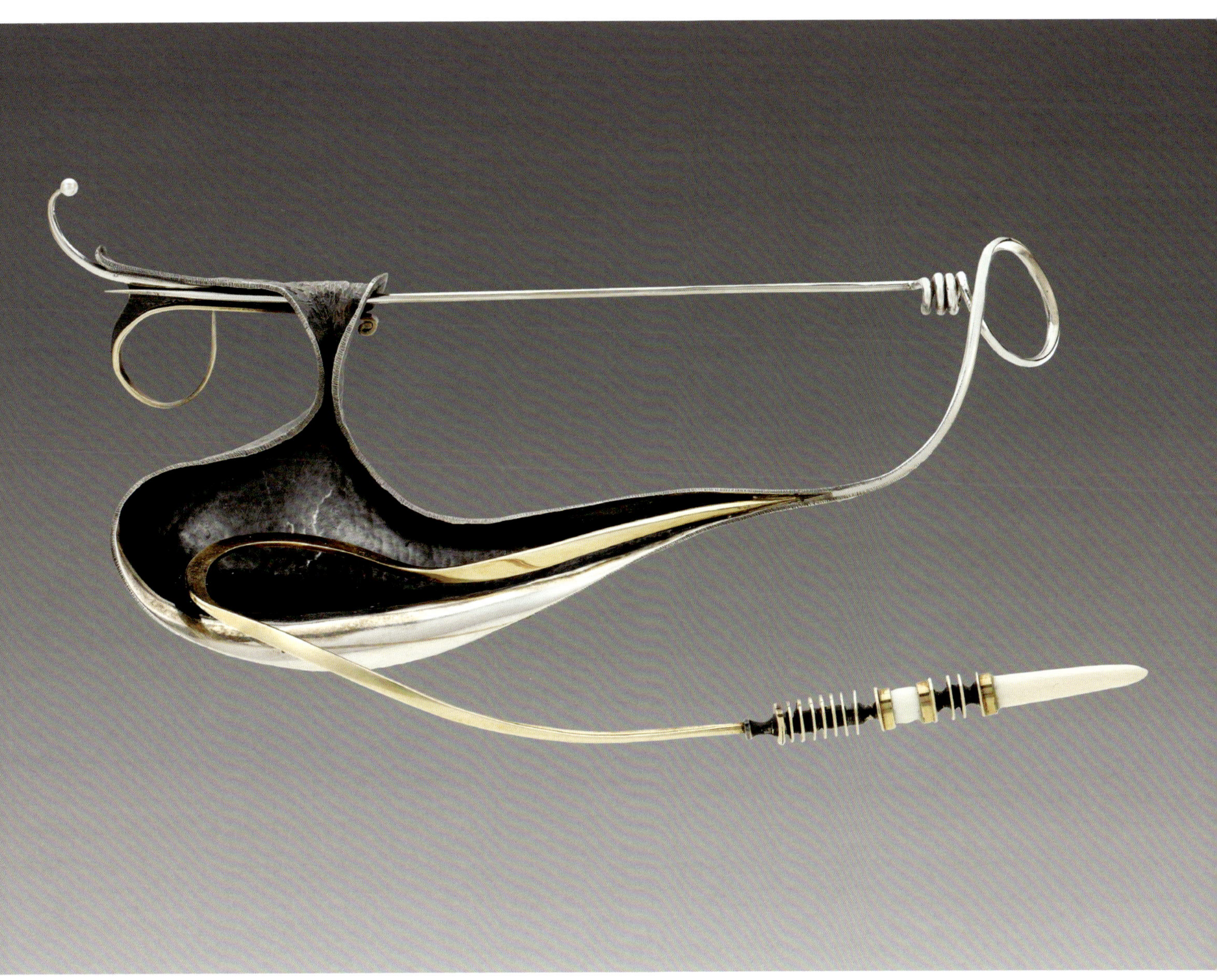

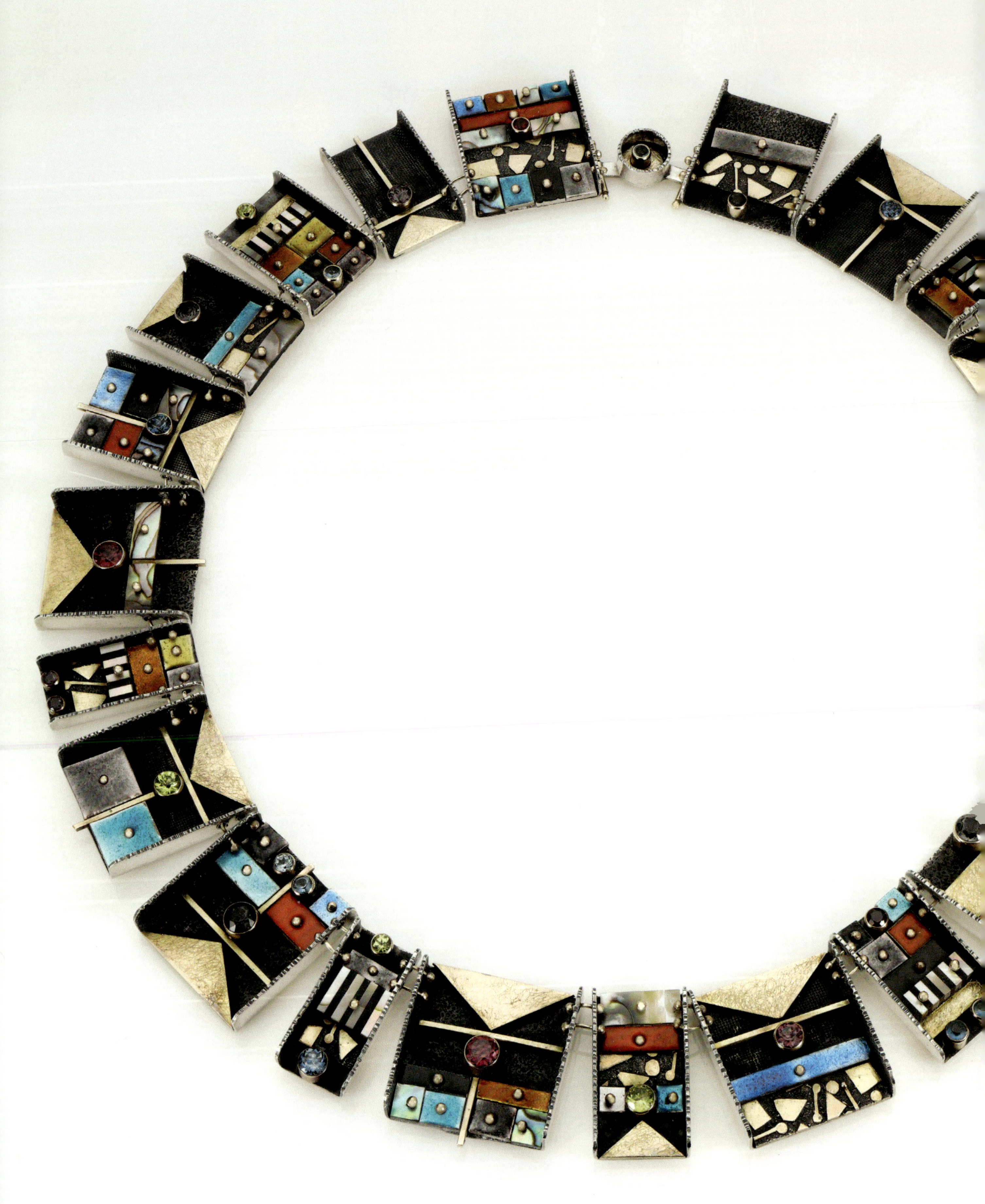

EARL PARDON
American, 1926–1991

Earl Pardon is among the pioneers of American studio jewelry, known equally for his innovative enamel work and his lifelong dedication to teaching. He was first introduced to jewelry in a required crafts course at the Academy of the Arts in Memphis, Tennessee, in the late 1940s. This event proved fortuitous, for though Pardon would later receive an MFA in painting at Syracuse University and would continue to work in a wide range of media throughout his life, ultimately he would establish his reputation in jewelry.

From 1951 to 1989, Pardon taught painting, sculpture, jewelry, and enameling at Skidmore College in Saratoga Springs, New York. The diversity of these courses and the enthusiasm with which he approached them are evident in his jewelry. With the zeal of an artistic polymath, he combined in his designs for necklaces, brooches, and bracelets a painterly interest in color with a sculptor's analysis of form. This strategy is apparent in pieces such as *Bracelet* (1960, see checklist no. 98) and *Mosaic Panel Necklace* (1987), whose fabricated silver forms serve as framing devices for brilliantly colored, abstract compositions punctuated by gleaming gold rivets, pearls, precious stones, and inlayed hardwoods. SJS

PLATE 42

MOSAIC PANEL NECKLACE
1987
Sterling silver, 14k gold, enamel,
semiprecious stones, ebony,
and mother-of-pearl
1/4 x 7 7/8 inches diameter
(0.6 x 20 cm)
The Leatrice S. and
Melvin B. Eagle Collection,
museum purchase funded
by the Caroline Wiess Law
Accessions Endowment Fund
2010.2106

TOM PATTI
American, born 1943

Since the 1970s, Tom Patti has investigated the phenomena of perception and the possibilities of glass in diminutive jewel-like sculptures and large-scale prismatic architectural interventions. Precise, geometric, and subtle, Patti's artworks stand out from other examples of early studio glass, in part as a result of their unusual method of manufacture. Trained as an industrial designer at the Pratt Institute in Brooklyn, New York, where he earned his BFA in 1967 and MFA in 1969, Patti developed a method to use discarded pieces of plate glass, rather than the traditional gather of molten glass, as the starting point of his works. From the 1970s through the 1990s, he fused small stacks of this material in a kiln and then used a blowpipe or compressed air to introduce singular bubbles into the composition. The resulting objects retain the character of their industrially produced material: the layers of plate glass create bands of color, and their heat-softened corners give the pieces an architectonic presence that transcends their small size.

The blend of artistry and technology at the heart of these works became even more pronounced in the sheet-glass objects and installations that Patti began to make in the late 1980s. Building on his experience completing a 1982 commission in fused plastic sheet for General Electric, titled *Genic Doran Divider—Sentinel*,[1] Patti expanded the scale of his pieces to up to several hundred feet long. He constructed these larger pieces primarily of laminated sheet glass, employing a wide range of specialized glass coatings to create the iridescent refraction in works such as *Spectral Panel* (1997). These works continue Patti's earlier inquiry into the poetics of space on a truly architectural scale. His endeavors to expand the vocabulary and interpretive possibilities of this material over the course of five decades have cemented him at the forefront of glass sculpture, and have made him an inspiration to other artists working in the medium. SJS

NOTE
1   This work is now in the collection of the Museum of Fine Arts, Houston.

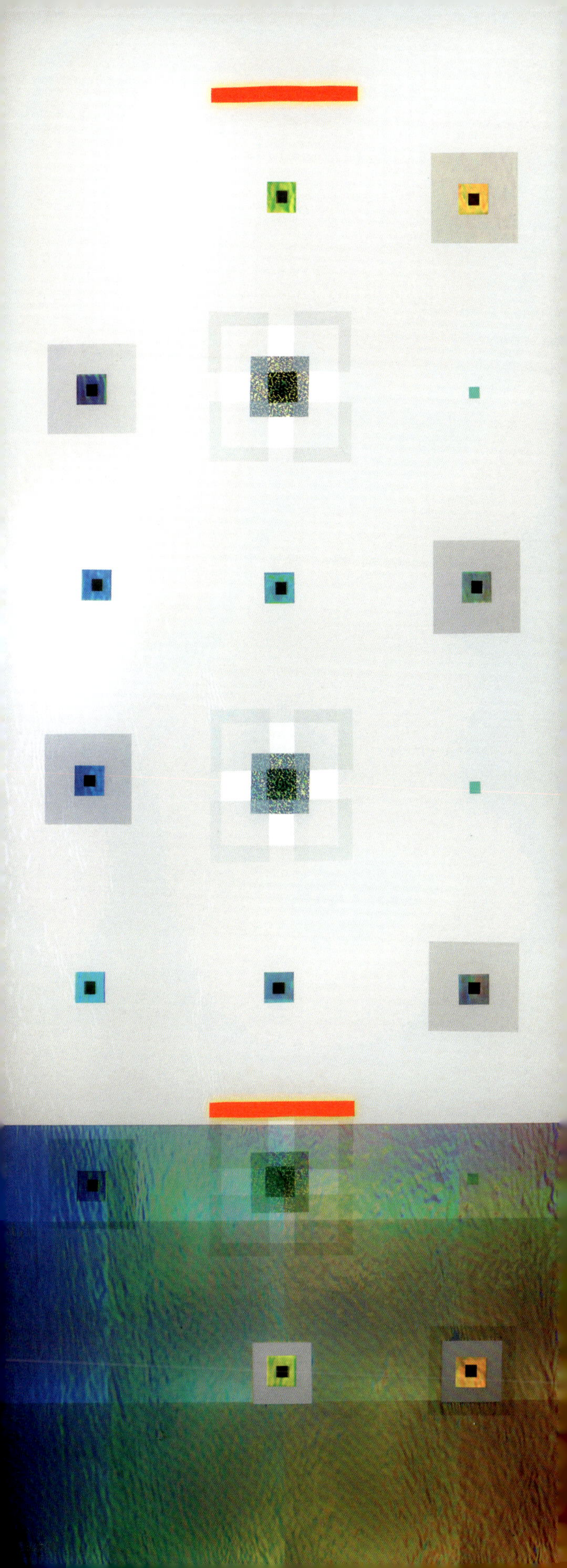

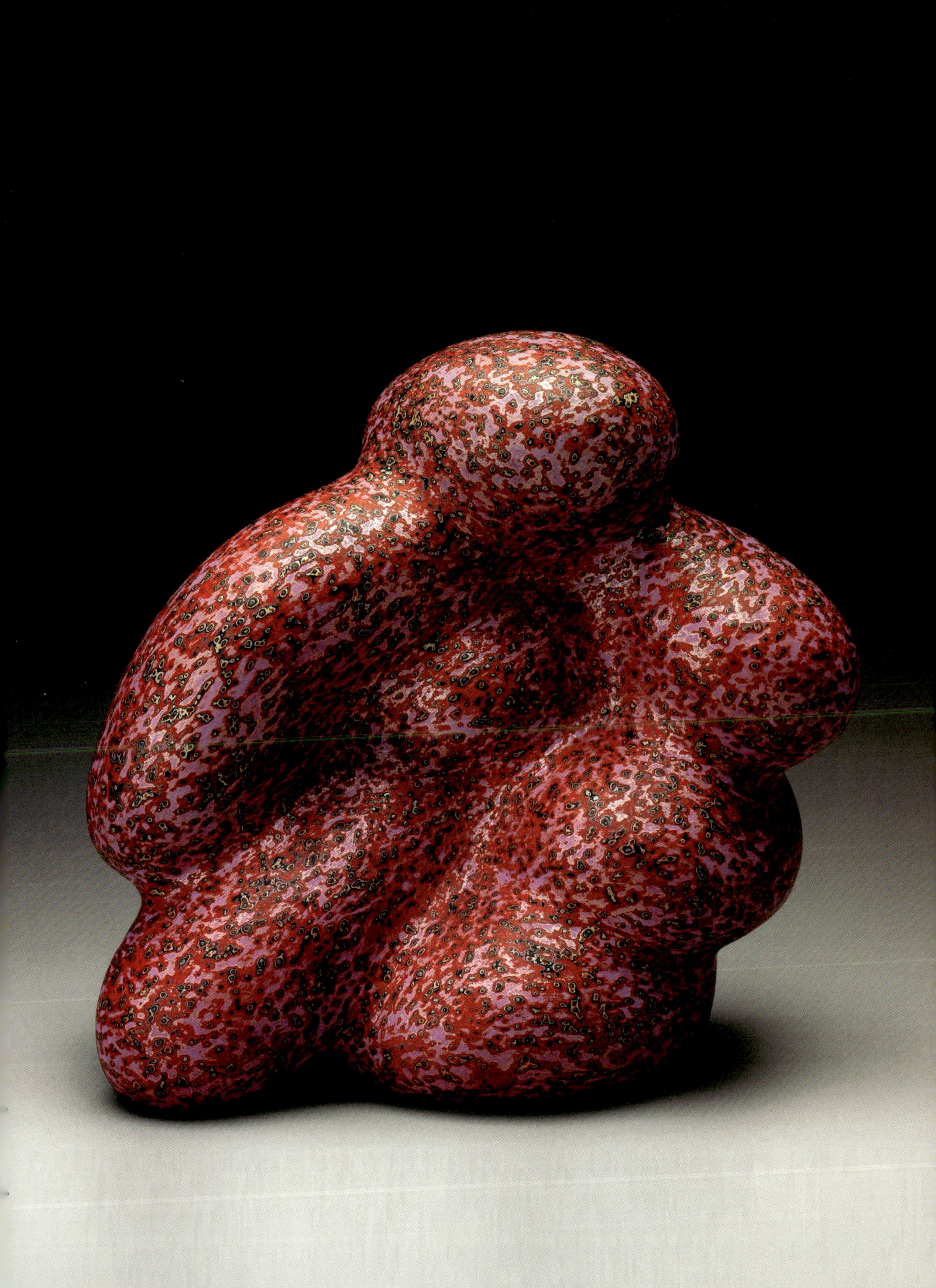

KEN PRICE
American, 1935–2012

Ken Price's first introduction to clay was at Santa Monica City College, but he began seriously working with ceramics at the University of Southern California, where he received his bachelor of fine arts degree in 1956. In 1957 Price studied ceramics at the Los Angeles County Art Institute (now Otis College of Art and Design) with Peter Voulkos. There, Price found himself in the crucible of avant-garde ceramics in America. However, feeling the need to receive traditional instruction in ceramic techniques and firing glazes, he left Los Angeles to pursue graduate work in ceramics at the New York State College of Ceramics at Alfred University, receiving his master of fine arts in 1959.

After returning to Los Angeles, Price began developing what would become his signature style, using bold automotive paint or glazed color and polished surfaces on witty, sensual, or inventively shaped cups, vases, teapots, and sculptures. With influences ranging from organic forms to constructivism, and from geologic formations to abstract figuration, the sculptures that he created beginning in the 1960s were celebrated equally among scholars and enthusiasts of clay and contemporary art. The art historian Lucy Lippard wrote in a 1966 catalogue for the *Robert Irwin/Kenneth Price* exhibition at the Los Angeles County Museum of Art, "It is a fact rather than a value judgment that no one else, on the east or west coast, is working like Kenneth Price."[1]

By the mid-to-late 1990s, Price had begun to create boldly colored, bulbous, and amorphously shaped sculptures. These new works emerged from a series of sculptures that he made in the late 1980s and early 1990s, when he increased the scale of his ceramics and began layering and sanding up to fifteen different colors so that dazzling patterns emerged on their surfaces. Price continued to explore surface patterns and coloration up until his death in 2012, combining these extraordinary effects with increasingly fluid and erotic shapes. This process offered him a chance for both experimentation and renewal, two pathways that ensured the ongoing vitality of his pieces. CS

NOTE

1 Stephanie Barron, *Ken Price Sculpture: A Retrospective* (Los Angeles: Los Angeles County Museum of Art, 2012), 18.

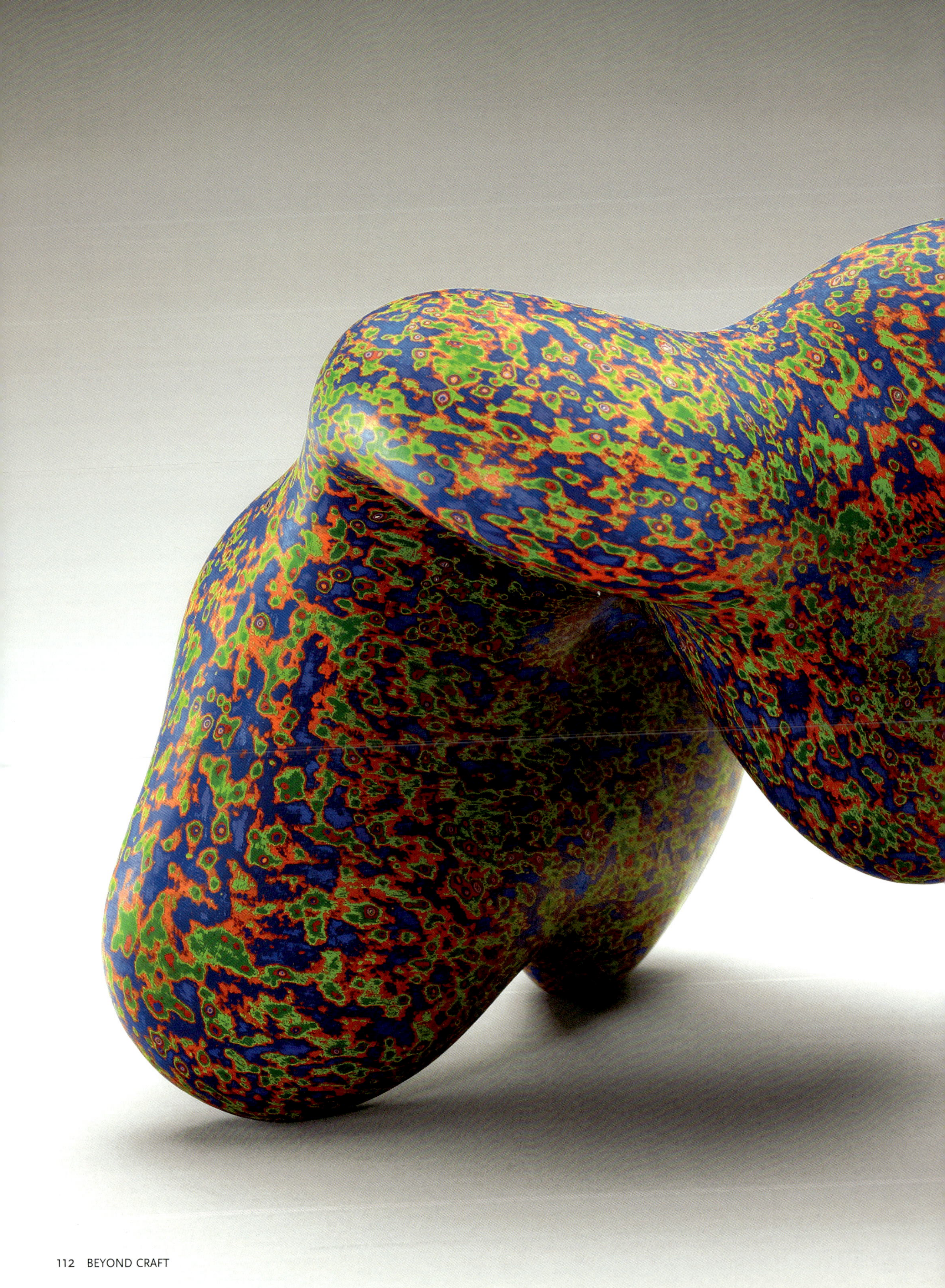

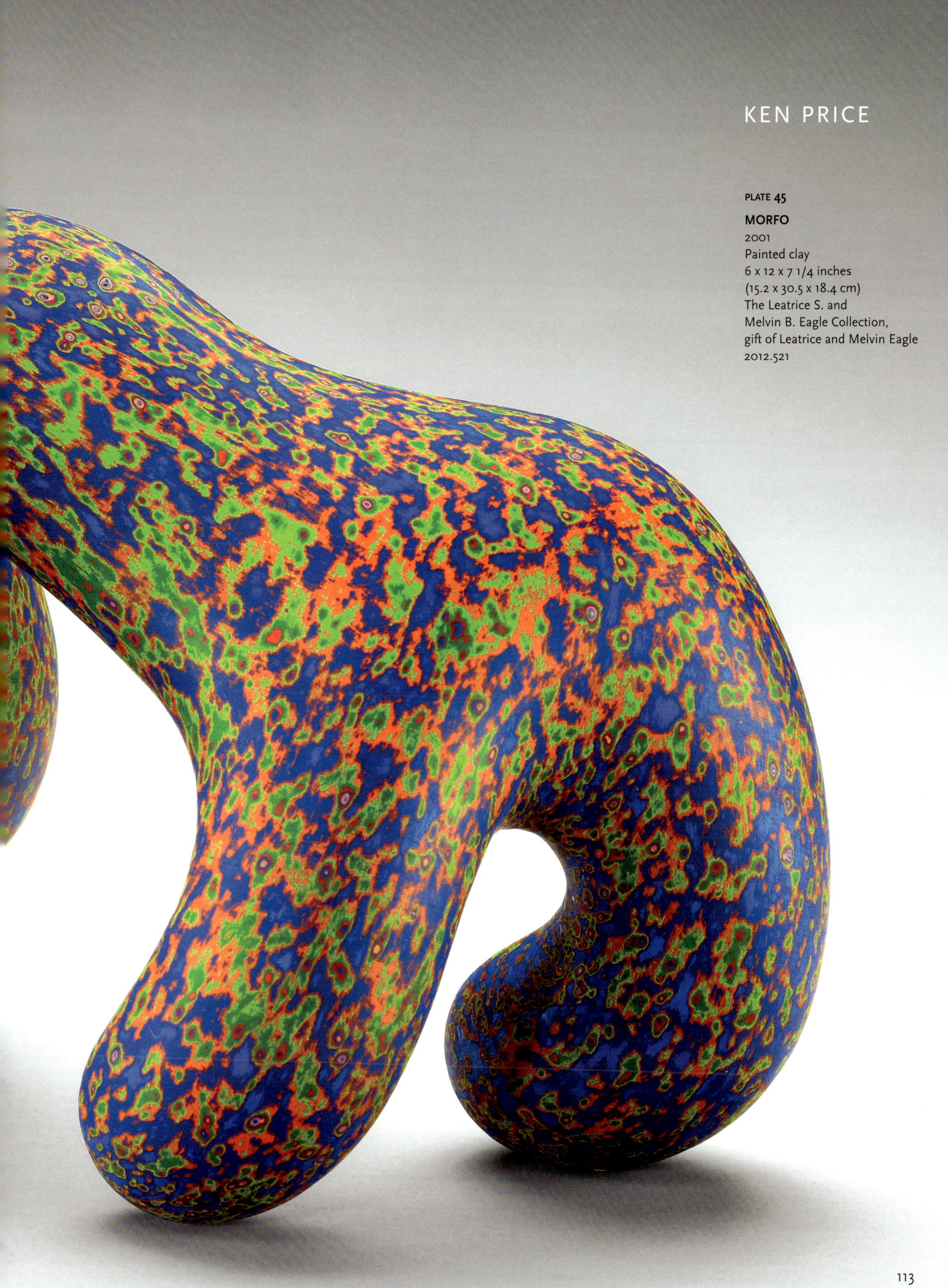

KEN PRICE

PLATE **45**

MORFO
2001
Painted clay
6 x 12 x 7 1/4 inches
(15.2 x 30.5 x 18.4 cm)
The Leatrice S. and
Melvin B. Eagle Collection,
gift of Leatrice and Melvin Eagle
2012.521

DON REITZ
American, born 1929

PLATE 46

PLATTER

1981
Salt-fired stoneware
3 1/4 x 21 3/4 inches diameter
(8.3 x 55.2 cm)
The Leatrice S. and
Melvin B. Eagle Collection,
museum purchase funded
by the Caroline Wiess Law
Accessions Endowment Fund
2010.2115

PLATE 47

UNTITLED VESSEL

c. 1980
Salt-fired stoneware
30 x 23 x 23 inches
(76.2 x 58.4 x 58.4 cm)
The Leatrice S. and
Melvin B. Eagle Collection,
gift of Leatrice and Melvin Eagle
2006.1270

Don Reitz is a potter's potter. For him, the process of hand-making a pot, the substance of the clay, and his incised surface decorations are all physical expressions of his emotions. Reitz has said, "I love what the clay does, because the clay, in fact, is me. It is my motion, my spirit, my energy, my mark, my signature's all over it."[1] In his belief in the expressive power of clay, Reitz takes an approach that echoes the forcefulness of Peter Voulkos, whose work Reitz playfully references in his adoption of the platter format and in the naming of his series *Tea Stacks*. Reitz, however, moderates Voulkos's aggressively sculptural stance with his commitment to the formal possibilities of utilitarian pottery, even as many of his own pieces are nonfunctional.

Reitz's love of the hand-worked clay surface led him to search for alternate finishes that would highlight his gestures and marks. Over the course of his lengthy career, Reitz would become associated with two processes that utilize firing alone to induce the clay to self-glaze: salt- and wood-firing. In particular, Reitz is widely credited with the revival of salt-firing, a practice in which sodium chloride is introduced into the kiln at the height of firing, initiating a reaction between the salt vapor and the silica in the clay to create a hard finish that reveals and enhances the worked surface. The fact that salt-firing is a standard ceramic practice today is a testament to Reitz's widespread teaching. During his twenty-eight-year tenure at the University of Wisconsin–Madison, Reitz also maintained an ambitious workshop and exhibition schedule that took him all over the United States and inspired new generations of potters. SJS

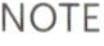

NOTE

1   Don Reitz, in an unpublished letter to Jack Troy (July 28, 1993) in response to his queries in preparation for writing *Wood-fired Stoneware and Porcelain* (Radnor, PA: Chilton, 1995), cited in Jody Clowes, *Don Reitz: Clay, Fire, Salt and Wood* (Madison: Elvehjem Museum of Art / University of Wisconsin–Madison, 2004), 56.

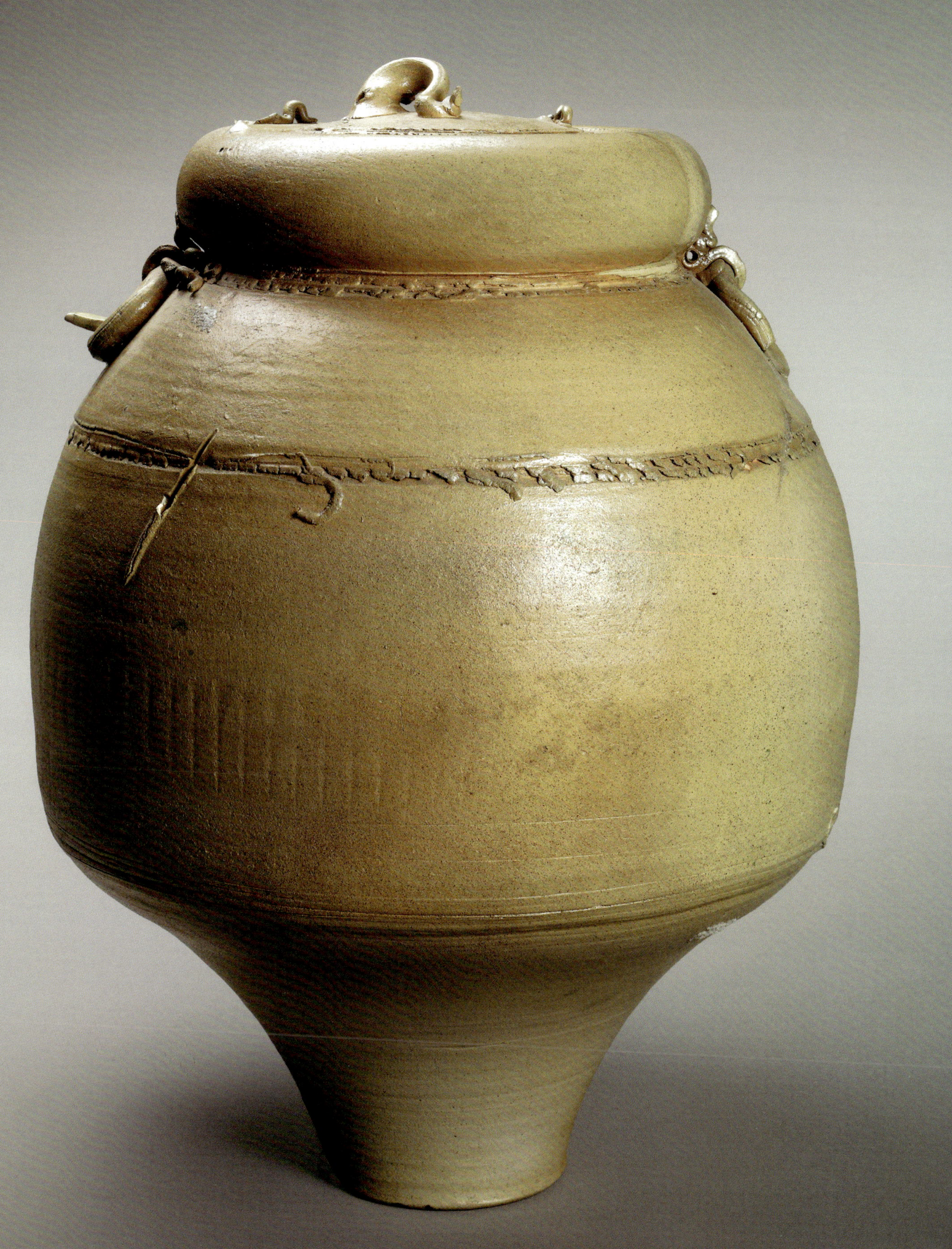

ADRIAN SAXE
American, born 1943

PLATE **48**

OIL LAMP #33
1983
Porcelain
9 1/8 x 4 5/8 x 2 1/4 inches
(23 x 11.7 x 5.7 cm)
The Leatrice S. and
Melvin B. Eagle Collection,
museum purchase funded
by the Caroline Wiess Law
Accessions Endowment Fund
2010.2123.A–.C

Recognized as a master of glaze and form, Adrian Saxe is often referred to as the quintessential postmodern artist in clay because of his eclectic combination of motifs and subject matter in vessels whose forms are writ large. By taking inspiration from historical decorative arts, Saxe transforms functional vessels into complex meditations on color and form, imbuing them with an often subversive sense of humor that renders them provocatively challenging and awe-inspiring.

Saxe's first exposure to ceramics as a student occurred at the Los Angeles County Art Institute (now Otis College of Art and Design) in 1957. He was drawn to functional works and to Japanese wares that he encountered upon moving to Hawaii with his family shortly thereafter. Saxe committed to studying ceramics and in the early 1960s returned to California to establish a studio. He ultimately entered the ceramic program directed by Ralph Bacerra at the Chouinard Art Institute (now California Institute of the Arts) in 1965, joining a group of passionate students who explored artistic trends both within and beyond the medium of clay.

Over the next years, Saxe developed a reputation for creating functional pieces and ceramic sculptures that addressed concerns shared by other contemporary artists. Ultimately, he shifted direction and, by the 1970s and 1980s, had developed his own style influenced by European and Asian porcelains, gourds, mortars, oil lamps, and other functional forms, which he embellished with elements derived from popular culture, faux gemstones, and found objects. He does not provide explicit explanations of his pieces, preferring to let their titles and motifs speak for themselves. Finials play a particularly important role, often signifying a specific narrative or point of view.

The Eagle collection is particularly rich in Saxe's ceramics, reflecting his output across the span of his career from the 1970s to 2000s. These pieces demonstrate the full range of his materials (raku to porcelain), forms (oil lamps, mugs, mortars, ampersands, ewers, jars, and gourds), and glazes, demonstrating the technical virtuosity of Saxe's ceramics and reaffirming his place in contemporary artistic practice. CS

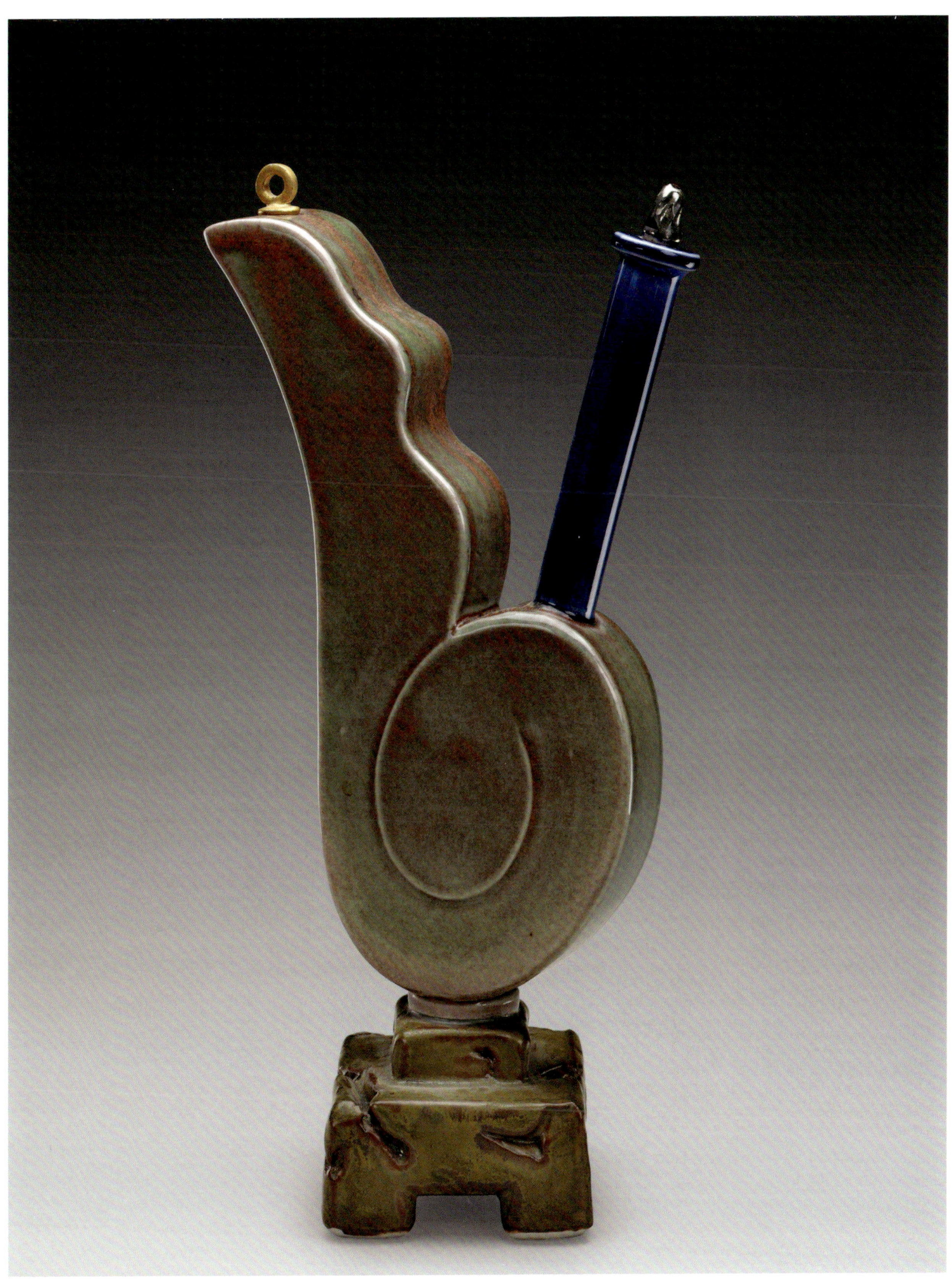

ADRIAN SAXE

PLATE **49**
UNTITLED EWER (DIJ)
1993
Porcelain, pearl, and
image-doubling calcite crystal
9 3/4 x 8 3/8 x 4 1/2 inches
(24.8 x 21.3 x 11.4 cm)
The Leatrice S. and
Melvin B. Eagle Collection,
museum purchase funded
by the Caroline Wiess Law
Accessions Endowment Fund
2010.2124.A.,B

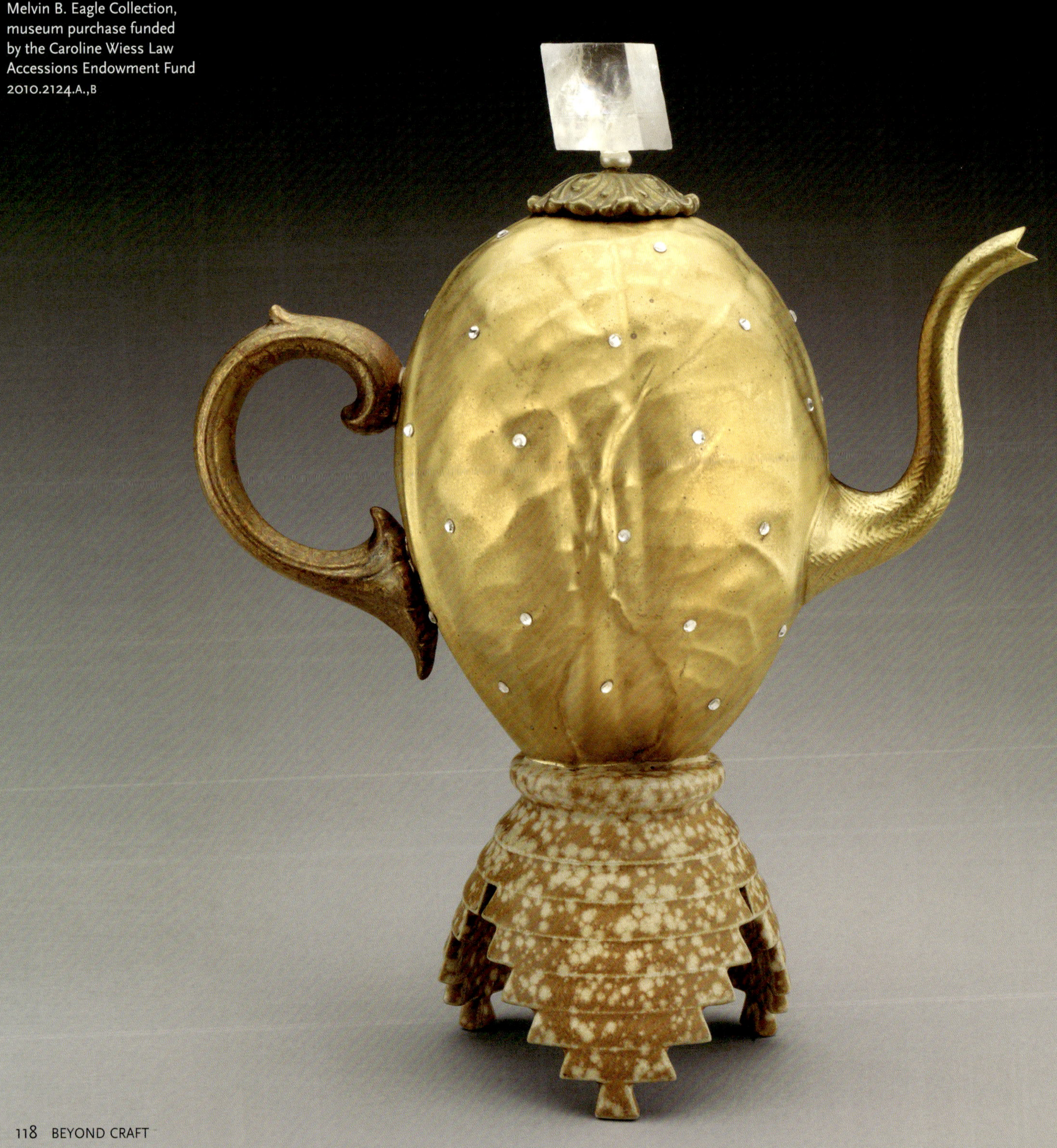

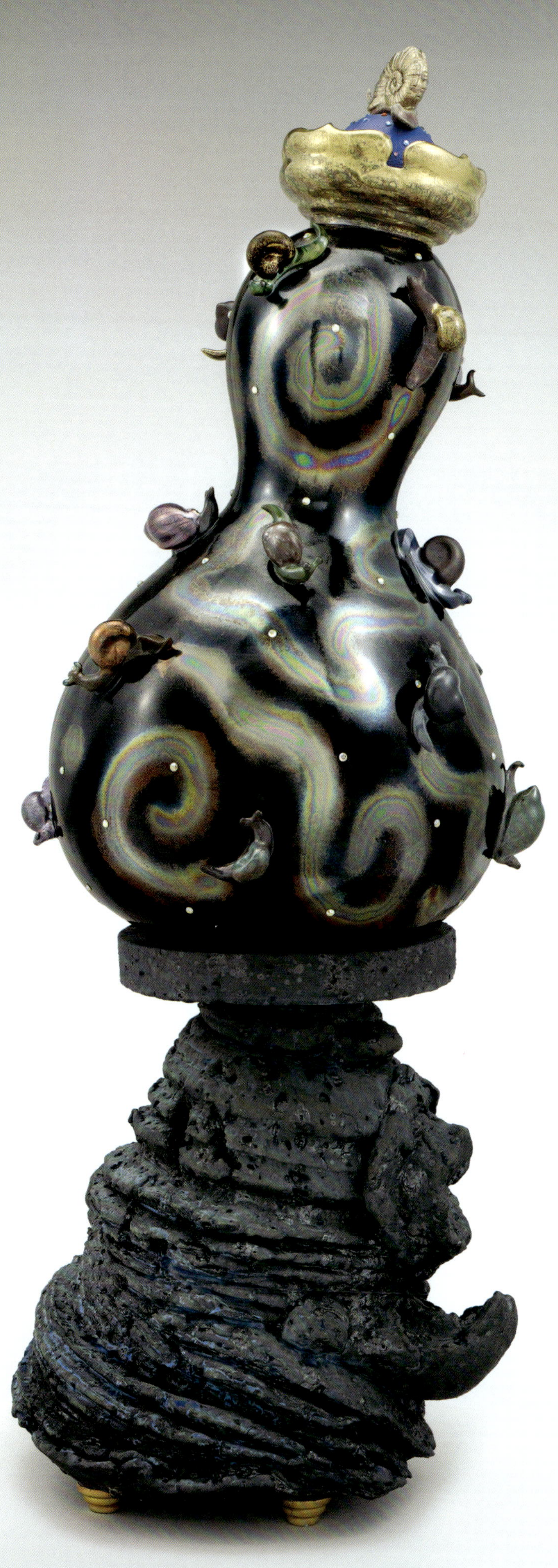

PLATE 50

MYXOCOCCUS JAMBOREE
2001
Porcelain and raku
29 x 11 x 9 3/4 inches
(73.7 x 27.9 x 24.8 cm)
The Leatrice S. and
Melvin B. Eagle Collection,
museum purchase funded
by the Caroline Wiess Law
Accessions Endowment Fund
2010.2129.A,.B

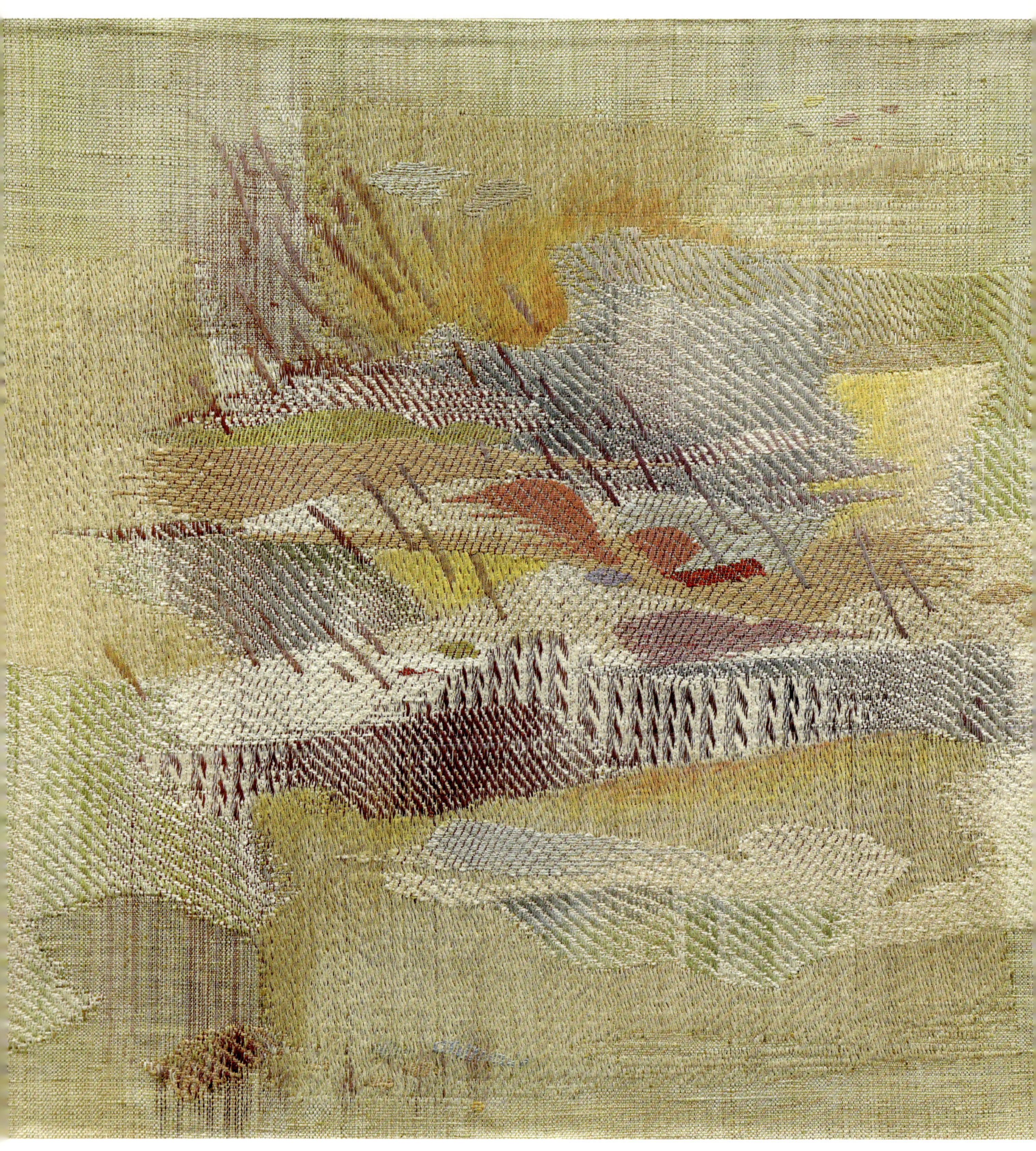

CYNTHIA SCHIRA
American, born 1934

A pioneer of contemporary textiles, Cynthia Schira seamlessly blends technology and artistry in ambitious tapestries that have alternately alluded to landscapes, codes, and ciphers. Though her training was traditional (she received a BFA in textiles from the Rhode Island School of Design in 1956 and pursued post-baccalaureate studies in tapestry at the École nationale d'art decoratif in Aubusson, France, the following year), her career can be categorized as one of continuous experimentation.

Throughout the 1970s and early 1980s, Schira created painterly weavings that involved unusual structures and nontraditional materials. Directly following her graduate studies, which she completed in 1967 at the University of Kansas, where she later served as a professor of textiles for twenty-seven years, Schira completed a body of work juxtaposing the metallic rigidity of aluminum with the naturalism of a linen warp. By the end of the 1970s, she was making atmospheric tapestries in a series titled *Supplemental Warps*, which explored color and texture through the addition of extra threads along the weavings' horizontal axis.

In 1982 Schira became one of the first textile artists to embrace the new technology of computer-aided weaving. In that year, with funding from her second grant from the National Endowment for the Arts, she purchased a computer and a computerized loom and spent several years investigating their possibilities.[1] The results of her first forays into computer-aided weaving, including the piece *Borderland* (1986), illustrated here, were exhibited in a solo exhibition at the Spencer Museum of Art in Lawrence, Kansas, in 1987. Since then, this technologically advanced method has been at the center of Schira's process as she continues to embrace the added complexity, abstraction, and sensuousness afforded by the computerized loom. SJS

NOTE

1 Cynthia Schira and Helen Foresman, *Cynthia Schira, New Work: Exhibition*, 1st ed. (Lawrence, KS: Spencer Museum of Art, 1987), unpaginated.

JOYCE J. SCOTT
American, born 1948

Throughout her career as an artist engaged in the realms of jewelry, sculpture, performance art, and installation, Joyce J. Scott has combined diverse influences such as Native American beadwork traditions, African art, and Mexican weavings into her provocative compositions. Identity is often a central theme of her work, and many of her pieces address complex issues related to African-American women, including feminism and apartheid, violence and intimacy. According to art historian Mary Jane Jacob, Scott's representation of the African-American experience in craft practice "allows her to exhume African-American memory, to elicit a response to social issues of today."[1] At other times, Scott's pieces simply focus on color, pattern, and the relationship between motifs, highlighting her mastery of composition and design. Her facility with combining and juxtaposing forms derives from lessons learned from her mother, the renowned fiber artist Elizabeth Talford Scott, who was known for her inventive combinations of techniques and materials in her quilts.

Scott began using beads in the mid-1970s after working with Native American and African artists at the Haystack Mountain School of Crafts in Deer Isle, Maine. She constructs her jewelry by using a traditional Native American peyote stitch to sew thousands of colored beads into individual structures that are then joined together. By using beadwork, which is traditionally the province of women, Scott also references gender studies in her work through her embrace of the associations that fiber art, sewing, and knitting have with femininity and domestic arts. CS

NOTE

1 Mary Jane Jacob, "The Critical Craftsmanship of Joyce Scott," in *Kickin' It with Joyce Scott* (Baltimore: The Baltimore Museum of At and the Maryland Art Institute, 2000), 78.

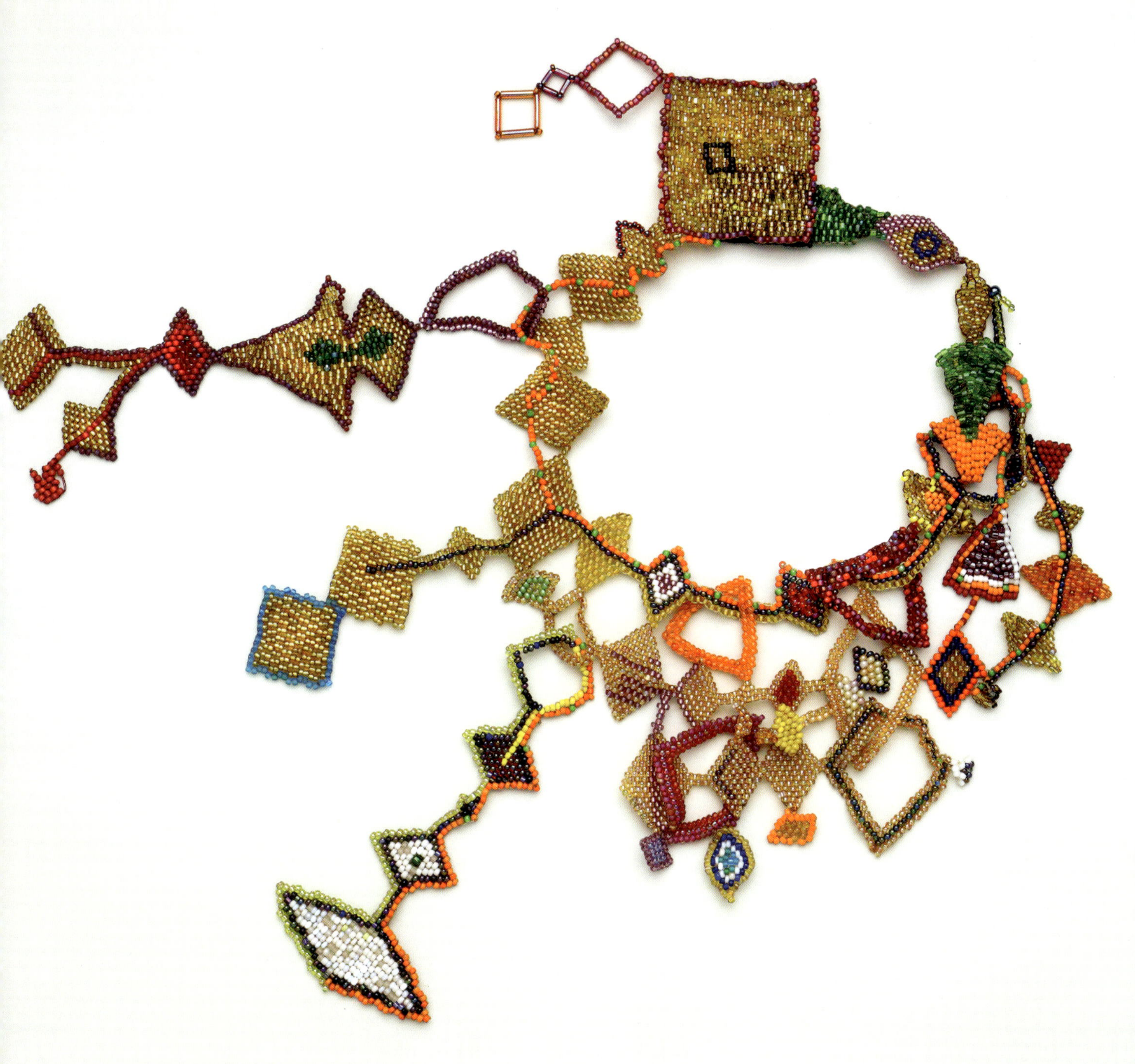

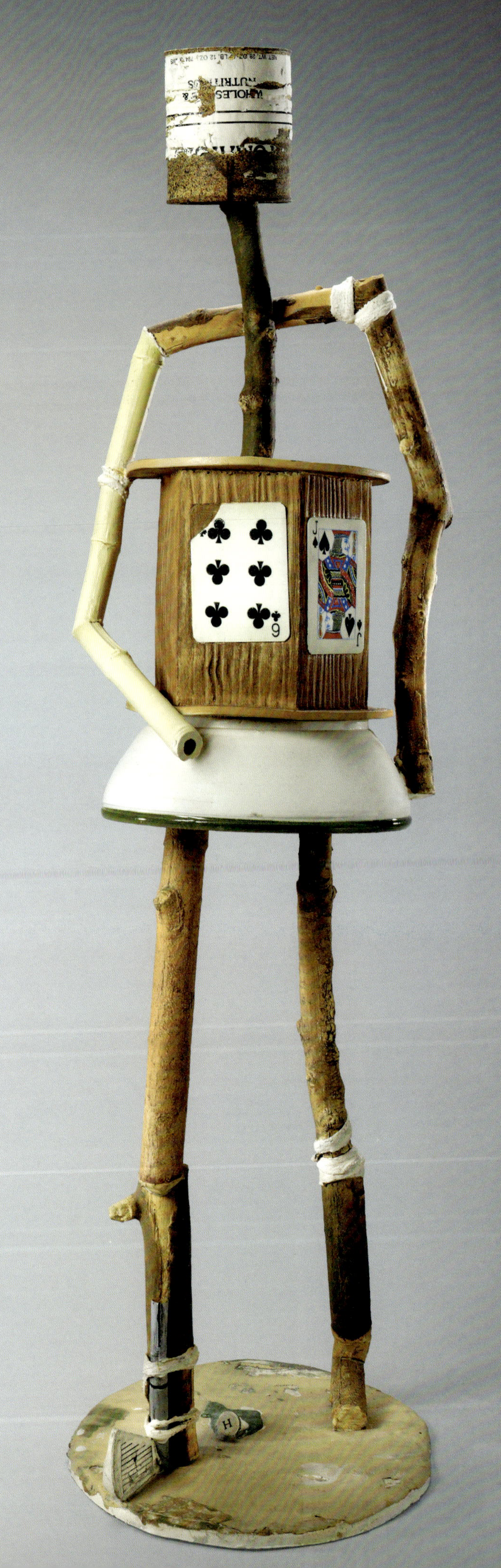

RICHARD SHAW
American, born 1941

Since the 1970s, Richard Shaw has been playfully upending viewer expectations with trompe l'oeil assemblages that incorporate the humorousness of Northern California Funk with the precise surfaces of Southern California ceramics.

Shaw is well known for the technical advancements that enable the impeccable detail in his works. In 1971, soon after finishing his graduate degree at the University of California, Davis, Shaw and the sculptor Robert Hudson spent eighteen months adapting the factory process of slip-casting porcelain for small-scale use in an artist studio. Using molds cast from everyday objects, they developed the mix-and-match style that forms the backbone of Shaw's mature works. By 1978 Shaw had refined his slip-casting method to create large, anthropomorphic sculptures such as *In the Family Way* (1980), whose verisimilitude makes it difficult to distinguish its porcelain replicas of wood legs, bamboo arms, and rusty tin-can head from their real-world counterparts.

Shaw's illusion is so convincing in part because of his focus on the surfaces of the pieces. In order to enhance their illusion, he worked with a master printer to develop a silkscreen method to accurately reproduce food labels, stamps, and other printed material on special decal paper, which could then be transferred to a bisque-fired surface. This process is especially successful in his signature playing cards, which he uses as both decoration and structure in his work (see checklist no. 133).

The success of Shaw's realism and the humor and wit with which it is deployed speak to his role within the history of West Coast ceramics. As one of Robert Arneson's leading students and as a professor at the University of California, Berkeley, for twenty-five years, Shaw had a significant influence in the Bay Area and throughout the country. SJS

PLATE 53

IN THE FAMILY WAY
1980
Porcelain
37 x 10 x 12 inches
(94 x 25.4 x 30.5 cm)
The Leatrice S. and
Melvin B. Eagle Collection,
museum purchase funded
by the Caroline Wiess Law
Accessions Endowment Fund
2010.2133

PAUL SOLDNER
American, 1921–2011

PLATE 54

UNTITLED
1980
Ceramic
18 x 23 1/2 x 2 1/4 inches
(45.7 x 59.7 x 5.7 cm)
The Leatrice S. and
Melvin B. Eagle Collection,
museum purchase funded
by the Caroline Wiess Law
Accessions Endowment Fund
2010.2138

Paul Soldner's career in ceramics encompassed three distinct but related roles: as a potter, he pioneered American-style raku and other low-fire techniques; as an inventor, he built easy-to-maneuver potting wheels and other tools; and as a teacher, he advocated for an open-source atmosphere of sharing information. For Soldner, the impetus to explore in all of these areas came from his own innate curiosity, opportunity and serendipitous accidents, encouragement from mentors, and the excitement of an intuitive approach.

Soldner's work has been defined by a series of formal and technical breakthroughs. Beginning with his time as Peter Voulkos's first graduate student at the Los Angeles County Art Institute (now Otis College of Art and Design) in 1954, he began to shape his ceramic vocabulary, learning when to decorate his pieces and when to leave them unornamented.[1] His development of a uniquely American raku style, complete with a different clay body, firing, and smoking methods, occurred in the early 1960s. For the next forty years, he used raku and salt-vapor firing to create vessels, plaques, and sculptures that sometimes featured a variety of calligraphic and figural drawings In addition to colors and surfaces. Soldner was able to achieve dramatic colors on his work by employing stains and oxides as well as innovative firing techniques. One method called for placing salt in front of the kiln's flame or layering it on the clay so that the chemical reaction during firing produced soft orange and pink hues on the surface. In 1986 Soldner also began experimenting with bronze casting (see checklist no. 139). This material and technique allowed him to explore form and movement differently, resulting in yet another opportunity to push beyond traditional boundaries of clay. CS

NOTE
1   Paul Soldner, "Romancing the Clay," *Studio Potter* 23, no. 2 (June 1995): 61.

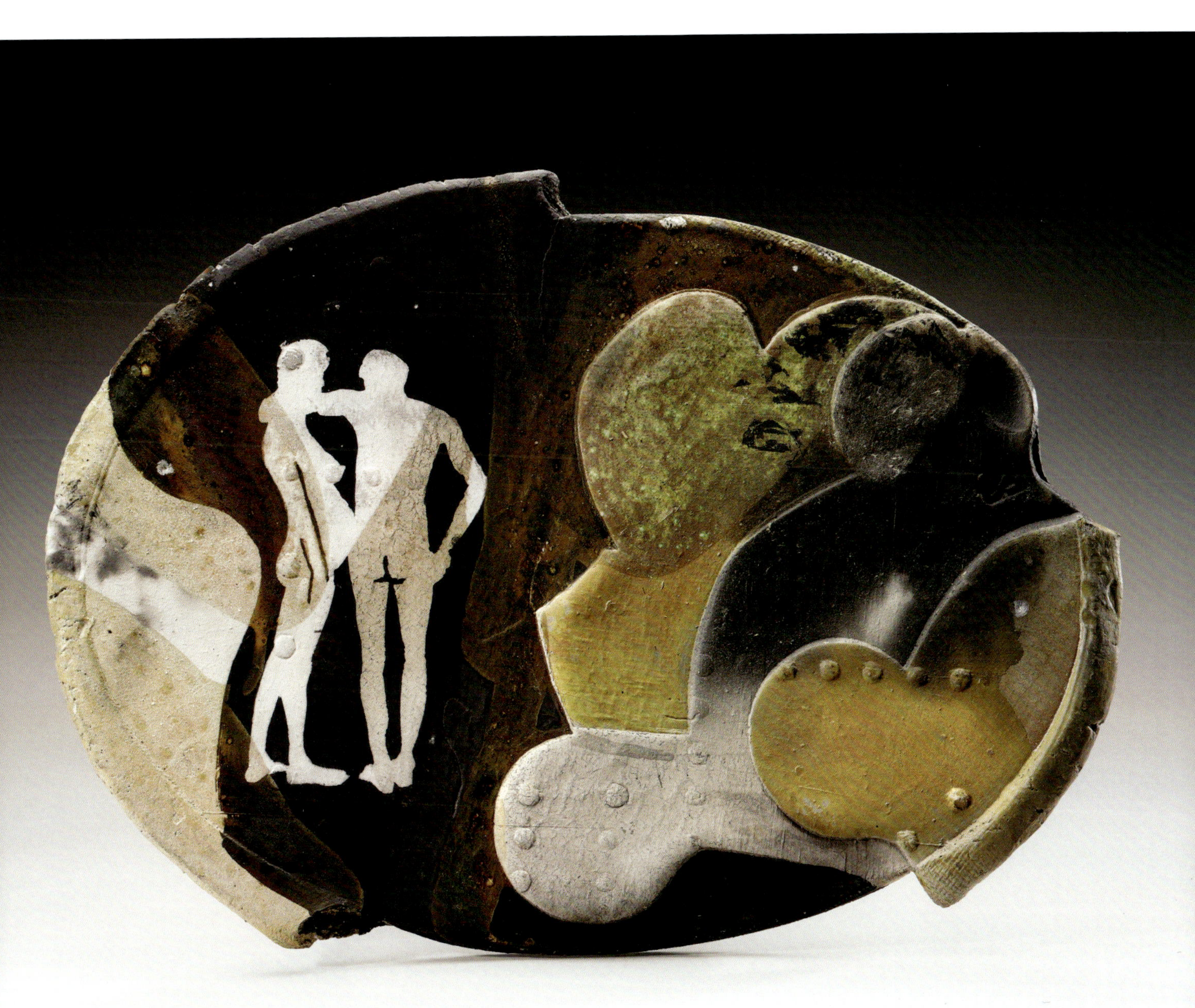

THERMAN STATOM
American, born 1953

PLATE 55

GLASS HOUSE
1994/98
Glass and paint
26 1/4 x 18 1/2 x 14 inches
(66.7 x 47 x 35.6 cm)
The Leatrice S. and
Melvin B. Eagle Collection,
museum purchase funded
by the Caroline Wiess Law
Accessions Endowment Fund
2010.2146

Therman Statom is best known for large-scale installations that transform their surroundings into landscapes of plate glass, blown-glass elements, and painted imagery.[1] Statom trained as a glass artist at Pilchuck Glass School and the Rhode Island School of Design just as studio glass was coming of age, yet he eschewed that movement's preoccupation with hot-working techniques in favor of the architectonic and expressive possibilities of transparent plate glass. He works in an additive and often improvisational manner, constructing an instantly recognizable mélange of objects: chairs, ladders, houses, and paintings (rectangular plate-glass boxes), which he embellishes with blown-glass elements and imagery culled from his highly developed personal lexicon as well as from art history and popular culture. Baseballs and playing cards, reproductions of Old Master paintings, classical vessel forms, and glass shards are all equally at home in his constructions.

Statom's works resemble dreamscapes. His use of watery colors and his juxtaposition of seemingly disparate household forms give a sense of familiarity that is nevertheless disorienting. He intentionally generates an atmosphere in which preconceived notions are destabilized and new ideas can be formed. He has a specific goal for viewers encountering his installations: "I want you to close your eyes and I want the substance of the show to parallel your imagination. I want your experience and your memory to blend into one."[2] SJS

NOTES

1 The work shown here was originally made in 1994. When the Eagles acquired it in 1998, it was damaged during shipping, and the artist added new elements during its repair.

2 Sarah Baker, "Gut Level: Glass Artist Therman Statom Brings More Than Meets the Eye," *Omaha Weekly Reader*, April 16, 2008.

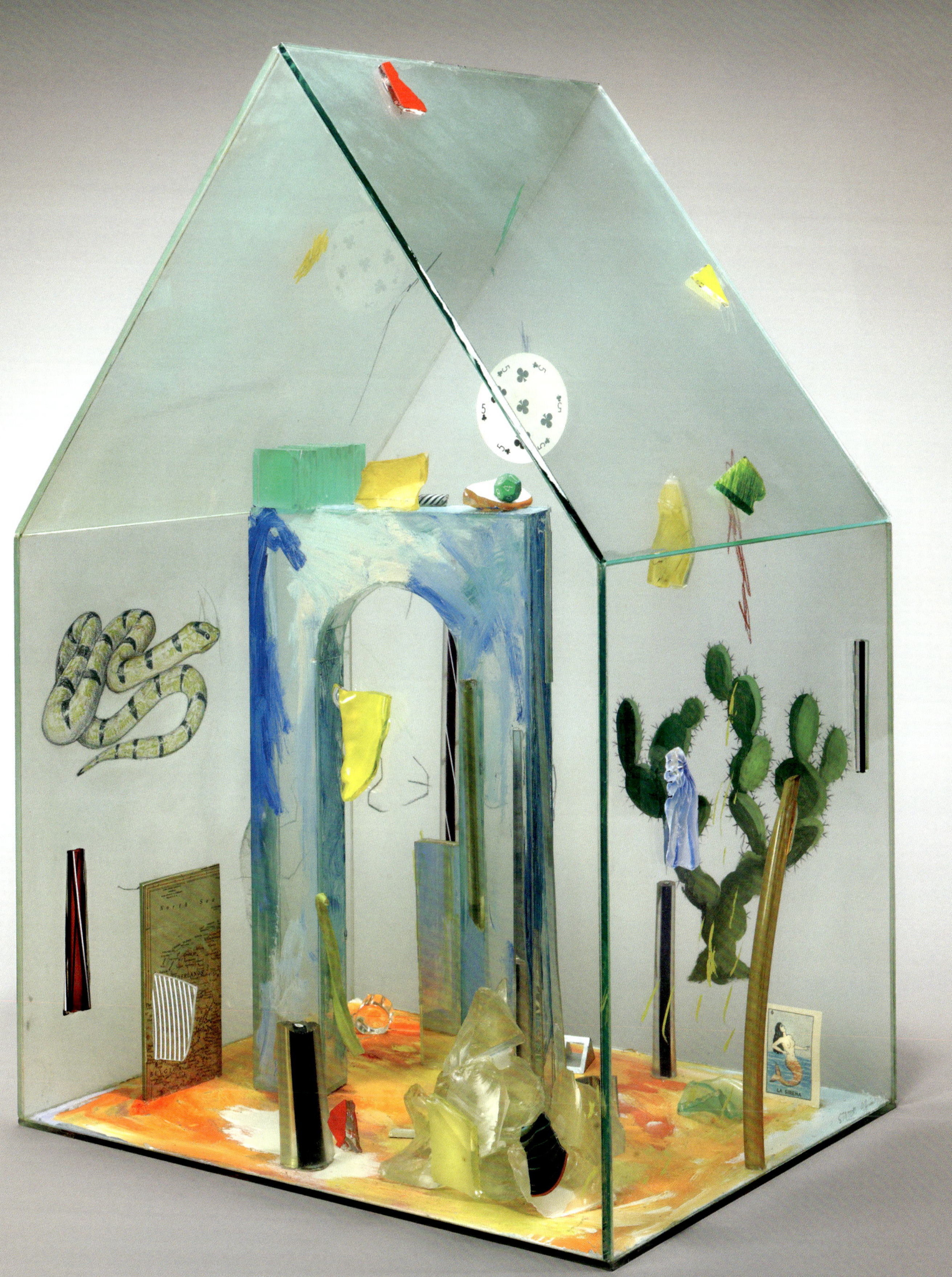
LA SIRENA

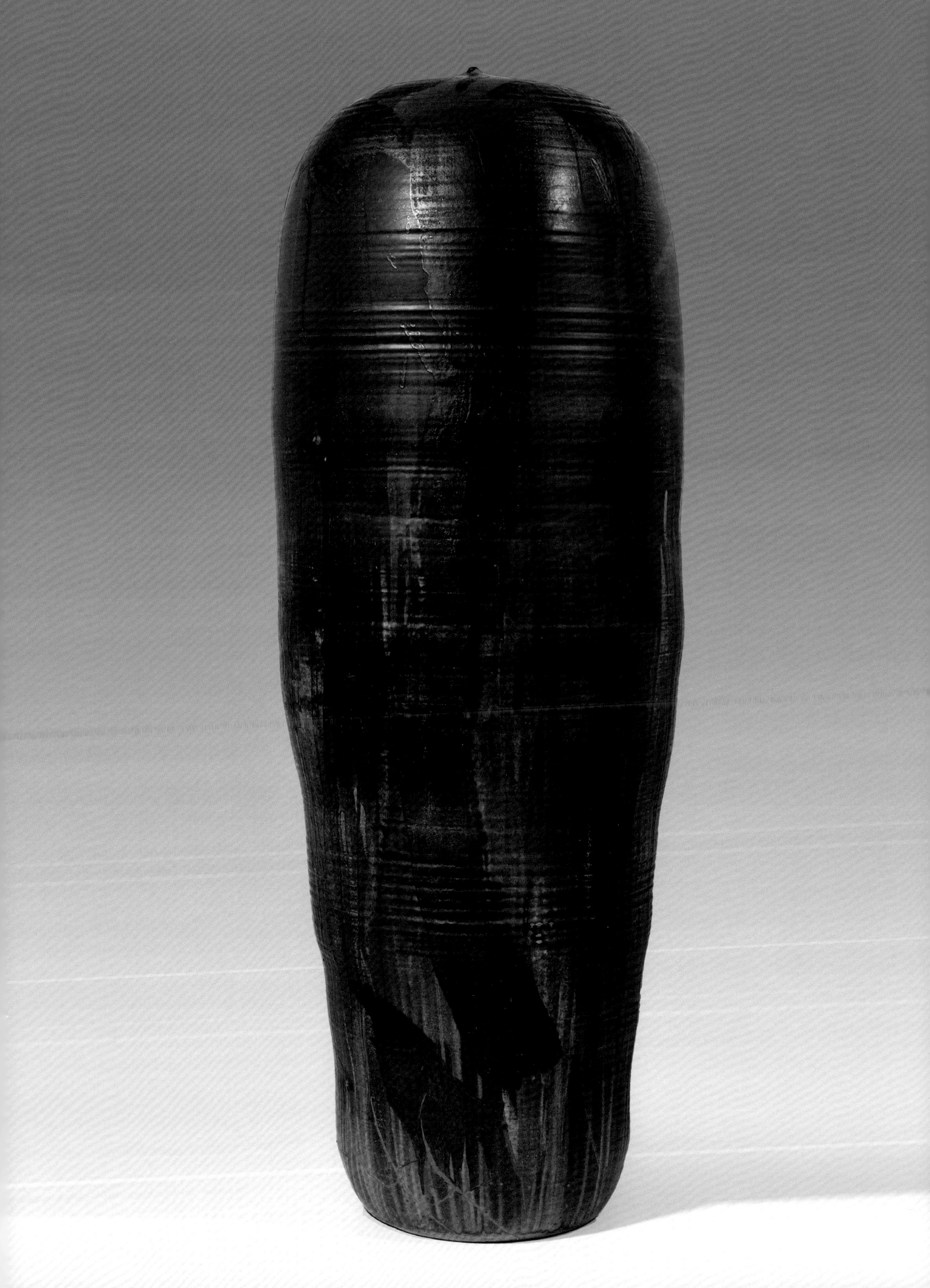

TOSHIKO TAKAEZU
American, 1922–2011

With quiet, wheel-thrown ceramic forms and bold surfaces, Toshiko Takaezu provided a considered counterpoint to the more overtly political works of her contemporaries Robert Arneson and Peter Voulkos. Born in Hawaii to Japanese parents, Takaezu worked in production potteries in Honolulu and studied at the University of Hawaii, Manoa, before moving to the mainland to study with Finnish ceramicist and avowed modernist Maija Grotell at Cranbrook Academy of Art in Bloomfield Hills, Michigan, in 1951.

Under the tutelage of Grotell, Takaezu began to see the vessel as a vehicle for artistic concerns beyond utility. Using the wheel as her primary tool, she began experimenting with compound thrown forms and with adding multiple spouts to create nonfunctional sculptural vessels. By the late 1950s, she had begun to develop the gently swollen closed forms with attenuated, vestigial spouts for which she is most well known. These vessels, along with the equally renowned sphere-shaped *Moon Pots* that she began producing in the following decade and her columnar *Tree Forests* that she began making in the 1970s, provided an uninterrupted canvas for her explorations in glaze. Surface treatment was of utmost importance to Takaezu. From the 1960s on, she expanded her palette and techniques, developing a painterly approach in which she applied brushstrokes of glaze or dipped, poured, and dripped glaze to achieve atmospheric effects reminiscent of landscapes and the confident mark-making of Abstract Expressionist painters.

Throughout her career, Takaezu continually renewed her restrained formal language through small adjustments to scale and shape, glaze and color. The result is a decades-long investigation of the expressive possibilities of the closed form, from the very small to the impressively grand. In the last decade of her life, she increased the size of her works to create room-size installations of her human-scale *Star Series* so that the pieces could be experienced as a group as well as individually. SJS

PLATE **56**

ZEUS
c. 1995
Stoneware
66 1/2 x 24 3/4 inches diameter
(168.9 x 62.9 cm)
The Leatrice S. and
Melvin B. Eagle Collection,
museum purchase funded
by the Caroline Wiess Law
Accessions Endowment Fund
2010.2147

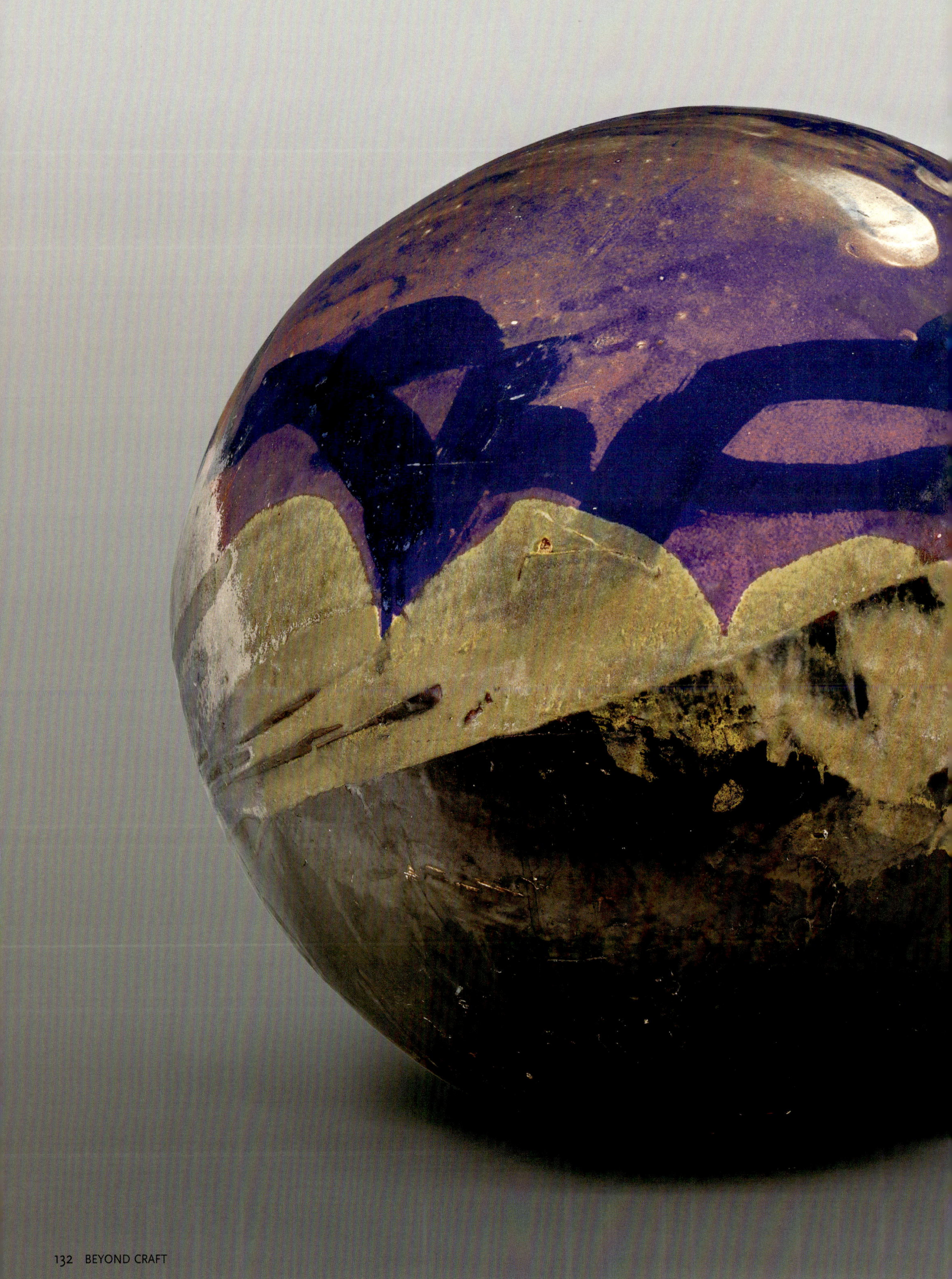

TOSHIKO TAKAEZU

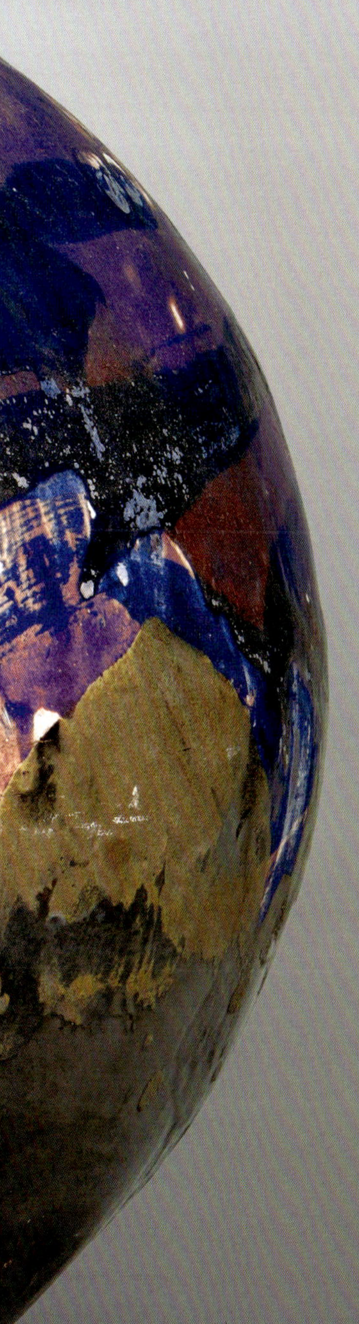

PLATE **57**

PURPLE MOON
1999
Stoneware
20 1/2 x 21 inches diameter
(52.1 x 53.3 cm)
The Leatrice S. and
Melvin B. Eagle Collection,
gift of Leatrice and Melvin Eagle
2010.2265

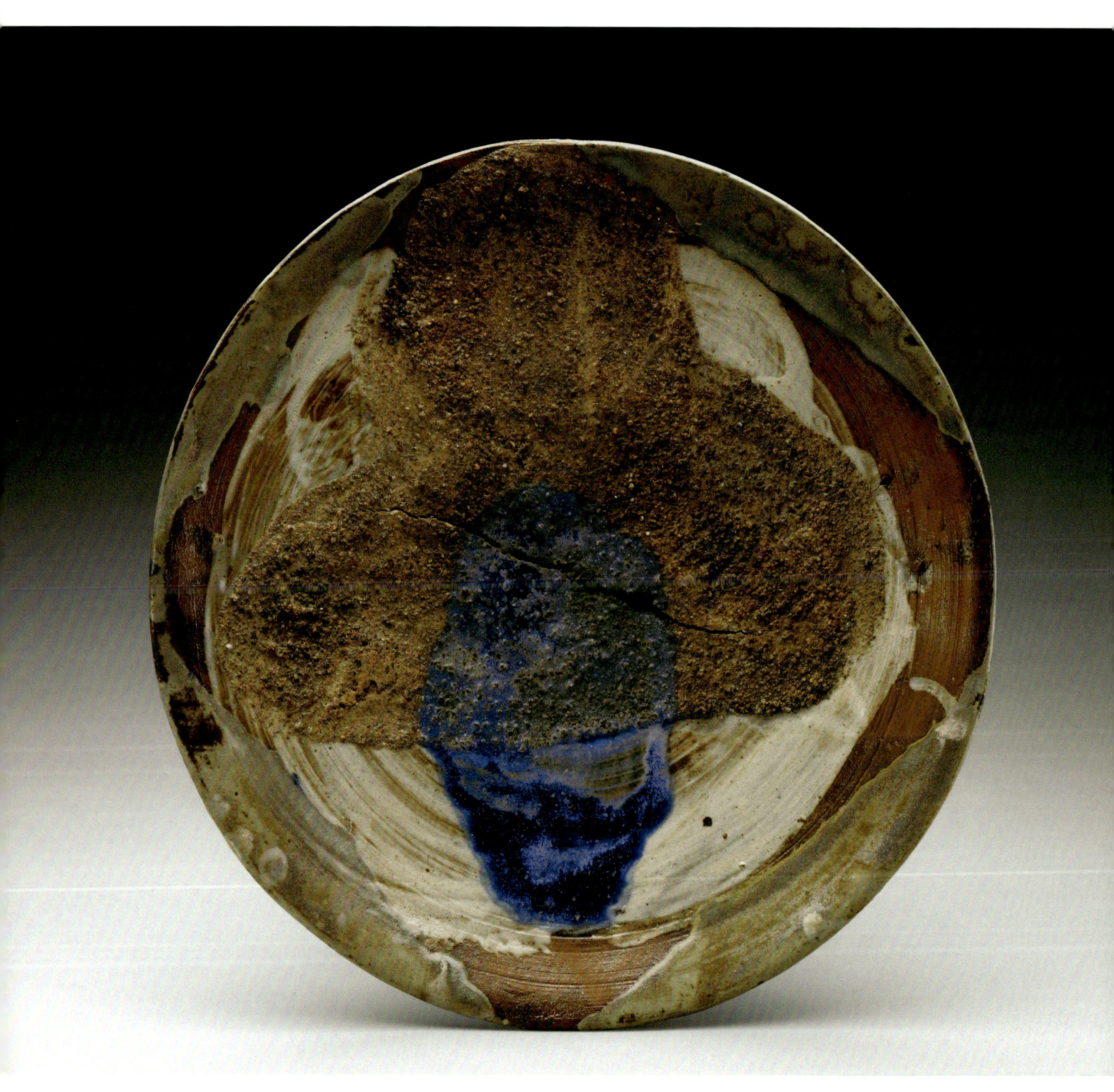

PETER VOULKOS
American, 1924–2002

Over the course of his fifty-year career, Peter Voulkos challenged historical attitudes about the nature of clay, revolutionized aesthetics, and established California as the center for avant-garde ceramic art in the United States. He first encountered clay as a student at Montana State University, and during the early 1950s he served as co–resident director at the Archie Bray Foundation in Helena, Montana. However, Voulkos's breakthrough ceramics emerged later, during the five years he spent in Los Angeles, from 1954 to 1959, as the chairman of the new ceramics department at the Los Angeles County Art Institute (now Otis College of Art and Design). His success there in building a new ceramic vocabulary, one that emphasized spontaneity and the material qualities of clay, freed him and his students from the constraints of functional ceramics and charted a new course for American ceramics.

Many of Voulkos's progressive inventions can be found in his plate and stack forms, which he began making in the 1950s. As seen in this 1961 example, his early plates often feature painted surfaces rendered in the abstract style of painters whom Voulkos admired at Black Mountain College in Black Mountain, North Carolina, and in New York. His plates soon grew to massive proportions, with thick rims that barely contain the energy of their designs. The 1973 example from the Eagle collection has knife strokes or action marks, ripped and punched holes, and windows that allow for shadows, which became hallmarks of Voulkos's style. His stack forms progressed along similar lines. Voulkos's stacked vessels of the 1960s and 1970s underwent a complete upheaval in the 1980s, becoming more abstract. During this process, his approach became looser and more expressive, ultimately culminating in some of the most powerful works of his career.

Voulkos created stacks and plates, as well as ice buckets, tea bowls, and a few other forms, until his death in 2002 (see checklist nos. 160–164). He never tired of certain shapes, which he returned to repeatedly over the length of his career, consistently seeking new information from them and "trying to get [a form] down to a simple gesture, one where the risks are great but spiritually rewarding."[1] CS

NOTE
1   Peter Voulkos, untitled artist statement, *Studio Potter* 13, no. 1 (December 1984): 46.

PLATE 58

UNTITLED PLATE
1961
Stoneware
2 1/2 x 12 1/4 inches diameter
(6.4 x 31.1 cm)
The Leatrice S. and
Melvin B. Eagle Collection,
museum purchase funded
by the Caroline Wiess Law
Accessions Endowment Fund
2010.2151

PETER VOULKOS

PLATE **59**

UNTITLED PLATE
1973
Stoneware and porcelain
3 3/8 x 18 1/2 inches diameter
(8.6 x 47 cm)
The Leatrice S. and
Melvin B. Eagle Collection,
museum purchase funded
by the Caroline Wiess Law
Accessions Endowment Fund
2010.2153

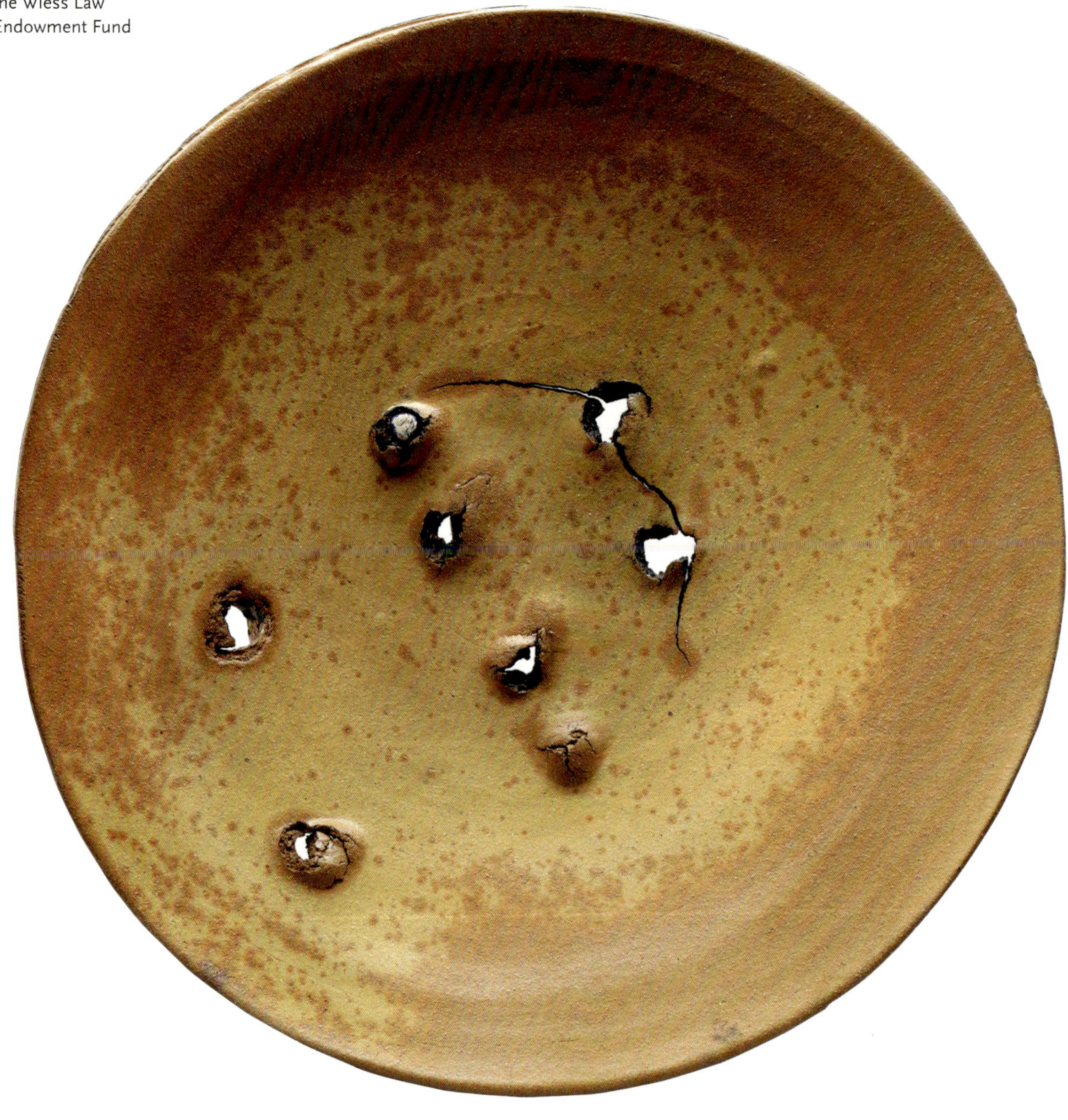

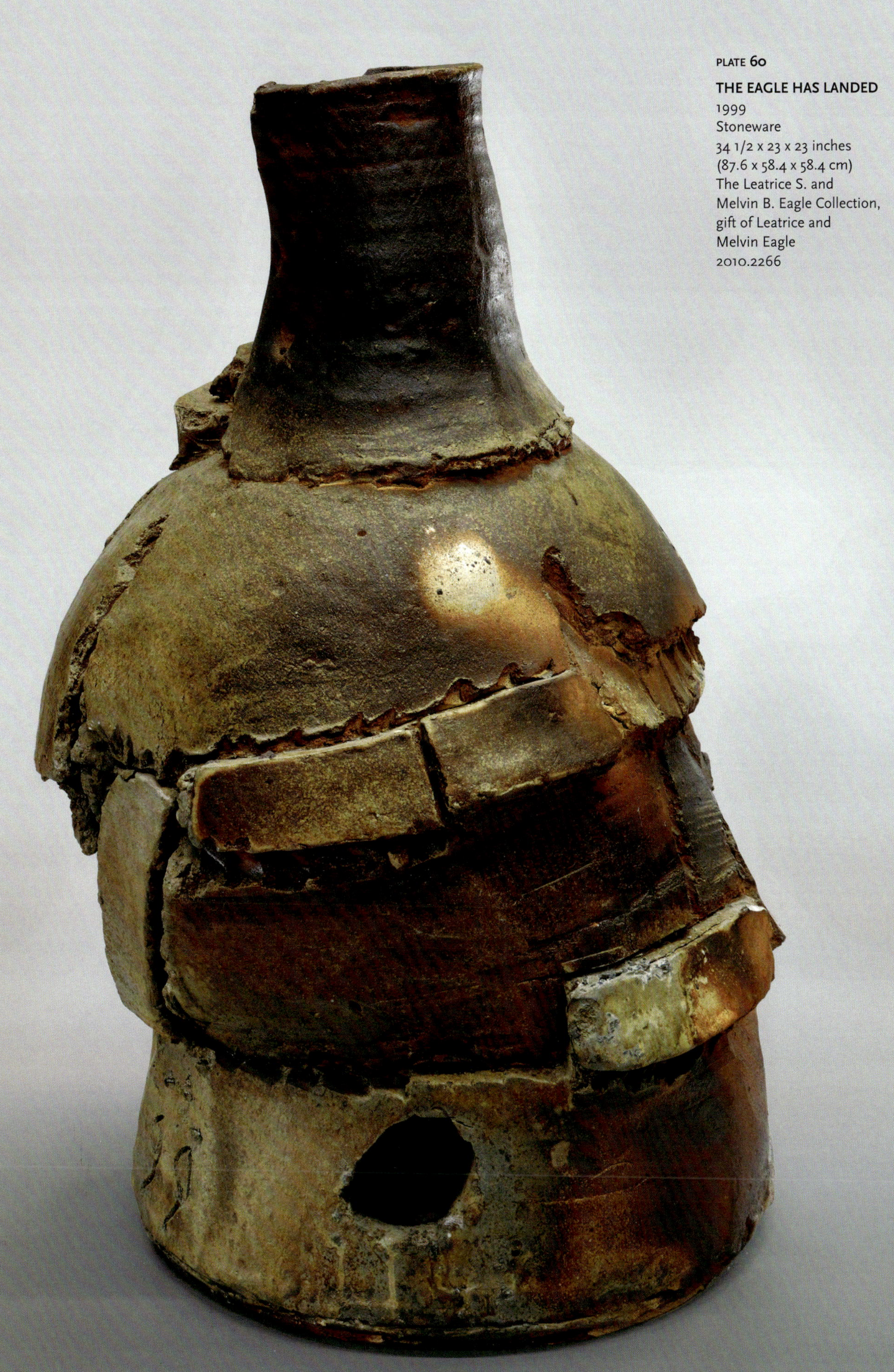

PLATE 60

THE EAGLE HAS LANDED
1999
Stoneware
34 1/2 x 23 x 23 inches
(87.6 x 58.4 x 58.4 cm)
The Leatrice S. and
Melvin B. Eagle Collection,
gift of Leatrice and
Melvin Eagle
2010.2266

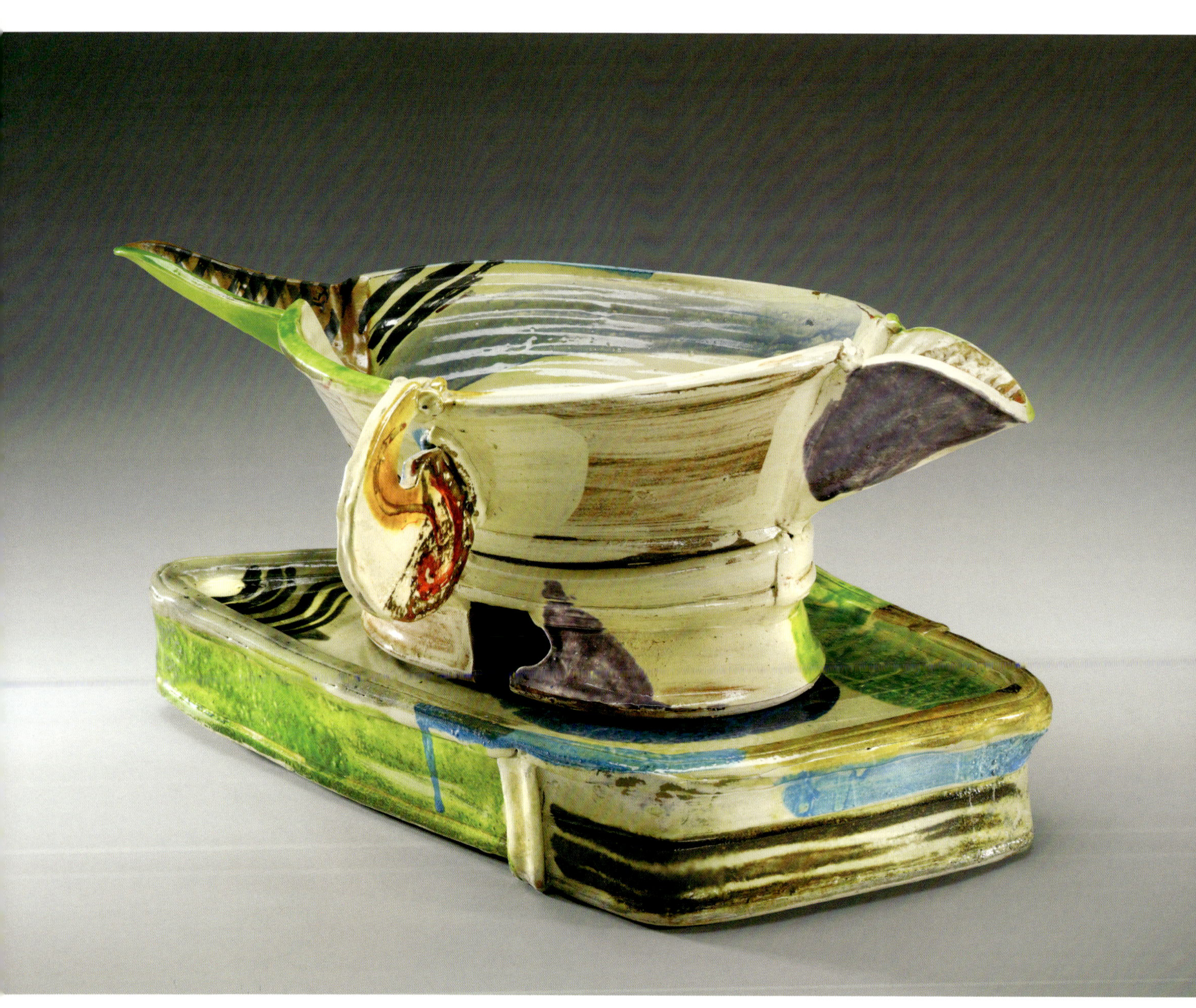

BETTY WOODMAN
American, born 1930

For more than fifty years, Betty Woodman has been creating exuberant ceramics that explore the vessel form. Each work in her oeuvre begins with that idea. Yet regardless of how she transforms or deconstructs them, her vessels still reference the history of functional ceramics. They also reflect such wide-ranging artistic influences as Greek and Etruscan sculpture, the paintings of Pablo Picasso and Henri Matisse, Italian majolica, and Baroque and Rococo architectural ornaments, among others.

Woodman is an extraordinary colorist whose ceramics often feature lush bursts of color. Her views on painting her work defy traditional ideas about ceramic glazes and are more closely aligned with artistic movements, such as the Pattern and Decoration movement, in which she participated while living in New York during the 1970s. Over the course of her career, gestural brushstrokes and the synthesis of color, drawing, and form have become her hallmarks.

Woodman's bold palette complements the energy found in her inventive shapes. Many of her ceramics are multipart compositions with dramatic, overscaled volumes and contours. Although Woodman does not work in series, she has revisited certain shapes and forms for decades, consistently rethinking and refining avenues for decoration. These bodies of work demonstrate her dedication to her craft; they also are open to a multiplicity of interpretations, thereby revealing their vast potential. CS

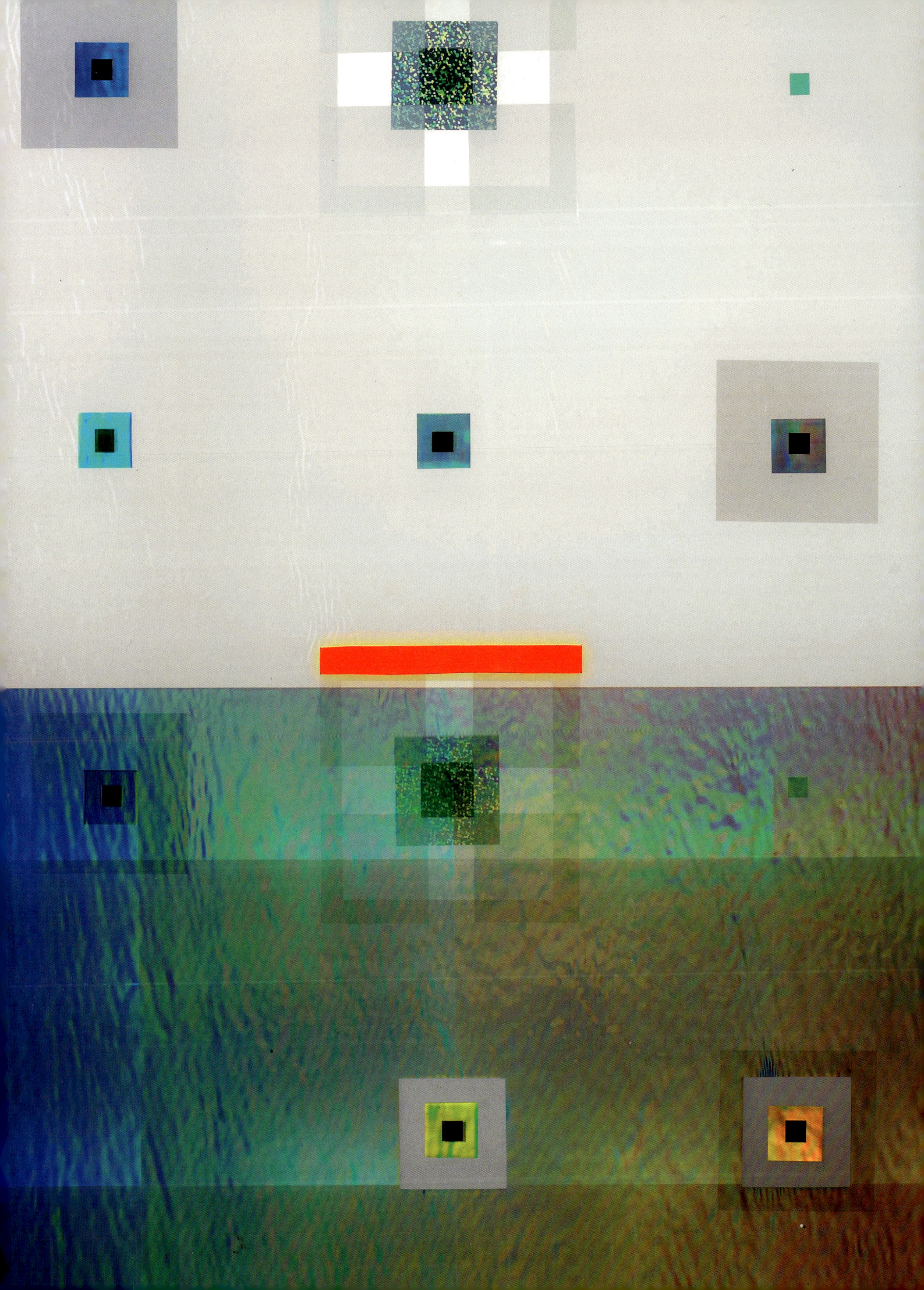

ILLUSTRATED CHECKLIST
OF THE COLLECTION

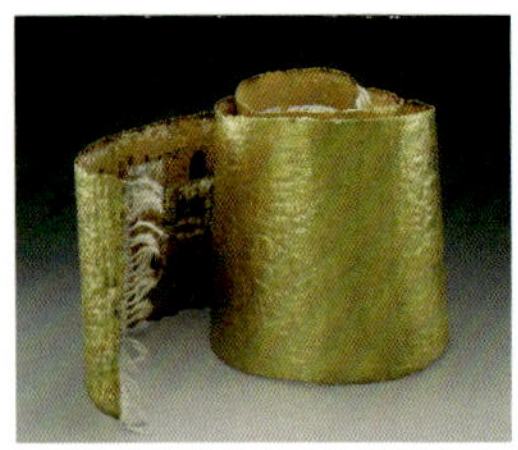

1 OLGA DE AMARAL,
Colombian, born 1932
R1062 Glyph IX, 2002
Linen, gold leaf, clay, and paint
13 x 96 inches
(33 x 243.8 cm)
Gift of Leatrice and Melvin Eagle
2008.901

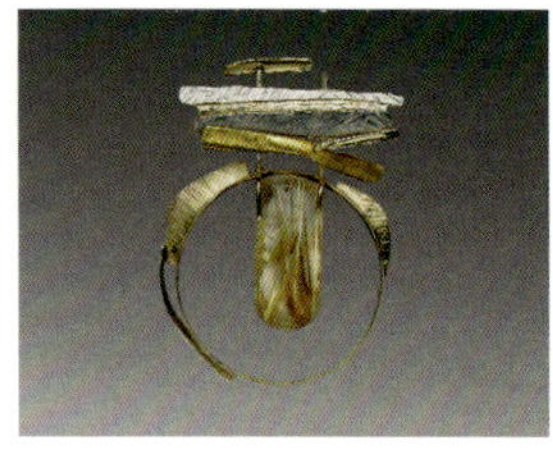

5 GLENDA ARENTZEN,
American, born 1941
Gemstone carving by Steve Walters
Pin, c. 2000
14k yellow gold, 24k gold, palladium,
quartz, and rutilated quartz
2 1/4 x 1 3/4 x 1/2 inches (5.7 x 4.4 x 1.3 cm)
Museum purchase funded
by the Caroline Wiess Law
Accessions Endowment Fund
2010.2019

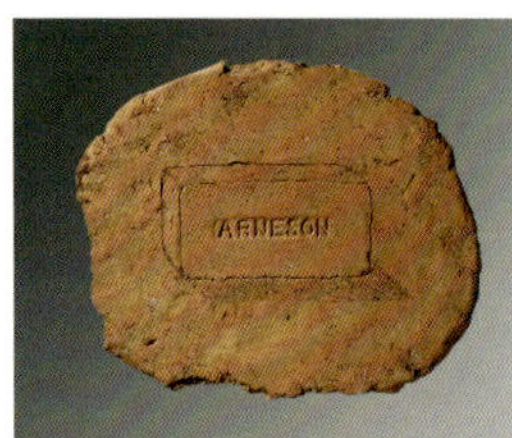

9 ROBERT ARNESON
American, 1930–1992
Brick, 1974
Ceramic
15 x 17 7/8 x 1 5/8 inches
(38.1 x 45.4 x 4.1 cm)
Museum purchase funded
by the Caroline Wiess Law
Accessions Endowment Fund
2010.2023

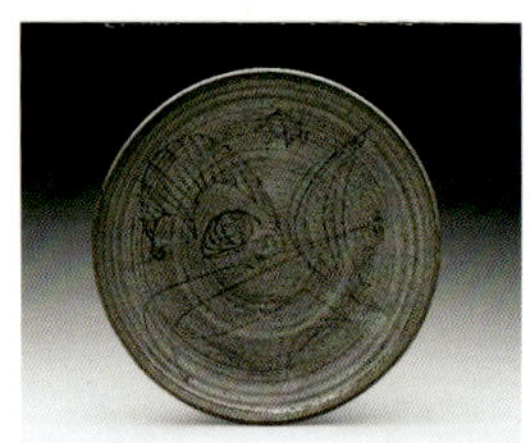

12 ROBERT ARNESON,
American, 1930–1992
Plate, 1960
Ceramic
1 3/4 x 12 inches diameter
(4.4 x 30.5 cm)
Museum purchase funded
by the Caroline Wiess Law
Accessions Endowment Fund
2010.2026

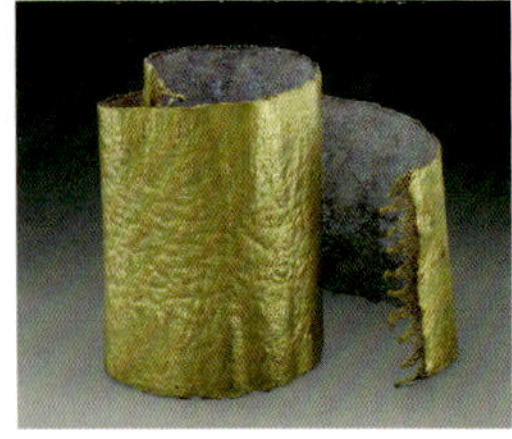

2 OLGA DE AMARAL,
Colombian, born 1932
1029 Glyph IV, 2002
Linen, gold leaf, clay, and paint
11 1/4 x 52 inches
(28.6 x 132.1 cm)
Gift of Leatrice and Melvin Eagle
2008.902

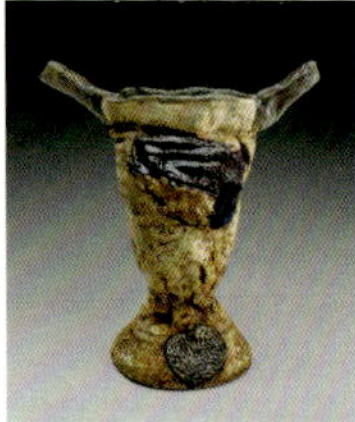

6 ROBERT ARNESON,
American, 1930–1992
Trophy Maquette, 1966
Ceramic
11 1/4 x 11 1/4 x 5 3/4 inches
(28.6 x 28.6 x 14.6 cm)
Museum purchase funded
by the Caroline Wiess Law
Accessions Endowment Fund
2010.2020

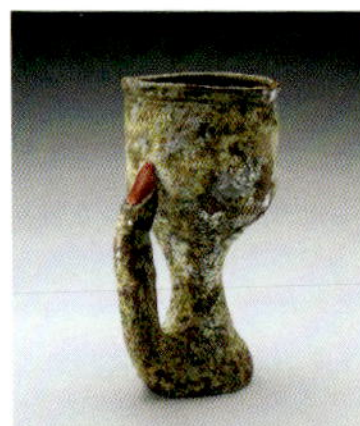

10 ROBERT ARNESON,
American, 1930–1992
Untitled, 1967
Ceramic
5 3/8 x 3 1/2 x 2 3/4 inches
(13.7 x 8.9 x 7 cm)
Museum purchase funded
by the Caroline Wiess Law
Accessions Endowment Fund
2010.2024

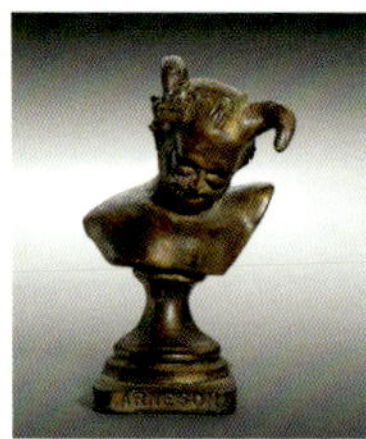

13 ROBERT ARNESON,
American, 1930–1992
Trophy Bust, c. 1971–1980
Ceramic
7 1/8 x 4 3/4 x 4 1/2 inches
(18.1 x 12.1 x 11.4 cm)
Museum purchase funded
by the Caroline Wiess Law
Accessions Endowment Fund
2010.2027

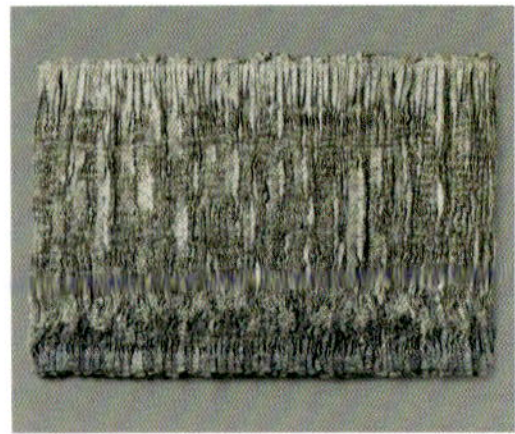

3 OLGA DE AMARAL,
Colombian, born 1932
Riscos y Tiempo, 1985
Fiber
47 x 75 inches
(119.4 x 190.5 cm)
Gift of Leatrice and Melvin Eagle
2010.2262

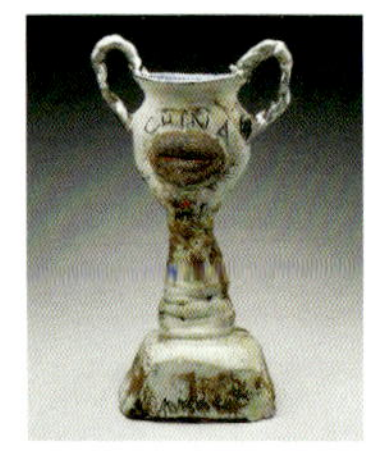

7 ROBERT ARNESON,
American, 1930–1992
China Trophy, 1964
Ceramic
18 5/8 x 11 1/4 x 7 3/4 inches
(47.3 x 28.6 x 19.7 cm)
Museum purchase funded
by the Caroline Wiess Law
Accessions Endowment Fund
2010.2021

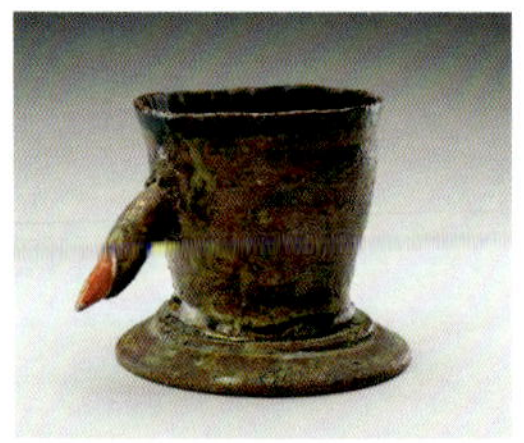

11 ROBERT ARNESON,
American, 1930–1992
Untitled, 1967
Ceramic
3 1/2 x 5 x 4 1/8 inches
(8.9 x 12.7 x 10.3 cm)
Museum purchase funded
by the Caroline Wiess Law
Accessions Endowment Fund
2010.2025

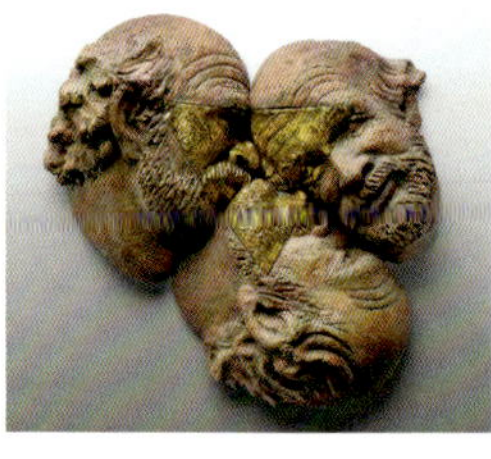

14 ROBERT ARNESON,
American, 1930–1992
Golden Triangle / Us Guys, 1991
Earthenware
20 x 23 x 5 inches
(50.8 x 53.3 x 12.7 cm)
Gift of Leatrice and Melvin Eagle
2011.970

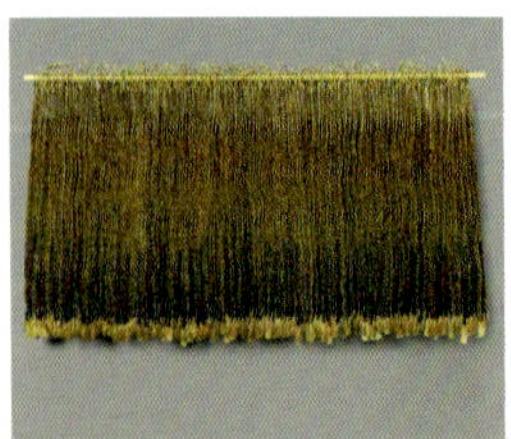

4 OLGA DE AMARAL,
Colombian, born 1932
Tierra y Oro #2, 1986
Fiber with gold leaf
40 x 70 1/4 x 1 1/2 inches
(101.6 x 178.4 x 3.8 cm)
Gift of Leatrice and Melvin Eagle
2012.520

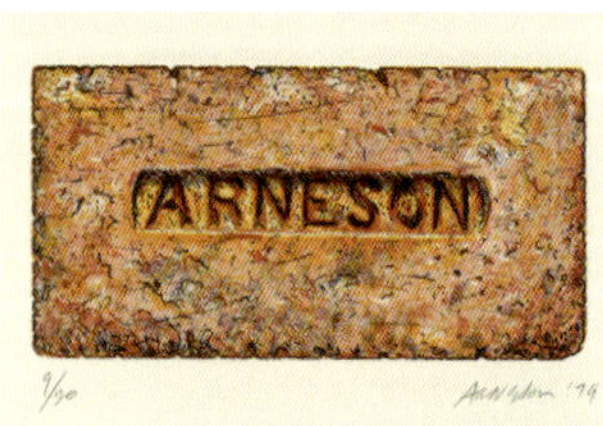

8 ROBERT ARNESON,
American, 1930–1992
Brick, 1979
Etching and aquatint in colors, ed. 9/20
10 1/2 x 15 inches
(26.7 x 38.1 cm)
Museum purchase funded
by the Caroline Wiess Law
Accessions Endowment Fund
2010.2022

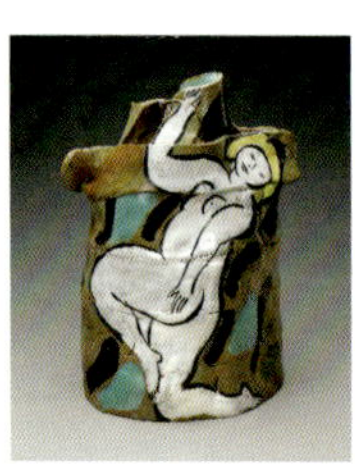

15 RUDY AUTIO,
American, 1926–2007
Lady with Green Band Vessel, 1981
Stoneware
26 1/2 x 22 x 14 1/2 inches
(67.3 x 55.9 x 36.8 cm)
Museum purchase funded
by the Caroline Wiess Law
Accessions Endowment Fund
2010.2028

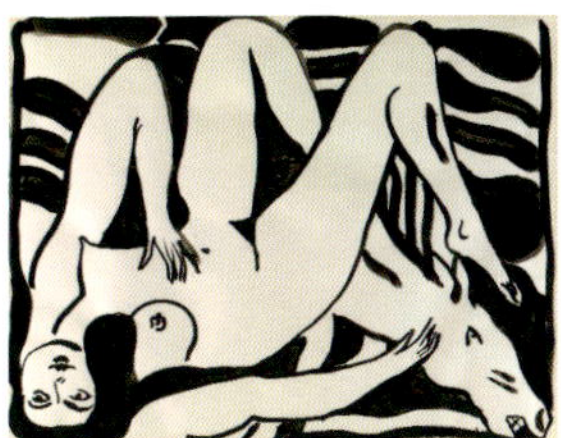

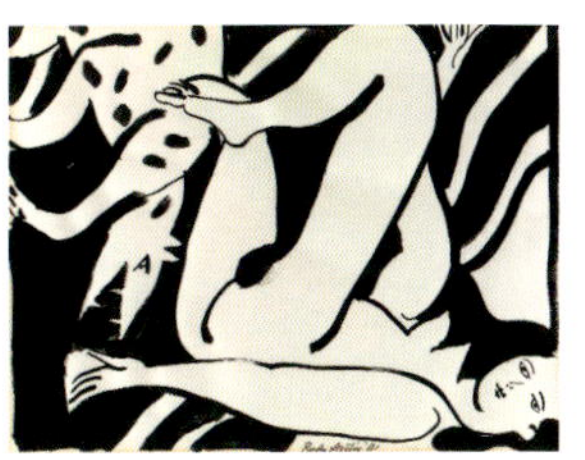

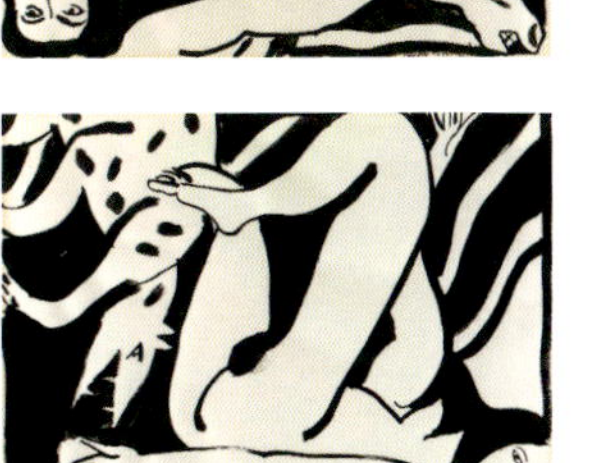

16 RUDY AUTIO,
American, 1926–2007
Untitled, 1981
Ink on paper
25 x 32 inches each
(63.5 x 81.3 cm)
Museum purchases funded
by the Caroline Wiess Law
Accessions Endowment Fund
2010.2029.1–.3

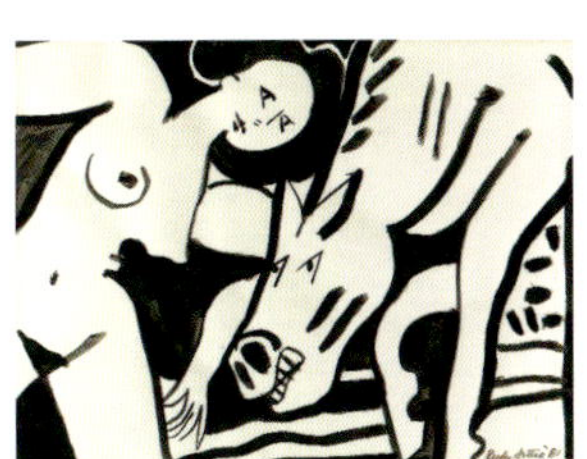

17 RUDY AUTIO,
American, 1926–2007
Horse, 1980
Crayon on paper
25 x 32 inches
(63.5 x 81.3 cm)
Museum purchase funded
by the Caroline Wiess Law
Accessions Endowment Fund
2010.2030

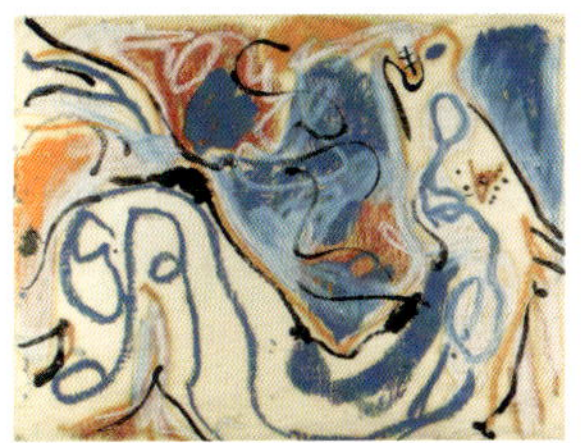

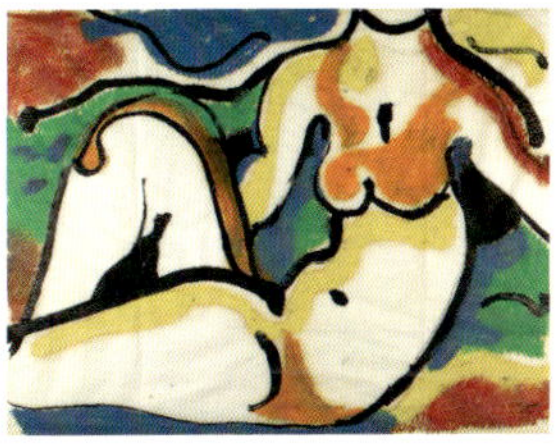

18 RUDY AUTIO,
American, 1926–2007
Torso, 1980
Oil crayon and tempera on paper
25 x 32 inches (63.5 x 81.3 cm)
Museum purchase funded
by the Caroline Wiess Law
Accessions Endowment Fund
2010.2259

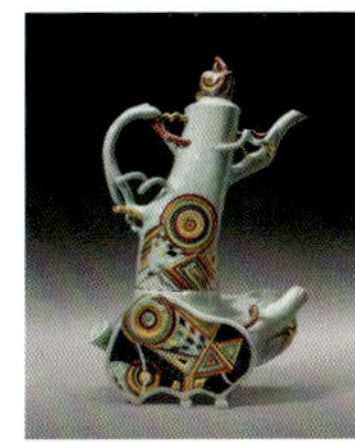

19 RALPH BACERRA,
American, 1938–2008
Teapot, 2000
Whiteware
18 1/4 x 11 1/2 x 5 1/2 inches
(46.4 x 29.2 x 14 cm)
Museum purchase funded
by the Caroline Wiess Law
Accessions Endowment Fund
2010.2031.A–.C

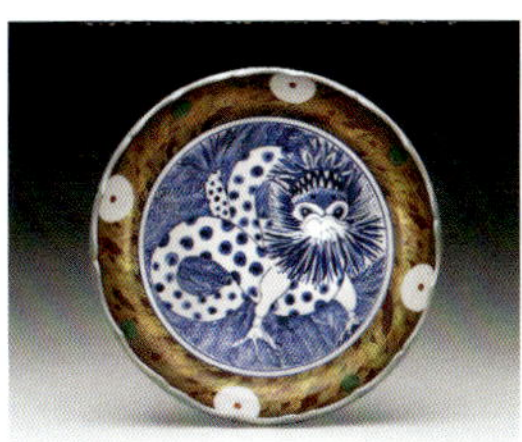

20 RALPH BACERRA,
American, 1938–2008
Dragon Bowl, 1979
Porcelain
3 3/4 x 16 1/8 inches diameter
(9.5 x 41 cm)
Museum purchase funded
by the Caroline Wiess Law
Accessions Endowment Fund
2010.2032

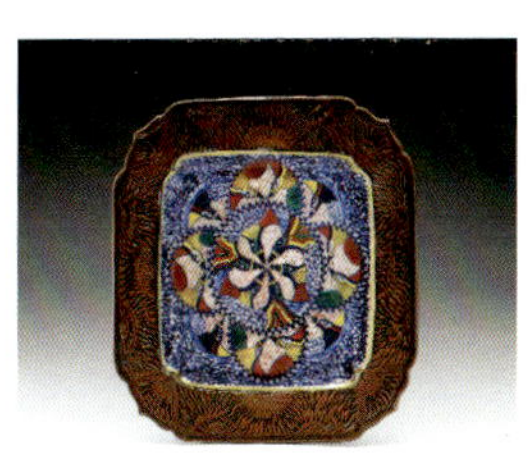

21 RALPH BACERRA,
American, 1938–2008
*Square Platter with Bird
Decoration*, 1979
Stoneware
2 1/8 x 12 1/2 x 12 1/2 inches
(5.2 x 31.8 x 31.8 cm)
Museum purchase funded
by the Caroline Wiess Law
Accessions Endowment Fund
2010.2033

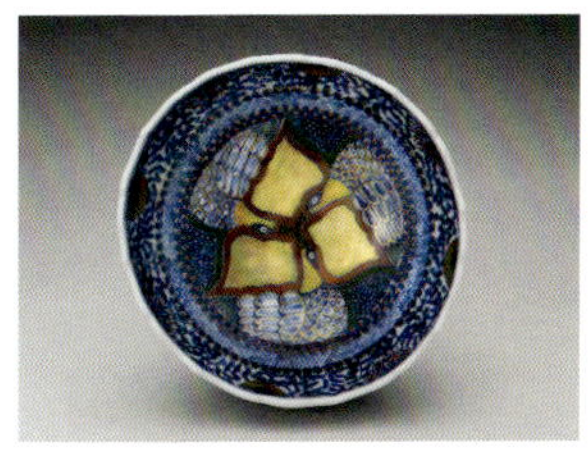

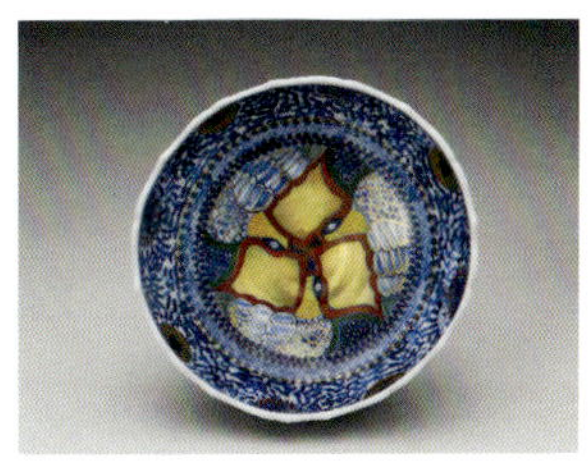

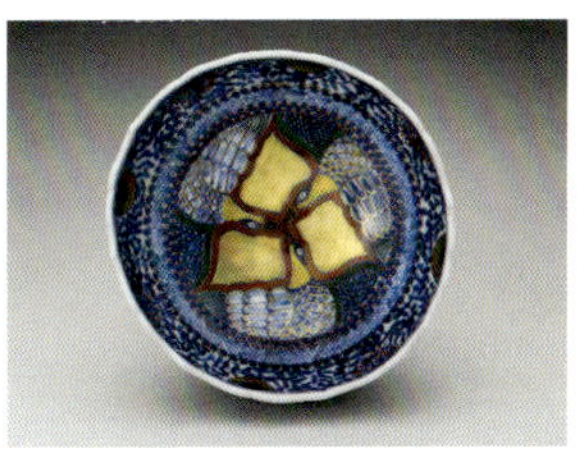

22 RALPH BACERRA,
American, 1938–2008
Three Bowls, 1979
Porcelain
3 7/8 x 10 inches diameter (9.8 x 25.4 cm)
3 1/2 x 8 1/2 inches diameter (8.7 x 21.6 cm)
3 1/8 x 7 inches diameter (7.8 x 17.8 cm)
Museum purchase funded
by the Caroline Wiess Law
Accessions Endowment Fund
2010.2034.1–.3

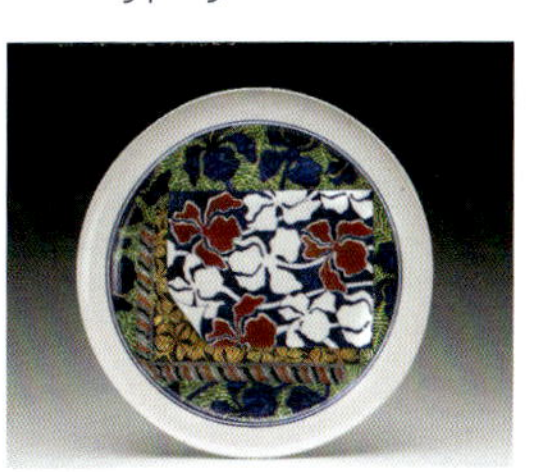

23 RALPH BACERRA,
American, 1938–2008
Iris Platter, 1980
Stoneware
2 3/4 x 21 3/4 inches diameter
(7 x 55.2 cm)
Gift of Leatrice and Melvin Eagle
2010.2261

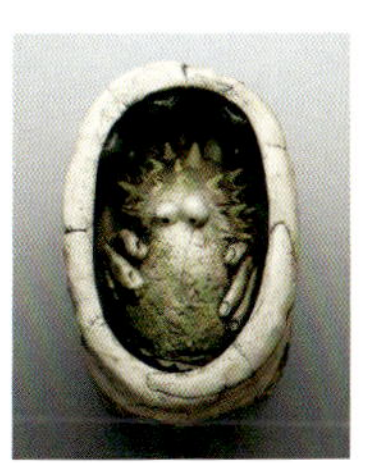

24 CLAYTON BAILEY,
American, born 1939
Monster ("Burping Bowl"), 1977
Ceramic
9 1/2 x 13 x 19 inches (24.1 x 33 x 48.3 cm)
Museum purchase funded
by the Caroline Wiess Law
Accessions Endowment Fund
2010.2035.A, .B

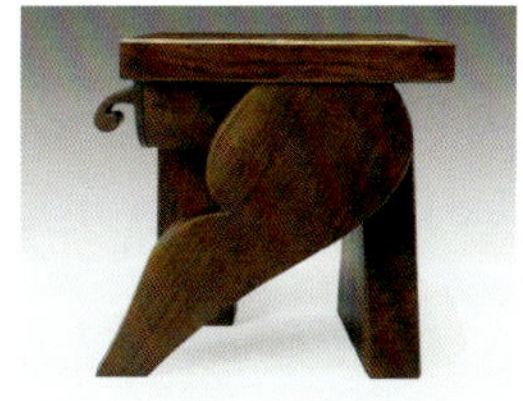

25 GARRY KNOX BENNETT,
American, born 1934
Side Table, 1997
Walnut
18 x 16 x 17 inches (45.7 x 40.6 x 43.2 cm)
Museum purchase funded
by the Caroline Wiess Law
Accessions Endowment Fund
2010.2036.A, .B

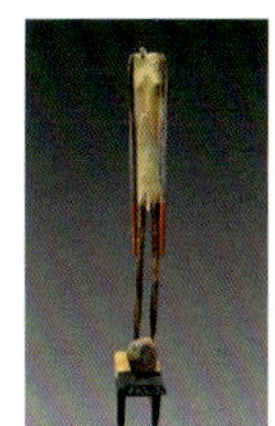

26 ROBERT BRADY,
American, born 1946
Darwin, 2003
Wood, paint, and stone
66 1/2 x 8 3/4 x 20 1/2 inches
(168.9 x 22.2 x 52.1 cm)
Museum purchase funded
by the Caroline Wiess Law
Accessions Endowment Fund
2010.2037.A, .B

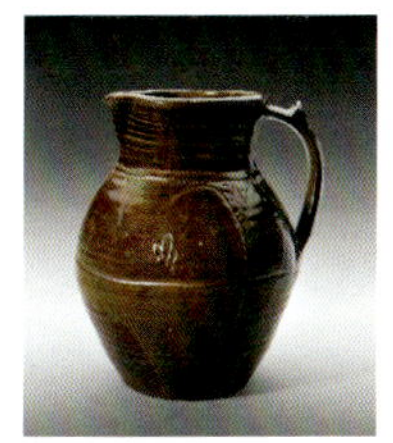

27 MICHAEL CARDEW,
British, 1901–1983
Pitcher, 1980
Earthenware
8 3/8 x 7 1/2 x 6 5/8 inches
(21.3 x 19.1 x 16.8 cm)
Museum purchase funded
by the Caroline Wiess Law
Accessions Endowment Fund
2010.2038

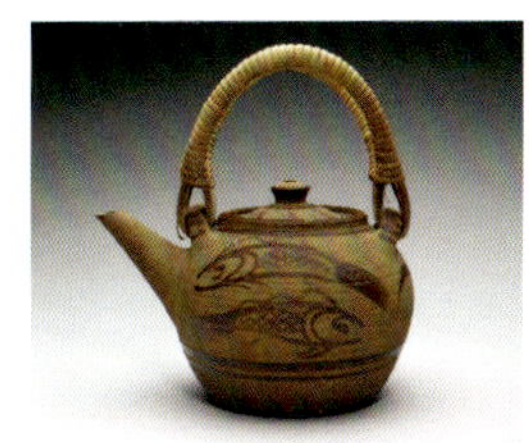

28 MICHAEL CARDEW,
British, 1901–1983
Teapot with Fish, 1950
Earthenware and cane
10 3/8 x 9 1/2 x 7 1/4 inches
(26.4 x 24.1 x 18.4 cm)
Museum purchase funded
by the Caroline Wiess Law
Accessions Endowment Fund
2010.2039.A, .B

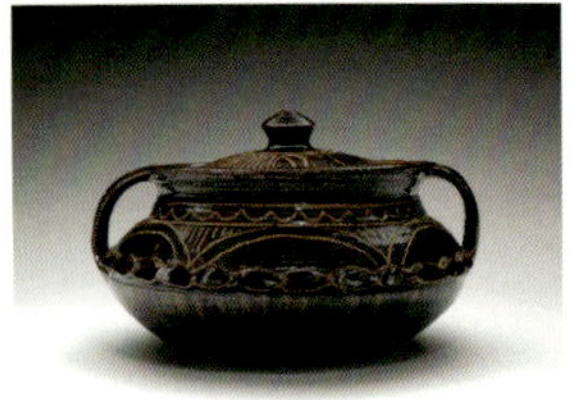

29 MICHAEL CARDEW,
British, 1901–1983
Gwari Casserole, 1973
Stoneware
7 x 11 5/8 x 11 1/8 inches
(17.8 x 29.5 x 28.3 cm)
Museum purchase funded
by the Caroline Wiess Law
Accessions Endowment Fund
2010.2040.A, .B

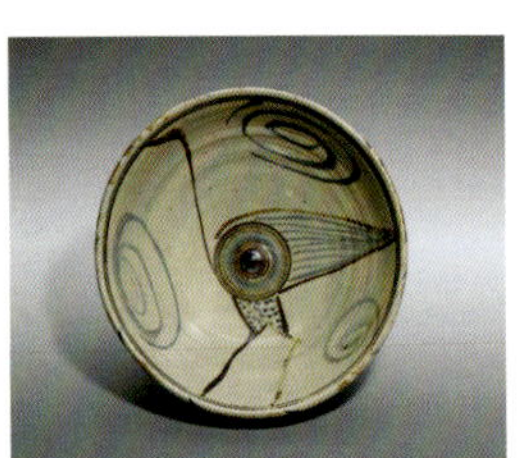

30 MICHAEL CARDEW,
British, 1901–1983
Bowl, 1973
Stoneware
5 3/4 x 11 3/4 inches diameter
(14.6 x 29.8 cm)
Museum purchase funded
by the Caroline Wiess Law
Accessions Endowment Fund
2010.2041

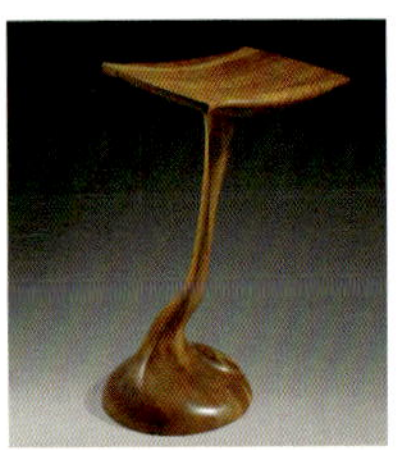

31 WENDELL CASTLE,
American, born 1932
Lectern, 1975
Cherry
39 x 22 x 19 inches
(99.1 x 55.9 x 48.3 cm)
Gift of Leatrice and Melvin Eagle
2008.900

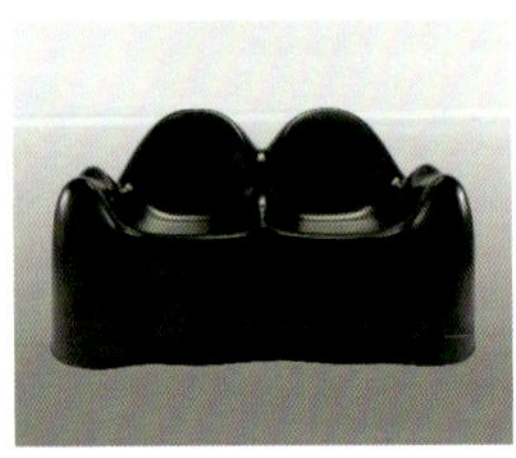

32 WENDELL CASTLE,
American, born 1932
Molar Couch, 1965
Fiberglass
25 1/2 x 54 x 33 inches (64.8 x 137.2 x 83.8 cm)
Museum purchase funded
by the Caroline Wiess Law
Accessions Endowment Fund
2010.2042

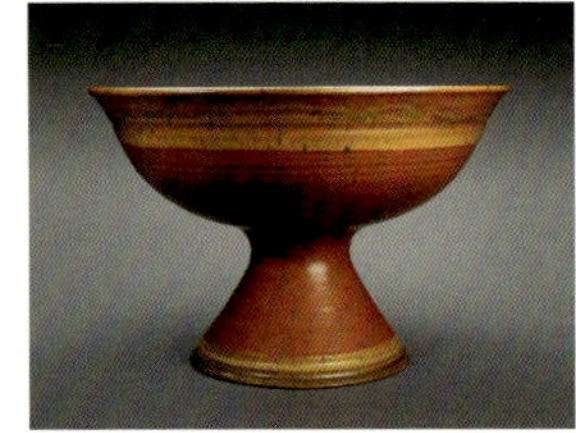

33 VAL MURAT CUSHING,
American, 1931–2013
Footed Bowl, 1979
Stoneware
11 1/4 x 18 1/4 inches diameter
(28.6 x 46.4 cm)
Museum purchase funded
by the Caroline Wiess Law
Accessions Endowment Fund
2010.2043

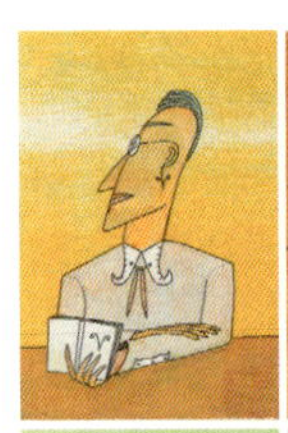
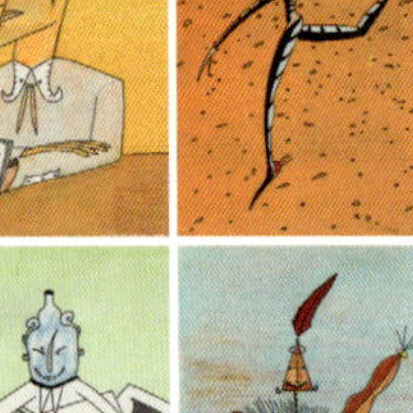
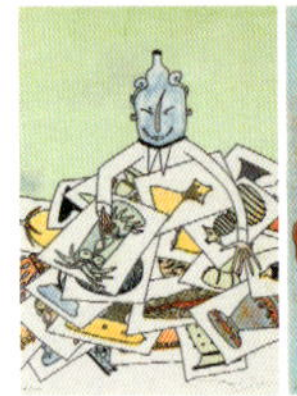
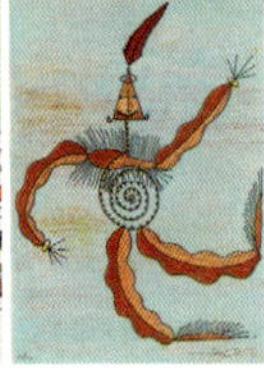

34 DAN DAILEY,
American, born 1947
Printed by Herbert A. Fox, American
Published by Fox Graphics
Merrimac Editions, American
Eye Poems, 1997
Series of 4 lithographs in colors,
ed. 14/100
14 1/4 x 10 3/4 inches each
(36.2 x 27.3 cm)
Museum purchase funded
by the Caroline Wiess Law
Accessions Endowment Fund
2010.2044.1–.4

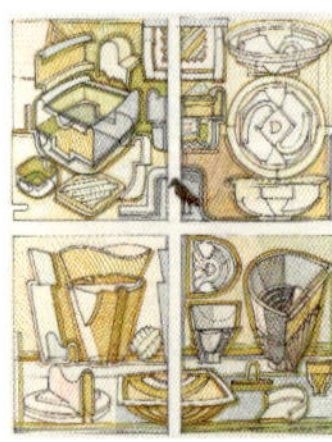

35 WILLIAM P. DALEY,
American, born 1925
Mine-d Pots, 1998
Ink on board
17 x 14 inches (43.2 x 35.6 cm)
Museum purchase funded
by the Caroline Wiess Law
Accessions Endowment Fund
2010.2045

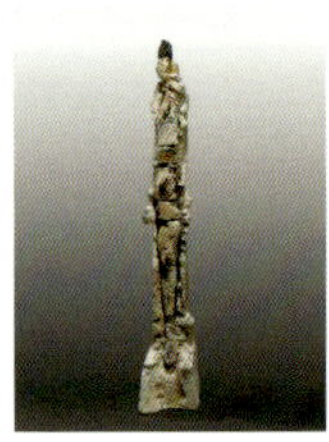

36 STEPHEN DE STAEBLER,
American, 1933–2011
Figure Column I, 2001
Stoneware
75 x 11 1/2 x 12 1/4 inches
(190.5 x 29.2 x 31.1 cm)
Museum purchase funded
by the Caroline Wiess Law
Accessions Endowment Fund
2010.2047

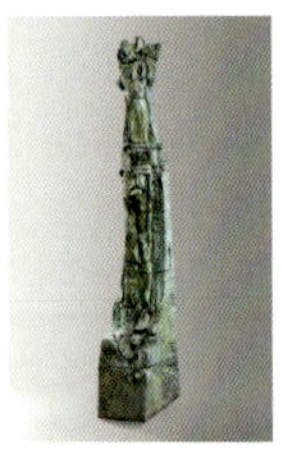

37 STEPHEN DE STAEBLER,
American, 1933–2011
*Standing Figure with
Segmented Knee*, 1983
Bronze
93 1/2 x 12 3/4 x 21 1/2 inches
(237.5 x 32.4 x 54.6 cm)
Museum purchase funded
by the Caroline Wiess Law
Accessions Endowment Fund
2010.2048

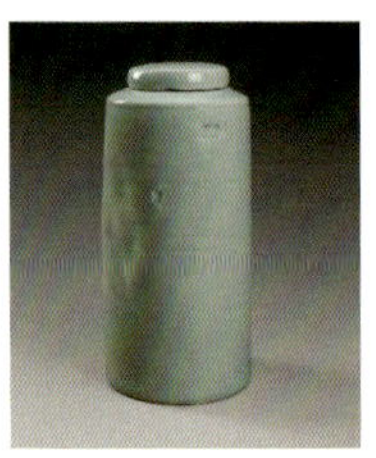

38 EDMUND DE WAAL,
British, born 1964
Lidded Jar, c. 2000
Porcelain
9 1/2 x 4 3/8 inches diameter
(24 x 11.1 cm)
Museum purchase funded
by the Caroline Wiess Law
Accessions Endowment Fund
2010.2046.A, .B

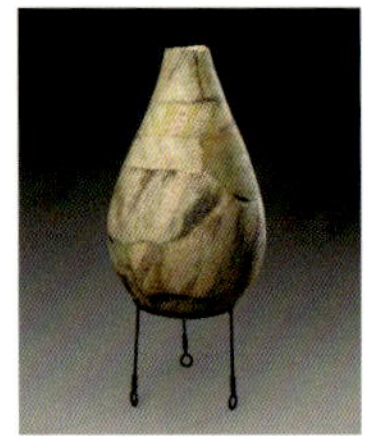

39 RICK DILLINGHAM,
American, 1952–1994
Vessel, 1976
Raku
12 x 7 inches diameter
(30.5 x 17.8 cm)
Museum purchase funded
by the Caroline Wiess Law
Accessions Endowment Fund
2010.2049.A, .B

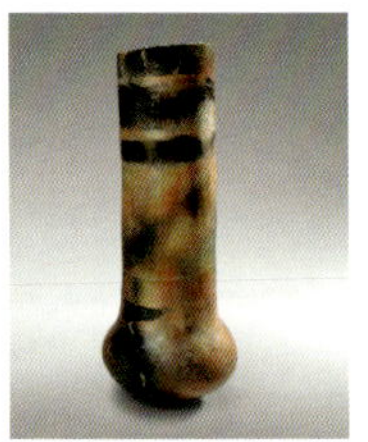

40 RICK DILLINGHAM,
American, 1952–1994
Vessel, 1976
Raku
17 7/8 x 7 1/4 inches diameter
(45.4 x 18.4 cm)
Museum purchase funded
by the Caroline Wiess Law
Accessions Endowment Fund
2010.2050

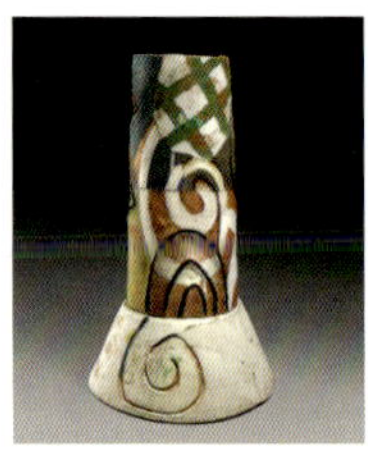

41 RICK DILLINGHAM,
American, 1952–1994
Vessel, 1985
Raku
23 x 13 1/2 x 13 1/4 inches
(58.4 x 34.3 x 33.7 cm)
Museum purchase funded
by the Caroline Wiess Law
Accessions Endowment Fund
2010.2051.A, .B

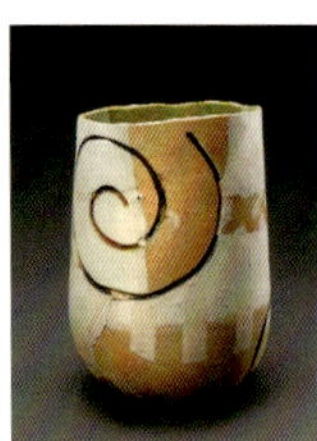

42 RICK DILLINGHAM,
American, 1952–1994
Vessel, 1984
Earthenware and silver leaf
14 3/8 x 10 inches diameter
(36.5 x 25.4 cm)
Museum purchase funded
by the Caroline Wiess Law
Accessions Endowment Fund
2010.2052

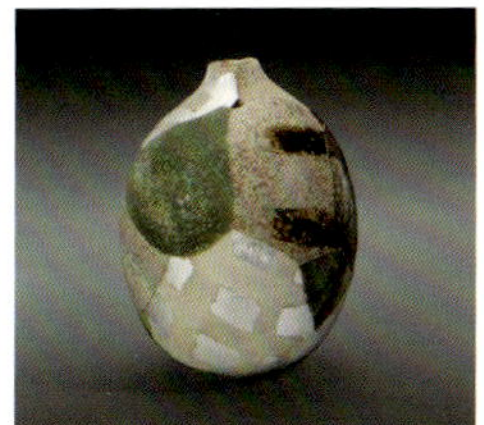

43 RICK DILLINGHAM,
American, 1952–1994
Vessel, 1985
Raku
6 1/4 x 5 1/8 inches diameter
(15.9 x 13 cm)
Museum purchase funded
by the Caroline Wiess Law
Accessions Endowment Fund
2010.2053

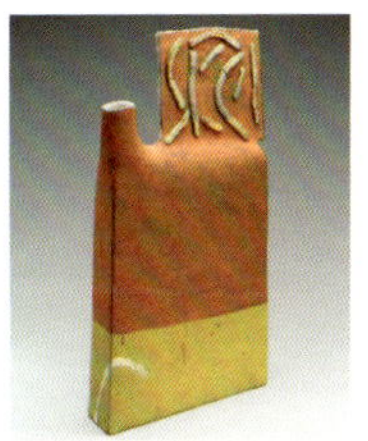

44 RICK DILLINGHAM,
American, 1952–1994
Gas Can, 1982
Earthenware and gold leaf
22 x 11 7/8 x 2 3/4 inches
(55.9 x 30.2 x 7 cm)
Museum purchase funded
by the Caroline Wiess Law
Accessions Endowment Fund
2010.2054

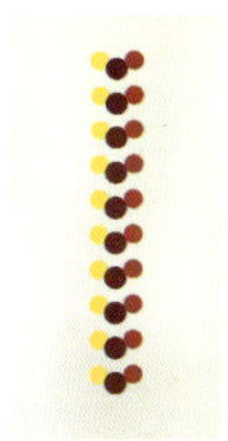

45 THOMAS DOWNING,
American, 1928–1985
Do, Do, Do, 1976
Acrylic on canvas
95 1/2 x 49 3/4 inches
(242.6 x 126.4 cm)
Museum purchase funded
by the Caroline Wiess Law
Accessions Endowment Fund
2010.2055

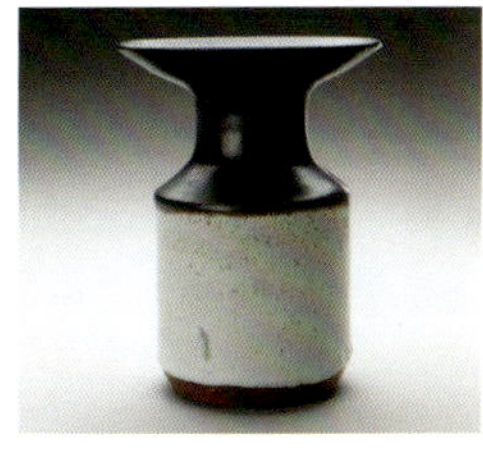

46 RUTH DUCKWORTH,
American, born Germany, 1919–2009
Vessel, c. 1980
Stoneware
4 3/8 x 3 3/8 inches diameter
(11.1 x 8.4 cm)
Museum purchase funded
by the Caroline Wiess Law
Accessions Endowment Fund
2010.2056

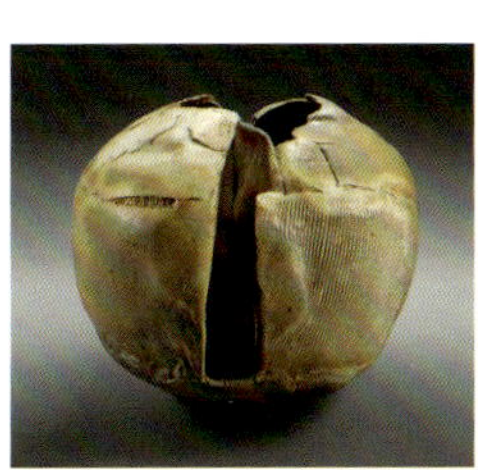

47 RUTH DUCKWORTH,
American, born Germany, 1919–2009
Vessel: Split #R81-735801, c. 1981
Stoneware
18 1/2 x 19 1/2 x 21 inches
(47 x 49.5 x 53.3 cm)
Museum purchase funded
by the Caroline Wiess Law
Accessions Endowment Fund
2010.2057

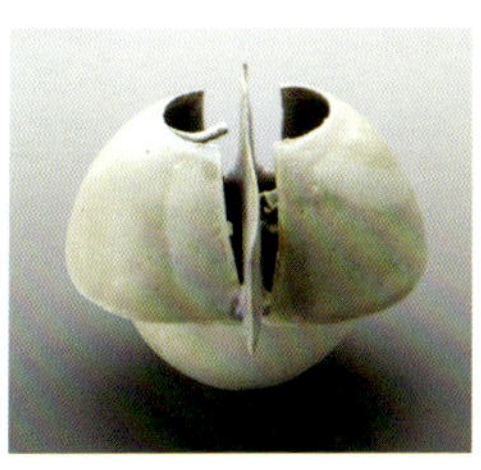

48 RUTH DUCKWORTH,
American, born Germany, 1919–2009
Organic Form—734801, c. 1980
Porcelain
4 1/4 x 5 7/8 x 5 1/2 inches
(10.8 x 14.9 x 14 cm)
Museum purchase funded
by the Caroline Wiess Law
Accessions Endowment Fund
2010.2058

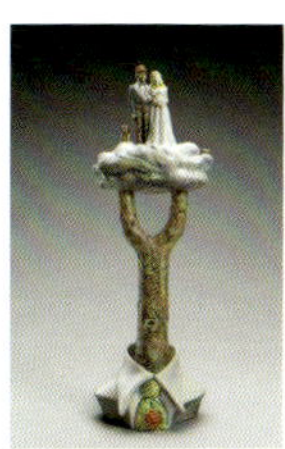

49 JACK EARL,
American, born 1934
Bird in the Dream Tree Man Myth, 1992
Porcelain with electronics
24 1/4 x 8 3/4 x 6 1/4 inches
(61.6 x 22.2 x 15.9 cm)
Museum purchase funded
by the Caroline Wiess Law
Accessions Endowment Fund
2010.2059

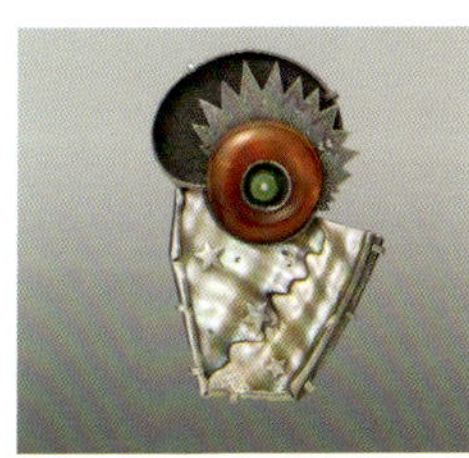

50 ROBERT EBENDORF,
American, born 1938
Brooch, 1994
Silver, shell, and colored stones
2 1/4 x 1 5/8 x 5/8 inches
(5.7 x 4.1 x 1.6 cm)
Museum purchase funded
by the Caroline Wiess Law
Accessions Endowment Fund
2010.2060

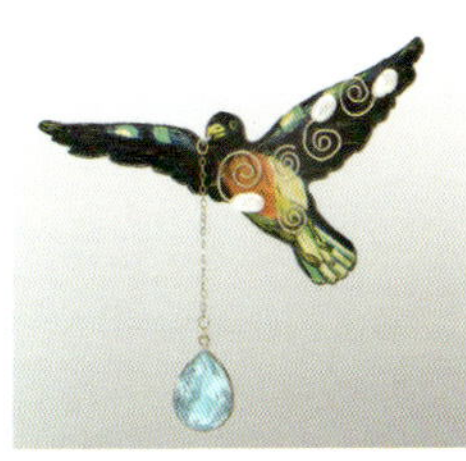

51 ROBERT EBENDORF,
American, born 1938
Bird Brooch, 1994
Sterling silver, 14k gold, pearls,
glass, and tin
2 3/4 x 3 1/4 x 3/8 inches
(7 x 8.3 x 1 cm)
Museum purchase funded
by the Caroline Wiess Law
Accessions Endowment Fund
2010.2061

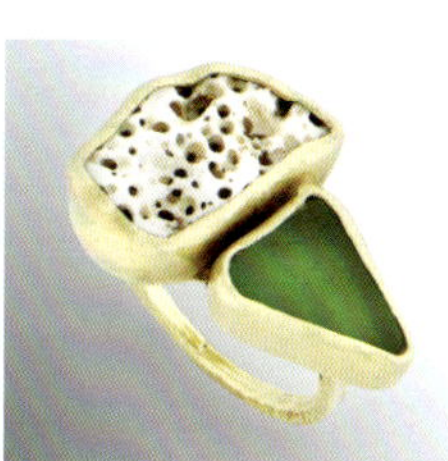

52 ROBERT EBENDORF,
American, born 1938
Ring, 1987
18k yellow gold, glass, and coral
3/4 x 1 1/8 x 1 inches
(1.9 x 2.9 x 2.5 cm)
Museum purchase funded
by the Caroline Wiess Law
Accessions Endowment Fund
2010.2062.1

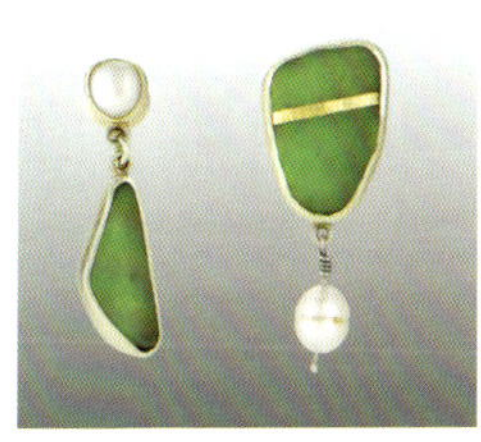

53 ROBERT EBENDORF,
American, born 1938
Pair of Earrings, 1987
14k yellow gold, 18k yellow gold,
glass, and pearl
(.A): 1 3/8 x 5/8 x 5/8 inches (3.5 x 1.6 x 1.6 cm)
(.B): 1 1/4 x 3/4 x 1/2 inches (3.2 x 1.9 x 1.3 cm)
Museum purchase funded by the Caroline
Wiess Law Accessions Endowment Fund
2010.2062.2.A, .B

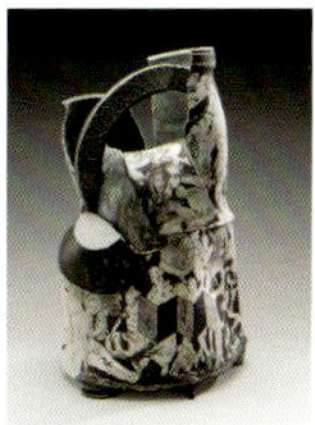

54 EDWARD S. EBERLE,
American, born 1944
Fire Hat and Full Moon, 2002
Porcelain
22 3/8 x 15 x 13 1/2 inches
(56.8 x 38.1 x 34.3 cm)
Museum purchase funded
by the Caroline Wiess Law
Accessions Endowment Fund
2010.2063

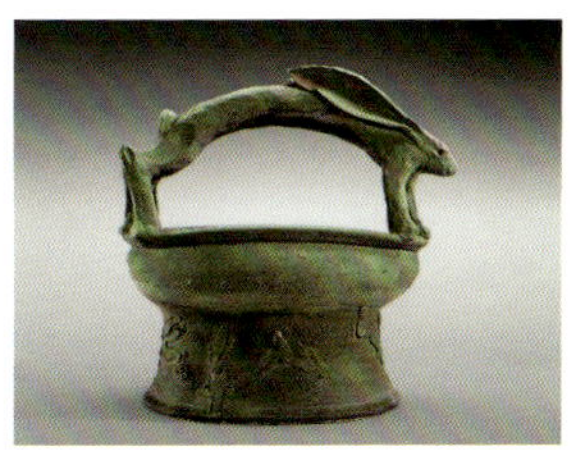

55 KEN FERGUSON,
American, 1928–2004
Rabbit Basket, 1992
Stoneware
15 1/2 x 17 1/8 x 12 5/8 inches
(39.4 x 43.5 x 32.1 cm)
Museum purchase funded
by the Caroline Wiess Law
Accessions Endowment Fund
2010.2064

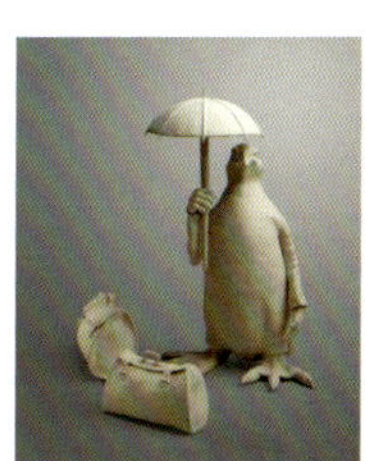

56 FRANK FLEMING,
American, born 1940
Penguin at the Bus Stop, 1979
Porcelain
Penguin
(A): 13 1/4 x 10 3/4 x 10 1/2 inches
(33.7 x 27.3 x 26.7 cm)
Bag 1
(B): 3 1/4 x 6 x 2 1/2 inches
(8.3 x 15.2 x 6.4 cm)
Bag 2
(C): 2 3/4 x 4 1/2 x 1 3/4 inches
(7 x 11.4 x 4.4 cm)
Museum purchase funded
by the Caroline Wiess Law
Accessions Endowment Fund
2010.2065.A–.C

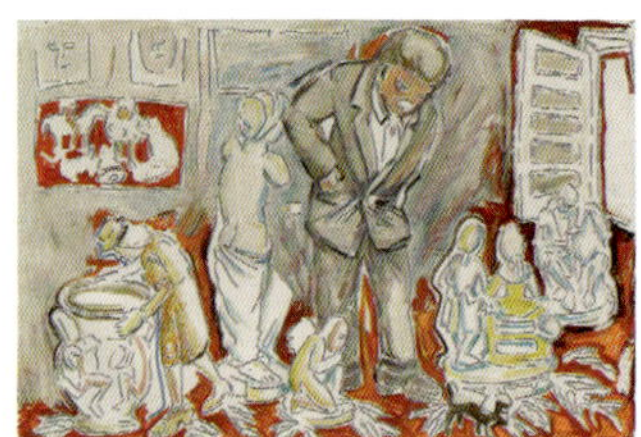

57 VIOLA FREY,
American, 1933–2004
Women Underneath Studio, 1982
Oil on paper
40 x 60 inches
(101.6 x 152.4 cm)
Museum purchase funded
by the Caroline Wiess Law
Accessions Endowment Fund
2010.2066

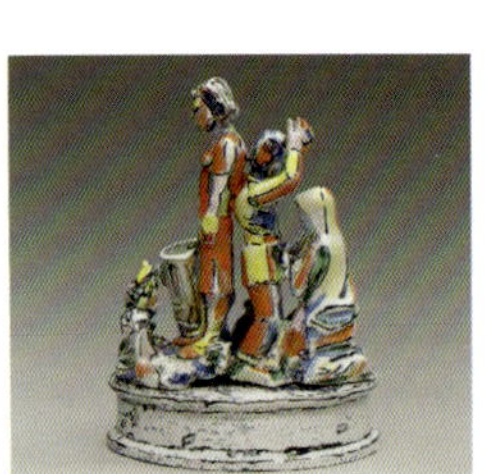

58 VIOLA FREY,
American, 1933–2004
Western Civilization (Clown Care), 1997
Ceramic
31 1/4 x 24 x 14 1/2 inches
(79.4 x 61 x 36.8 cm)
Museum purchase funded
by the Caroline Wiess Law
Accessions Endowment Fund
2010.2067.A, .B

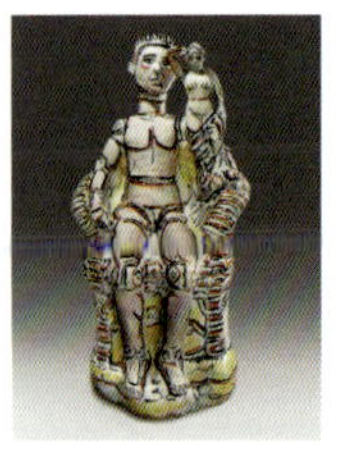

59 VIOLA FREY,
American, 1933–2004
Seated Manikin Man and Venus, 1975
Ceramic
32 1/2 x 16 x 14 inches
(82.6 x 40.6 x 35.6 cm)
Museum purchase funded
by the Caroline Wiess Law
Accessions Endowment Fund
2010.2068

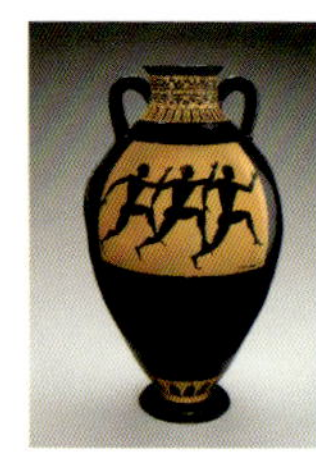

60 MICHAEL FRIMKESS,
American, born 1937
Decorated by Magdalena Frimkess,
American, born Venezuela, 1929
Neck and Neck, 1977
Stoneware with china paint
24 7/8 x 15 1/8 inches diameter
(63.2 x 38.4 cm)
Museum purchase funded by the Caroline
Wiess Law Accessions Endowment Fund
2010.2069

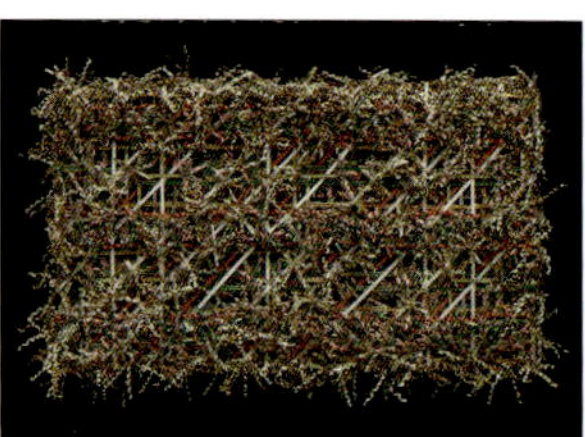

61 JOHN GARRETT,
American, born 1950
Desert Garden Gate, 1985
Plastic and wire mesh
45 x 70 1/2 x 10 inches
(114.3 x 179.1 x 25.4 cm)
Museum purchase funded
by the Caroline Wiess Law
Accessions Endowment Fund
2010.2070

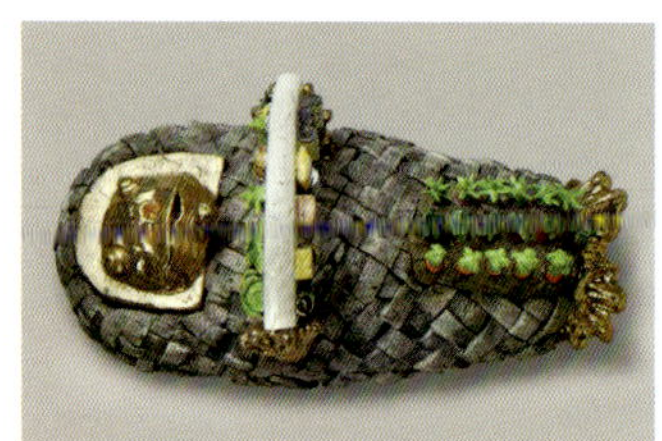

62 DAVID GILHOOLY,
American, 1943–2013
The Miracle of Production, 1973
Earthenware
13 5/8 x 13 5/8 x 30 inches
(34.6 x 34.6 x 76.2 cm)
Museum purchase funded
by the Caroline Wiess Law
Accessions Endowment Fund
2010.2071

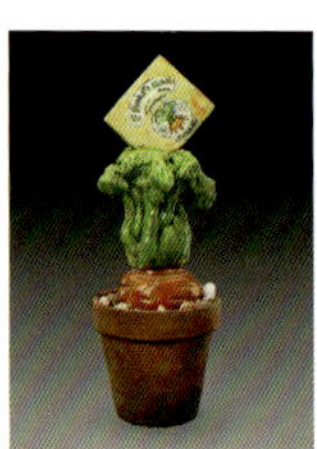

63 DAVID GILHOOLY,
American, 1943–2013
The Miracle of Production: Frozen Carrots,
1972
Earthenware
17 1/4 x 6 3/8 inches diameter
(43.8 x 16.2 cm)
Museum purchase funded by the Caroline
Wiess Law Accessions Endowment Fund
2010.2072

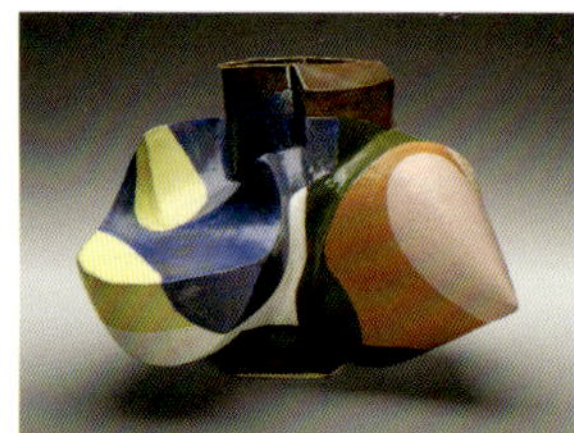

64 JOHN PATRICK GILL,
American, born 1949
Vase, 1993
Ceramic
14 x 18 1/2 x 14 inches
(35.6 x 47 x 35.6 cm)
Museum purchase funded
by the Caroline Wiess Law
Accessions Endowment Fund
2010.2073

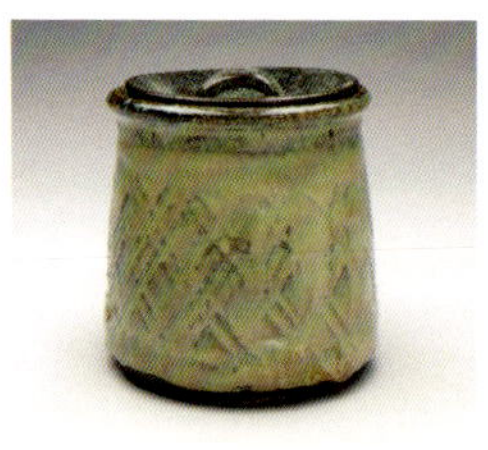

65 HAMADA SHŌJI,
Japanese, 1894–1978
Tea Caddy, 1945
Stoneware
5 1/4 x 5 1/4 inches diameter
(13.3 x 13.2 cm)
Museum purchase funded
by the Caroline Wiess Law
Accessions Endowment Fund
2010.2074.A, .B

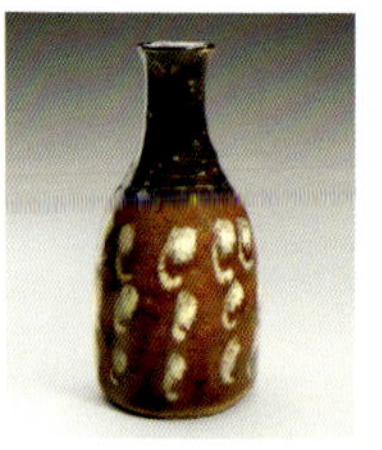

66 HAMADA SHŌJI,
Japanese, 1894–1978
Bottle, 1945
Stoneware
5 1/8 x 2 5/8 inches diameter
(13 x 6.7 cm)
Museum purchase funded
by the Caroline Wiess Law
Accessions Endowment Fund
2010.2075

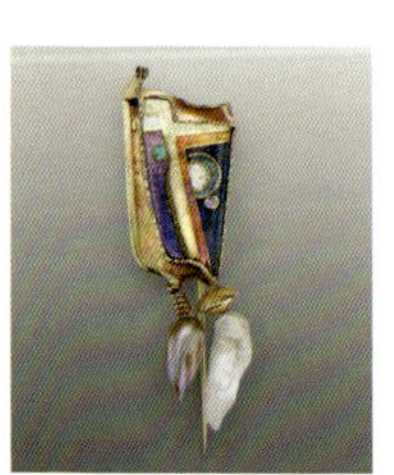

67 WILLIAM HARPER,
American, born 1944
September Sketch #5, 1985
Gold, enamel, fine silver, and pearl
2 1/2 x 3/4 x 1/2 inches
(6.4 x 1.9 x 1.3 cm)
Museum purchase funded by the Caroline
Wiess Law Accessions Endowment Fund
2010.2076

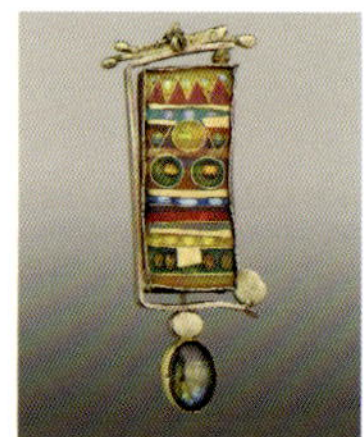

68 WILLIAM HARPER,
American, born 1944
Kilim III, 1995
Gold, enamel, fine silver and gold, 14k and
22k gold, sterling silver, and labradorite
3 1/4 x 1 1/4 x 1/2 inches
(8.3 x 3.2 x 1.3 cm)
Museum purchase funded
by the Caroline Wiess Law
Accessions Endowment Fund
2010.2077

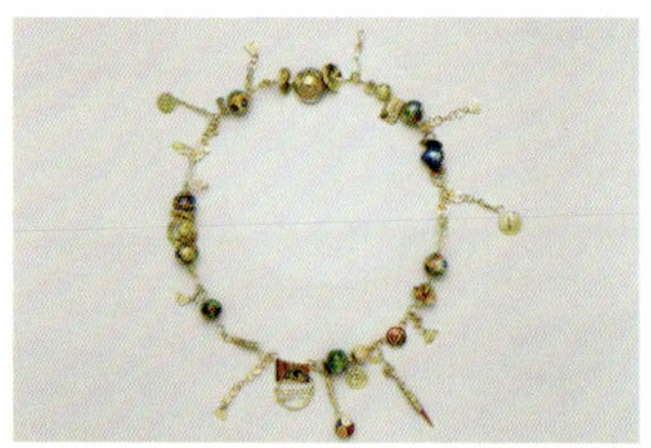

69 WILLIAM HARPER,
American, born 1944
The Magician's Chain, 2003
Gold, enamel, fine silver, 14k, 18k, and
24k gold, and carnelian
15 x 10 x 1 inches (38.1 x 25.4 x 2.5 cm)
Museum purchase funded
by the Caroline Wiess Law
Accessions Endowment Fund
2010.2078

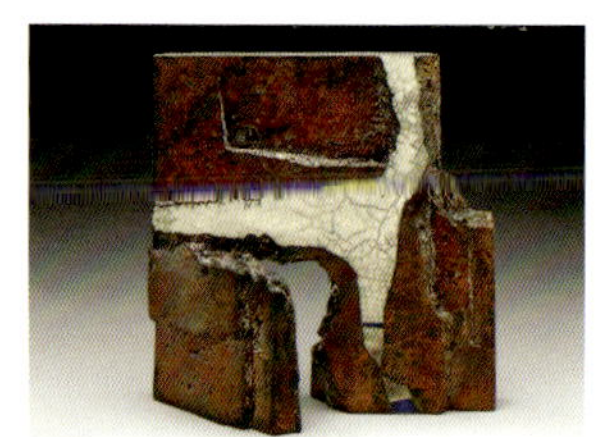

70 WAYNE HIGBY,
American, born 1943
Entry Rock, 1997
Earthenware
8 x 8 x 3 inches
(20.3 x 20.3 x 7.6 cm)
Museum purchase funded
by the Caroline Wiess Law
Accessions Endowment Fund
2010.2079

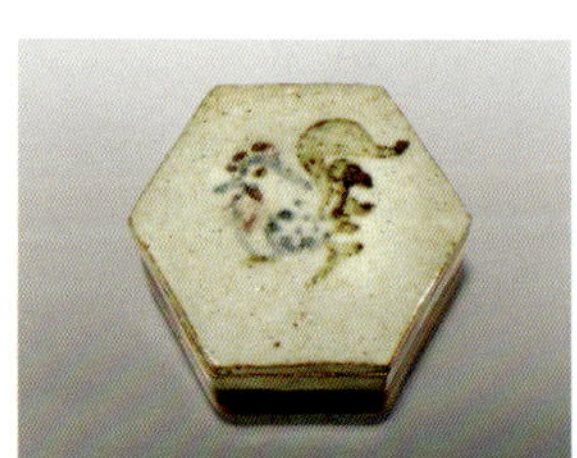

71 KAWAI KANJIRŌ,
Japanese, 1890–1966
Box, c. 1931
Stoneware
2 1/8 x 2 5/8 x 3 inches
(5.4 x 6.7 x 7.5 cm)
Museum purchase funded
by the Caroline Wiess Law
Accessions Endowment Fund
2010.2080.A–.C

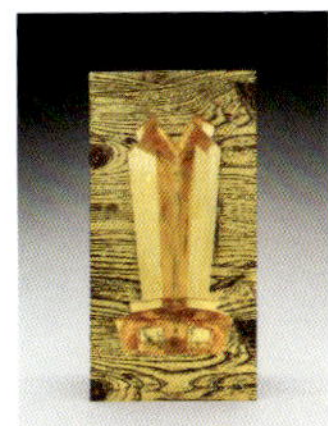

72 HOWARD KOTTLER,
American, 1930–1989
Royal Wood Vase, 1987
Earthenware
12 3/8 x 6 3/8 x 3 1/2 inches
(31.5 x 16.2 x 8.9 cm)
Museum purchase funded
by the Caroline Wiess Law
Accessions Endowment Fund
2010.2081

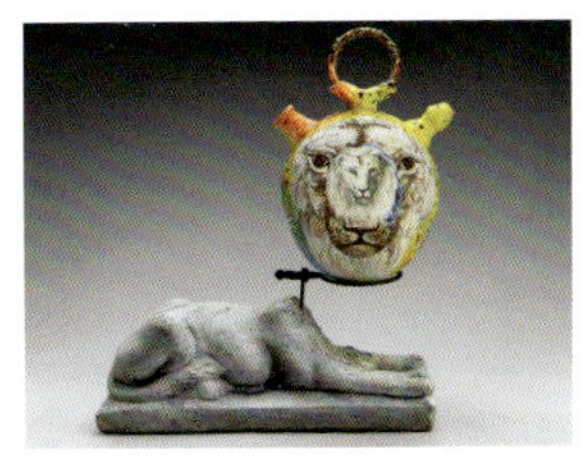

75 MICHAEL LUCERO,
American, born 1953
Lion, from the series *Reclamation*, 1997
White earthenware and found object
29 x 23 x 13 inches
(73.7 x 58.4 x 33 cm)
Museum purchase funded
by the Caroline Wiess Law
Accessions Endowment Fund
2010.2084.A–.C

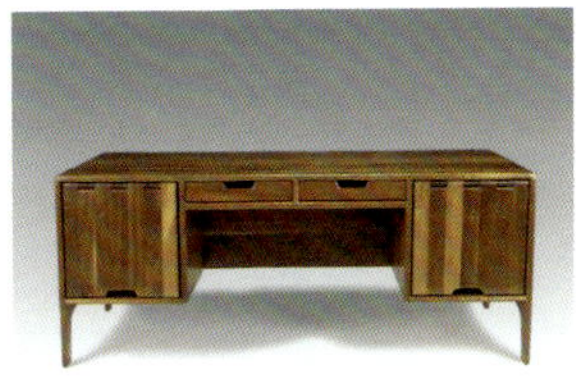

79 SAM MALOOF,
American, 1916–2009
Desk, 1975
Walnut
29 1/2 x 72 x 36 inches
(74.9 x 182.9 x 91.4 cm)
Museum purchase funded
by the Caroline Wiess Law
Accessions Endowment Fund
2010.2087.A–.K

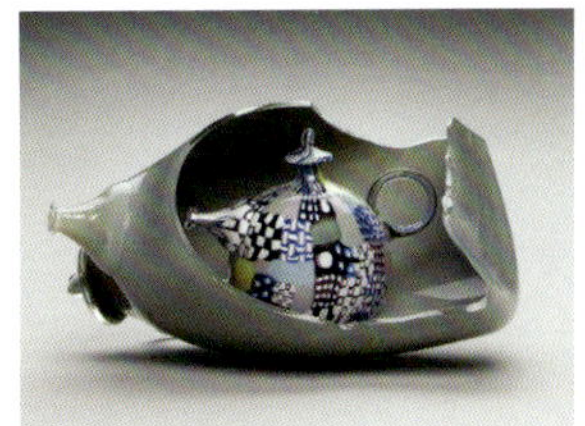

83 RICHARD MARQUIS,
American, born 1945
Broken Grey #1, 1979
Glass
5 3/8 x 10 1/4 x 7 inches
(13.7 x 26 x 17.8 cm)
Gift of Leatrice and Melvin Eagle
2011.972

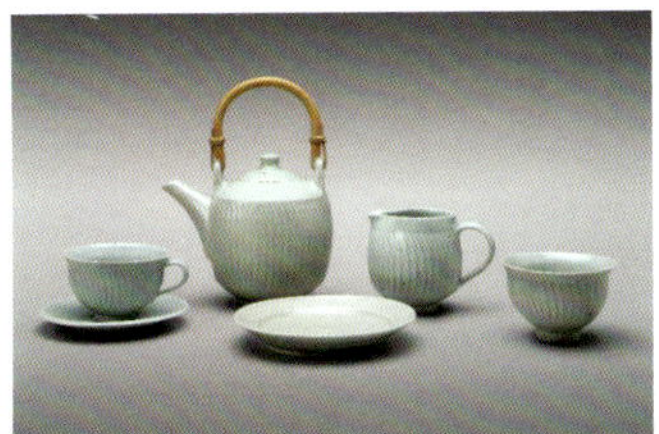

73 DAVID LEACH,
British, 1911–2005
Tea Service, 1980
Porcelain
Dimensions vary
Museum purchase funded
by the Caroline Wiess Law
Accessions Endowment Fund
2010.2082.1–.21

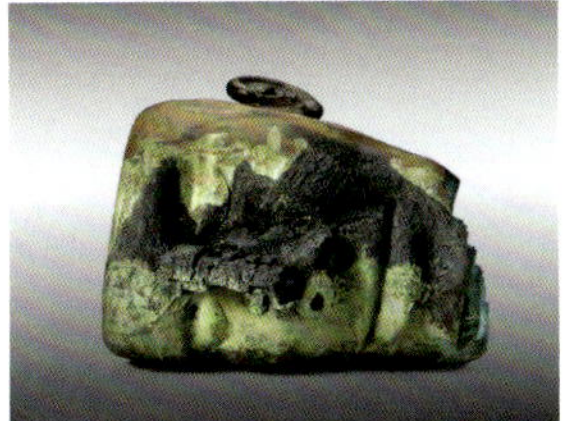

76 MICHAEL LUCERO,
American, born 1953
Night Train—Dreamer, 1986
Bronze
20 3/4 x 25 x 23 1/2 inches
(52.7 x 63.5 x 59.7 cm)
Museum purchase funded
by the Caroline Wiess Law
Accessions Endowment Fund
2010.2085

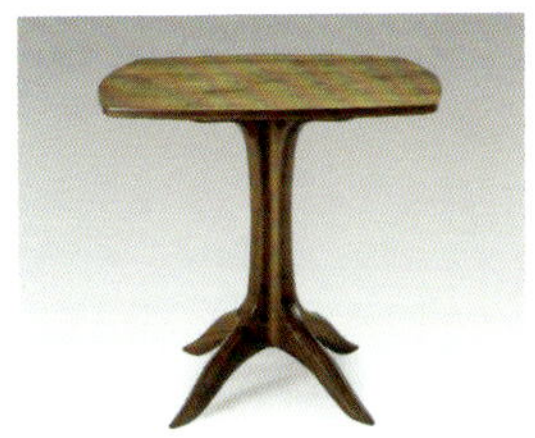

80 SAM MALOOF,
American, 1916–2009
Side Table, 2007
Walnut
24 x 24 x 24 inches
(61 x 61 x 61 cm)
Museum purchase funded
by the Caroline Wiess Law
Accessions Endowment Fund
2010.2088

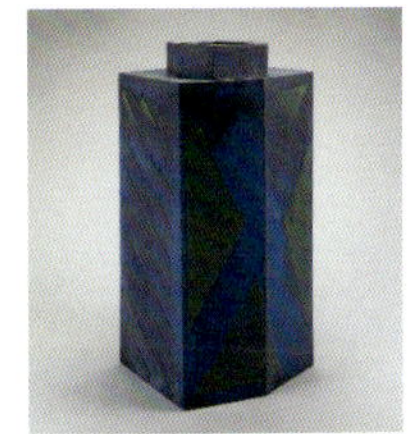

84 JOHN MASON,
American, born 1927
Torque Vessel, 1986
Stoneware
44 x 21 x 22 inches
(111.8 x 53.3 x 55.9 cm)
Gift of Leatrice and Melvin Eagle
2007.1785

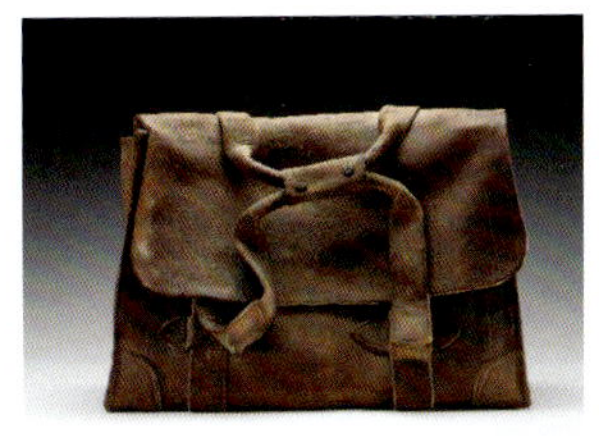

74 MARILYN ANNE LEVINE,
American, born Canada, 1935–2005
Flea Market Bag, 1971
Stoneware and string
12 3/4 x 17 1/4 x 9 inches
(32.4 x 43.8 x 22.9 cm)
Museum purchase funded
by the Caroline Wiess Law
Accessions Endowment Fund
2010.2083

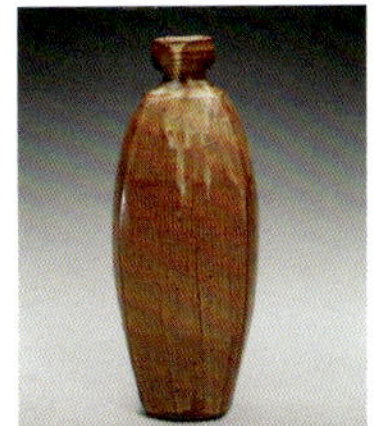

77 WARREN MACKENZIE,
American, born 1924
Shino Vessel, 1995
Stoneware
16 x 6 3/4 x 6 3/4 inches
(40.6 x 17.1 x 17.1 cm)
Museum purchase funded
by the Caroline Wiess Law
Accessions Endowment Fund
2010.2086

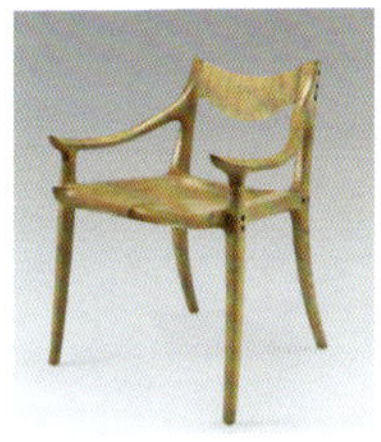

81 SAM MALOOF,
American, 1916–2009
Low-Back Chair, 1998
Curly maple
30 x 22 1/4 x 23 inches
(76.2 x 56.5 x 58.4 cm)
Museum purchase funded
by the Caroline Wiess Law
Accessions Endowment Fund
2010.2089

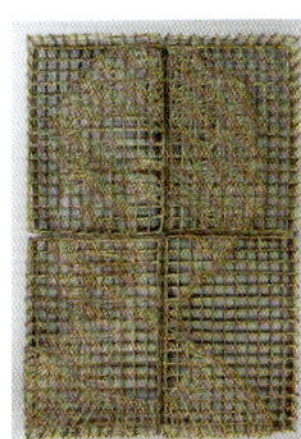

85 JOHN MCQUEEN,
American, born 1943
Self-Portrait, 1998
Willow and waxed string
41 1/2 x 29 1/4 x 7 1/2 inches
(105.4 x 74.3 x 19.1 cm)
Museum purchase funded
by the Caroline Wiess Law
Accessions Endowment Fund
2010.2091.A–.D

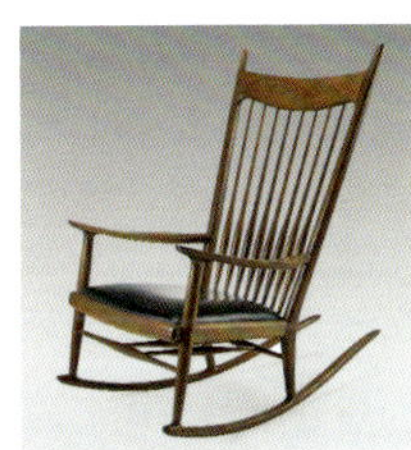

78 SAM MALOOF,
American, 1916–2009
Upholstered by Ballard
Upholstering, American
Rocking Chair, 1968
Walnut and leather
45 x 27 1/4 x 42 3/8 inches
(114.3 x 69.2 x 107.6 cm)
Gift of Leatrice and Melvin Eagle
2009.1704

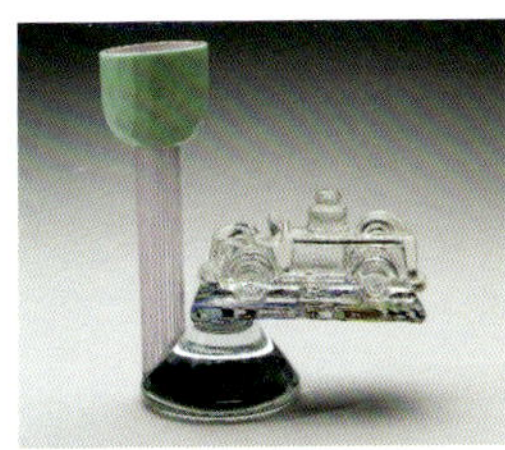

82 RICHARD MARQUIS,
American, born 1945
Fire Engine Cup, 1980
Glass
7 x 6 3/4 x 3 3/8 inches
(17.8 x 17 x 8.6 cm)
Museum purchase funded
by the Caroline Wiess Law
Accessions Endowment Fund
2010.2090.A, .B

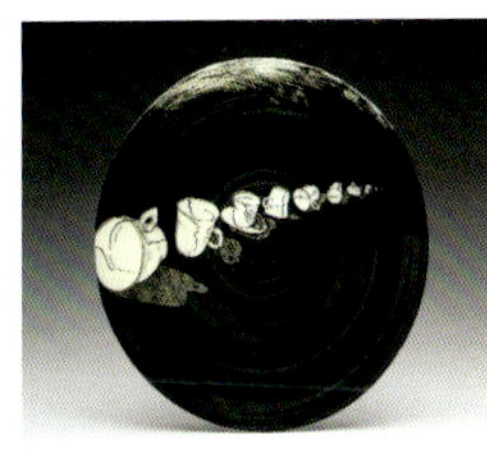

86 MINEO MIZUNO,
American, born Japan, 1944
Charger, 1982
Porcelain
2 1/4 x 21 1/8 inches diameter
(5.7 x 53.7 cm)
Museum purchase funded
by the Caroline Wiess Law
Accessions Endowment Fund
2010.2092

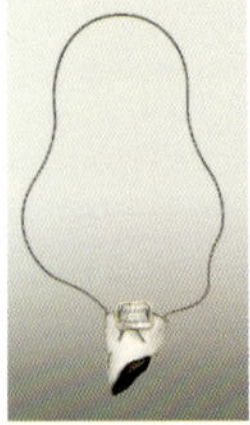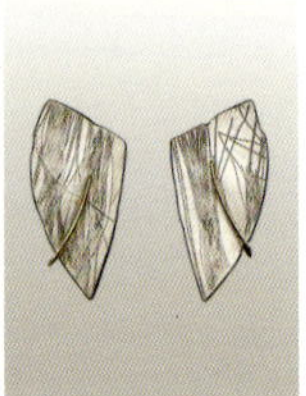

87 ELEANOR H. MOTY,
American, born 1945
*Night Cloud Brooch /
Pendant and Earrings*, 1993
Sterling silver, 18k gold, tourmalinated
quartz, and black micarta
Brooch: 2 7/8 x 2 x 1/2 inches
(7.3 x 5.1 x 1.3 cm)
Earrings: 1 5/8 x 3/4 x 3/8 inches each
(4.1 x 1.9 x 0.8 cm)
Museum purchases funded
by the Caroline Wiess Law
Accessions Endowment Fund
2010.2093.1.A, .B–.2,A, .B

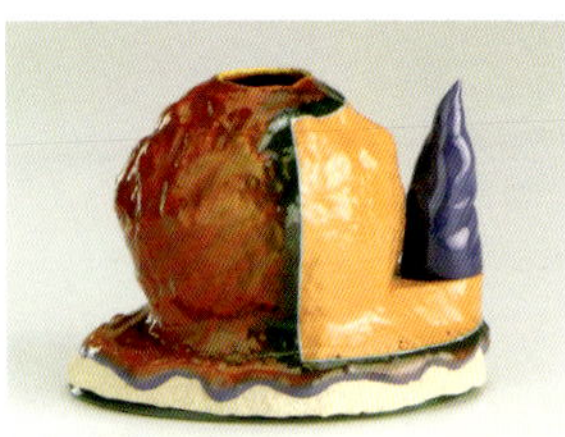

88 RON NAGLE,
American, born 1939
Knucklehead Jr., 2000
Earthenware with overglaze
3 1/2 x 5 1/8 x 3 3/4 inches
(8.9 x 13 x 9.7 cm)
Museum purchase funded
by the Caroline Wiess Law
Accessions Endowment Fund
2010.2094.A, .B

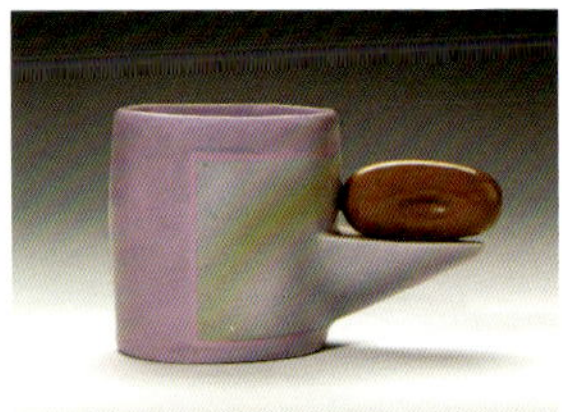

89 RON NAGLE,
American, born 1939
Untitled, Johnson Commission, c. 1970
Earthenware
2 5/8 x 4 1/4 x 2 3/8 inches
(6.7 x 10.8 x 5.9 cm)
Museum purchase funded
by the Caroline Wiess Law
Accessions Endowment Fund
2010.2095

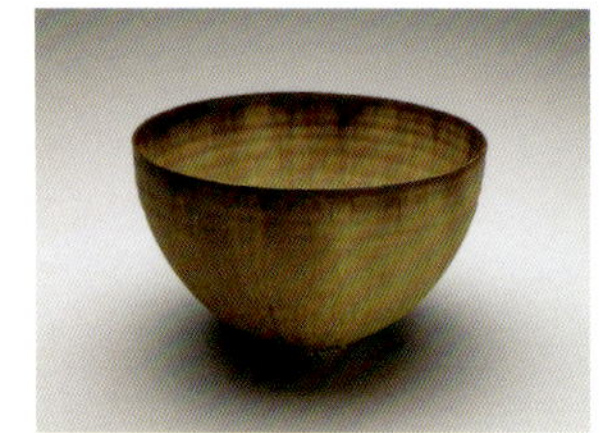

90 OTTO NATZLER,
Austrian, 1908–2007
GERTRUD NATZLER,
Austrian, 1908–1971
Bowl, model 2449, 1942
Earthenware with Pompeian glaze
3 3/4 x 7 inches diameter (9.5 x 17.8 cm)
Museum purchase funded
by the Caroline Wiess Law
Accessions Endowment Fund
2010.2096

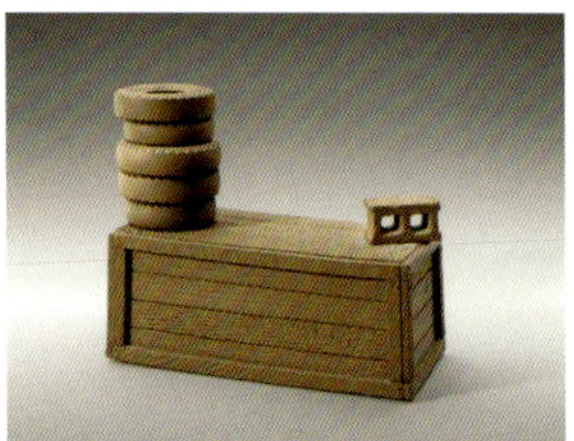

91 RICHARD T. NOTKIN,
American, born 1948
Five Tires on Crate Cup, 1998
Stoneware
4 1/4 x 5 1/4 x 2 1/4 inches
(10.8 x 13.2 x 5.7 cm)
Museum purchase funded
by the Caroline Wiess Law
Accessions Endowment Fund
2010.2097

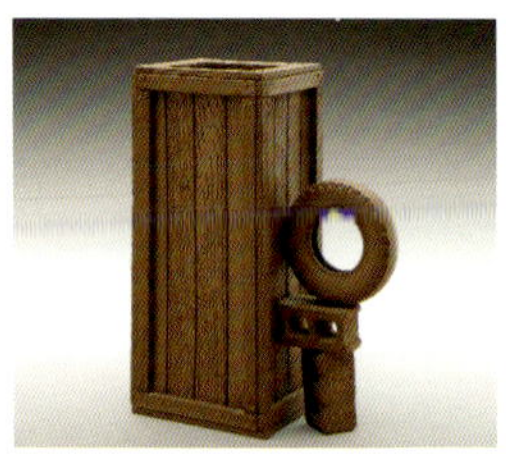

92 RICHARD T. NOTKIN,
American, born 1948
Cup, 1984
Stoneware
5 x 3 1/4 x 1 7/8 inches
(12.7 x 8.3 x 4.8 cm)
Museum purchase funded
by the Caroline Wiess Law
Accessions Endowment Fund
2010.2098

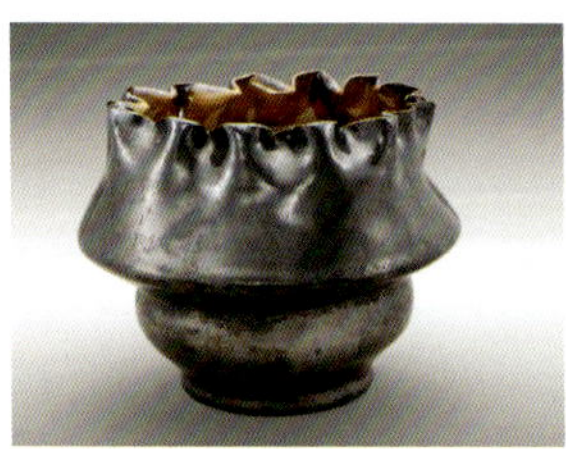

93 GEORGE OHR,
American, 1857–1918
Vase, 1910
Earthenware
4 3/8 x 5 3/4 inches diameter
(11.1 x 14.6 cm)
Museum purchase funded
by the Caroline Wiess Law
Accessions Endowment Fund
2010.2099

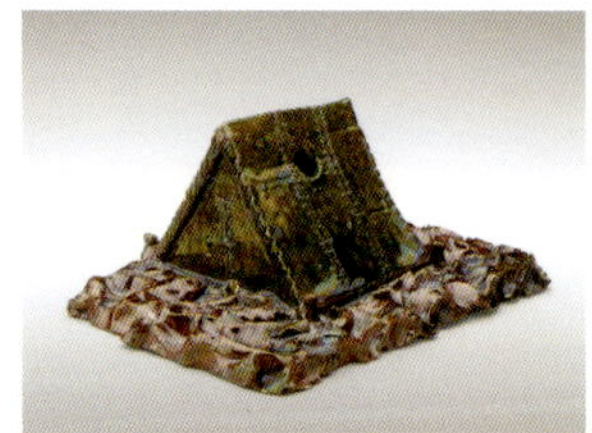

94 GEORGE OHR,
American, 1857–1918
House-Tent Inkwell, c. 1900
Earthenware
6 3/4 x 6 5/8 x 4 7/8 inches
(17.1 x 16.8 x 12.4 cm)
Museum purchase funded
by the Caroline Wiess Law
Accessions Endowment Fund
2010.2100

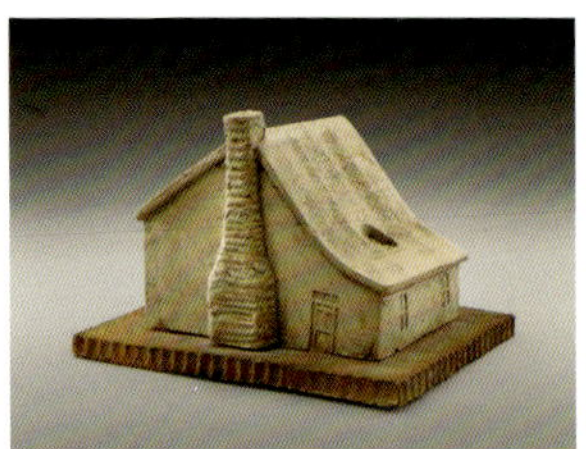

95 GEORGE OHR,
American, 1857–1918
Log Cabin Inkwell, c. 1900
Earthenware
4 1/4 x 5 1/4 x 2 1/4 inches
(10.8 x 13.2 x 5.7 cm)
Museum purchase funded
by the Caroline Wiess Law
Accessions Endowment Fund
2010.2101

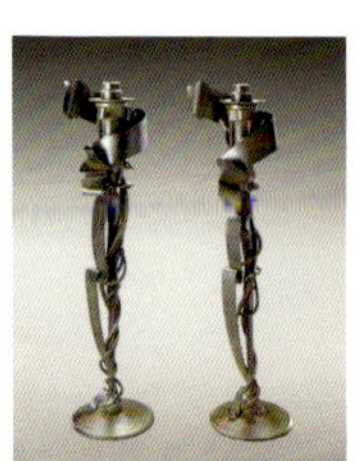

96 ALBERT PALEY,
American, born 1944
Pair of Millennium Candleholders, 1998
Steel and brass
21 1/8 x 6 x 5 1/4 inches each
(53.7 x 15.2 x 13.3 cm)
Museum purchases funded
by the Caroline Wiess Law
Accessions Endowment Fund
2010.2102.1–.2

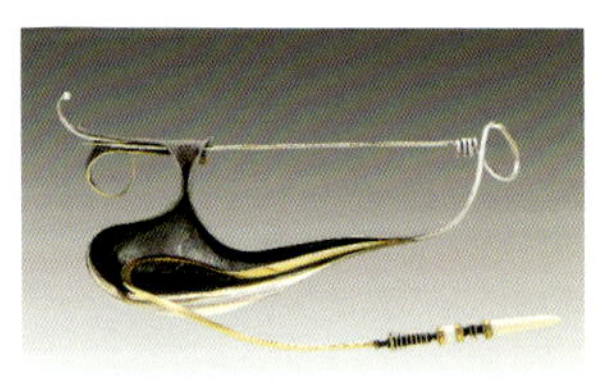

97 ALBERT PALEY,
American, born 1944
Pin, 1969
Silver, gold, ivory, and pearl
6 x 3 1/4 inches
(15.2 x 8.3 cm)
Gift of Leatrice and Melvin Eagle
2011.973

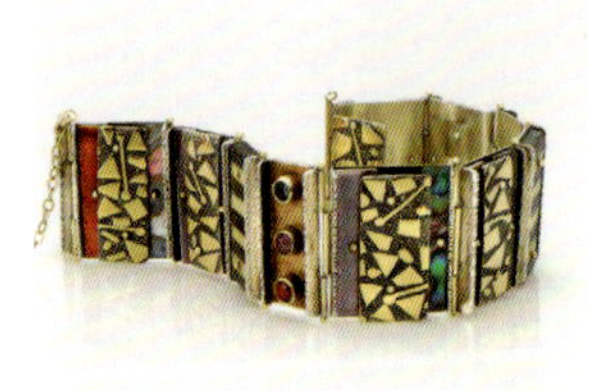

98 EARL PARDON,
American, 1926–1991
Bracelet, 1960
Sterling silver, 14k gold, enamel,
shell, ebony, and colored stones
7 3/4 x 1 x 1/8 inches
(19.7 x 2.5 x 0.3 cm)
Museum purchase funded
by the Caroline Wiess Law
Accessions Endowment Fund
2010.2103

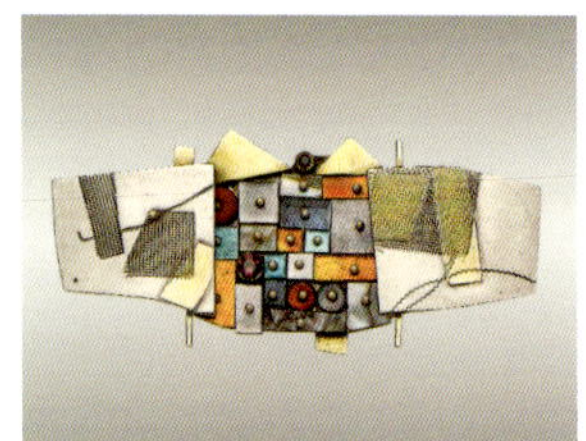

99 EARL PARDON,
American, 1926–1991
Pin, 1960
Sterling silver, 14k gold, shell,
colored stones, and enamel
3 1/8 x 1 1/4 x 1/4 inches
(7.9 x 3.2 x 0.6 cm)
Museum purchase funded
by the Caroline Wiess Law
Accessions Endowment Fund
2010.2104

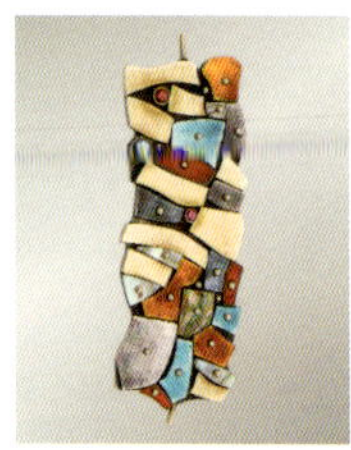

100 EARL PARDON,
American, 1926–1991
Pin, 1960
Sterling silver, 14k gold, enamel, and stones
3 x 1 x 3/8 inches
(7.6 x 2.5 x 1 cm)
Museum purchase funded
by the Caroline Wiess Law
Accessions Endowment Fund
2010.2105

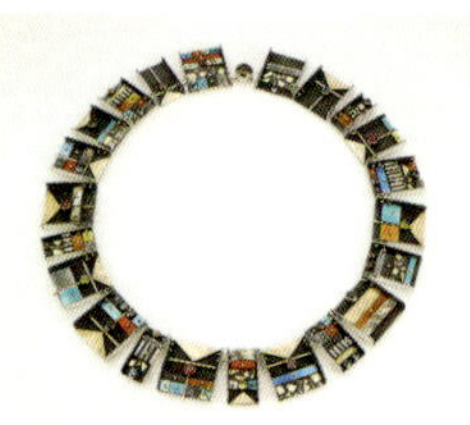

101 EARL PARDON,
American, 1926–1991
Mosaic Panel Necklace, 1987
Sterling silver, 14k gold, enamel, semiprecious
stones, ebony, and mother-of-pearl
1/4 x 7 7/8 inches diameter
(0.6 x 20 cm)
Museum purchase funded by the Caroline
Wiess Law Accessions Endowment Fund
2010.2106

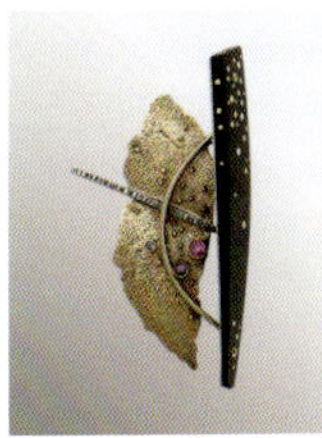

102 EARL PARDON,
American, 1926–1991
Pin, c. 1980–83
Sterling silver, 14k gold,
colored stones, and ebony
3 1/8 x 1 3/4 x 1/2 inches
(7.9 x 4.4 x 1.3 cm)
Museum purchase funded
by the Caroline Wiess Law
Accessions Endowment Fund
2010.2107

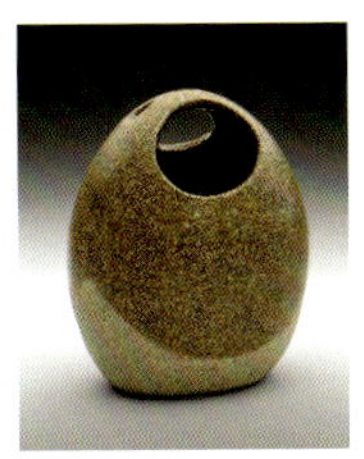

103 JANE PARSHALL,
American, 1916–1993
Untitled, 1960
Stoneware
7 1/4 x 6 1/4 x 4 1/8 inches
(18.4 x 15.9 x 10.5 cm)
Museum purchase funded
by the Caroline Wiess Law
Accessions Endowment Fund
2010.2108

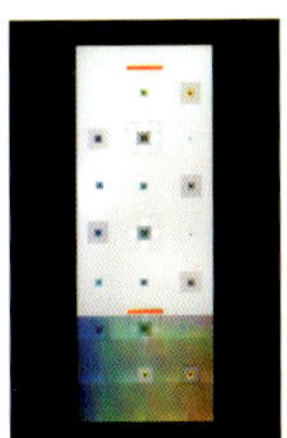

104 TOM PATTI,
American, born 1943
Spectral Panel, 1997
Glass
53 1/2 x 21 x 1 inches
(135.9 x 53.3 x 2.5 cm)
Museum purchase funded
by the Caroline Wiess Law
Accessions Endowment Fund
2010.2109

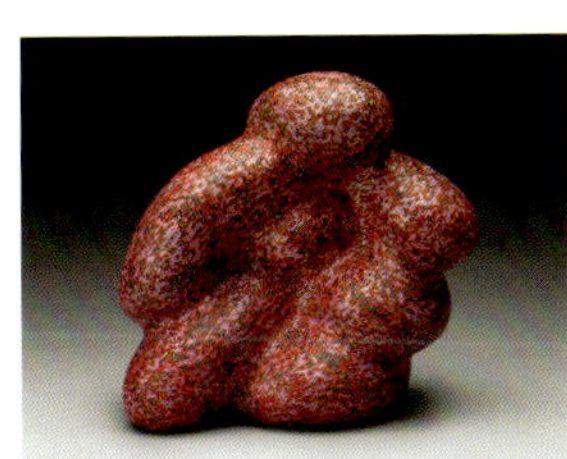

105 KEN PRICE,
American, 1935–2012
Sag, 2007
Painted clay
6 1/2 x 6 7/8 x 5 1/8 inches
(16.5 x 17.5 x 13 cm)
Museum purchase funded
by the Caroline Wiess Law
Accessions Endowment Fund
2010.2110

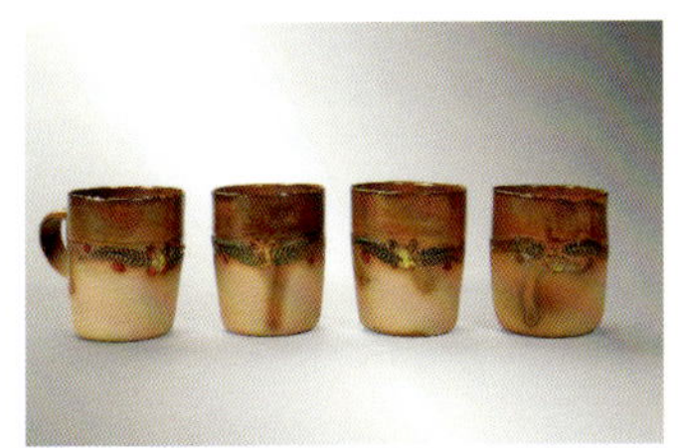

106 KEN PRICE,
American, 1935–2012
Four Coffee Cups, c. 1970–77
Ceramic
3 1/8 x 2 1/2 inches diameter each
(7.9 x 6.4 cm)
Museum purchase funded
by the Caroline Wiess Law
Accessions Endowment Fund
2010.2111.1–.4

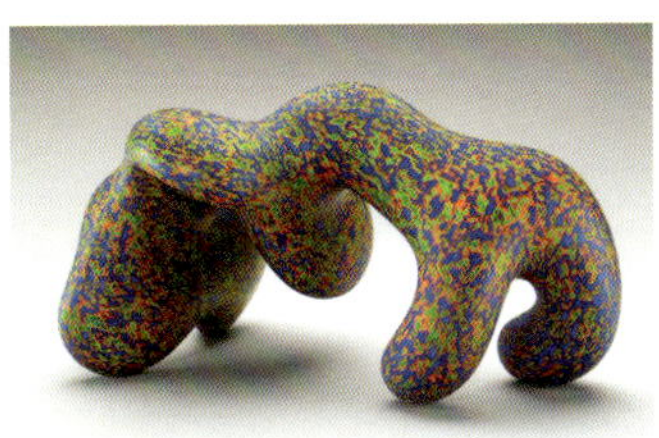

107 KEN PRICE,
American, 1935–2012
Morfo, 2001
Painted clay
6 x 12 x 7 1/4 inches
(15.2 x 30.5 x 18.4 cm)
Gift of Leatrice and Melvin Eagle
2012.521

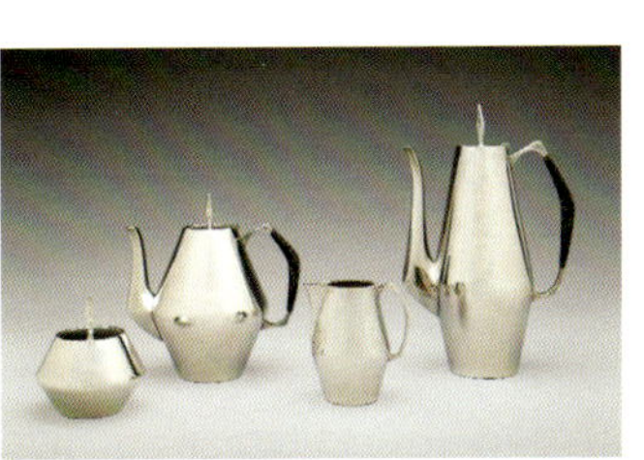

108 JOHN AXEL PRIP,
American, 1922–2009
Manufactured by Reed & Barton,
American, est. 1824
"The Diamond" Tea and Coffee Service, 1960
Sterling silver and plastic
11 3/8 x 7 3/4 x 4 1/2 inches
(28.9 x 19.7 x 11.4 cm)
7 5/8 x 8 x 5 1/4 inches
(19.4 x 20.3 x 13.3 cm)
4 1/2 x 4 1/2 x 3 1/4 inches
(11.4 x 11.4 x 8.3 cm)
4 1/8 x 4 1/8 inches diameter
(10.5 x 10.5 cm)
Gift of Leatrice and Melvin Eagle in honor
of the memory of Lottie and Benjamin Eagle
2010.2263.1–.4

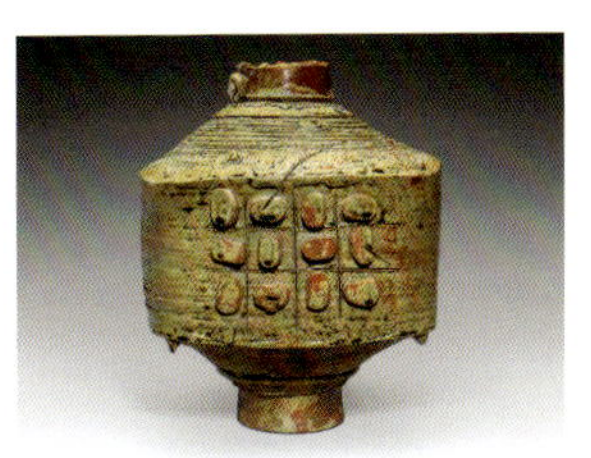

109 THEODORE RANDALL,
American, 1914–1985
Pot, 1970
Stoneware
10 7/8 x 9 3/4 x 10 1/8 inches
(27.6 x 24.8 x 25.7 cm)
Museum purchase funded
by the Caroline Wiess Law
Accessions Endowment Fund
2010.2112

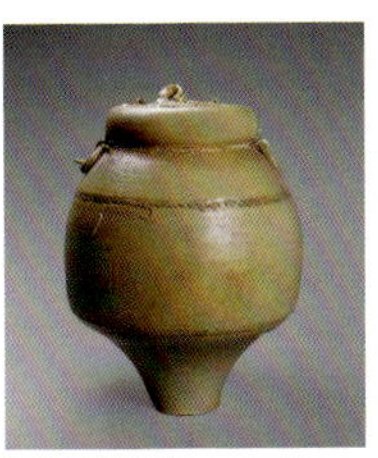

110 DON REITZ,
American, born 1929
Untitled Vessel, c. 1980
Salt-fired stoneware
30 x 23 x 23 inches
(76.2 x 58.4 x 58.4 cm)
Gift of Leatrice and Melvin Eagle
2006.1270

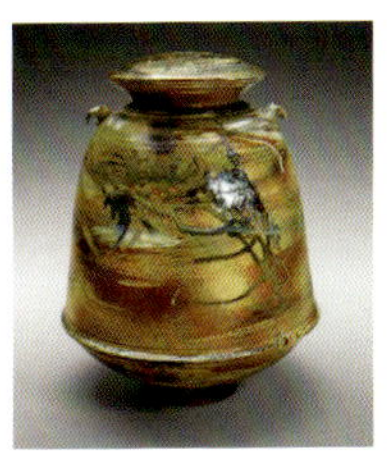

111 DON REITZ,
American, born 1929
Covered Jar, 1966
Salt-fired stoneware
18 1/2 x 14 1/2 inches diameter
(47 x 36.8 cm)
Museum purchase funded
by the Caroline Wiess Law
Accessions Endowment Fund
2010.2113.A, .B

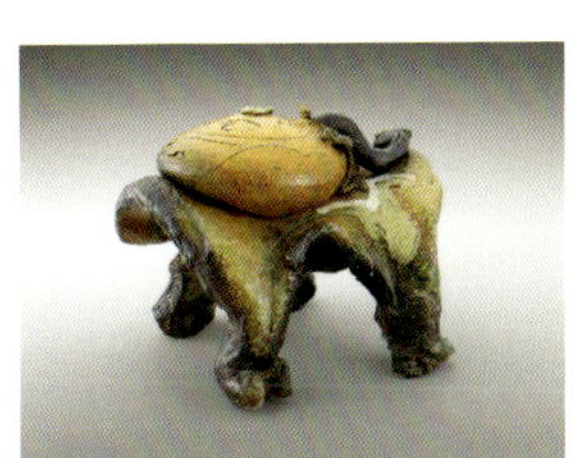

112 DON REITZ,
American, born 1929
Animal, 1964
Salt-fired stoneware with uranium glaze accent
5 3/4 x 8 1/2 x 6 5/8 inches
(14.6 x 21.6 x 16.8 cm)
Museum purchase funded
by the Caroline Wiess Law
Accessions Endowment Fund
2010.2114

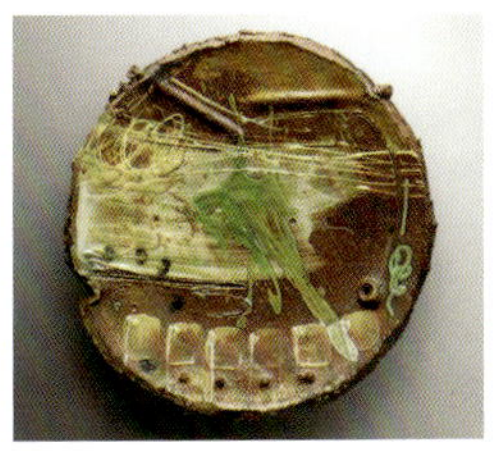

113 DON REITZ,
American, born 1929
Platter, 1981
Salt-fired stoneware
3 1/4 x 21 3/4 inches diameter
(8.3 x 55.2 cm)
Museum purchase funded
by the Caroline Wiess Law
Accessions Endowment Fund
2010.2115

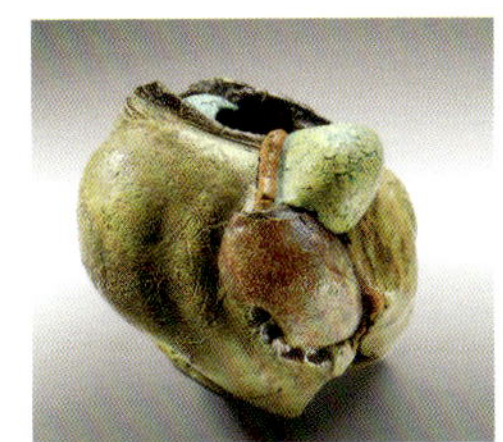

114 DON REITZ,
American, born 1929
Untitled, 1964
Salt-fired stoneware with
uranium glaze accent
11 x 13 3/4 x 11 3/4 inches
(27.9 x 34.9 x 29.8 cm)
Museum purchase funded
by the Caroline Wiess Law
Accessions Endowment Fund
2010.2116

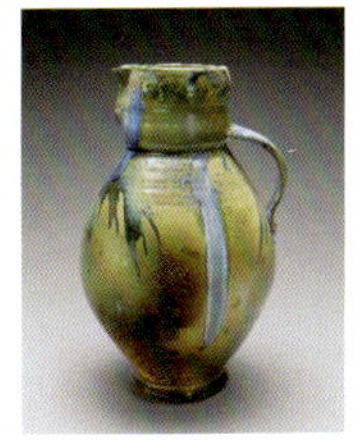

115 DON REITZ,
American, born 1929
Pitcher, 1999
Salt-fired stoneware
18 1/8 x 12 1/8 x 11 1/2 inches
(46 x 30.8 x 29.2 cm)
Museum purchase funded
by the Caroline Wiess Law
Accessions Endowment Fund
2010.2117

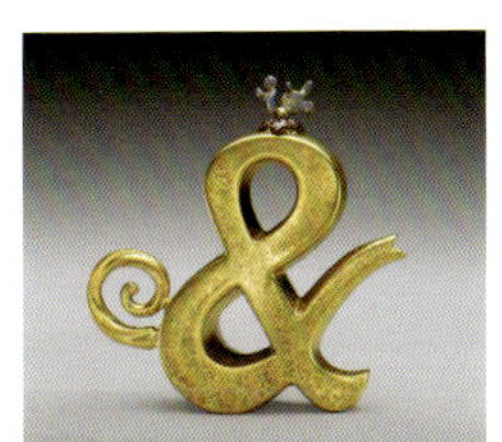

116 ADRIAN SAXE,
American, born 1943
*Untitled Ewer (Franklin Gothic
Italic Ampersand, MT)*, 2001
Porcelain
10 1/8 x 10 1/2 x 2 3/4 inches
(25.7 x 26.7 x 7 cm)
Museum purchase funded by the Caroline
Wiess Law Accessions Endowment Fund
2010.2118.A, .B

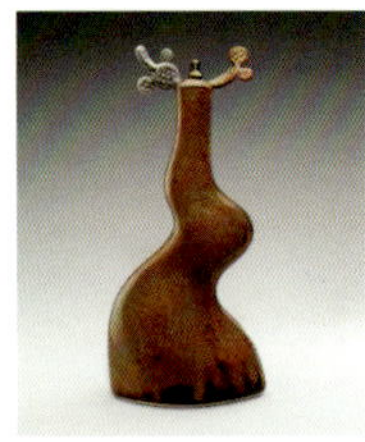

117 ADRIAN SAXE,
American, born 1943
Untitled Oil Lamp (Tenmoku), 1983
Porcelain
8 1/2 x 3 7/8 x 2 1/8 inches
(21.6 x 9.8 x 5.4 cm)
Museum purchase funded
by the Caroline Wiess Law
Accessions Endowment Fund
2010.2119

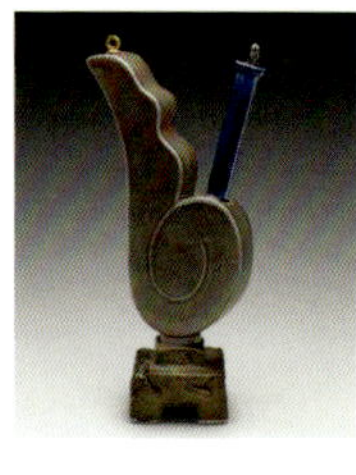

121 ADRIAN SAXE,
American, born 1943
Oil Lamp #33, 1983
Porcelain
9 1/8 x 4 5/8 x 2 1/4 inches
(23 x 11.7 x 5.7 cm)
Museum purchase funded
by the Caroline Wiess Law
Accessions Endowment Fund
2010.2123.A–.C

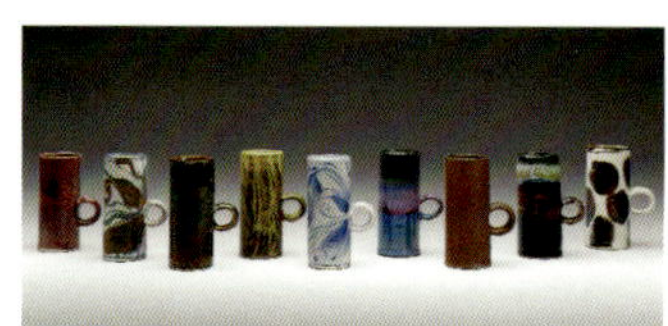

125 ADRIAN SAXE,
American, born 1943
Nine Mugs, 1971–79
Porcelain and gold lusters
Dimensions vary
Museum purchase funded
by the Caroline Wiess Law
Accessions Endowment Fund
2010.2127.1–.9

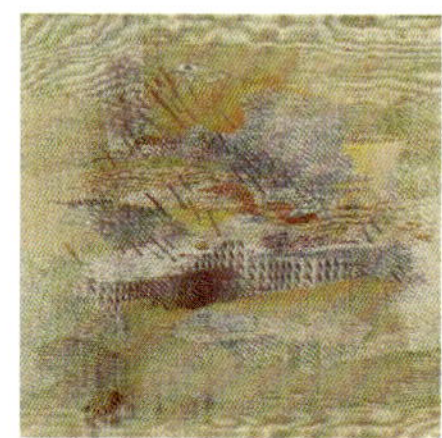

129 CYNTHIA SCHIRA,
American, born 1934
Borderland, 1986
Cotton, linen, rayon, and
mixed fibers
65 x 66 x 1/4 inches
(165.1 x 167.6 x 0.6 cm)
Museum purchase funded
by the Caroline Wiess Law
Accessions Endowment Fund
2010.2130

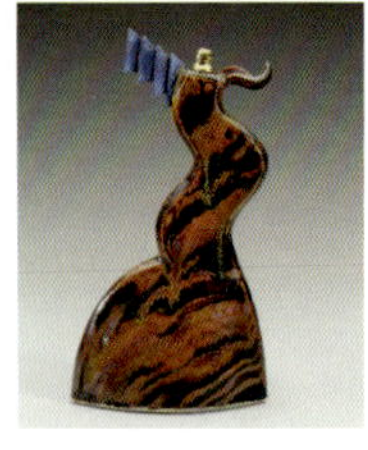

118 ADRIAN SAXE,
American, born 1943
Untitled Oil Lamp (Tenmoku), 1979
Porcelain
6 5/8 x 4 5/8 x 1 5/8 inches
(16.8 x 11.6 x 4 cm)
Museum purchase funded
by the Caroline Wiess Law
Accessions Endowment Fund
2010.2120.A, .B

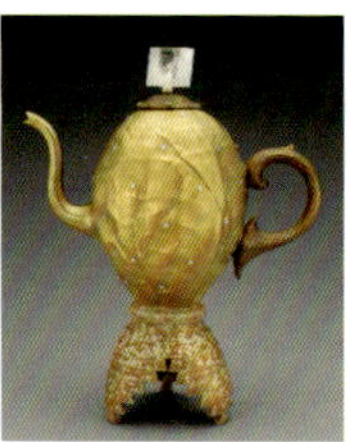

122 ADRIAN SAXE,
American, born 1943
Untitled Ewer (DIJ), 1993
Porcelain, pearl, and image-doubling
calcite crystal
9 3/4 x 8 3/8 x 4 1/2 inches
(24.8 x 21.3 x 11.4 cm)
Museum purchase funded
by the Caroline Wiess Law
Accessions Endowment Fund
2010.2124.A, .B

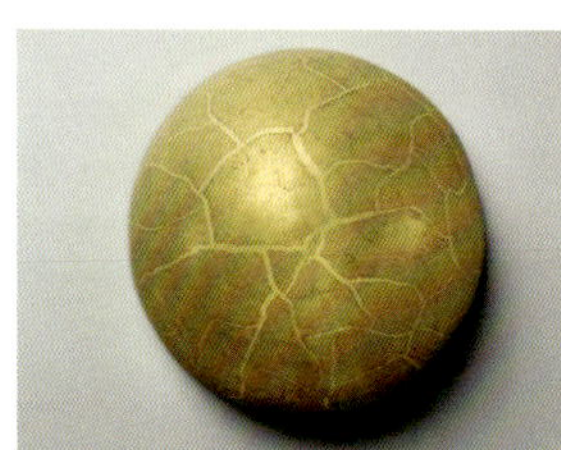

126 ADRIAN SAXE,
American, born 1943
Queen's Gambit Declined, 1995
Porcelain and gold lusters
7 1/4 x 13 5/8 inches diameter
(18.4 x 34.6 cm)
Museum purchase funded
by the Caroline Wiess Law
Accessions Endowment Fund
2010.2128

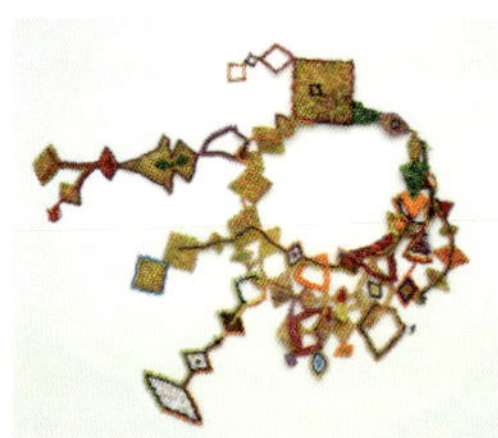

130 JOYCE J. SCOTT,
American, born 1948
Necklace, c. 2002
Glass beads and thread
11 1/4 x 9 x 1/8 inches
(28.6 x 22.9 x 0.3 cm)
Museum purchase funded
by the Caroline Wiess Law
Accessions Endowment Fund
2010.2131

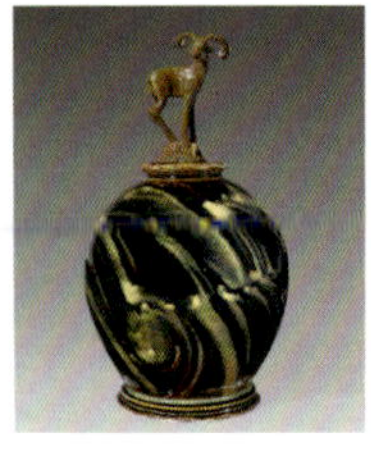

119 ADRIAN SAXE,
American, born 1943
Antelope Jar, 1979
Porcelain and stoneware
13 3/4 x 7 3/4 inches diameter
(34.9 x 19.7 cm)
Museum purchase funded
by the Caroline Wiess Law
Accessions Endowment Fund
2010.2121.A, .B

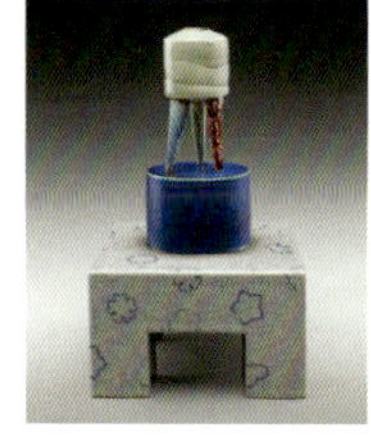

123 ADRIAN SAXE,
American, born 1943
Untitled Tripod Oil Lamp, 1979
Porcelain
10 x 6 1/4 x 6 1/4 inches
(25.4 x 15.7 x 15.7 cm)
Museum purchase funded
by the Caroline Wiess Law
Accessions Endowment Fund
2010.2125.A, .B

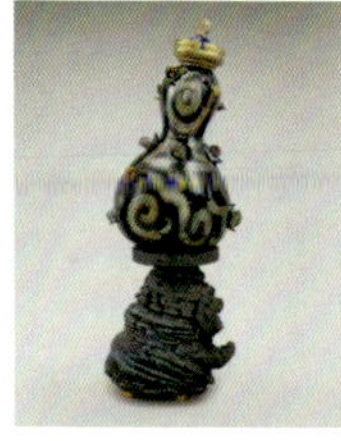

127 ADRIAN SAXE,
American, born 1943
Myxococcus Jamboree, 2001
Porcelain and raku
29 x 11 x 9 3/4 inches
(73.7 x 27.9 x 24.8 cm)
Museum purchase funded
by the Caroline Wiess Law
Accessions Endowment Fund
2010.2129.A, .B

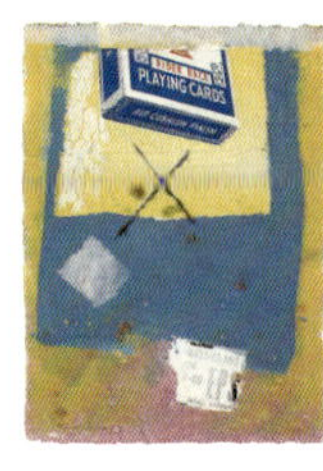

131 RICHARD SHAW,
American, born 1941
Collage Cards, 1984
Collage on paper
40 x 30 inches
(101.6 x 76.2 cm)
Museum purchase funded
by the Caroline Wiess Law
Accessions Endowment Fund
2010.2132

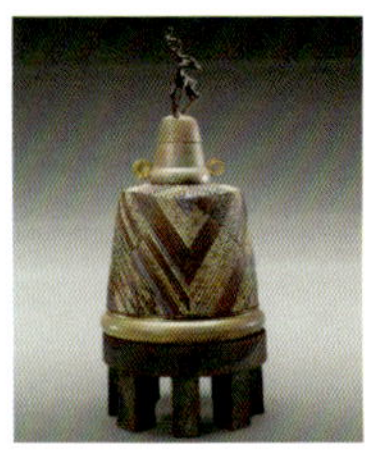

120 ADRIAN SAXE,
American, born 1943
Antelope Jar, 1980
Porcelain, stoneware, and raku
20 5/8 x 8 5/8 x 8 1/4 inches
(52.4 x 21.9 x 21 cm)
Museum purchase funded by the Caroline
Wiess Law Accessions Endowment Fund
2010.2122.A–.C

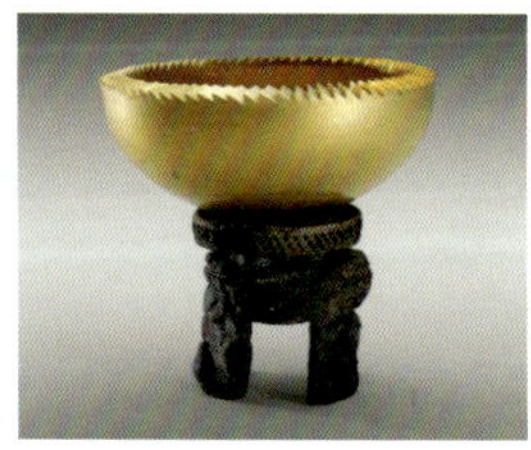

124 ADRIAN SAXE,
American, born 1943
Mortar Bowl on Stand, 1980
Porcelain and raku
4 3/8 x 4 7/8 inches diameter
(11.2 x 12.4 cm)
Museum purchase funded
by the Caroline Wiess Law
Accessions Endowment Fund
2010.2126

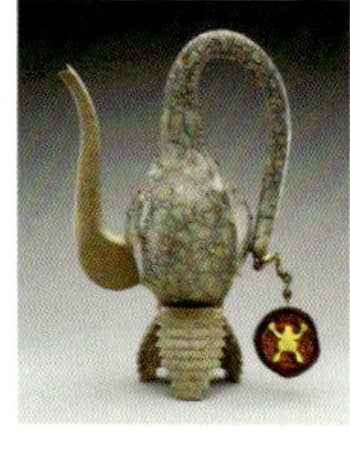

128 ADRIAN SAXE,
American, born 1943
Untitled Mystery Ewer, 1993
Porcelain, plastic, and metal
12 x 8 1/4 x 4 1/2 inches
(30.5 x 21 x 11.4 cm)
Gift of Leatrice and Melvin Eagle
2010.2264

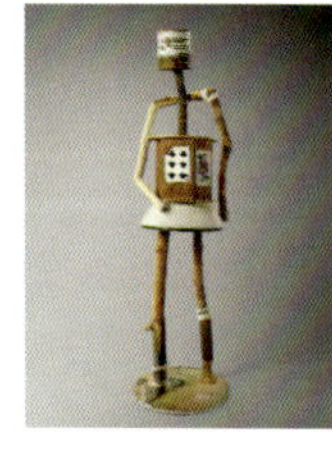

132 RICHARD SHAW,
American, born 1941
In the Family Way, 1980
Porcelain
37 x 10 x 12 inches
(94 x 25.4 x 30.5 cm)
Museum purchase funded
by the Caroline Wiess Law
Accessions Endowment Fund
2010.2133

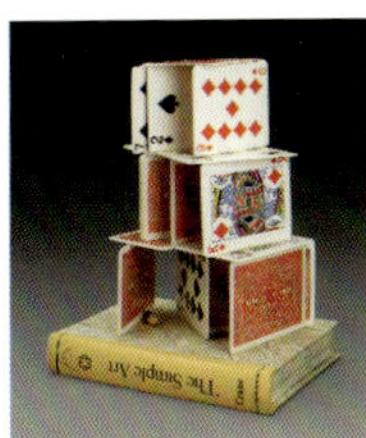

133 RICHARD SHAW,
American, born 1941
Stack of Cards (Mel/Lee), 2001
Porcelain
8 3/4 x 7 1/4 x 5 1/4 inches
(22.2 x 18.3 x 13.3 cm)
Museum purchase funded
by the Caroline Wiess Law
Accessions Endowment Fund
2010.2134

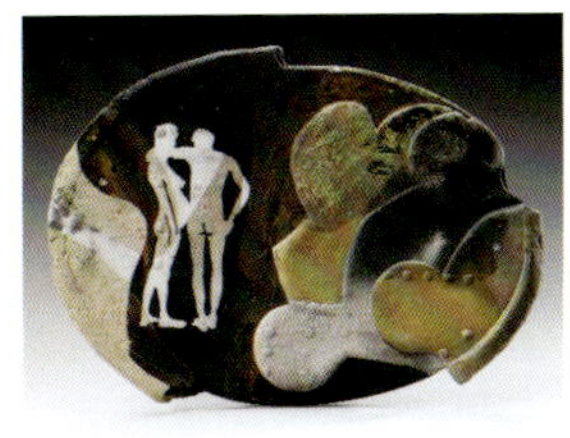

137 PAUL SOLDNER,
American, 1921–2011
Untitled, 1980
Ceramic
18 x 23 1/2 x 2 1/4 inches
(45.7 x 59.7 x 5.7 cm)
Museum purchase funded
by the Caroline Wiess Law
Accessions Endowment Fund
2010.2138

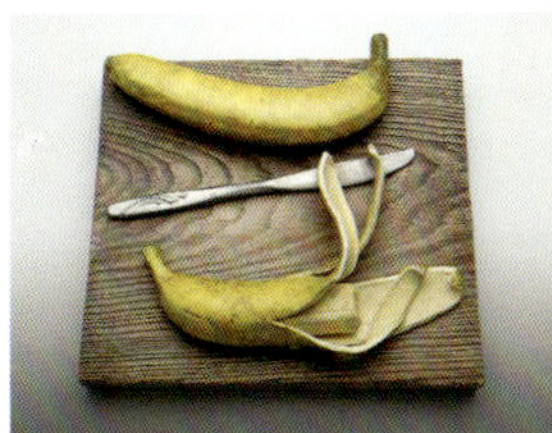

141 VICTOR SPINSKI,
American, 1940–2013
Still Life with Banana, 1981
Earthenware
3 1/8 x 10 1/8 x 9 inches
(7.9 x 25.6 x 22.7 cm)
Museum purchase funded
by the Caroline Wiess Law
Accessions Endowment Fund
2010.2142

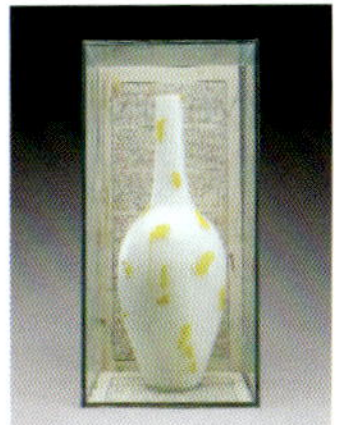

145 THERMAN STATOM,
American, born 1953
Untitled, from the series *Winter Boxes*, 1994
Glass, paper, and pencil
16 x 8 x 6 1/8 inches
(40.6 x 20.3 x 15.6 cm)
Museum purchase funded
by the Caroline Wiess Law
Accessions Endowment Fund
2010.2145.3

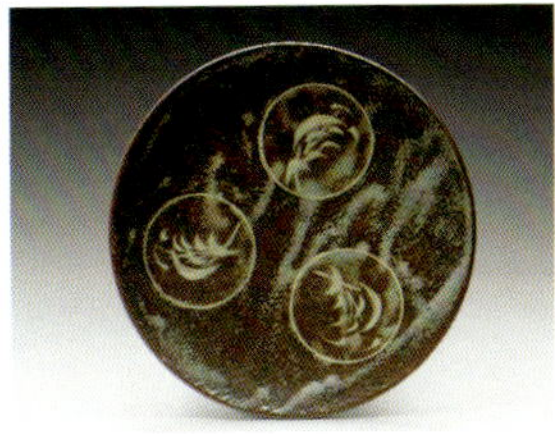

134 SHIMAOKA TATSUZŌ,
Japanese, 1919–2007
Plate with Rope Design, 1980
Stoneware
1 3/4 x 10 1/2 inches diameter
(4.4 x 26.7 cm)
Museum purchase funded
by the Caroline Wiess Law
Accessions Endowment Fund
2010.2135

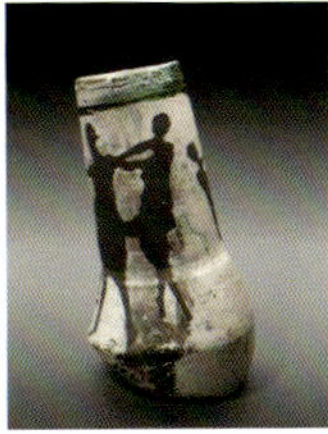

138 PAUL SOLDNER,
American, 1921–2011
Vase, 1979
Ceramic
11 1/4 x 6 3/4 x 6 1/2 inches
(28.6 x 17.1 x 16.5 cm)
Museum purchase funded
by the Caroline Wiess Law
Accessions Endowment Fund
2010.2139

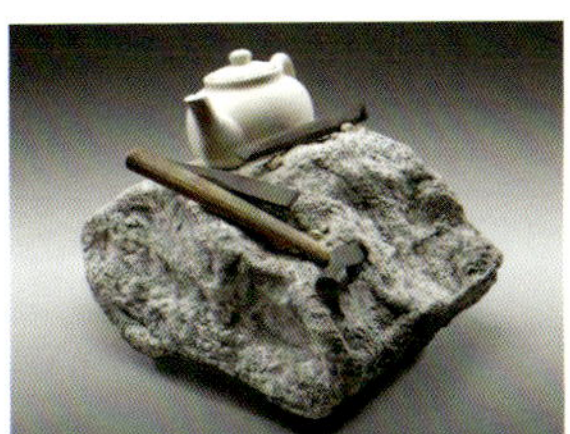

142 VICTOR SPINSKI,
American, 1940–2013
Rock, 2000
Earthenware
10 1/2 x 15 1/8 x 13 3/4 inches
(26.7 x 38.4 x 34.9 cm)
Museum purchase funded
by the Caroline Wiess Law
Accessions Endowment Fund
2010.2143

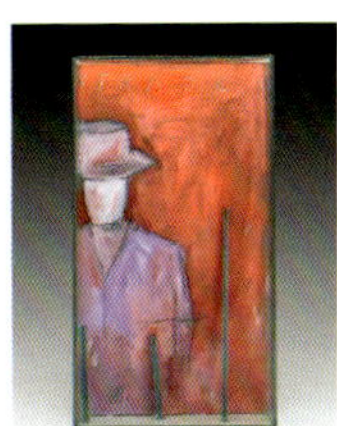

146 THERMAN STATOM,
American, born 1953
Self-Portrait, from the series *Winter Boxes*,
1994
Glass and paint
18 x 10 x 2 1/8 inches
(45.7 x 25.4 x 5.4 cm)
Museum purchase funded
by the Caroline Wiess Law
Accessions Endowment Fund
2010.2145.4

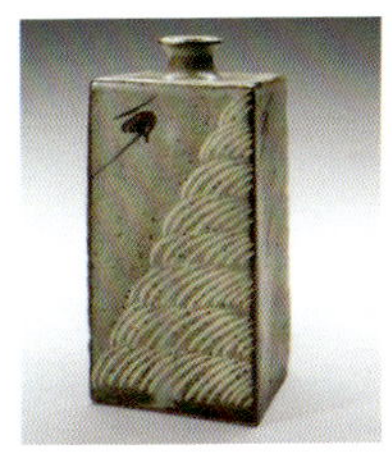

135 SHIMAOKA TATSUZŌ,
Japanese, 1919–2007
Vase, 1980
Stoneware
8 1/4 x 4 x 3 3/8 inches
(21 x 10.2 x 8.4 cm)
Museum purchase funded
by the Caroline Wiess Law
Accessions Endowment Fund
2010.2136

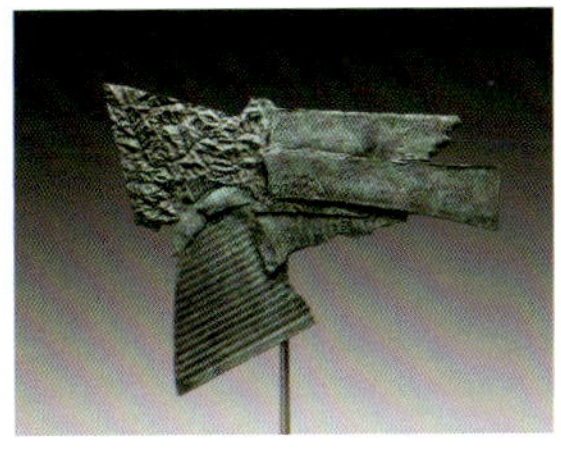

139 PAUL SOLDNER,
American, 1921–2011
Untitled, 1995
Bronze
20 1/2 x 28 x 3/4 inches
(52.1 x 71.1 x 1.9 cm)
Museum purchase funded
by the Caroline Wiess Law
Accessions Endowment Fund
2010.2140.A, .B

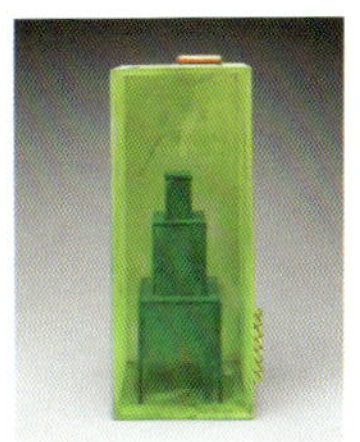

143 THERMAN STATOM,
American, born 1953
Green Stairs, from the series
Winter Boxes, 1994
Glass and paint
12 3/8 x 5 1/2 x 5 1/4 inches
(31.4 x 14 x 13.3 cm)
Museum purchase funded
by the Caroline Wiess Law
Accessions Endowment Fund
2010.2145.1

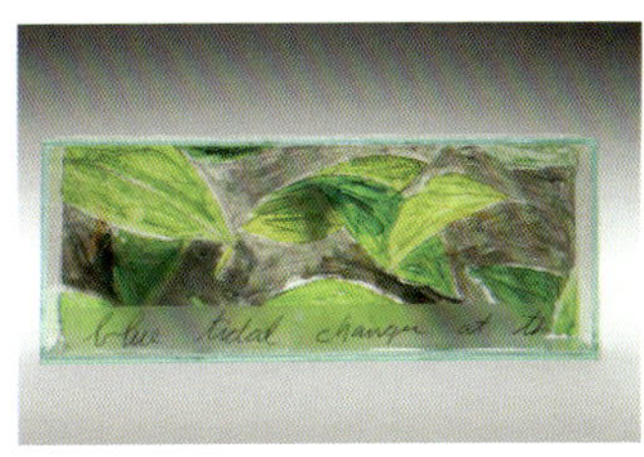

147 THERMAN STATOM,
American, born 1953
Fall, from the series *Winter Boxes*, 1994
Glass, pencil, and paint
6 x 16 x 2 1/8 inches
(15.2 x 40.6 x 5.4 cm)
Museum purchase funded
by the Caroline Wiess Law
Accessions Endowment Fund
2010.2145.5

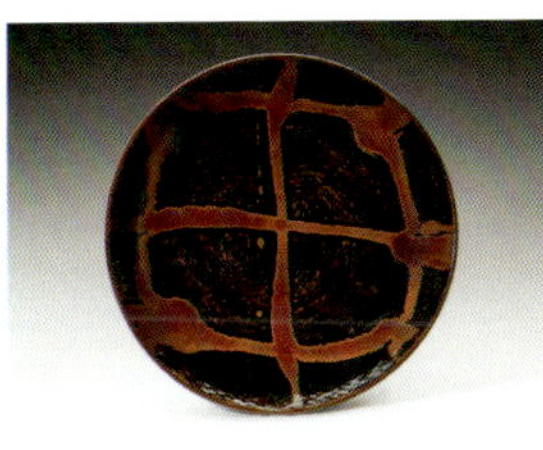

136 SHIMAOKA TATSUZŌ,
Japanese, 1919–2007
Plate, 2000
Stoneware
2 1/4 x 12 inches diameter
(5.7 x 30.5 cm)
Museum purchase funded
by the Caroline Wiess Law
Accessions Endowment Fund
2010.2137

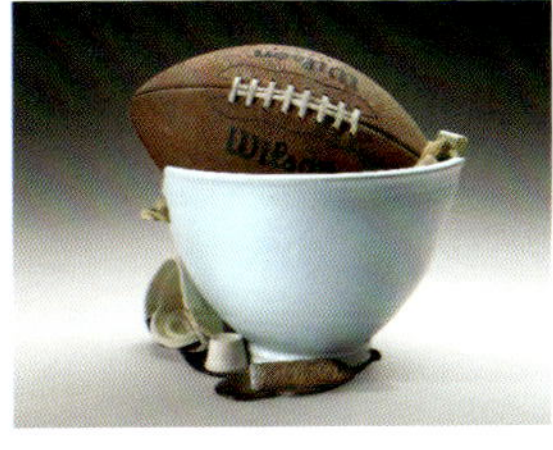

140 VICTOR SPINSKI,
American, 1940–2013
Misdirected Forward Pass, 1995
White clay
10 x 10 x 10 1/2 inches
(25.4 x 25.4 x 26.7 cm)
Museum purchase funded
by the Caroline Wiess Law
Accessions Endowment Fund
2010.2141

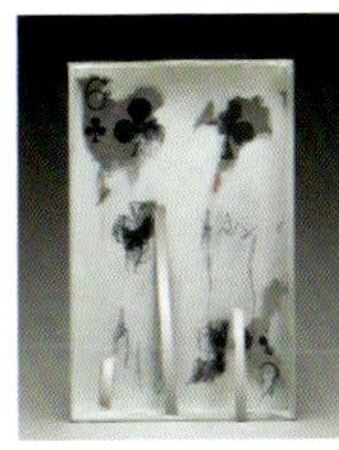

144 THERMAN STATOM,
American, born 1953
Six of Clubs, from the series *Winter Boxes*, 1994
Glass, pencil, and paint
15 1/4 x 9 3/4 x 1 3/4 inches
(38.7 x 24.8 x 4.4 cm)
Museum purchase funded
by the Caroline Wiess Law
Accessions Endowment Fund
2010.2145.2

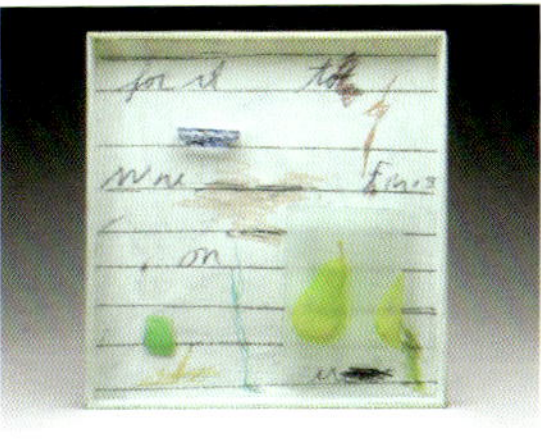

148 THERMAN STATOM,
American, born 1953
Cross Words, from the series *Winter Boxes*, 1994
Glass, pencil, and paint
12 1/4 x 12 1/4 x 1 1/4 inches
(31.1 x 31.1 x 3.2 cm)
Museum purchase funded
by the Caroline Wiess Law
Accessions Endowment Fund
2010.2145.6

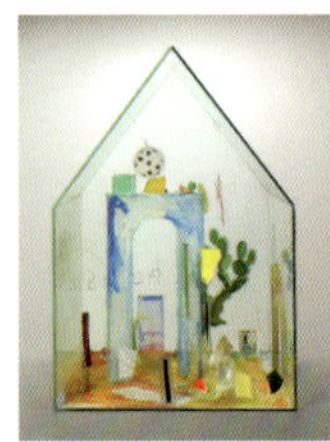

149 THERMAN STATOM,
American, born 1953
Glass House, 1994/98
Glass and paint
26 1/4 x 18 1/2 x 14 inches
(66.7 x 47 x 35.6 cm)
Museum purchase funded
by the Caroline Wiess Law
Accessions Endowment Fund
2010.2146

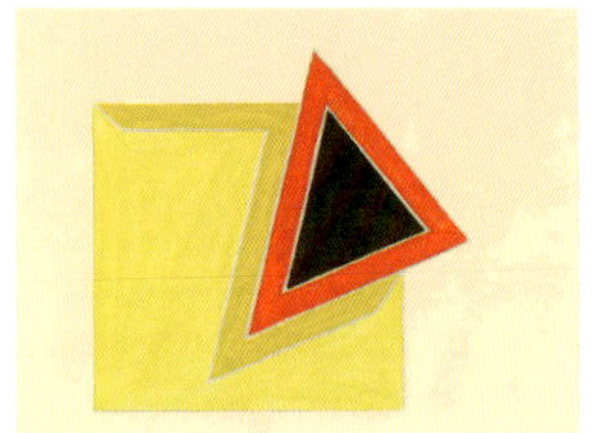

150 FRANK STELLA,
American, born 1936
Study, for *Moultonboro IV,* from the series
Irregular Polygon: Moultonboro, 1971
Gouache on paper
17 x 22 inches (43.2 x 55.9 cm)
Museum purchase funded
by the Caroline Wiess Law
Accessions Endowment Fund
2010.2144

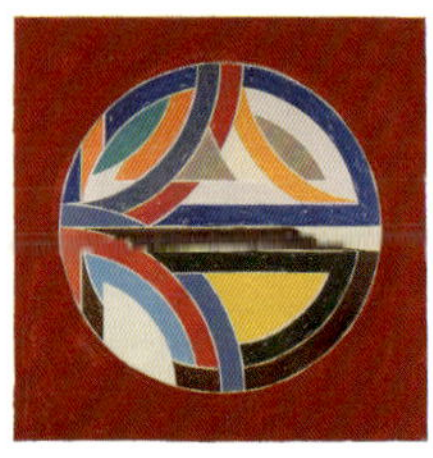

151 FRANK STELLA,
American, born 1936
Printed by Bruce Porter, James Welty,
and John Campione
Published by Petersburg Press,
American
Study, for *Sinjerli Variations Squared with
Colored Ground III,* from the series *Sinjerli
Variations Squared with Colored Grounds,*
1980
Offset lithograph and screenprint
in colors with acrylic on 320 gram
Arches Cover paper
32 3/4 x 32 3/4 inches
(83.2 x 83.2 cm)
Gift of Leatrice and Melvin Eagle
2012.522

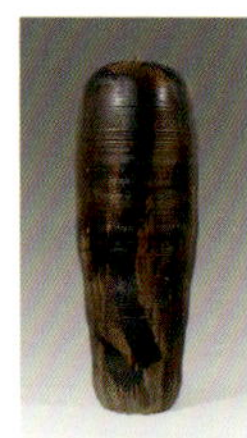

152 TOSHIKO TAKAEZU,
American, 1922–2011
Zeus, c. 1995
Stoneware
66 1/2 x 24 3/4 inches diameter
(168.9 x 62.9 cm)
Museum purchase funded
by the Caroline Wiess Law
Accessions Endowment Fund
2010.2147

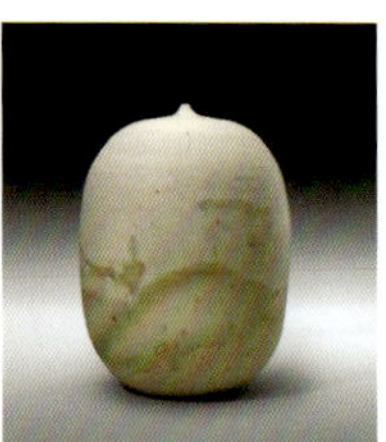

153 TOSHIKO TAKAEZU,
American, 1922–2011
Bottle, 1980
Stoneware
6 1/2 x 5 1/8 inches diameter
(16.5 x 13 cm)
Museum purchase funded
by the Caroline Wiess Law
Accessions Endowment Fund
2010.2148

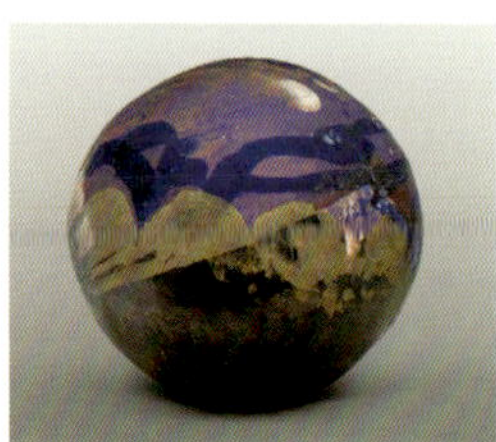

154 TOSHIKO TAKAEZU,
American, 1922–2011
Purple Moon, 1999
Stoneware
20 1/2 x 21 inches diameter
(52.1 x 53.3 cm)
Gift of Leatrice and Melvin Eagle
2010.2265

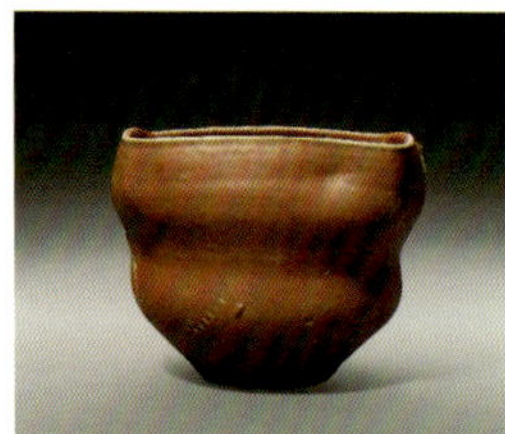

155 ROBERT TURNER,
American, 1913–2005
Bowl Squared, 1978
Stoneware
7 1/4 x 9 3/8 x 9 5/8 inches
(18.3 x 23.8 x 24.4 cm)
Museum purchase funded
by the Caroline Wiess Law
Accessions Endowment Fund
2010.2149

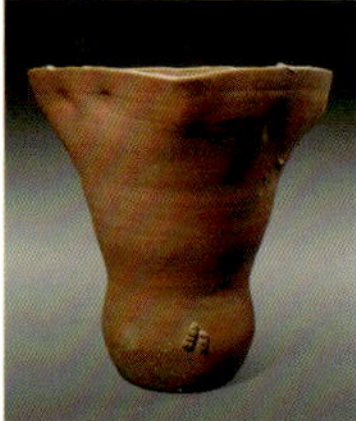

156 ROBERT TURNER,
American, 1913–2005
High Square, c. 1980
Stoneware
16 1/2 x 15 3/4 x 16 1/4 inches
(41.9 x 40 x 41.3 cm)
Museum purchase funded
by the Caroline Wiess Law
Accessions Endowment Fund
2010.2150

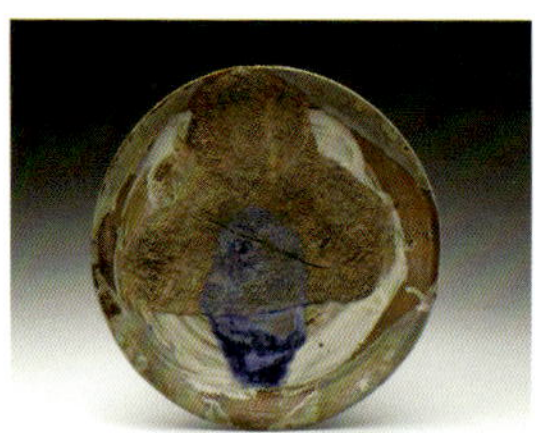

157 PETER VOULKOS,
American, 1924–2002
Untitled Plate, 1961
Stoneware
2 1/2 x 12 1/4 inches diameter
(6.4 x 31.1 cm)
Museum purchase funded
by the Caroline Wiess Law
Accessions Endowment Fund
2010.2151

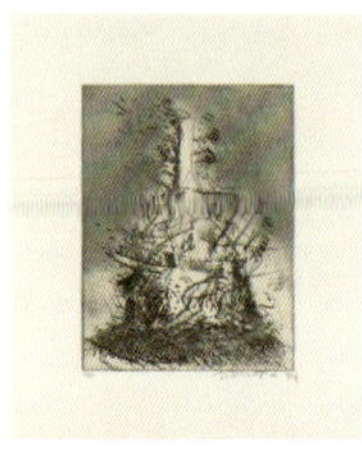

158 PETER VOULKOS,
American, 1924–2002
Untitled, 1994
Etching on Arches paper, ed. 11/30
19 x 15 inches
(48.3 x 38.1 cm)
Museum purchase funded
by the Caroline Wiess Law
Accessions Endowment Fund
2010.2152

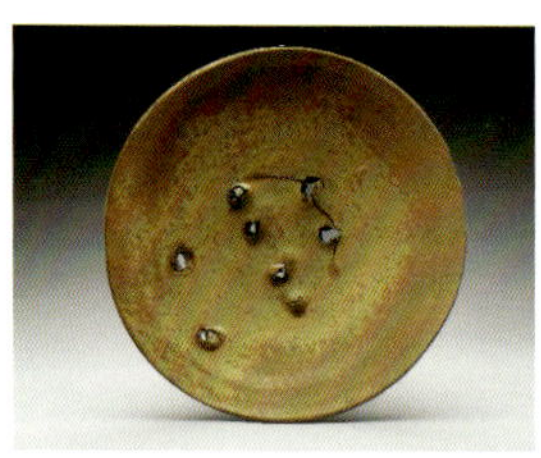

159 PETER VOULKOS,
American, 1924–2002
Untitled Plate, 1973
Stoneware and porcelain
3 3/8 x 18 1/2 inches diameter
(8.6 x 47 cm)
Museum purchase funded
by the Caroline Wiess Law
Accessions Endowment Fund
2010.2153

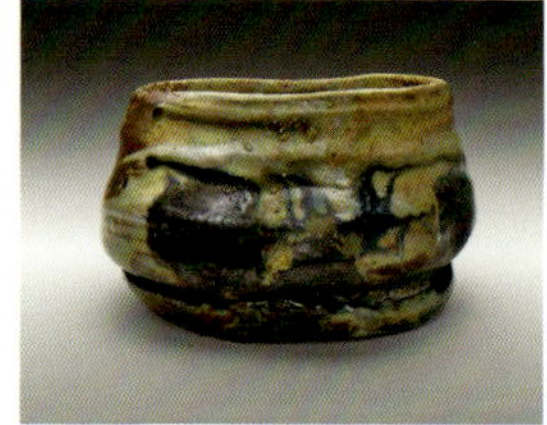

160 PETER VOULKOS,
American, 1924–2002
Tea Bowl, 1994
Stoneware
3 3/4 x 6 3/8 x 5 7/8 inches
(9.5 x 16.2 x 14.9 cm)
Museum purchase funded
by the Caroline Wiess Law
Accessions Endowment Fund
2010.2154

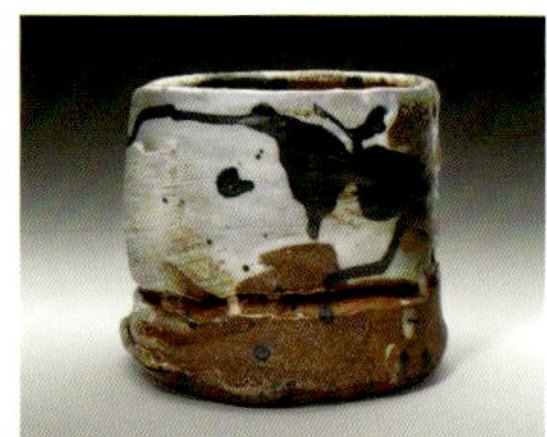

161 PETER VOULKOS,
American, 1924–2002
Untitled Tea Bowl, 1996
Stoneware
5 1/8 x 6 x 5 5/8 inches
(12.9 x 15.2 x 14.3 cm)
Museum purchase funded
by the Caroline Wiess Law
Accessions Endowment Fund
2010.2155

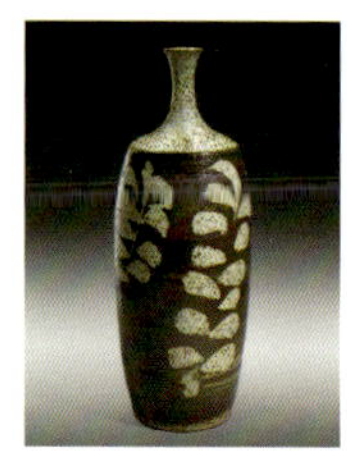

162 PETER VOULKOS,
American, 1924–2002
Vase, 1952–53
Stoneware
14 7/8 x 5 3/4 inches diameter
(37.8 x 14.6 cm)
Museum purchase funded
by the Caroline Wiess Law
Accessions Endowment Fund
2010.2156

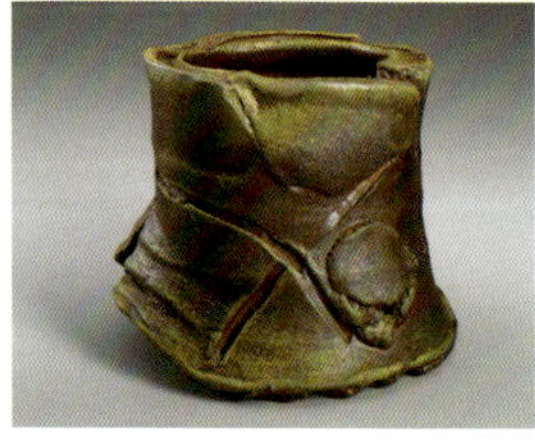

163 PETER VOULKOS,
American, 1924–2002
Untitled Ice Bucket, 1979
Stoneware
8 x 10 inches diameter
(20.3 x 25.4 cm)
Museum purchase funded by the Caroline
Wiess Law Accessions Endowment Fund
2010.2157

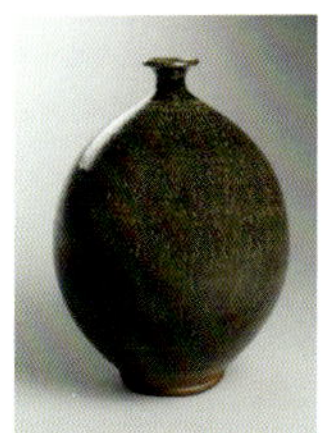

164 PETER VOULKOS,
American, 1924–2002
Vase, c. 1952–54
Stoneware
12 1/4 x 9 1/4 inches diameter
(31.1 x 23.5 cm)
Museum purchase funded
by the Caroline Wiess Law
Accessions Endowment Fund
2010.2158

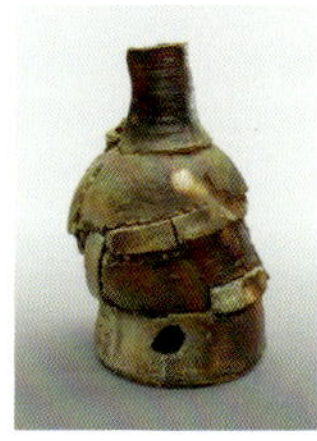

166 PETER VOULKOS,
American, 1924–2002
The Eagle Has Landed, 1999
Stoneware
34 1/2 x 23 x 23 inches
(87.6 x 58.4 x 58.4 cm)
Gift of Leatrice and Melvin Eagle
2010.2266

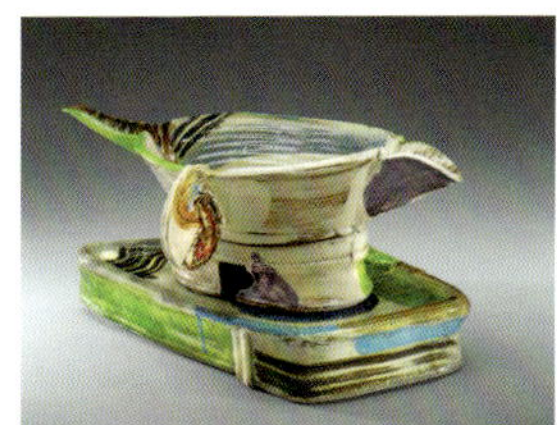

168 BETTY WOODMAN,
American, born 1930
Shark Soup Tureen, 1992
Earthenware
9 1/2 x 21 x 16 1/4 inches
(24.1 x 53.3 x 41.3 cm)
Gift of Leatrice and Melvin Eagle
2008.903.A, .B

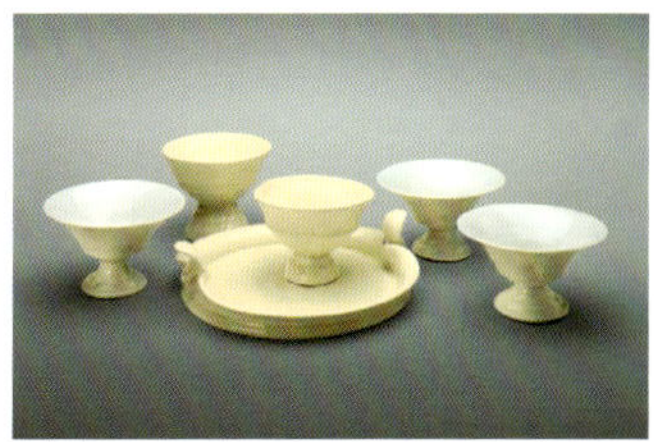

170 TAKESHI YASUDA,
British, born Japan, 1943
Five Bowls and Platter, 1975
Creamware
Dimensions vary
Museum purchase funded
by the Caroline Wiess Law
Accessions Endowment Fund
2010.2162.1–.6

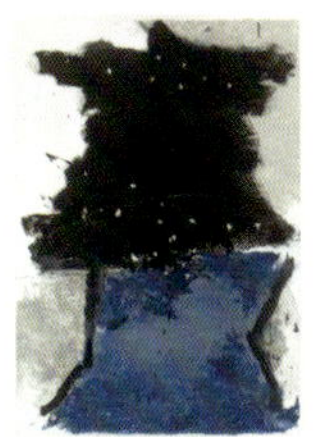

165 PETER VOULKOS,
American, 1924–2002
Untitled, 1994
Monotype in color
30 x 44 inches
(76.2 x 111.8 cm)
Museum purchase funded
by the Caroline Wiess Law
Accessions Endowment Fund
2010.2159

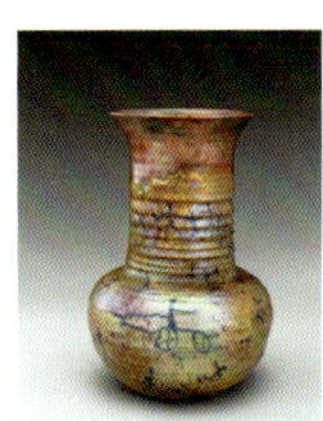

167 BEATRICE WOOD,
American, 1893–1998
Vase, 1970
Earthenware
8 x 5 1/2 inches diameter
(20.3 x 14 cm)
Museum purchase funded
by the Caroline Wiess Law
Accessions Endowment Fund
2010.2160

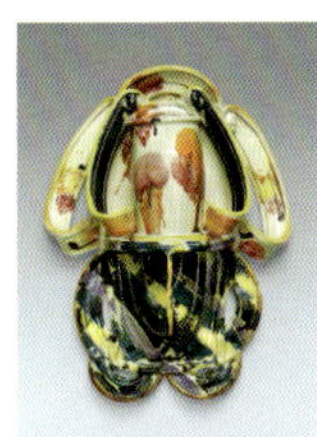

169 BETTY WOODMAN,
American, born 1930
Antella Wall Vase and Holder, 1985
Earthenware
27 1/2 x 21 x 6 5/8 inches
(69.9 x 53.3 x 16.8 cm)
Museum purchase funded
by the Caroline Wiess Law
Accessions Endowment Fund
2010.2161.A, .B

SELECTED BIBLIOGRAPHY

Adamson, Glenn. *The Craft Reader*. Oxford and New York: Berg, 2010.

————. *Thinking through Craft*. Oxford and New York: Berg, 2007.

Adamson, Jeremy. *The Furniture of Sam Maloof*. New York: W.W. Norton & Company, 2006.

Adlin, Jane. *Contemporary Ceramics: Selections from The Metropolitan Museum of Art*. New York: The Metropolitan Museum of Art, 1998.

Allen, Jane Addams. *William Harper: Self Portraits of the Artist Sacred & Profane*. New York: Franklin Parrasch Gallery, 1990.

Amaral, Olga de. *Threaded Words: Works by Olga de Amaral*. Washington, D.C.: Colombian Embassy, 2004.

Bacerra, Ralph. Interview by Frank Lloyd. Nanette L. Laitman Documentation Project for Craft and Decorative Arts in America, Smithsonian Archives of American Art, Washington, D.C., April 12–19, 2004.

————. *Ralph Bacerra: A Survey*. New York: Garth Clark Gallery, 1999.

Barron, Stephanie, ed. *Ken Price Sculpture: A Retrospective*. Los Angeles: Los Angeles County Museum of Art, 2012.

Bell, Robert. *Transformations: The Language of Craft*. Canberra: National Gallery of Australia, 2005.

Benezra, Neal, and Robert Arneson. *Robert Arneson: A Retrospective*. Des Moines, IA: Des Moines Art Center, 1986.

Burgard, Timothy Anglin. *The Art of Craft: Contemporary Works from the Saxe Collection*. San Francisco: Fine Arts Museum of San Francisco, 1999.

Clark, Garth. *American Potters: The Work of Twenty Modern Masters*. New York: Watson-Guptill Publications, 1981.

————. ed. *Ceramic Millennium: Critical Writings on Ceramic History, Theory, and Art*. Halifax: Press of the Nova Scotia College of Art and Design, 2005.

————. *Michael Cardew: A Portrait*. Tokyo and New York: Kodansha International, 1976.

————. *The Potter's Art: A Complete History of Pottery in Britain*. London: Phaidon Press, 1995.

Clark, Garth, and John Pagliaro, eds. *Shards: Garth Clark on Ceramic Art*. New York: D.A.P. and Ceramic Arts Foundation, 2004.

Clark, Garth, and Oliver Watson. *American Potters Today*. London: Victoria and Albert Museum, 1986.

Clark, Vicky A. *Edward Eberle*. Pittsburgh: The Carnegie Museum of Art, 1991.

Clowes, Jody, and Mark Leach. *Don Reitz: Clay, Fire, Salt, and Wood*. Madison, WI: Chazen Museum of Art, 2005.

Danto, Arthur Coleman, and Janet Koplos. *Betty Woodman*. New York: Monacelli Press, 2006.

Del Vecchio, Mark. *Postmodern Ceramics*. New York: Thames and Hudson, 2001.

Dietz, Ulysses Grant. *Great Pots: Contemporary Ceramics from Function to Fantasy*. Newark, NJ: Newark Museum, 2003.

Dormer, Peter. *The New Ceramics: Trends and Traditions*. London: Thames and Hudson, 1986.

Dunham, Judith L. "Ceramic Bricolage: The Protean Art of Viola Frey." *American Craft* 41, no. 4 (August–September 1981): 29–33.

Ebendorf, Robert. *Ebendorf: The Jewelry of Robert Ebendorf: A Retrospective of Forty Years*. Raleigh: Gallery of Art and Design, North Carolina State University, 2002.

Faberman, Hilarie. *Fired at Davis: Figurative Ceramic Sculpture*. Stanford, CA: Iris and B. Gerald Cantor Center for Visual Arts, 2005.

Failing, Patricia. *Howard Kottler: Face to Face*. Seattle and London: University of Washington Press, 1995.

————. "Michael Lucero: Homage to Ancient Arts." *American Craft* 55, no. 1 (February–March 1995): 32–37.

Fineberg, Jonathan. *A Troublesome Subject: The Art of Robert Arneson*. Davis: University of California Press, 2013.

Galusha, Emily, and Mary Ann Nord, eds. *Clay Talks: Reflections by American Master Ceramists*. Minneapolis: Northern Clay Center, 2000.

Gordon, Alastair, and Evan Snyderman. *Wendell Castle: Wandering Forms, Works from 1959–1979*. Ridgefield, CT: The Aldrich Contemporary Art Museum, 2012.

Halper, Vicki. *Look Alikes: The Decal Plates of Howard Kottler*. Tacoma, WA: Tacoma Art Museum, 2004.

Halper, Vicki, and Diane Douglas, eds. *Choosing Craft: The Artist's Viewpoint*. Chapel Hill: The University of North Carolina Press, 2009.

Harper, William. Interview by Harold B. Nelson. The Nanette L. Laitman Documentation Project for Craft and Decorative Arts in America, Smithsonian Archives of American Art, Washington D.C., January 12–13, 2004.

Harrod, Tanya. *The Crafts in Britain in the Twentieth Century*. New Haven, CT: Yale University Press, 1999.

Held, Peter, ed. *Humor, Irony and Wit: Ceramic Funk from the Sixties and Beyond*. Tempe: Arizona State University, 2004.

————. *The Art of Toshiko Takaezu: In the Language of Silence*. Chapel Hill: The University of North Carolina Press, 2011.

Jönsson, Love, ed. *Craft in Dialogue: Six Views on a Practice in Change*. Stockholm: Craft in Dialogue, 2005.

Joris, Yvonne G. J. M., ed. *Who's Afraid of American Pottery?* 's Hertogenbosch, Netherlands: Dienst Beeldende Kunst, 1983.

Kuspit, Donald. *Stephen De Staebler: The Figure*. San Francisco: Chronicle Books, 1988.

Lauria, Jo. *Color and Fire: Defining Moments in Studio Ceramics, 1950–2000*. Los Angeles: Los Angeles County Museum of Art, 2000.

————. *Ruth Duckworth: Modernist Sculptor*. Hampshire, UK: Lund Humphries, 2004.

Leach, Mark Richard, and Barbara J. Bloemink. *Michael Lucero: Sculpture 1976–1995*. New York: Hudson Hills Press; Charlotte, NC: Mint Museum of Art, 1996.

Lebow, Edward. *Ken Ferguson*. Kansas City, MO: Nelson-Atkins Museum of Art, 1995.

Levin, Elaine. "Paul Soldner." *Ceramics Monthly* 27, no. 6 (June 1979): 59–69.

Long, Timothy, ed. *Mariyn Levine: A Retrospective.* Saskatoon, Canada: PrintWest Communications, 1998.

Longhauser, Elsa Weiner. *It's All Part of the Clay: Viola Frey.* Philadelphia: Moore College of Art, 1984.

Lucie-Smith, Edward. *Olga de Amaral: Strata.* Bogotá, Colombia: Galeria La Cometa, 2008.

Lynn, Martha Drexler. *The Clay Art of Adrian Saxe.* New York: Thames and Hudson; Los Angeles: Los Angeles County Museum of Art, 1993.

————. *Clay Today: Contemporary Ceramists and Their Work.* Los Angeles: Los Angeles County Museum of Art, 1990.

MacNaughton, Mary Davis, ed. *Clay's Tectonic Shift: John Mason, Ken Price, and Peter Voulkos, 1956–1968.* Los Angeles: The J. Paul Getty Museum, 2012.

Marshall, Richard, and Suzanne Foley. *Ceramic Sculpture: Six Artists.* New York: Whitney Museum of American Art, 1981.

Mazow, Lee G., and Robert Arneson. *Arneson and the Object.* College University Park, PA: Pennsylvania State University Press, 2000.

McCready, Karen. *Contemporary American Ceramics: Twenty Artists.* Newport Beach, CA: Newport Harbor Art Museum, 1985.

McTwigan, Michael. *Ron Nagle: A Survey Exhibition 1958–1993.* Oakland, CA: Mills College Art Gallery, 1993.

Monroe, Michael W. *William Harper: Volumes of Souls.* New York: Kennedy Galleries, 1998.

Newby, Rick, Timothy Anglin Burgard, and Dore Ashton. *Matter and Spirit: Stephen De Staebler.* Los Angeles: University of California Press, 2012.

Nordness, Lee. *Jack Earl: The Genesis and Triumphant Survival of an Underground Ohio Artist.* Racine, WI: Perimeter Press, 1985.

————. *Objects: USA.* New York: Viking Press, 1970.

Norton, Deborah L., and Matthew Drutt. *Albert Paley: Sculptural Adornment.* Washington, D.C.: Renwick Gallery, 1991.

Notkin, Richard. *Strong Tea: Richard Notkin and the Yixing Tradition.* Seattle: Seattle Art Museum, 1990.

Odom, Michael. "Edward Eberle: In the Realm of Myth." *American Craft* 52, no. 2 (April–May 1992): 36–39.

Oldknow, Tina. *Richard Marquis Objects.* Seattle: University of Washington Press, 1998.

Oldknow, Tina, Cristine Russell, and David Whitehouse. *Voices of Contemporary Glass: The Heineman Collection.* Easthampton, MA: Hudson Hills Press, 2009.

Paley, Albert. *Albert Paley: The Art of Metal.* Springfield, MA: Springfield Library and Museums Association for the Museum of Fine Arts, 1985.

Paley, Albert, with Robert A. Sobieszek and Helen Williams Drutt. *The Metalwork of Albert Paley.* Sheboygan, WI: John Michael Kohler Arts Center, 1980.

Pardon, Earl. *Earl Pardon: A Retrospective Exhibition.* Saratoga Springs: Art Gallery, Skidmore College, 1980.

Porges, Maria. "Ron Nagle: Fishing Around for Chords." *American Craft* 69, no. 6 (December 2009–January 2010): 40–47.

Price, Ken, Walter Hopps, and Edward Lebow. *Ken Price.* Houston: The Menil Collection, 1992.

Ramljak, Suzanne. *Crafting a Legacy: Contemporary American Crafts in the Philadelphia Museum of Art.* Philadelphia: Philadelphia Museum of Art, 2002.

Reynolds, Jock. *Robert Hudson and Richard Shaw: New Ceramic Sculpture.* Andover, MA: Addison Gallery of American Art, 1998.

Sargent, Richard. "A Short Survey of San Francisco Bay Area Potters and Artists." *The Studio Potter* 32, no. 3 (September 2004): 8–19.

Saxe, Adrian, Jeff Perrone, and Peter Schjeldahl. *Adrian Saxe.* Kansas City: University of Missouri-Kansas City Gallery of Art, 1987.

Schaffner, Ingrid, and Janelle Porter. *Dirt on Delight: Impulses That Form Clay.* Philadelphia: Institute of Contemporary Art, 2009.

Scott, Joyce, George Ciscle, and Leslie King-Hammond. *Joyce J. Scott: Kickin' It with the Old Masters.* Baltimore: The Baltimore Museum of Art and Maryland Institute College of Art, 2000.

Selz, Peter. *Funk.* Berkeley, CA: University Art Museum, 1967.

Simon, Joan, Cynthia Schira, and Christa C. Mayer Thurman. *Cynthia Schira.* Brighton, England: Telos Art Publishing, 2003.

Sims, Patterson. *Viola Frey.* New York: Whitney Museum of American Art, 1984.

Slivka, Rose. *Peter Voulkos: A Dialogue with Clay.* Boston: Bullfinch Press, 1978.

Slivka, Rose, and Karen Tsujimoto. *The Art of Peter Voulkos.* Tokyo: Kodansha International, 1995.

Smith, Paul J. *American Craft Today: Poetry of the Physical.* New York: Weidenfeld and Nicholson, 1986.

Soldner, Paul. *Paul Soldner: A Retrospective.* Pomona, CA: Lang Gallery Scripps College, 1991.

Strauss, Cindi. *Ornament as Art: Contemporary Jewelry from the Helen Williams Drutt Collection, The Museum of Fine Arts, Houston.* Houston: The Museum of Fine Arts, Houston; Stuttgart, Germany: Arnoldsche Art Publishers, 2007.

Strauss, Cindi, and Garth Clark. *Shifting Paradigms in Contemporary Ceramics: The Garth Clark and Mark Del Vecchio Collection.* New Haven and Houston: Yale University Press and the Museum of Fine Arts, Houston, 2012.

Taragin, Davira S., ed. *Contemporary Crafts and the Saxe Collection.* Toledo: The Toledo Museum of Art, 1993.

Taragin, Davira S., Edward S. Cooke, Jr., and Joseph Giovannini. *Furniture by Wendell Castle.* New York: Hudson Hills, 1996.

Taragin, Davira S., and Patterson Sims. *Bigger, Better, More: The Art of Viola Frey.* Racine, WI: Racine Art Museum, 2009.

Traugott, Joseph. *Rick Dillingham 1952–1994: A Retrospective Exhibition.* Albuquerque: University of New Mexico Art Museum, 1994.

Turner, Ralph. *Jewelry in Europe and America: New Times, New Thinking.* London: Thames and Hudson, 1996.

Williams, Tony, Kenneth Baker, and John Natsoulas. *David Gilhooly.* San Francisco: John Natsulas Gallery, 1994.

ILLUSTRATION CREDITS

The Museum of Fine Arts, Houston, has made every effort to contact all copyright holders for images reproduced in this book. If proper acknowledgment has not been made, we ask copyright holders to contact the museum. We regret any omissions. Certain illustrations are covered by claims to copyright listed by page number below.

COPYRIGHT CREDITS

© Olga de Amaral, pages 37–39, 142 (Checklist nos. 1–4)
© American Craft Council, pages 20, 21
© Glenda Arentzen, page 142 (Checklist no. 5)
© Estate of Robert Arneson / Licensed by VAGA, New York, NY, cover art and
  pages 15, 41–43, 142 (Checklist nos. 6–14)
© Lela Autio, pages 45–47, 142, 143 (Checklist nos. 15–18)
© Estate of Ralph Bacerra, pages 6, 13, 48, 49, 143 (Checklist nos. 19–23)
© Clayton G. Bailey, pages 51, 143 (Checklist no. 24)
© Garry Knox Bennett, pages 52, 143 (Checklist no. 25)
© Robert Brady, courtesy of Stremmel Gallery, pages 55, 143 (Checklist no. 26)
© Seth Cardew, pages 56, 57, 143, 144 (Checklist nos. 27–30)
© Wendell Castle, Inc., pages 29 (top), 58, 144 (Checklist nos. 31–32)
© Val Cushing, page 144 (Checklist no. 33)
© Dan Dailey, page 144 (Checklist no. 34)
© William P. Daley, page 144 (Checklist no. 35)
© Estate of Stephen De Staebler, pages 61–63, 144 (Checklist nos. 36–37)
© Edmund de Waal, page 144 (Checklist no. 38)
© Estate of Rick Dillingham, pages 64, 65, 143, 145 (Checklist nos. 39–44)
© Estate of Thomas Downing, page 145 (Checklist no. 45)
© Estate of Ruth Duckworth, pages 67, 145 (Checklist nos. 46–48)
© Jack Earl, page 145 (Checklist no. 49)
© Robert Ebendorf, pages 69, 145 (Checklist nos. 50–53)
© Edward S. Eberle, pages 70, 71, 145 (Checklist no. 54)
© Estate of Kenneth R. Ferguson, page 145 (Checklist no. 55)
© Frank Fleming, pages 73, 145 (Checklist no. 56)
© Artists' Legacy Foundation / Licensed by VAGA, New York, NY, pages 74–77, 146
  (Checklist nos. 57–59)
© Michael Frimkess and Estate of Magdalena Frimkess, pages 78, 79, 146 (Checklist no. 60)
© John G. Garrett, pages 80–81, 146 (Checklist no. 61)
© David Gilhooly, pages 82, 83, 146 (Checklist nos. 62–63)
© John Gill, page 146 (Checklist no. 64)
© Estate of Hamada Shōji, page 146 (Checklist nos. 65–66)
© William Harper, pages 30 (bottom), 85, 146 (Checklist nos. 67–69)
© Wayne Higby, page 146 (Checklist no. 70)
© Kawai Kanjiro's House, page 146 (Checklist no. 71)
© Estate of Howard Kottler, page 147 (Checklist no. 72)
© Estate of David Leach, page 147 (Checklist no. 73)
© 2014 Marilyn Levine, pages 87, 147 (Checklist no. 74)
© Michael Lucero, pages 89–91, 147 (Checklist nos. 75–76)
© Warren MacKenzie, page 147 (Checklist no. 77)
© Sam Maloof Woodworker Inc., pages 93–95, 147 (Checklist nos. 78–81)
© Richard Marquis, pages 96, 97, 147 (Checklist nos. 82–83)
© John Mason, pages 99, 147 (Checklist no. 84)
© John McQueen, pages 100, 147 (Checklist no. 85)
© Mineo Mizuno, page 147 (Checklist no. 86)
© Eleanor Moty, page 148 (Checklist no. 87)
© Ron Nagle, pages 103, 148 (Checklist nos. 88–89)
© Gail Reynolds Natzler, Trustee, The Natzler Trust, page 148 (Checklist no. 90)
© Richard T. Notkin, page 148 (Checklist nos. 91–92)
© Albert Paley, pages 105, 148 (Checklist nos. 96–97)
© Estate of Earl Pardon, pages 18, 28 (bottom right), 148 (Checklist nos. 98–100)
© Pardon Design, Inc., pages 106–7, 148, 149 (Checklist nos. 101–102)
© Estate of Jane Parshall, pages 12, 149 (Checklist no. 103)
© Tom Patti, pages 109, 140, 149 (Checklist no. 104)
© Estate of Ken Price, pages 2, 110, 112–13, 149 (Checklist nos. 105–107)

© Estate of John Axel Prip, pages 28 (top), 149 (Checklist no. 108)
© Estate of Theodore Randall, page 149 (Checklist no. 109)
© Don Reitz, pages 16, 114, 115, 149 (Checklist nos. 110–115)
© Adrian Saxe, pages 30 (top), 117–19, 149, 150 (Checklist nos. 116–128)
© Cynthia Schira, pages 34, 120, 150 (Checklist no. 129)
© Joyce J. Scott, pages 123, 150 (Checklist no. 130)
© Richard Shaw, pages 124, 150, 151 (Checklist nos. 131–133)
© Estate of Shimaoka Tatsuzō, pages 14, 151 (Checklist nos. 134–136)
© Soldner Descendants' Trust, pages 127, 151 (Checklist nos. 137–139)
© Victor Spinski, page 151 (Checklist nos. 140–142)
© Therman Statom, pages 129, 151, 152 (Checklist nos. 143–149)
© 2014 Frank Stella / Artists Rights Society (ARS), New York, page 152
  (Checklist nos. 150–151)
© Toshiko Takaezu, pages 130, 132–33, 152 (Checklist nos. 152–154)
© Estate of Robert C. Turner, pages 29 (bottom left), 152 (Checklist nos. 155–156)
© The Voulkos Family Trust, pages 30 (top), 134, 136, 137, 152, 153
  (Checklist nos. 157–166)
© Courtesy Beatrice Wood Center for the Arts / Happy Valley Foundation, page 153
  (Checklist no. 167)
© Betty Woodman, pages 138, 153 (Checklist nos. 168–169)
© Takeshi Yasuda, page 153 (Checklist no. 170)

PHOTOGRAPHY CREDITS

Sasha Borodulin, courtesy American Craft Council, page 20
Courtesy American Craft Council, 21 (top)
Courtesy American Craft Museum / Museum of Arts and Design, page 27
Courtesy New York: Dutton, page 26
Courtesy Penguin Group (USA) / Viking Press, pages 22, 23, 24
Image courtesy University of California, Berkeley Art Museum and Pacific Film Archive
  (BAM/PFA), page 21 (bottom)
© The Museum of Fine Arts, Houston, Thomas R. DuBrock, cover and pages 2, 6, 12–16,
  18, 28–30, 34, 37–39, 41–43, 45, 48, 49, 51, 52, 55–58, 61–65, 67, 69–71, 73, 76–83, 85, 87,
  89–91, 93–97, 99, 100, 105–7, 109, 110, 112–15, 117–20, 123, 124, 127, 129, 130, 132–34,
  136–38, 140, 142–53 (Checklist nos. 1–7, 9–15, 19–33, 36–44, 46–56, 58–87, 89–130,
  132–149, 152–157, 159–164, 166–170)
© The Museum of Fine Arts, Houston, Will Michels, pages 46–47, 74–75, 142–46,
  150, 152, 153 (Checklist nos. 8, 16–18, 34, 35, 45, 57, 131, 150, 151, 158, 165)
© Don Tuttle, pages 103, 148 (Checklist no. 88)